Praise for *American Exceptionalism and American Innocence*

"Danny Haiphong and Roberto Sirvent are two of the most courageous and truthful intellectuals in the belly of the U.S. imperial beast! In this powerful text they lay bare the hidden realities and concealed miseries of poor and working peoples even as revolutionary fire remains strong! This book keeps alive so much of the best of the radical tradition in the neo-fascist age of Trump!"

—Cornel West, Professor of the Practice
of Public Philosophy at Harvard University

"*American Exceptionalism and American Innocence* provides an astute, engaging, and provocative look into how the human toll of U.S. colonial occupation, imperial expansion, and structural racism is subsumed into an overarching narrative of the 'greater good.' By exposing the ideology of innocence that inevitably accompanies exceptionalism, Roberto Sirvent and Danny Haiphong move us beyond the constraints of liberal engagement to question our presumptions about what 'America' means. These short, topical essays expose the American exceptionalism we encounter in everyday life, thereby providing a roadmap for how it can be challenged. A unique resource for students and teachers, grassroots activists, and anyone who wants to stop circling the same rock and have an actually interesting conversation."

—Natsu Taylor Saito, author of *Meeting the Enemy:*
American Exceptionalism and International Law

"The extreme danger of America to the rest of us remains the great unspoken, lost in myths, or what Larry David called 'a babbling brook of bullshit.' Witty terms such as 'exceptionalism' and 'democracy' are deployed as the bombs fall and the blood never dries. In this outstanding study, Danny Haiphong and Roberto Sirvent tell us why: and why Trump is merely a symptom and that only our urgent enlightenment can defy the inevitable."

—John Pilger, Australian journalist and
BAFTA award-winning documentary filmmaker

"Roberto Sirvent and Danny Haiphong deliver a stirring indictment of ruling class propaganda. By carefully exposing the destructive myths that sustain

U.S. empire, this book provides an intellectual anchor that will surely disrupt and unsettle the powers that be."

—Cynthia McKinney, Professor and Activist, former six-term member of the United States House of Representatives

"In this timely, multi-layered, brilliantly argued counter-history, Sirvent and Haiphong draw on case studies ranging from the nation's settler colonial past to the Trumpist present so as to open spaces needed to imagine socially transformative alternatives to the white-supremacist, imperial policies that the discourse of American exceptionalism and the doctrine of American innocence have worked relentlessly to normalize."

—Donald E. Pease, Avalon Foundation Professor of the Humanities at Dartmouth College and director of the Futures of American Studies Institute

"America's decline toward national madness has become so multi-faceted that narrow analysis can no longer explain it. This wide-ranging book seeks to weave our history and our modern-day reality together. It may seem radical, but it is not as radical as what our leaders are doing today to suppress human freedom at home and abroad."

—Stephen Kinzer, former *New York Times* correspondent, author of *Overthrow* and *All the Shah's Men: An American Coup and the Roots of Middle East Terror*

"A varied offering of America's real history, with sharp arguments and revealing information drawn down through the centuries—a rich treat for both beginners and the well-informed."

—Michael Parenti, author of *History as Mystery* and *Contrary Notions*

"*American Exceptionalism and American Innocence* does what is so needed in this, the late stage of American Empire—it blasts a hole through the notion that the US is some unique beacon for democracy and freedom in the world, and that it is therefore privileged to intervene throughout the world at will. Rather, as this book demonstrates, the US has never been such a beacon, either nationally or internationally. The US was built on genocide and slavery, and, accordingly, has invaded weaker countries to impose systems which protect the privileged few from the just demands of the struggling masses. The result has been vast inequality and suffering in both the US and abroad, and the undermining, if not wholesale destruction, of democracy. As this book shows us, US Empire is the greatest threat to the survival of humanity, and it is only the citizens of the US who can, and indeed must, dismantle it."

—Dan Kovalik, author of *The Plot to Scapegoat Russia* and *The Plot to Attack Iran*

"Timely, historic, and analytically rich, Roberto Sirvent and Danny Haiphong rightfully challenge the hegemonic narrative of American innocence and American exceptionalism that pervade contemporary culture. Examining monuments, memory, media, and movies, alongside of political slogans, sports culture and social movements, this book offers a powerful intervention, demanding that we account for the bipartisan project of hyper nationalism and narratives of America's unique greatness. Providing historic lessons, tools of literary analysis, a critical gaze, and so much more, this book takes you on an important journey, preparing all readers for the current moment and a progressive future."

—David J. Leonard, author of *Playing While White: Privilege and Power on and off the Field*

"In their essays on race, empire and historical memory, Roberto Sirvent and Danny Haiphong skillfully unveil the profound hypocrisy and inherent barbarism of the US state, stripping away its respectable forms and forcing it to go naked. The book is a must read for anyone who wants to understand the US empire as it is, rather than as it would like to be understood."

—Stephen Gowans, author of *Washington's Long War on Syria* and *Patriots, Traitors and Empires: The Story of Korea's Fight for Freedom*

AMERICAN EXCEPTIONALISM *AND* AMERICAN INNOCENCE

AMERICAN EXCEPTIONALISM *AND* AMERICAN INNOCENCE

A PEOPLE'S HISTORY OF FAKE NEWS—FROM THE REVOLUTIONARY WAR TO THE WAR ON TERROR

ROBERTO SIRVENT
AND DANNY HAIPHONG

Skyhorse Publishing

Skyhorse Publishing books may be purchased in bulk at special discounts for sales promotion, corporate gifts, fund-raising, or educational purposes. Special editions can also be created to specifications. For details, contact the Special Sales Department, Skyhorse Publishing, 307 West 36th Street, 11th Floor, New York, NY 10018 or info@skyhorsepublishing.com.

Visit our website at www.skyhorsepublishing.com.

10 9 8 7 6 5 4 3 2 1

Library of Congress Cataloging-in-Publication Data is available on file.

Cover design by Mona Lin

ISBN: 978-1-5107-4236-9
Ebook ISBN: 978-1-5107-4237-6

Printed in the United States of America

This book is dedicated to Margaret Kimberley, Glen Ford, Bruce Dixon, Mumia Abu-Jamal, and all the political prisoners in the United States.

CONTENTS

FOREWORD

Countering the Violence of Imposed Forgetting
by Ajamu Baraka

"The civilized have created the wretched, quite coldly and deliberately, and do not intend to change the status quo; are responsible for their slaughter and enslavement; rain down bombs on defenseless children whenever and wherever they decide that their 'vital interests' are menaced, and think nothing of torturing a man to death; these people are not to be taken seriously when they speak of the 'sanctity' of human life, or the conscience of civilized world."

—James Baldwin

While the 20th century was a century of unparalleled human depravity with literally millions of lives lost in two planetary wars, and millions more in smaller wars, the 21st century was supposed to be different. History had supposedly ended with the victory of the United States as the sole great power—its civilization the envy of all. However, the century slated to be the dawn of expanded greatness for the United States has seen the nation at war for 17 of the last 18 years with the real possibility that death by war in this century could vastly exceed the millions lost during the last.

The invasion of Afghanistan and then Iraq, drone warfare, torture, and black sites, as part of the War on Terror, complemented the militarized urban warfare and poverty imposed on people of color that characterized the new normal supported by both "major" political parties, the corporate media, and large sections of the U.S. public.

How can this be?

How could a nation that claims its fidelity to "universal values" of human rights, international law, democracy, freedom, and human progress, also be the main protagonist in the systematic global assaults on those very same values without any apparent psychological tension between those two contradictory realities?

Roberto Sirvent and Danny Haiphong provide an explanation.

Like a thunderbolt that penetrates the dark fog of ideological confusion, *American Exceptionalism and American Innocence: A People's History of Fake News—From the Revolutionary War to the War on Terror*, illuminates the hidden spaces of the official story of the territory that came to be known as the United States of America.

Meticulously researched, *American Exceptionalism and American Innocence* utilizes a de-colonial lens that debunks the distorted, mythological liberal framework that rationalized the U.S. settler-colonial project. The de-colonized frame allows them to critically root their analysis in the psychosocial history, culture, political economy, and evolving institutions of the United States of America without falling prey to the unrecognized and unacknowledged liberalism and national chauvinism that seeps through so much of what is advanced as radical analysis today.

That is what makes this work so "exceptional" and so valuable at this moment of institutional and ideological crisis in the U.S. This crisis is indeed more severe and potentially more transformative than at any other moment in this nation's history.

With unflinching clarity, Sirvent and Haiphong go right to the heart of the current social, political, economic, and ideological crisis. They strip away the obscurantist nonsense pushed by liberal and state propagandists that the Trump phenomenon represents a fundamental departure from traditional "American values" by demonstrating that "Trumpism" is no departure at all, but only the unfiltered contemporary and particular expression of the core values that the nation was "founded" on.

What Sirvent and Haiphong expose in their work is that American exceptionalism and its corollary American innocence are the interconnected frames that not only explain why the crude white nationalism of a Donald Trump is consistent with the violence and white supremacy of the American experience, but also why that violence has been largely supported by large sections of the U.S. population repeatedly.

As the exceptional nation, the indispensable nation, the term President Obama liked to evoke to give humanitarian cover to the multiple interventions, destabilization campaigns, and unilateral global policing operations on behalf of U.S. and international capital, it is expected and largely accepted by the citizens of the U.S. that their nation-state has a right and, actually, a moral duty to do whatever it deems appropriate to uphold the international order. It can do that because this cause is noble and righteous. Lest we forget the words of Theodore Roosevelt, considered a great architect of American progressiveness, "If given the choice between righteousness and peace, I choose righteousness."

In a succinct and penetrating observation, Sirvent and Haiphong point out:

> American exceptionalism has always presumed national innocence despite imposing centuries of war and plunder. The American nation-state has been at war for over ninety percent of its existence. These wars have all been justified as necessary ventures meant to defend or expand America's so-called founding values and beliefs. A consequence of centuries of endless war has been the historical tendency of the U.S. to erase from consciousness the realities that surround American domestic and international policy, not to mention the system of imperialism that governs both.

But the acceptance of state violence in the form of economic sanctions and direct and indirect military interventions is not the only consequence of the cultural conditioning process informed by the arrogance of white privilege, white rights, and the protection of white Western civilization. The racist xenophobia, impunity for killer-cops, mass incarceration, ICE raids and checkpoints, left-right ideological convergence to erase "blackness," are all part of the racial management process that still enjoys majoritarian support in the U.S.

American Exceptionalism and American Innocence's focus on the insidious and corrosive impact of white supremacy throughout the book is a necessary and valuable corrective to the growing tendency toward marginalizing the issue of race, even among left forces under the guise of being opposed to so-called identity politics.

Centering the role of white supremacist ideologies and its connection to American exceptionalism and innocence, Sirvent and Haiphong argue that "communities and activists will be better positioned to dismantle them." American exceptionalism and notions of U.S. innocence not only provide ideological rationalizations for colonialism, capitalism, empire, and white supremacy, but also a normalized theoretical framework for how the world is and should be structured that inevitably makes criminals out of the people opposing U.S. dominance, within the nation and abroad.

Paul Krugman, a leading liberal within the context of the U.S. articulates this normalized framework that is shared across the ideological spectrum from liberal to conservative and even among some left forces. I have previously referred to this view of the world as representative of the psychopathology of white supremacy:

> "We emerged from World War II with a level of both economic and military dominance not seen since the heyday of ancient Rome. But our role in the world was always about more than money and guns. It was also about ideals: America stood for something larger than itself—for freedom, human rights and the rule of law as universal principles . . . By the end of World War II, we and our British allies had in effect conquered a large part of the world. We could have become permanent occupiers, and/or installed subservient puppet governments, the way the Soviet Union did in Eastern Europe. And yes, we did do that in some developing countries; our history with, say, Iran is not at all pretty. But what we mainly did instead was help defeated enemies get back on their feet, establishing democratic regimes that shared our core values and became allies in protecting those values. The Pax Americana was a sort of empire; certainly America was for a long time very much first among equals. But it was by historical standards a remarkably benign empire, held together by soft power and respect rather than force."[1]

American Exceptionalism and American Innocence refutes this pathological view of the U.S. and demonstrates that this view is a luxury that the colonized peoples of the world cannot afford.

The bullet and the bomb—the American military occupation and the police occupation—are the bonds that link the condition of Black Americans to oppressed nations around the world. This is the urgency in which the authors approached their task. The physical and ideological war being waged against the victims of the colonial/capitalist white supremacist patriarchy is resulting in real suffering. Authentic solidarity with the oppressed requires a rejection of obfuscation. The state intends to secure itself and the ruling elite by legal or illegal means, by manipulating or completely jettisoning human freedom and democratic rights. Sirvent and Haiphong know that time is running out. They demonstrate the intricate collaboration between the state and the corporate and financial elite to create the conditions in which ideological and political opposition would be rendered criminal as the state grapples with the legitimacy crisis it finds itself in. They know that Trump's "make America great again" is the Republican version of Obama's heralding of U.S. exceptionalism, and that both are laying the ideological foundation for a cross-class white neofascist solution to the crisis of neoliberal capitalism.

The U.S. is well on its way toward a new form of totalitarianism that is more widespread than the forms of neofascist rule that was the norm in the Southern states of the U.S. from 1878 to 1965. Chris Hedges refers to it as "corporate totalitarianism." And unlike the sheer social terror experienced by the African American population as a result of the corporatist alignment of the new Democratic party and national and regional capital in the South, this "new" form of totalitarianism is more benign but perhaps even more insidious because the control rests on the ability to control thought. And here lies the challenge. Marxist thinker Fredrick Jamison shares a very simple lesson, "The lesson is this, and it is a lesson about system: one cannot change anything without changing everything." This simple theory of system change argues that when you change one part of a system you by necessity must change all parts of the system, because all parts are interrelated.

The failure of the Western left in general and the U.S. left in particular to understand the inextricable, structural connection between empire, colonization, capitalism, and white supremacy—and that all elements of that oppressive structure must be confronted, dismantled, and defeated—continues to give lifeblood to a system that is ready to sweep into the dustbins of history. This is why *American Exceptionalism and American Innocence* is nothing more than an abject subversion. It destabilizes the hegemonic assumptions and imposed conceptual frameworks of bourgeois liberalism and points the reader toward the inevitable conclusion that U.S. society in its present form poses an existential threat to global humanity.

Challenging the reader to rethink the history of the U.S. and to imagine a future, decolonial nation in whatever form it might take, Sirvent and Haiphong include a quote from Indigenous rights supporter Andrea Smith that captures both the subversive and optimistic character of their book. Smith is quoted saying:

> Rather than a pursuit of life, liberty, and happiness that depends on the deaths of others . . . we can imagine new forms of governance based on the principles of mutuality, interdependence, and equality. When we do not presume that the United States should or will continue to exist, we can begin to imagine more than a kinder, gentler settler state founded on genocide and slavery.

American Exceptionalism and American Innocence gives us a weapon to reimagine a transformed U.S. nation, but it also surfaces the ideological minefields that we must avoid if we are to realize a new possibility and a new people.

INTRODUCTION

"Americans are a confused people because they can't admit this contradiction. They believe in a universe of divine justice where the human race is guilty of sin, but they also believe in a secular justice where human beings are presumed innocent. You can't have both. You know how Americans deal with it? They pretend they are eternally innocent no matter how many times they lose their innocence. The problem is that those who insist on their innocence believe anything they do is just. At least we who believe in our own guilt know what dark things we can do."

—Viet Thanh Nguyen[1]

"If we feel calm, what must we forget to inhabit such a restful feeling?"

—Jasbir Puar[2]

Fake news existed long before Donald Trump. In fact, Donald Trump didn't even come up with the term. According to the BBC, it was Hillary Clinton who first lamented over the "real world consequences" of "fake news," or false information spread on the internet.[3] Fake news has become the primary explanation as to why Hillary Clinton lost the 2016 election. The notion that devious hackers associated with Russia used fake news to help Trump win the election has deflected attention from the real shortcomings of the Clinton campaign in particular and the two-party political system in general. What is ironic is that *fake* news has indeed been the *only* news disseminated by the rulers of U.S. empire. We've been exposed to this fake news for as long as we've been told that the U.S. is a force for good in the world—news that slavery is a thing of the past, that we don't really live on stolen land, that wars are fought to spread freedom and democracy, that a rising tide lifts all boats, that prisons keep us safe, and that the police serve and protect. Thus, the only "news" ever reported by various channels of U.S. empire is the news of American exceptionalism and American innocence. And as this book will hopefully show, it's all fake.

Gil Scott Heron famously coined the statement, "the revolution will not be televised." Millions of people in the U.S. have learned innumerable lessons about American exceptionalism and American innocence from prominent television personalities. Bill O'Reilly, for example, taught us how to defend American "greatness" in his response to Michelle Obama's public reminder that slaves built the White House. O'Reilly quickly retorted that slaves who built it were "well fed" and provided with "decent" lodging. Millions more learned about the pervasiveness of American exceptionalism from a *60 Minutes* interview with former Secretary of State Madeleine Albright. It was here on national TV where she famously declared the deaths of 500,000 Iraqi children by way of U.S. sanctions as a sacrifice that was "worth it." Albright was subsequently awarded the Presidential Medal of Freedom by Barack Obama in 2012. For O'Reilly and Albright, the inherent superiority and good intentions of the U.S. provide absolution for crimes against humanity.

Narratives of exceptionalism and innocence are evident in all spheres of American society. They were embedded in Donald Trump's 2016 electoral slogan, "Make America Great Again," and Hillary Clinton's rebuttal that "we don't need to make America great again. America never stopped being great." More recently, former candidate for U.S. Senate in Alabama, Roy Moore, attempted to defend Trump's "Make America Great Again" slogan by wishing we could go back to the country's good ol' days, a "time when families were united—even though we had slavery. They cared for one another. People were strong in the families. Our families were strong. Our country had a direction."

The nation's multibillion dollar sports industry also plays a crucial role in reinforcing exceptionalist myths. Americans sing the national anthem at every sporting event regardless of the venue. The nation's military is celebrated and venerated prior to nearly every game in professional sports leagues. When MLB player Bruce Maxwell joined NFL players in kneeling during the national anthem in protest of police brutality, he felt the need to clarify that there was nothing anti-American about his protest: "At the end of the day, this is the best country on the planet. I am and forever will be an American citizen and grateful to be here, but my kneeling is what's getting the attention, and I'm kneeling for the people who don't have a voice."

The mainstream corporate media is one of the chief propagators of

American exceptionalism and innocence. Flipping through the pages of the *New York Times* or watching personalities such as Oprah Winfrey are often the best ways to spot this propaganda. For example, in a *New York Times* editorial, the staff responded to Donald Trump's rather uncontroversial claim that the Russian state is not the only one made up of "killers." "There are a lot of killers," Trump remarked. "Do you think our country is so innocent?" The *Times* went on the defensive, acknowledging the "mistakes" of U.S. foreign policy yet reaffirming its exceptional character:

> There's no doubt that the United States has made terrible *mistakes*, like invading Iraq in 2003 and torturing terrorism suspects after Sept. 11 [. . .] [But] in recent decades, American presidents who took military action *have been driven by the desire to promote freedom and democracy*, sometimes with extraordinary results, as when Germany and Japan evolved after World War II from vanquished enemies into trusted, prosperous allies.[4]

After reading this editorial, one can't help but recall Michael Corleone's conversation with his future wife Kay Adams in *The Godfather*. Attempting to temper Kay's fear about Michael joining the family business, Michael says, "My father is no different than any powerful man, any man with power, like a president or senator." Kay responds, "Do you know how naive you sound, Michael? Presidents and senators don't have men killed." Michael, without any hesitation, asks, "Oh. Who's being naive, Kay?"

But one need not subscribe to the *New York Times* to be bombarded by narratives of American exceptionalism and American innocence. We also have entertainment television and Hollywood for that. Oprah Winfrey, for example, has based her entire career as a promoter of the American Dream, which can be summarized in one statement made by a guest on her show: "Where else but America can someone have no money, not know the language, grow up, work hard, respect other people, and end up getting a scholarship to go to college? That's only possible in America. That's the American Dream that people have been dreaming about for years."[5] Or take the latest Hollywood blockbusters as another example, whether it be *Captain America* or the *Transformers* franchise. Not only are these films used as prime military recruitment tools, but the U.S. military is directly involved in the production of the films themselves. The more the film paints the armed forces in a favorable light, the more military props are made available to the studio for use.[6] Sounds like a win-win situation, doesn't it? So, if we're going to seriously examine the ideological work of American exceptionalism and innocence, we would be wise to heed Saidiya Hartman's observation that "99.5% of U.S. cinema is a totally instrumental pernicious propaganda machine."[7]

It's almost impossible for Americans to avoid complicity and participation in these patriotic ideologies. Holidays are celebrated every year honoring the American military, the birth of American "independence," and the birthday of the first American president, George Washington. Every American president has extolled the founding origins of the U.S., as do the majority of school textbooks, mainstream media sources, and Hollywood's latest blockbuster releases. In other words, American exceptionalism and American innocence are deeply embedded into the fabric of the institutions that govern the nation's economic, political, and cultural life. Even in the bastion of "higher learning," the university, we find the sanctity of American exceptionalism and innocence hardly ever questioned.

This book is a response to the spectre currently haunting those who benefit most from promoting the myths of American exceptionalism and American innocence. Corporate executives, millionaire politicians, and military war-hawks have all voiced concerns in recent years over the fragility of American power both domestically and internationally. Despite the pervasiveness of American exceptionalism and innocence in all aspects of society, there are numerous signs that the environmental stability needed for these ideologies to thrive is in a state of breakdown. Contradictions in society are becoming more difficult to bare and broader sections of the population are standing up in protest. The Occupy Wall Street Movement in 2011, the Black Lives Matter movement beginning in 2014, and the rise of the word "socialism" in Bernie Sanders's 2016 presidential campaign brought these contradictions to light.

Young people were at the center of these movements. It was students and student-aged populations who made their way to Zuccotti Park to express their disgust with mounting student debt and dwindling living-wage job opportunities. Young Black Americans organized a mass movement against racist policing after the officer who killed 18-year old Michael Brown walked away without an indictment. A number of polls have confirmed that young people have begun identifying with the word "socialism" in higher numbers, which explains the excitement generated during the Bernie Sanders 2016 presidential campaign.

These developments are indicative of a groundswell of opposition to the system that promotes American exceptionalism and innocence. However, narratives of American exceptionalism and American innocence have played a vital role in dampening the advancement of such opposition toward the goal of social transformation. A new generation of activists and scholars is emerging from a centuries-long development process in which both of these narratives have been *the* dominant narratives. It is important, then, that American exceptionalism and innocence not be allowed to cloud historical memory, political understanding, and the struggle for social justice. This is where the following pages come in.

Argument and Goals

Our goal is to show how narratives of American exceptionalism and American innocence work together to serve white supremacy, empire, capitalism, and the U.S. war machine. Sometimes these two ideologies work together in obvious and explicit ways. Other times they are more deceptive and seductive. By taking a more topical approach to our study, we look at how narratives of exceptionalism and innocence show up in conversations about slavery, Indigenous genocide, the Super Bowl, comic books, human caging, and even our former celebrity TV star-turned-president, Donald Trump. Readers—especially liberals—who think these are "easy targets" would be wise to brace themselves for what's ahead. Our book also takes full aim at Barack Obama, the broadway musical *Hamilton*, romantic narratives of racial progress, and the "humanitarian" efforts of Bill Gates, Angelina Jolie, and many well-meaning college students hoping to "change the world."

Ultimately, we want to equip our readers with the tools to locate, critique, and dismantle the twin ideologies of American exceptionalism and American innocence. In short, we hope that everyone who reads this book will be convinced to let go of these ideologies. And while the process of "letting go" won't be easy, we try to show why it's necessary for imagining and building a more just world. To be sure, we might not be able to imagine what that world looks like just yet. After all, our conception of what is possible has been severely limited by such dominant and destructive ideologies like American exceptionalism and American innocence. These ideologies must be dismantled so a thirst for a political alternative can emerge among a larger segment of the population. And with this thirst, we will be better positioned to imagine alternative arrangements rooted in history and solidarity with those who have attempted to chart their own course of political and economic development.

This book draws on the vast and rich scholarly literature examining American exceptionalism. Yet this book is different in at least four ways. First, too few works exist that not only explain American exceptionalism, but also analyze the enduring impact that the ideology has on popular discourse. We hope that the book's topical approach provides a succinct, non-exhaustive treatment of what American exceptionalism *looks like* in everyday life—whether it be in the way we consume media, organize our communities, spend our money, or debate U.S. foreign policy. Second, this book attempts to show that the "fantasy" of American exceptionalism is best viewed as a "dual fantasy" of American exceptionalism *and* American innocence. By illuminating how both of these ideologies *work together,* we argue, communities and activists will be better positioned to dismantle them. Third, while some scholarly critiques of American exceptionalism address the colonial, imperial, and racial roots of the ideology, we attempt to show an *inherent connection* between American exceptionalism on the one hand, and empire, colonialism, capitalism, and white supremacy (especially anti-black racism) on the other. In other words, we do not think it is possible to be a staunch feminist, anti-racist, or peace activist while maintaining one's ideological devotion to the United States as an exceptional, superior, civilized, and civilizing force for good in the world. Fourth and finally, this book is not intended primarily for scholars and professors. Rather, the book is meant to be a guide for activists, community organizers, and intellectuals who are genuinely concerned about the vacuum that currently exists in American politics. It is meant for those who dream of a world without war, without borders, without prisons, without police, and a world without private property.

American Exceptionalism

Before moving forward, it might be helpful to provide some definitions. When we employ the term "American exceptionalism," we mean the ideological tool used to present and sustain a particular narrative about the United States. This narrative, according to legal theorist Natsu Taylor Saito, "presumes that human history is best understood as a linear progression toward higher stages of civilization, that Western civilization represents the apex of this history, and that the United States embodies the best and most advanced stage of Western civilization and, therefore, human history to date."[8] The grand narrative of exceptionalism is often rooted in other myths like that of "Manifest Destiny," the supposed saving grace of free markets and free enterprise, and even the myth of the United States serving as God's "chosen nation." Not all scholars of American exceptionalism, nor the millions of Americans who are devoted to it, hold exceptionalist attitudes in the same way. Nor do they always manifest in the same manner. That said, the point we hope to make is that American exceptionalism—in all its stripes—operates under a "colonial logic":

> This is a logic that organizes society and that makes sense of the geopolitical space and of everything that it appears in its horizon according to perceptions of degrees of humanity. The closer to an ideal of the human subjects and groups are, the more they can enjoy a certain condition considered normal for humans, and the farther away from that ideal subjects and groups are, the closer they will be to a condition of death or early death, misery, dispossession, and permanent slavery and war. This is a form of colonialism that involves racially motivated genocide and racial slavery and that can continue even after the formal end of slavery and colonialism.[9]

For our purposes, we adopt Joy James's description of American exceptionalism as a "cultural drug," one from which our imagination needs to be freed.[10] Ultimately, our task is to expose what Donald Pease calls the "psychosocial logics" of this pernicious national "fantasy."[11]

Readers might object to the way we use the term "American exceptionalism," for a few reasons. First, some might suggest that the the term "U.S. exceptionalism" is more appropriate than "American exceptionalism." We're well aware that the Americas encompass more than the United States, and therefore the term "U.S." exceptionalism might be better suited. But as Hortense Spillers observes in her analysis of novelist Ralph Ellison, for many people, "*America* . . . is quite a lot more than the nation-state entity called *the United States*."[12] It involves an idea, she adds, and "a sublime *possibility* . . . in human becoming."[13] Other readers might object to our definition on grounds that American exceptionalism entails believing not that the *government* is exceptional but that its *people* and *culture* are. We'll show this is problematic in a few respects, not least because it assumes the people of a country can be so easily separated from the actions of their government. For example, one might claim that our government is founded on anti-Black racism but that the people of the U.S. are not racists. We might even admit that white people are unintentional *beneficiaries* of anti-Black racism or even that they are unwillingly *complicit* in it, but the truth is that—in many ways—white Americans are conscious, active *participants* in these very structures. American exceptionalism, therefore, doesn't just assume that the U.S. government is exceptional, but that its white citizens are, too.

Others might say that our country has never been exceptional in its current state, but that our founding ideals are. This is a naive claim in many respects. Not only does it suggest that these ideals are uniquely American (i.e., are Americans the only ones that value freedom?) but it also assumes the most effective way to judge a society is by its rhetoric rather than its *actions*. Moreover, few people realize that these ideals are actually rooted in the modern philosophy of liberalism, which many scholars have shown is deeply tied to—and dependent on—exclusion, dispossession, and slavery. In other words, the right to "freedom" in the U.S. has always entailed the "un-freedom" of others and involved complex and violent processes of determining who is and is not "human." Again, we keep all these objections in mind throughout the book.

Finally, this book may be dismissed as "un-American" or just a petty attempt to defame the United States. Accusations of being "un-American" usually come as a knee-jerk response to criticisms of U.S. domestic and foreign policy. They are themselves a manifestation of American exceptionalism. To be "un-American" is to insult everything that is mythologically great about the American nation-state, such as "democracy" and "freedom." This framework assumes that the U.S. is beyond criticism or that its supposed "flaws" are mere "shortcomings," "imperfections," or "stains" that can be washed away. To be "American" is to be loyal to the nation regardless of the exploitation and oppression that lies at its foundations. Anyone who believes otherwise, the argument goes, doesn't deserve to live in the exceptional "land of the free, and the home of the brave." To be called "un-American," then, is to be delegitimized by those who have, or believe to have, vested interests in the preservation of American exceptionalism.

Many avoid being labeled "un-American" by remaining silent about war, poverty, racism and the many ills that U.S. imperialism inflicts upon the world. Some activists have even suggested that approaching people from "where they are" by appealing to American exceptionalism will help recruit more Americans to the cause of social justice and transformation. If Americans believe "democracy" and "freedom" are worthwhile goals, we are told, then these sentiments should be utilized in service of the development of a more just social order. We believe that this is a monumental error in political thought and action. It not only assumes that the American population, especially the oppressed, primarily identify as "American" and will identify as such for the foreseeable future, but it also assumes that the American nation-state is in fact capable of ever bringing about true freedom, justice, or peace. The racist oppression of Black people at the hands of the cops, the endless war waged against people around the world at the hands of U.S. military, and the impoverishment of workers at the hands of American corporations are deceptively and unconsciously disassociated from "America" itself. This is nothing but fear masked as opportunism, a fear that takes American exceptionalist values like "liberty" out of their proper liberal context. It is a fear driven by the reality that one group's "freedom" fundamentally depends on the "un-freedom" of another.

The following essays place American exceptionalism in its proper context. We show that American exceptionalism is indeed a weapon of oppression, allowing readers to see just *how* that weapon is wielded and in whose interests. Only after this is realized can we begin to develop new tools and weapons capable of building a new society free from the confines of U.S. imperialism and its exceptionalist mythologies. A society where "American" and "un-American" no longer exist because the relations of power and oppression that they signify have been eradicated all together. If building such a society is "un-American," then we must begin to question what it means to be "American" and whether it is desirable at all. The following essays attempt to answer this question.

American Innocence

Throughout this book, we attempt to show the importance of examining American exceptionalism and American innocence *together*, as two ideologies that work in tandem to reinforce one another. As a result, both operate in the service of empire, white supremacy, and the U.S. military. So why is it important to study exceptionalism and innocence together? Popular rhetoric demonstrates that the ideological tool of American innocence "kicks in" or is "triggered" when the supposedly exceptional nation is forced to explain a past, present, or future action that many people deem morally abhorrent. American innocence, then, involves the stories told—to the world and ourselves—to justify or excuse these actions.

To cite just a few examples, American innocence has us remember slavery and settler colonialism as *events of the past*, not as *structures of domination that haunt our present*. It has us view our violent overthrows of democratically elected leaders around the globe as mere "aberrations" of what we truly represent as a country, or as "unfortunate transitional developments on the way to full-fledged liberal democracy."[14] American innocence has us view the Iraq War as a simple "mistake." It has us view Abraham Lincoln as the one who freed the slaves. It tells us that our laws are neutral, that our police "serve and protect," and that our military "fights for our rights." It tells us that everyone can make it in this country, if they just work hard enough. It tells us that our history, like every other nation's is a "mixed bag," so it's time to move on. In short, the ideological work of American innocence is to remind us of the pure, benevolent intentions behind our imperial and genocidal actions, while at the same time assigning the most impure and evil motives to the violence of others. In other words, Martin Luther King may have been right that the United States is the world's greatest perpetrator of violence, but at least we always mean well.

Roadmap

The following essays attempt to expose the ideological work of American exceptionalist discourse. Rather than harken on a specific historical moment or analyze events chronologically, each essay addresses critical historical and contemporary questions related to the development of American exceptionalist ideology. Four interrelated parts form the skeleton of the ideology. These parts include: (1) a presumption of American innocence in the ways we remember genocide, slavery, and war; (2) the myth of a meritocracy cloaked in the "American Dream"; (3) a lust for military conquest all around the world; and (4) the ongoing requirement for imperialism or the rule of monopoly capitalism to expand the United States' civilizing mission.

In twenty-one essays, we break down four essential parts of American exceptionalism and American innocence to provide a framework for understanding history and the contemporary world. We attempt to show that the presumption of American innocence so popularized in American society provides a smokescreen for the suffering and exploitation that occurs within and beyond America's borders. This presumption of innocence is deeply related to how ordinary people in America are then repeatedly encouraged to strive for an "American Dream" that is further and further out of reach. Finally, American exceptionalism and innocence not only render military ventures publicly acceptable, but also serve as the primary basis from which the super profits of banks and corporations are masked amid mass suffering.

The first section of the book deals with the question of American exceptionalism in the context of historical memory. We address whether the "American Revolution" was revolutionary for African slaves so critical to the origins myths of the U.S. We examine how "they," what Frantz Fanon called the "wretched (or 'damned') of the earth," have been painted as threats to humanity, and therefore consistently face exploitation and annihilation by a nation reliant upon war. Popular myths, such as the American military's role in World War II, Korea, and the War on Terror are examined to provide evidence of how the most heinous crimes of U.S. imperialism have been preserved by shrouding them in American exceptionalist discourse.

The next section focuses on a specific pillar of U.S. imperialism: white supremacy. White supremacy has taken center stage in mainstream political conversation since the election of Donald J. Trump. However, the primary drivers of the conversation have sought to preserve the myths of American exceptionalism and innocence rather than challenge them. Essays in this section highlight the importance of viewing white supremacy and privilege from a materialist perspective, rooting the system of white dominance in recent developments such as NFL quarterback Colin Kaepernick's protest during the national anthem and the dwindling existence of Black wealth in America. We suggest that it is impossible to understand the twin narratives of American exceptionalism and innocence without a grasp of modern manifestations of white supremacy.

The final two sections serve to place a final blow to the "common sense" (to paraphrase Antonio Gramsci) of American exceptionalism and American innocence, and offer a way forward for emerging activist leaders and organizers. American militarism and capitalism, while while two common threads throughout prior sections, are given primary attention. Critical questions that determine the fate of billions of people worldwide, such as the American military's provocations toward Russia, the rise of "humanitarian intervention" as demonstrated in Libya and Syria, and the stagnation and decline of American capitalism are examined. Both in popular and scholarly discourses, these questions are often overlooked or tackled as separate, disconnected phenomena. We believe that the impulse to preserve American exceptionalism's enduring legacy is a big reason why. Thus, our project should not be seen primarily as an attempt to prove that the U.S. is not really exceptional or that it is not really innocent. Rather, to borrow from Lisa Lowe, we're more interested in how the twin ideologies of American exceptionalism and American innocence shape "the limits of what can be thought and imagined."[15]

Historical Memory

One of our primary goals is to encourage readers to think critically about what narratives need to be told for ideologies of American exceptionalism and American innocence to perform their work—for these ideologies to become so internalized and to feel so natural that they become "common sense." We invite readers to consider what narratives must be erased, hidden, excluded, emphasized, repeated, distorted, justified, excused, punished, and forgotten in order for the twin ideologies of exceptionalism and innocence to thrive. In short, we invite readers to examine what Lowe calls "the economy of affirmation and forgetting" that creates and structures these ideologies, and which threatens to leave alternative narratives unknown or unthought.[16]

As long as people have been telling stories of American exceptionalism and American innocence, there have been people contesting these stories. There have been people telling *counter-stories* or counternarratives. There have been people telling stories of the U.S. as a *civilized* nation, and there have been people telling stories of the U.S. as a *barbaric* nation. There have been stories of the U.S. as a force for *good* in the world and stories about the U.S. being a force for *terror* in the world. Some have talked about the United States becoming gradually more inclusive, while others have told stories of the U.S. continuing its domination in other, more creative forms. While some have told the story of the U.S. being chosen by God, others have narrated the U.S. as being damned from the beginning.

This collection of essays is designed to be provocative. It is designed to further conversations that we believe deserve popular, national, and international attention. To challenge American exceptionalism and American innocence is to challenge the system from which they rest. That system, U.S. imperialism, remains a scary, if not unheard of, concept to many of the young people currently taking center stage in the resistance to oppression occurring around the country. There is no better time than now to deconstruct—and dismantle—American exceptionalism and American innocence, and identify the myriad of ways it has normalized imperial policy since the nation's inception. A central aim of this book is to confront the reality that violence, empire, genocide, slavery, dispossession, and white supremacy are not *aberattions* of the U.S. nation-state but *central to* its very identity and structure. It is common nowadays to hear well-intentioned rhetoric about how torture, anti-Black racism, and Muslim immigration bans do not reflect "who we really are" as a country. Yet, as we will see, this is a paramount example of how ideologies of American exceptionalism and innocence work together to paint a distorted picture of our nation's history, its current social structures, and what possibilities exist without them.

The essays in this book seek to develop a new anti-war consciousness as more young people become curious about alternatives to the conditions before them. The American way of war is more complicated and indeed more expansive than in any other period of history. Yet the virtue of the American military is one of the most difficult narratives to challenge. It strikes a sensitive nerve with broad sections of the population precisely because militarism is such a critical component to the foundations of American exceptionalist ideology and the class interests behind it. As the American war machine inches closer to even more dangerous confrontations, the revival of an anti-war movement becomes more critical.

Radical politics lead to radical possibilities. This book seeks to bring together historical and contemporary issues related to American exceptionalism and American innocence to help inject a radical consciousness into the discontent of our times. It isn't meant as a replacement for activism or even a "how-to" in the mechanics of organizing a new movement. After all, oppressed communities don't need to be told that American exceptionalism and American innocence are blatant lies. Many already know this, consciously or unconsciously. State violence has been at the center of these communities' analysis because state violence has been at the center of their *experience*. Our goal, then, is to amplify their voices, to share with others what these victims of U.S. imperialism have been saying all along but have not been heard due to the intentional and ruthless suppression of their narratives.

Something that often goes unsaid is the wide gap that exists between the worlds of scholarship and activism. This is a gap between ideology and practice, between knowing and doing. Yet one cannot exist without the other. Social transformation certainly cannot, either. The following pages hope to close that gap and contribute to current efforts to dismantle oppressive ideologies, structures, and institutions. In the process, we join all those in the academy and on the streets who, in the words of the Zapatistas, are trying to create a new world where many worlds are possible.

AMERICAN EXCEPTIONALISM *AND* AMERICAN INNOCENCE

CHAPTER 1

"'Why Do They Hate Us?' American Innocence and Historical Memory"

"So American exceptionalism rewrites history and time lines to make immediacy and punitive reflex action normative and to place the wounded and traumatized American body center while denying the terror it has inflicted and does inflict on other bodies."

—Joy James[1]

"Despite the absence of public debate about sexuality and the war on terrorism, the 'Abu Ghraib prisoner sexual torture/abuse scandal,' as it is now termed, vividly reveals that sexuality constitutes a central and crucial component of the machinic assemblage that is American patriotism."

—Jasbir Puar[2]

Few events in history have affected the American psyche more than what transpired on September 11th, 2001, now known as "9/11." Nearly 3,000 Americans died in the terrorist attack on the World Trade Center Towers. The tragedy was exploited mightily by the American power structure, for it raised to the surface the deeply chauvinistic, racist, and imperialist attitudes of many Americans that could be manipulated and directed. Since its inception, the U.S. had enjoyed geographical and political advantages that allowed it to become a powerful aggressor without repercussion. The U.S. committed acts of aggression abroad in the name of freedom and democracy but rarely had to worry about being attacked for its hypocrisy on American soil. To be attacked on the mainland was a direct assault on American superiority and only intensified the desire for many Americans to feel special and powerful again.

So strong was the fear promoted by the American power structure in the aftermath of 9/11 that the mere sight of burning buildings reignited trauma. In a fascinating controversy that erupted more than ten years after 9/11, a movie poster for the 2014 film *Teenage Mutant Ninja Turtles* was redacted after thousands on social media decried the imagery as offensive to the victims of the attack. The poster of the turtles jumping out of a skyscraper with a release date of September 11th evoked such strong feelings that the director yelled at the studio executives for their "mistake." It was as if buildings had never burned before during the dozens of American wars of aggression against nations in Asia, Africa, and Latin America. It was as if Chile didn't have its own 9/11—September 11th of 1973—when the U.S. government overthrew the democratically elected Salvador Allende and replaced him with the brutal dictator, Augusto Pinochet. No, *our* 9/11 was different. It involved Americans as the *victims* of terror, not as *perpetrators*. This narcissism led many Americans to think that any picture of a burning building anywhere in the world next to the date of September 11th, even with animated turtles jumping out of it, was an insult to the trauma of the World Trade Center getting hit. It didn't matter that this poster came out thirteen years after the attack. And apparently it didn't matter that the poster was promoting the film's release in *Australia*.

The imagery of buildings burning was nothing more than a metaphor for the inherently special quality of the American nation-state and the shaky ground from which it stood. September 11th, 2001, was indeed a day that shook the world. On the one hand, the U.S. was rattled by a vulnerability in what had been advertised for decades as the world's most secure and powerful military. On the other hand, a war was unleashed that forever changed the international polity. Then-President George W. Bush declared a "War on Terror." This new war was a reform of an old one. U.S. imperialism had already laid plenty of blood soaked tracks that could be traced back to major corporations and their quest for profit and dominance. The "War on Terror" laid the blame for 9/11 on whatever people or whichever nation the American military had not yet placed under its submission. An intense military buildup on all fronts was masked by the heavily promoted notion that the American nation-state and everything it represented was under attack from a foreign entity. Yet as Kyoo Lee writes, "We will not forget that we have been attacked, but we have forgotten that we have often been attackers, justly or not."[3]

With the fall of the Soviet Union, U.S. imperialism became the unquestioned hegemon in world politics and economy. This reality created a new set of political challenges as much as it greatly expanded the influence and profits of American enterprise. The American nation-state needed a new enemy to justify the growth of domestic and global exploitation. The events on 9/11 provided this enemy and gave the rulers of U.S. imperialism the political cover necessary to modify American exceptionalism in service of their interests. Such political cover existed during the Cold War, which, as Aslı Bâli and Aziz Rana argue,

> was no doubt filled with defections from international legality, anti-democratic overthrows, and support for American-aligned dictatorships. Indeed, in many ways the defining feature of American Cold War power was the degree to which the promotion of liberal constitutionalism in actuality produced coercion and widespread violence on the ground.[4]

And just as the threat of communism was utilized to wage war on dissidents in the American mainland and dissident nations abroad, so too did the War on Terror give the American ruling class an avenue from which to expand its war apparatus. American innocence and exceptionalism not only narrated the expansion of war as an aberration but also intensified the notion that the U.S. only waged war in response to threats to its existence. This is a key component of American exceptionalism and innocence. Not only is the violence inherent to American domestic and foreign policy presented as a deviation from the norm, but also as a tactic wielded only when it is necessary to protect the exceptional character of the "national interest." As Joy James so aptly notes, 9/11 gave America the chance to paint itself as both "the recognizable victim and inevitable victor."[5]

The idea of the United States as a perpetual "victim" of enemy aggression that is compelled to "play defense" on the international stage is a quintessential example of American exceptionalism and American innocence working together. "Exceptionalist states portray themselves as innocent victims. They are never the sources of international insecurity, but only the targets of malign forces," writes K. J. Holsti. "They do not act so much as react to a hostile world," he continues. "They are exceptional, in part, because they are morally clean as the objects of others' hatreds."[6] Of course, it's not just presidential rhetoric that perpetuates these ideologies. Author Jason Dittmer shows how one of the most popular comic book heroes, Captain America, contributes to political narratives of innocence as well. In contrast to most superheroes that carry around "glamorous offensive weapons," Dittmer writes, Captain America's prop is "a rather unglamorous (yet patriotically covered) shield."[7] As consumers of popular culture, we should not underestimate the impact such representations play in how we understand the world. If Captain America is to serve as the embodiment of what values we present and what our country is *really* about, then "it is important for the narrative of America that he embodies defense rather than offense."[8] Just like the former Texas governor George W. Bush after 9/11, Captain America is placed "in the heroic tradition of the American cowboy killer, the man of purely innocent intention who draws second in the gun battle but shoots more quickly and accurately than the dastardly foe."[9]

When the World Trade Center Towers fell, George W. Bush faced political dilemmas that could only be remedied by a full embrace of American exceptionalism. He needed an event that would change the trajectory of his administration, which was hampered by accusations that votes were stolen from Democratic Party candidate Al Gore in the state of Florida during the general election. Bush had yet to give the ruling class anything definitive in terms of policy. The 9/11 attacks provided the newly sworn-in president an opportunity to remake the nation's most coveted ideologies: American exceptionalism and American innocence. In his response to the attacks, Bush lamented, "Why do they hate us?" His answer: "They hate what they see right here in this chamber: a democratically elected government. Their leaders are self-appointed. They hate our freedoms: our freedom of religion, our freedom of speech, our freedom to vote and assemble and disagree with each other."[10]

It was in this speech that Bush taught the world an important lesson about the function of American exceptionalist ideology. Donald Pease, author of many books and articles on American exceptionalism, roots the ideology within the context of history. He explains:

> Before 9/11, expositors of American exceptionalism represented the unfolding of American history as the progressive development of American

> principles guided by Manifest Destiny. The triumphalism of the post-Cold War 1990s summoned Americans to envision . . . the evangelical spread of American democracy across the world. But the Global War on Terror the Bush Administration declared after 9/11 shattered the image of a providential future as an expendable delusion.[11]

Beginning a declaration of war with the question "Why do they hate us?" suggests that the spread of American democracy required war. But as Carrie Tirado Bramen argues, that war was started with a question that operates less as an inquiry and more so as "a way of making sense of a complex incident by personalizing the political." In her book, *American Niceness: A Cultural History*, Bramen observes how "[t]he global, structural, and historical dimensions of the event are reduced to an interpersonal matter of envy and hatred. It translates a political crisis into a problem of sociability." "'Why do they hate us?'" she writes, "is another way of asking 'Why don't they like us?' [. . .] To know us, the question assumes, is to love us."[12]

The assumption that the American nation-state is a loveable representative of the American people reinforces the racialized character of American innocence. It simplifies the "us" and "them" dichotomy. It is conveniently vague. And it leaves no room for either introspection or diplomacy. As K. J. Holsti writes,

> Bush's only public explanation for the al-Qaeda attack was that these evil people hate everything America stands for, particularly its freedom. Framed this way, one is the innocent victim, and one thus does not have to indulge in any self-examination or enter into any dialogue with the enemy. The enemy has no issues to discuss, but is only driven by hatred. All that remains to be done is to root out the evildoers and bring them to justice.[13]

Thus, rather than explore the roots of U.S. foreign policy in possibly instigating the attack, American exceptionalism defines the enemy as anyone or anything that is presumed to "hate" the American way of life. And those who "hate" the American way of life have no rights that the American nation-state is bound to respect.

American exceptionalism has always presumed national innocence despite imposing centuries of war and plunder. The U.S. has been at war for over ninety percent of its existence. These wars have all been justified as necessary ventures meant to defend or expand America's so-called founding values and beliefs. A consequence of centuries of endless war has been the historical tendency of the U.S. to erase from consciousness the realities that surround American domestic and international policy, not to mention the system of imperialism that governs both.

The declaration of a War on Terror was (and remains) a defining moment for the legacy of American exceptionalism. It utilized a period of crisis to cement the image that the U.S. and its representative values were in perpetual danger. The threat to American "national security" lay in the rise of Islamic fundamentalism and terrorism. As practitioners of "Jihad," or holy war, these demonized "others" from foreign lands served as the scapegoat for War on Terror imperial policy. And for the first time, American exceptionalism was promoted not just as a service to humanity, but rather a convenient excuse to expand American power at the expense of the people and planet on every coast.

The erasure of historical memory that has taken place during the War on Terror is a key component to the preservation of American innocence and exceptionalism. Ordinary Americans rarely think about the roots of the American nation-state as being firmly planted in the colonial conquest of Native populations and the enslavement of African populations. Ordinary Americans rarely ponder the consequences of the millions that were murdered during the Korean and Vietnam wars, or any American war abroad for that matter. Even when acknowledged, rarely has the power of American exceptionalism been challenged on a mass basis. Indeed, the War on Terror merely offered the United States another way to apply its colonial logic to a different set of circumstances.

These circumstances were largely a product of the September 11th attacks which led to an intense ideological assault on the part of officials in Washington. This ideological assault sought to bury the masses in hysteria draped in American exceptionalism. The War on Terror, which has been dutifully enforced by three presidential administrations thus far, required an intense demonization of Arab and Muslim peoples to justify domestic and foreign aggression. Policies such as The Patriot Act and new provisions in the National Defense Authorization Act greatly scaled back civil liberties on the American mainland while the invasions of Afghanistan and Iraq led to massive amount of civilian casualties abroad. Importantly, the War on Terror also led to mass systems of torture at Abu Ghraib, a scandal that Jasbir Puar argues should not be seen as exceptional to the U.S. war machine. Rather, it "needs to be contextualized within a range of practices and discourses . . . that lasso sexuality in the deployment of U.S. nationalism, patriotism, and, increasingly, empire."[14]

The construction of what Puar calls the "monstrous terrorist" involves the interconnection of multiple ideologies and forms of domination. This process, which Puar and Amit Rai explain, is worth quoting in full:

> First, the monster is not merely an other; it is one category through which a multiform power operates. As such, discourses that would mobilize monstrosity as a screen for otherness are always also involved in circuits of normalizing power as well: the monster and the person to be corrected are close cousins. Second, if the monster is part of the West's family of abnormals, questions of race and sexuality will have always haunted its figuration. The category of monstrosity is also an implicit index of civilizational development and cultural adaptability. As the machines of war begin to narrow the choices and life chances people have here in America and in decidedly more bloody ways abroad, it seems a certain grid of civilizational progress organized by such keywords as "democracy," "freedom," and "humanity" have come to superintend the figure of the monster.[15]

The War on Terror was therefore, in large part, a psychological assault that justified military expansion and further distorted the economic realities that undergirded such expansion. As Puar and Rai argue, the study of counterterrorism was immediately undertaken not just by the media but also by academic universities across the country. Counterterrorism became a "civilizational" knowledge.[16] It drew new contours in the racial, class, and gender hierarchies that exist in American society. The terrorist became the object of scorn and the target of war, with a flexible definition that served a variety of purposes.

That the War on Terror meant the creation of new enemies (i.e., monsters) and greater military spending and buildup at the expense of poor, exploited, and oppressed people everywhere meant that the project for a "New American Century" had to rely on an altered form of American exceptionalism for legitimacy. No longer could the American ruling circles point to an alternative, evil system as it did in the Cold War period as the main threat to the American way of life. This time the threat had to extend beyond borders and economic arrangements. American dominance had been achieved, and the "end of history" declared after the fall of the Soviet Union. Terrorism was an action that could be carried out by whoever the U.S. deemed to threaten its "security." Its definition could be easily adjusted to fit the needs of power and profit at any point and time.

The premise that the American way of life was under attack by a foreign yet stateless threat provided exactly what was needed to fuel the spread of U.S. empire. U.S. imperialism, or the system of social relations governed by monopoly corporations and financial firms, received a facelift amid a sharp decline in living standards and conditions both in the American mainland and around the world. U.S. imperialism's social relations have been marked by constant military and economic expansion worldwide, a process that precipitates an even higher degree of concentration of wealth and power in the hands of a few corporations and nation-states. The last vestiges of 20th-century socialism had been attacked by the Clinton Administration in its NATO-backed bombing of Yugoslavia. China stood alone as the last major power to be governed by a communist state. American cartels and monopolies found ample room around the world to rake in record profits yet the living standards of the industrialized capitalist world continued to plummet, especially for the Black poor. Something had to be done to maintain the illusion of American invincibility.

The politics of the War on Terror have attempted to stabilize U.S. imperialism by reinforcing the white supremacist, imperialist, and militaristic interests which shape American exceptionalist ideology. This has led to an intense psychological assault characterized by a fear of "the other." The assault isn't new, as U.S. imperialism has indeed used fear of the "other" to enrich the ruling class since its inception. In fact, this history has its roots in anti-Black racism. As Nikhil Pal Singh argues, the fear of slave rebellions required the colonial elite to frame Africans as inherent "thieves":

> The slave was "by nature a thief," Benjamin Franklin argued, later amending this assertion to argue that a propensity for thieving was a consequence of slavery as an institution. Thomas Jefferson claimed that the emancipation

> of slaves would threaten U.S. society itself [. . .] Blacks being unable to forget the terrible wrongs done to them would nurse murderous wishes . . . while whites would live in a state of anticipatory fear that urged preemptive violence.[17]

In other words, fear of the "other" has been a staple of American exceptionalism since the very founding of the nation. The War on Terror provides a contemporary example of how American exceptionalism is utilized in service of the profit, power, and pleasure of a few. Militarism is the primary means by which the few—better described as capitalists and the state functionaries who do their bidding—enforce the interests of imperialism beyond the borders of the nation-state. The military and the police act as the armed body of the state. Their function has always been to enforce the rule of a minority at the expense of genuine peace and justice of the majority.

Narratives of American innocence and exceptionalism preserve this arrangement by effectively placing the U.S. as the most advanced and progressive arrangement known in the history of humanity. "Terrorism" thus possesses only one definition, the definition derived from the political class that occupies the American nation-state. According to their definition, "terrorism" finds definition in portrayals of radical "Islamic" fundamentalists one day and undocumented migrants the next. Black American mass movements have been called "Black Identity Extremists" by the FBI, a slight variant of the label "terrorist." "What is called 'terrorism' is often the uprising of defenseless, subjugated people fighting against state-sanctioned violence," writes Lisa Lowe. "[T]hey are named 'terrorists' not only to delegitimize their actions and to justify 'war' against them, but also to gain popular support for the exercise of state and military violence as a means for dominating regions, populations, and resources."[18] The NSA has continuously cited the threat of terrorism to justify the mass surveillance of the entire population's digital communications. And of course, military ventures in Iraq, Afghanistan, and the oil and mineral rich Middle East region were explained away as necessary preconditions for the defense of "national interests" from terrorism.

Terrorism has thus served as a convenient political project of U.S. imperialism. This project took full advantage of the 9/11 attacks to create what Junaid Rana terms "the terror industrial complex."[19] The terror industrial complex, as an outgrowth of American militarism, found its foundations in the racialization of Muslims. As Rana explains, "the figure of the Muslim enables the policing of people of color at an ever expanding level" and "continuously operates from within the figures of criminality and social death that depend on the racialization of Black and brown bodies."[20] These alterations in the infrastructure of American white supremacy led not only to the police and FBI surveillance of Arab and Muslim populations in New York City and across the country, but also a steep decline in civil liberties for the population at large.[21]

The white supremacist logic of the War on Terror has become accepted fact. When former NATO commander Wesley Clark revealed that the plan to overthrow the governments of seven nations in the Middle East and North Africa after 9/11 had been realized in 2007, it was met with little opposition from ordinary Americans. Mass surveillance and police militarization has produced a semblance of resistance but none with the power to influence official policy. Too many Americans still search for rationalizations for the domestic and international wars wrought by the U.S. As Neferti X. M. Tadiar reminds us, "a general embrace of empire as status quo, whatever its valence as a positive or a negative reality, marks this dire political, historical hour."[22]

The embrace of empire has been a general condition in American society since the War on Terror began almost twenty years ago. A Democratic Party Administration under Barack Obama quieted the War on Terror's message but intensified each and every policy of the war. White supremacy and militarism have been the driving forces of this project. American exceptionalism is the anchor. This anchor has been distorting and erasing our memories of U.S. imperialism's wretched conditions since the conquest of the colonies. "They" do not hate us, they hate our anchor.

CHAPTER 2

"Conquest, Genocide, and the Formation of America"

"The United States is a nation defined by its original sin: the genocide of American Indians [. . .] American Indian tribes are viewed as an inherent threat to the nation, poised to expose the great lies of U.S. democracy: that we are a nation of laws and not random power; that we are guided by reason and not faith; that we are governed by representation and not executive order; and finally, that we stand as a self-determined citizenry and not a kingdom of blood or aristocracy [. . .] From the perspective of American Indians, 'democracy' has been wielded with impunity as the first and most virulent weapon of mass destruction."

—Sandy Grande[1]

"But it is not permissible that the authors of devastation should also be innocent. It is the innocence which constitutes the crimes."

—James Baldwin[2]

The colonial genocide of Indigenous people was the first root planted in the formation of America. That root remains a fundamental anchor of American society and one that permeates American culture. The National Football League (NFL) is a case in point. A struggle between tribal organizations and the Washington Redskins has been ongoing over the controversy of the team's name since the 1960's. "Redskins," as sports journalist Dave Zirin notes, refers to "a time when European and then American men skinned Native men, women, and children and produced them as 'proof of Indian kill' in order to collect bounties issued first by colonies and companies and then by states and territories."[3] Much of the Indigenous population describes the term "Redskin" as a racial slur.

Redskins owner Dan Snyder has repeatedly refused to sit down with tribal leaders to discuss the name. Yet in 2017, the NFL awarded the team the Thanksgiving Day game. The NFL's decision to have the Redskins play on a holiday so representative of colonial conquest has not been lost on those Indigenous to this land. The league's decision reaffirmed what Indigenous peoples have always known: the colonial ideology that justified the conquest of Indigenous land and nations has been culturally reproduced by American institutions to give Americans the opportunity to "disengage themselves from historic and ongoing marginalization of American Indians." In the process, DaShanne Stokes explains, "a false sense of unity is forged between American Indians and European Americans through the assumption that American Indians feel honored and respected by racialized mascotery."[4]

Because Indigenous people are either ignored or tokenized, most Americans feel no compulsion to pay any mind to their existence. American exceptionalism has been crucial in the reproduction of this ongoing reality. Indigenous people are viewed as a fossil or an artifact. As C. Richard King writes regarding the Washington football team controversy, "Native American mascots and other stereotypes persist because most Americans remain thoughtless, lacking the resources, knowledge, and skills to think critically about them." "Most Americans," he continues, "have not received adequate historical instruction nor had exposure to Indigenous peoples and perspectives as living, vital, and valuable." This indictment of the American educational system explains why so many Americans are unable to critically analyze the words and actions of politicians, corporate media outlets, and other cultural producers of the system they live in. "In many ways," King concludes, "while most Americans can read, they remain illiterate."[5] Roxanne Dunbar-Ortiz and Dina Gilio-Whitaker join King in placing blame on the U.S. media and education system for spreading "master narratives" of American exceptionalism in relation to Native American history. These master narratives, or "state mythologies," they argue, are strategically "designed to undergird the patriotism and emotional commitment necessary in a loyal citizenry."[6]

But while the American education system is certainly culpable for the historical illiteracy of the American population, the problem is much bigger than a lack of information—or what Alexis Shotwell calls "benign ignorance." It's too simplistic to think that if people were just taught the *right* version of history, or presented enough facts about what *really* happened to Indigenous populations, then people would want to join struggles for social justice. According to Shotwell, "we don't just have a knowledge problem—we have a habit-of-being problem":

> We white people might, on some level, *like* living with annihilated social and historical memories—we might like to think that the present can be innocent of the past that produced it. We might like to think, though we're ashamed to admit it, that we don't need to tell or hear the painful stories of the actions that created the world we live in. That feeling, of wanting to be people unmoored from history, of endorsing the pretense that we have nothing to do with the past that constitutes our material conditions and our most intimate subjectivities, is a feeling that defines us. The social organization of forgetting means that our actual histories are lost, and it means that we have a feeling of acceptance and normalness about living with a lie instead of an unforgetting.[7]

This "social organization of forgetting" leads many innocent white American settlers to frame colonization as a "civilizing mission," where the benefits far outweigh whatever consequences resulted from the decimation and destruction of vibrant Indigenous communities. It is this logic that has shaped the very essence of American exceptionalist ideology. The late author and journalist Christopher Hitchens, no doubt seduced by both ideologies of American exceptionalism and innocence, justified Indigenous genocide in a way that is very familiar to many Americans:

> [It] is sometimes unambiguously the case that a certain coincidence of ideas, technologies, population movements and politico-military victories leaves humanity on a slightly higher plane than it knew before. The transformation of part of the northern part of this continent into "America" inaugurated a nearly boundless epoch of opportunity and innovation, and thus deserves to be celebrated with great vim and gusto, with or without the participation of those who wish they had never been born.[8]

Such calls to "celebrate" the nation's "successful" civilizing mission are part and parcel of what American exceptionalism is all about. American exceptionalism leaves nothing for which to celebrate the lives of the Indigenous people who were dispossessed along the way. Indigenous people possess zero representation in the U.S. political system. Whatever "citizenship" has been endowed on them is merely an extension of their colonial erasure. Indigenous people face extreme poverty and notoriously high police homicide rates in the "reservations" where they were forced to reside by way of state terror and colonial displacement. Indigenous people in fact do exist, but that existence under the conditions of present day American empire remains precarious.[9]

American exceptionalism helped lay the foundations for this precarity by extolling the virtues of the American colonial project. The liberty, freedom, and democracy that supposedly characterized the formation of the U.S. did not include the Indigenous people whose land made "independence" possible. English settlers spent centuries decimating the Indigenous people of the North American mainland prior to formal independence. Natsu Taylor Saito explains that between 1513 and 1900, an Indigenous population of fifteen million people was reduced to 250,000 in what now belongs to the United States and Canada.[10] Settler warfare, whether in the form of exposing Indigenous populations to disease or waging bloody invasions, was accompanied by a narrative that assigned Indigenous land as "free" or "unoccupied."

The very existence of Indigenous people was thus an impediment to the initial development of the American empire. As Patrick Wolfe describes, settler colonialism required the racialization of the Native to justify expansion. Varied racial classifications were bestowed on Africans and Natives, whereby "as opposed to enslaved people, whose reproduction augmented their owners' wealth, Indigenous people obstructed settlers' access to land, so their increase was counterproductive."[11] Discovery and conquest was not about liberty, but profit. Colonists sought to profit from the land of the Indigenous and the labor of the enslaved to enrich the planters and traders who spearheaded the colonial project.

Settler colonialism is often boxed into a narrow category of history (the "colonial era") instead of viewed as an enduring structure in the development of the American way of life. Perhaps no other example best illuminates the importance of colonialism to the foundations of American exceptionalism than the Thanksgiving holiday. Every year, millions of working Americans are given Thanksgiving Day off to celebrate the nation's colonial origins. The celebration commemorates the historical account of the supposedly peaceful relations enjoyed between the Plymouth colonists, backed by the Virginia Company corporation of England, and the Native Wampanoag. The United American Indians of New England, however, remember the event not as a day of celebration but a "Day of Mourning" for Indigenous people.

It is a "Day of Mourning" because that fateful event marks a dark period for the survival of the Indigenous across New England. According to John Two-Hawks, who leads the educational website "Native Circle," the Indigenous people who are said to have attended the celebrated meal in 1621 were likely not invited.[12] In fact, the meal did not even initiate the celebration of Thanksgiving. Thanksgiving officially began after the massacre of the Pequot people in what is now Connecticut in 1637. The Pequot war led by Governor Winthrop killed upwards of 700 Pequots and ended with the colonists feasting in celebration of their spoils. The Indigenous of New England mounted a valiant resistance up until the end of "King Philip's War" of 1675 but suffered fatal losses in both land and life in the process.

Settler conquest of Native land was not merely a precursor to the American nation-state. Colonization laid the basis for the very formation of the state itself. The Proclamation of 1763 issued by the British Crown prohibited the colonists from expanding west into Indigenous territory beyond the Allegheny and Appalachian Mountains. Saito notes that the colonists saw this policy as an unacceptable infringement on their expansionist ambitions.[13] In fact, the "Founding Fathers" accuse King George in their Declaration of Independence of inciting "domestic insurrections amongst us . . . to bring on the inhabitants of our frontiers, the merciless Indian Savages whose known rule of warfare, is an undistinguished destruction of all ages, sexes and conditions."[14] American exceptionalism and innocence have distorted the centrality of settler colonialism to the formation of the U.S. by framing both the "Founding Fathers" and the founding of the nation as a democratic experiment.

The reality remains, however, that the spoils of colonialism and the eradication of Indigenous people were organizing principles in the country's formation. Western liberalism was one of the ideological principles that helped carry forth the process. Liberalism cemented the dominance of private property and created a society that modeled the Western world "in claiming the individual 'free' when s/he is unfettered by social ties."[15] While "the rest of the world has regarded this situation as akin to death," this individualistic construction of freedom created the condition of possibilities for Indigenous dispossession. As Donald F. Tibbs and Tryon P. Woods explain,

> liberalism's emphasis on individual rights and autonomy emerges through Western Europe's clash with Africa and the Americas, not prior to, or simply as a result of, this conquest. In this way the very notion of what it means to be "free," to possess liberty, is dependent upon an understanding of unfreedom and knowing which subjects not only are incapable of possessing themselves, but are, moreover, justly acquired and used by others.[16]

Whereas prior to colonial contact, Indigenous nations organized their societies and lands on a communal basis, the liberal promise of freedom involved a radically different social order. This is why it becomes problematic when some Americans say they don't necessarily believe in the exceptional nature of the U.S. but that they believe in its exceptional *ideals* and *values*. The ideals of U.S. society cannot be separated from the society itself. American "ideals" and "values" are fundamentally rooted in classical liberal thought. "Western notions of freedom, liberty, individual rights, and property are all profoundly bound up with the enslavement of the racialized Other."[17]

The promotion of freedom for colonialists and the un-freedom of the Indigenous continued into the American Republic's first presidential administration. George Washington and his secretary of war Henry Knox wasted no time in laying the basis for "Manifest Destiny." Manifest Destiny was an alteration to the colonial ideology that led to the formation of the American nation-state. It was rooted in the expansionist interests of the newly "independent" American ruling class. Manifest Destiny presupposed that American expansion from coast to coast was a matter of ordained fate justified by the Republic's superior "civilization."

A combination of Indigenous resistance and systemic limitations related to competition between the colonial powers limited settler expansion prior to the "American Revolution." While Indigenous resistance to settler colonialism continued, Native nations found themselves increasingly isolated without Spanish and British aid, as limited as it may have been prior to the formation of the U.S. The economic foundations of the new republic intensified lust for Indigenous territory as "[o]wners of large, slave-worked plantations sought to expand their landholdings while small farm owners who were unable to compete with the planters . . . desperately sought cheap land to support their families."[18] Furthermore, tensions between unregulated settler militias and the burgeoning military authorities prompted a number of settlements on the peripheries of Indigenous nations to threaten secession from the republic.[19] This made expansion into Indigenous territories an important method for quelling class cleavages among the settler population.

Washington's Administration focused its energy on fully conquering the territory of Ohio Country. The Miami, Shawnee, Iroquois, and Seneca people repeatedly beat back the advance of Washington's army, which was primarily composed of Kentucky squatters excited about the potential to score stolen land and bounty from Indigenous scalps. Secretary of War Henry Knox sent his commanders to recruit hundreds of Kentucky "rangers" (mercenaries) to loot and burn Miami towns and fields to the ground. Over forty women and children were kidnapped under the threat that even more would suffer cruel deaths should the Indigenous nations fail to surrender. It was such irregular, terror-induced warfare that would produce the Treaty of Greenville of 1795 and provide the nascent republic with the confiscated land necessary to generate tax revenue.[20]

American exceptionalism and innocence gave the American settler-state a powerful force from which to rewrite and erase its blood soaked history. Settler colonialism formed the basis of American capitalism and imperialism. The ruling class required a narrative that would both erase the existence of Indigenous people and forgive the supposedly "superior civilization" of its crimes. That's because settler colonialism would continue unabated as the U.S. sought expansion further South and West of its colonial borders. In 1862, the Lincoln Administration executed 38 Dakota men accused of rape, robbery, and other crimes related to the US-Dakota War.[21] Boyd Cothran explains how the American ruling class memorialized the so-called heroism of those settlers who waged war on the Indigenous in the Modoc War of 1872–73.[22] The memorialization of settler incursions on Indigenous territory cemented the portrayal of Indigenous people as criminal threats to the enlightened, white citizens of the colonizing Republic.

Cothran's study shows how the 19th century in many respects "perfected" the myth of American innocence. During this period, the U.S. media was obsessed with reporting instances of violent settlers being "murdered" by Indigenous resisters. Media discourse was able "to convince white Americans that they were the victims of the Indian wars and not in fact the victorious aggressors."[23] What makes Cothran's analysis even more compelling is how he connects early colonial formations of American innocence with its manifestations in today's War on Terror. Inferring it was no accident that the U.S. military gave Osama Bin Laden the code name "Geronimo," Cothran argues that interrogating these "longer-held traditions of claiming American innocence pushes us all to reckon with the continuing importance of redemptive violence to American's [sic] cultural and historical understandings of their wars of aggression." "In other words," he concludes, "the Indian wars still matter, try as we might to forget them."[24]

American innocence and exceptionalism have worked hand in hand to help Americans forget that the settler colonial genocide of Indigenous people has first and foremost served the interests of U.S. imperialism. Indigenous nations presented the first threat to the economic needs of a system based on profit accumulation through the acquisition, sale, and exploitation of the land through the use of slave labor. The "Founding Fathers" and their allies devised a narrative that essentially rebranded settler colonialism. White, male settlers were the first to be endowed the special privileges of developing what the Puritans called a "City on a Hill." The massacre and plunder of Indigenous nations were conducted with impunity and their people were forever marked as savages that possessed neither history nor humanity. As Sylvia Wynter shows us, "all other human beings who did not look, think, and act as the peoples of Western Europe did were now to be classified not as *Enemies-of-Christ* but, rather, as the Lack of 'true humanness,' allegedly because of their lack of a Western European order of rationality."[25] Andrea Smith highlights the persistence of sexual terror within processes of settler colonialism. "The goal of colonialism is not just to kill colonized peoples but to destroy their sense of being people," she writes. "It is through sexual violence that a colonizing group attempts to render a colonized people as inherently rapable, their lands inherently invadable, and their resources inherently extractable."[26]

Centuries of war and plunder have been unable to break the spirit of resistance of Indigenous people. Indigenous people resisted U.S. settler colonialism throughout the 17th and 18th centuries in what are called the "Indian Wars." The American Indian Movement of the 1960s and 1970s and the struggle to replace Columbus Day with Indigenous Peoples' Day in cities across America prove that Indigenous resistance to land and cultural theft will continue as long as settler colonialism exists. Today, the most visible front of resistance to settler colonialism has been Standing Rock Sioux's fight to preserve their ancestral lands in the face of the U.S. Army Corps approval of the Dakota Access Pipeline in 2014.

American exceptionalism and innocence remain major ideological forces that inform the contemporary development of settler colonialism and U.S. imperialism. Leonard Peltier, for example, has spent over forty years in America's prisons for his activity in the American Indian Movement.[27] He is at risk of dying in prison precisely because the narrative of American exceptionalism has washed away the legacy of Indigenous resistance and the centrality of settler colonialism from the historical memory of most Americans. The mass incarceration state which Peltier occupies is a prime example of settler colonialism. As historian Kelly Lytle Hernández notes, mass *incarceration* might be better described as mass *elimination*. For Hernández, the U.S. prison regime definitely has roots in slavery, but it can also be traced back to settler colonial logics.[28] Incarceration is a form of elimination which, in her words, "has been deployed in different ways in different times against different Indigenous and racially disparaged communities, but the punch line has been the same: elimination in the service of establishing, defending, and reproducing a settler society."[29] American innocence casts the elimination of Indigenous people as a "necessary evil," one that brought forth the greatest civilization ever born. Thus, even those settlers guilty of occupying Indigenous land can be forgiven for their crimes against humanity.

Saito reminds us that these crimes were extensive, as by 1890 the Federal Government estimated

> that fewer than 250,000 Indians remained, residing on less than 3% of their original land base. This had been accomplished directly by military force; by purportedly "rogue" settlers who were, in fact, encouraged to occupy Indian lands; and by individuals motivated by the scalp bounties offered by local governments and "civic" organizations throughout the country. Most of the remaining Indigenous peoples had been forcibly removed from their homelands, interned en masse in unlivable conditions, and confined to alien and inhospitable reservations-processes that predictably resulted in the deaths of 40 to 50% of those removed or interned.[30]

The American nation-state and the imperialist system it governs thus rests on the foundations of settler colonialism and war. American exceptionalism and innocence were critical weapons in this war. These related ideologies helped convince settlers across class lines of the graciousness of the conqueror and the inhumanity of the conquered. The Indigenous blood spilled from the terror of colonial plunder shaped American identity and citizenship. Thankfully, however, the reality that American identity was founded upon the destruction of Indigenous people and the enslavement of Africans has been more readily acknowledged by activists and scholars alike in recent years.

Of course, settlers exist in America to this very day. The common tendency is to blame settlers of the past without seeing *ourselves* as settlers, even though we live on stolen land. But if Patrick Wolfe is right that settler colonialism is a *structure*, not an *event*, then we have to come to terms with the remnants of settler colonialism.[31] We have to own up to the violence *we* are implicated in and the violence *we* perpetrate every day. In their article, "Decolonization is Not a Metaphor," Indigenous scholar-activists Eve Tuck and K. Wayne Yang identify a series of what they coin "settler moves to innocence." Tuck and Yang describe these "moves to innocence" as "those strategies or positionings that attempt to relieve the settler of feelings of guilt or responsibility without giving up land or power or privilege, without having to change much at all." While such "moves" might make us feel more self-aware, sensitive, and repentant of our complicity, they are nonetheless "hollow" and "only serve the settler."[32] Yet if decolonization is the end goal, exposing these "moves to innocence" are absolutely necessary since they only serve as "excuses, distractions, and diversions from" the undoing, unlearning, and dismantling of the U.S. colonial regime.[33]

Contemporary manifestations of settler colonialism, whether in the endless wars waged by U.S. imperialism abroad or the continued displacement of Indigenous people in the U.S. mainland, are generally addressed without requisite knowledge of the history and ideology that shaped these very problems. Saito reminds us that one cannot understand present day American influence over "international law" without incorporating the colonization of Indigenous people. The original "civilizing mission" of colonialism remains intact, albeit in different form. To fail to acknowledge this is to fall into the trap of American exceptionalism and negate essential lessons of the past and present. In short, we have to be very careful about how stories are told and who exactly is telling them. As Lisa Lowe reminds us,

> to understand these settler practices as having totally eliminated Indigenous peoples to the point of extinction, as some modern histories have suggested, or to ignore the ongoing nature of settler colonialism by consigning Native people exclusively to the past, is to continue to erase Indigenous people and history in a manner that echoes and reproduces earlier dispossessions. What we might identify as residual within the histories of settler or colonial capitalism does not disappear. To the contrary, it persists and endures, even if less legible within the obfuscations of a new dominant.[34]

Such negation obscures our vision toward a more radical and just future, a future that will not be born if we don't begin questioning and challenging how many Americans rationalize and justify living on stolen land. Only then can we raise American exceptionalism and American innocence to the surface of popular discourse and replace its interpretive frameworks with demands for reparations, sovereignty, and new Native futures—"lives to be lived once the settler nation is gone."[35]

CHAPTER 3

"Was the Revolutionary War Revolutionary for Slaves? A Few Thoughts on Slavery and Its Afterlives"

"If slavery persists as an issue in the political life of black America, it is not because of an antiquarian obsession with bygone days or the burden of a too-long memory, but because black lives are still imperiled and devalued by a racial calculus and a political arithmetic that were entrenched centuries ago."

—Saidiya Hartman[1]

"A great deal of one's energy is expended in reassuring white Americans that they do not see what they see. This is utterly futile, of course, since they do see what they see. And what they see is an appallingly oppressive and bloody history, known all the world over."

—James Baldwin[2]

The making of U.S. imperialism was dependent not only on the genocide of Indigenous peoples. Another and no less devastating policy characterized the formation of America's national identity. That policy was the enslavement of African peoples. Slavery birthed the capitalist economy that still dominates the Western world. The historical development of England's thirteen colonies at the backbone of the American republic was especially dependent on the practice. How can one speak of the *exceptionalism* or *innocence* of the United States when slavery was a driving force in the formation of the very nation-state itself? What stories have we been told that ignore, obscure, or minimize this great evil?

The U.S. is supported by an origins myth which is perhaps the most valuable narrative for the architects of American exceptionalism. It rests on the premise that the "American Revolution" was a positive step forward in the history of humanity. Free-market zealots and left-wing political thinkers alike have heralded the break from the British Empire as an "anti-colonial" rebellion. This rebellion has been deemed a breakthrough in democracy and a cornerstone in the progressive development of unfettered capitalism in the Western hemisphere. As historian Tisa Wenger writes,

> Pundits, politicians, and some scholars have regularly denied that the United States, past or present, should be called an empire. But these denials, and the assurances of American benevolence that so often accompany them, are in no way distinctive to the United States. Rather, they have been part of the discursive mechanics of many empires around the world and help to sustain an exceptionalism that rationalizes the global exercise of U.S. military and economic power. In fact, the colonies that declared their independence from British rule in 1776 were founded in the crucible of empire, out of the mix of Europe's competitions for empire in the Atlantic world. Thomas Jefferson famously described the new republic as a distinctive "Empire of Liberty," and by the late nineteenth century it had joined in the European contest for imperial possessions around the globe.[3]

Despite the imperial ambitions of America's founders, many people assign the purest and most benevolent of motives to their country's first "revolutionaries." America's "revolution" has retained its progressive character even though the colonial elites leading the rebellion had grown rich from the trade of African slaves and the theft of Indigenous land for over a century prior to the Declaration of Independence in 1776.

Still, the American nation-state has been upheld as a beacon of hope from which the principles of liberty, democracy, and freedom have flourished. Historians and scholars have largely accepted the premise that the "American Revolution" instituted these principles into law when the colonists severed ties with the British Crown. While it has been difficult to mask the horrors of slavery on subjugated Africans, it has been equally difficult to pierce through the narrative that the institution of slavery was a mere mistake or an aberration in an otherwise flawless American design. Thus, many Americans proudly look back at the "independence" movement forged by the colonists and call it a "revolution," while offering little regret for the slave economy that was so crucial to the nation's founding.

Constitutional law scholar Aziz Rana, commenting on his book, *The Two Faces of American Freedom*, explains how there are three fundamental problems with our country's origins myth.[4] The first is that it glorifies the so-called founding values of the nation, making institutions such as slavery appear as nothing more than a mere aberration in a larger, redemptive journey. Second, the narrative "reads American founding as an anti-imperial act and the republic as the first post-colonial society" when in fact colonialism and imperialism would remain crucial features of the nation's development into the present day. Finally, the origins myth provides a framework for social change in America where the redemptive promise of the American nation-state is the ideal goal set for future reform projects. As a consequence, the narrative has us believe that social justice requires tweaking a system that is becoming more and more inclusive, rather than organizing to dismantle the system itself. American "revolutionaries" or the "Founding Fathers" are thus seen as the standard bearer representatives of "freedom" and "justice," despite the subjugation and un-freedom they imposed on the colonized Native and the enslaved African.

The dominant narrative of the "American Revolution" is the first attempt to interpret the American story as one of freedom overcoming slavery rather than freedom rooted in slavery.[5] Lisa Lowe argues that this narrative "at once denies colonial slavery, erases the seizure of lands from Native peoples, and develops freedoms for man in modern Europe and North America, while relegating others to geographical and temporal spaces that are constituted as backward, uncivilized, and unfree."[6] Yet the continued relevance of American exceptionalism and American innocence depends on this myth. Whether it's the "American Revolution," the Emancipation Proclamation, the Thirteenth amendment (supposedly) abolishing slavery, the civil rights struggle, or the election of the first Black president, the American story is characterized as a progressive journey toward "a more perfect union." This trope is even reinforced in popular culture, as Salamishah Tillet notes in her analysis of the film "Race," which chronicles Jesse Owens and the 1936 Olympics. Contesting the idea that one person or even one movement can triumph over something as powerful as American anti-blackness, Tillet places Owens's legacy in historical context. "That the Holocaust and World War II were right on the horizon, while Jim Crow legally reigned for almost 30 more years after Owens's Olympic victories," she writes, "proves that one man or one moving image could not stop the tide of history."[7]

This is perhaps why George Shulman invites us to tell the American story in a different way. "Better to begin with American slavery and tell a story not of progress against failures," he writes, "but of continuing domination and struggles (partly effective) against it."[8] Rejection of the origins myth means centering the resistance of the enslaved in the development of the U.S. and taking seriously what Saidiya Hartman calls "the afterlives of slavery." To be sure, it is a lot more convenient to believe that America has become more and more free and that only a little more time is needed to establish our "perfect union." It is not easy to reject America's claim to racial progress, nor to admit that the state has consistently found new, creative ways of deriving power, pleasure, and profit from the domination of Black people. To do so would mean to lose faith in the promise of mere reforms or tweaks of the system and instead imagine a different world altogether. As Hartman writes in her book, *Lose Your Mother: A Journey Along the Atlantic Slave Route*:

> I knew that no matter how far from home I traveled, I would never be able to leave my past behind. I would never be able to imagine being the kind of person who had not been made and marked by slavery. I was black and a history of terror had produced that identity. Terror was "captivity without the possibility of flight," inescapable violence, precarious life. There was no going back to a time or place before slavery, and going beyond it no doubt would entail nothing less momentous than yet another revolution.[9]

Whether the "American Revolution" can be labeled a revolution at all is a question that brings to light the connection between American exceptionalism and historical memory. American educational institutions at all levels often present the formation of the U.S. as a glorious event completely detached from historical context. The fact that many of the "Founding Fathers" such as George Washington owned African slaves is explained away as a small deviation from the democratic order of the American republic rather than a troubling contradiction.[10] Yet narratives such as these have always played a critical role in positioning the U.S. as *different than* and *superior to* other nations. "A main component of early Americans' self-perception," writes K. J. Holsti, "was that they were uniquely free and that in their constitution they had created historically progressive political institutions and practices. America was free, virtuous, and peaceful. Europe was in contrast fallen, corrupt, and warlike."[11]

The American colonizer has historically assumed the identity of a freedom fighter who heroically frees its subjects after it secures freedom for itself. This identity has been ascribed to historical icons such as Abraham Lincoln. Stories of Lincoln often conclude that it was *he* who freed African slaves during the Civil War period. But as Joy James notes, these stories indicate that "Emancipation is *given* by the dominant, it being a legal, contractual, and social agreement." "Freedom," on the other hand, "is *taken* and created. It exists as a right against the captor and/or enslaver and a practice shared in community by the subordinate captives [. . .] Freedom is an ontological status—only the individual or collective—and perhaps a god—can create freedom."[12] In other words, neither Washington nor Lincoln, as heads of the oppressive state itself, have ever been in a position to "grant" freedom to those they oppress.

Presuming the "American Revolution" and its leaders as agents of liberty and freedom erases the role of the oppressed in the making of history. History is not a series of singular, disconnected events. Nor is history determined by the whims of the dominant class alone. American exceptionalism relies heavily on the notion that the roots of the nation's ruling elites directly sprout from the democratic struggle against the British Crown. This effectively minimizes the role the enslavement of Africans played in the making of the U.S. and severs the ties between this history and the continued oppression of Black Americans under present day U.S. imperialism. In today's fights for social justice, then, we must not forget that "Western notions of freedom, liberty, individual rights, and property are all profoundly bound up with the enslavement of the racialized Other."[13]

American exceptionalism and its origins myth protect the racist American power structure by diffusing a special character to the U.S. As a republic, the story goes, America was not constrained by the interests of a monarchy or held down by familial inheritance to state power. Yet this same republic that claimed to bestow freedom upon all citizens had to contend with the contradiction between the founding values of the nation-state and the interests of the class which led its drive to "independence." That contradiction has not become any less relevant in the present day. As Angela Davis and others have pointed out, the Thirteenth Amendment made slavery a crime except as punishment for criminal charges.[14] That penal servitude remained legal after the institution of the Thirteenth Amendment had severe consequences for Black life, whether in the Black Codes that sanctioned slave labor in the penal systems in the post–Civil War period or the present day incarceration regime that many activists have deemed "The New Jim Crow" or centers of "prison slavery."[15]

The afterlives of slavery so foundational to the current structure of U.S. empire cannot be truly understood without analyzing the framework of American exceptionalism and innocence. American virtues of liberty and freedom are bound together with the origins myth to help center attention to the malleability of the American settler colonial project. Even when the interests of white supremacy and private property are attributed to the roots of the project, rarely are they questioned. David Oshinsky's account of the backlash to Reconstruction in Mississippi shows that while emancipation protected Black freedmen from enslavement and forced labor, it by no means guaranteed equality on a social and political basis.[16] Black "freed" people continued to experience slavery's afterlives. The institution of Jim Crow laws and Black Codes kept the majority of Blacks in a state of bondage both within and outside of the American penal system through the proliferation of white vigilante terror.

Conditions for Black Americans remain precarious in the 21st century. Race relations and white privilege are consistent themes of discussion on many college campuses. The Black Lives Matter movement has nationalized this conversation. An opportunity exists for a mass movement to place slavery's afterlives in their proper context. That context bursts asunder the origins myth of the U.S. and should be widely discussed so more activists and scholars find the clarity necessary to envision a new, more just social order. The exceptional and innocent American nation-state would have us believe that slavery is a *past event*, one for which we deeply regret. But slavery—if viewed not just as an economic arrangement but as a form of domination—is not of the *past*; it lives on today. And slavery is also not an *event*; it is a *structure* that forms the very core of what the U.S. is as a country. Even after so-called "emancipation,"

Calvin Warren writes, "the form of terror might change, but the necessity and manifestation of terror remains." "A change in terroristic tactics and strategies is not progress or freedom," he adds, drawing on the work of Frantz Fanon and Hortense Spillers. Instead, "it is the metaphysical holocaust 'showing itself in endless disguises.'"[17]

The origins myth of the U.S. is especially pernicious because it masks the true motivations that spurred the settler drive to independence from London. These motivations, when coupled with the historical context that shaped world politics at the time, indicate that the settler revolt was a not a *revolution* but a *counterrevolution* to the tide of abolition. As Gerald Horne explains, the roots of the "American Revolution" lay in the desire for settlers of the thirteen colonies to preserve slavery:

> London had created an inherently unstable colonial project, based on mass enslavement of Africans—who could then be appealed to by Spanish neighbors and wreak havoc—and an inability to hedge against the fiasco . . . by building a buffer class of free Negros and mulattoes [. . .] That is to say, before 1763, mainland settlers were huddling in fear of Negro insurrection combined with foreign invasion, particularly from Spanish Florida or, possibly from French Canada; afterward, it appeared to a number of colonists—particularly as abolitionist sentiment grew in London—that Negro insurrection would be coupled with the throttling of the colonies by redcoats, many of them bearing an ebony hue.[18]

A host of historical events thus gave rise to the drive toward American "independence." The revolt against British rule was ultimately an effort to maintain the slave trade in opposition to London's incipient trend toward abolition. Africans stolen from their homeland and enslaved in both the mainland colonies and the Caribbean were prone to insurrection. Spain and France took advantage by arming Africans and Indigenous peoples against London's rule. This created a crisis of an internal enemy and an external foe that had the potential of sending London's mainland colonies into political and economic crisis. As London responded by arming Africans and seeking gradual abolition of chattel slavery in the mid to late 18th century, the planter and merchant capitalist class of the mainland colonies began to see London as a threat to its existence. The "Founding Fathers" sought to eliminate this threat by creating a perfect "whiteness" in the form of a republican state. It would do this by granting rights and privileges to European migrants of all classes (now deemed "white") to protect the slave-owning class from the rapidly growing African population, which by the year 1776 outnumbered white settlers in important colonies such as South Carolina.[19]

The Somerset case of 1772 solidified settler resentment toward London. James Somerset, originally a Virginia slave, was given freedom by English courts after escaping to London by sea. The ruling effectively outlawed slavery in the mother country. Settlers already fearing the possibility of seeing their 1600, sometimes 1700 percent, profit margins stripped from them by London's abolitionism saw no other option but to secede from the Union Jack.[20] England's need to arm Africans to preserve colonial possessions in the Caribbean decades prior to 1776 had cemented the notion in the colonies that to stay under the banner of the Crown was to submit to the same kind of slavery that mainland settlers forced upon Africans. White supremacy, which had already been institutionalized for decades as a key weapon for settlers in their unending struggle to subdue rebellious Africans, is at the very core of why the "American Revolution" was fought in the first place.

If no revolution occurred in 1776 or any point thereafter, then the roots of the American colonial project remain firmly intact. As Saidiya Hartman explains, "the seizing hold of the past is a way of lamenting current circumstance and countering the regular disqualification of claims for redress as complaint, envy, and a barrier to social advancement."[21] History possesses lessons that are critical toward forging successful movements to transform the conditions of slavery that have, historically, been critical to the development of U.S. imperialism. American exceptionalism and innocence, with their rhetoric of progress, makes it easier to dismiss or refute what Hartman calls "slavery's enduring legacy." And "by doing so," she continues, "[it] establishes the remoteness and irrelevance of the past. As a consequence of this posture, claims for redress based on this history and its enduring legacy are disqualified and belittled as ridiculous or unintelligible, with some conservative critics going so far as to denigrate these claims as racist acts themselves."[22] Indeed, claims that the American way of life is the most superior form of social organization, or that slavery is of a bygone era, ignore the "skewed life chances, limited access to health and education, premature death, incarceration, and impoverishment" which have plagued the Black condition in America since the nation's inception.[23]

The story of Erica Garner is an example of slavery's legacy on the Black condition in America. In 2014, Erica's father Eric was strangled to death by the NYPD. His cry "I can't breathe" in his last moments of life propelled masses of Black Americans into the street in protest, including his daughter. Erica Garner would become an advocate against racist policing, a system rooted in the nation's slave patrols of the 17th and 18th centuries. Her life, however, was cut short in 2017 when the 27-year-old suffered a heart attack on Christmas Eve, passing away six days later. Prior to her death, Erica reported to the media that "the system beats you down." Her statement amplified the real world consequences of the afterlife of slavery. Slavery's legacy wore down, beat down, and killed Erica Garner. Today, not only are Black Americans more likely to be murdered by police forces, mired in poverty, and incarcerated disproportionately, but the stress from these conditions has led to the lowest life expectancy rate among racialized groups in the country. For these reasons, Christina Sharpe invites us to "think anew what it means to be a (black) post-slavery subject positioned within everyday intimate brutalities who is said to have survived or to be surviving the past of slavery, that is not yet past, bearing something like freedom."[24]

Erica Garner also reminds us that it is not possible to fully comprehend slavery and its continued relation to Black America under modern day U.S. imperialism without acknowledging the centrality of African resistance in the making of history. The counter revolution to abolitionism was sparked by the resistance of the enslaved in all corners of the world where systems of slavery existed. Rebellions led by slaves in the English colonies of both the Caribbean and North American mainland ultimately created the conditions for London's slow retreat toward abolition. Despite popular discourse about how British politicians were swayed by compelling moral arguments to abolish slavery, Lisa Lowe argues otherwise in her book *The Intimacies of Four Continents.* These "liberal abolitionist arguments were less important to the passage of the Slave Trade Act and the Slavery Abolition Act," she shows, "than were the dramatic revolts and everyday practices of enslaved peoples themselves."[25] Thus, the colonial powers did not terminate the slave trade out of the benevolence of their hearts. They did so out of the necessity to protect colonial possessions in the face of unending resistance from those they so brutally chained and forced into wageless labor.

Black resistance to the afterlives of slavery has been an enduring theme in the history of U.S. imperialism as well. In fact, as Sylvia Frey shows, Pan-Africanism and international solidarity between Black communities in the U.S. and other nations began as early as America's founding.[26] "African Americans of the American Revolutionary era played a significant part in the foundational wave of pan-Africanism," Frey writes. Not only did they help "create and spread a diasporic consciousness unified by a collective memory of a lost homeland;" they "implicitly invoked the inalienable right of revolution espoused by white revolutionaries and so established two distinct processes of racial construction, one nonviolent and the other revolutionary."[27] Social movements from Reconstruction to Black Liberation also fought tirelessly to break the chains of white supremacy and class oppression after formal emancipation. We must ask ourselves why so many former Black Panthers like Herman Bell remain behind prison walls. These movements and their leaders faced backlash from the U.S. imperialist state similar to the colonial backlash against the British Crown that produced the "American Revolution." The preservation of anti-Black racism and private property has consistently undergirded the suppression of Black resistance. Dominant narratives of America's exceptional democracy and commitment to freedom have put a national blinder on the undemocratic regime that regulates Black life.

When the Black Lives Matter movement emerged in 2014 to challenge the near daily killings of Black Americans by law enforcement, activists and community members challenged the enduring strength of American exceptionalism and innocence head on. The SWAT teams and militarized police forces deployed to occupy the streets of Ferguson to put down the resistance only amplified the rage caused by acquitting the police officer who murdered Michael Brown. Meanwhile, the Obama Administration called for "law and order" and condemned the "violence" of protesters. Black Lives Matter movement activists and organizers learned quickly that the maintenance of America's exceptional image took precedence over their demands for justice. U.S. imperialism's response to the legal lynchings committed by police officers signaled that it was in fact Black American resistance that so disturbed the system, not the lynchings themselves.

The afterlives of slavery are in fact the afterlives of a counter revolution to preserve the system that produced slavery. That counter revolution created a special nation, the American nation. None other like it had existed before—but not for the reasons outlined in American exceptionalist discourse. The foundations of U.S. imperialism rest in the genocide of Indigenous Peoples and the enslavement of Africans. This has made U.S. imperialism not only a uniquely prosperous system but also a uniquely dangerous system to the lives of oppressed people both in the mainland and outside of it. The colonists that forged independence from enslavement did not stop at independence in their quest to expand far and wide under the banner of white superiority and capital accumulation. Their thirst for profit made the expansion of the capitalist enterprise of settler colonialism a permanent necessity. All corners of the planet and their inhabitants were plundered with these interests in mind. Black resistance in the post-emancipation period thus relied on global alliances with movements in Africa, Asia, and Latin America to strengthen Black freedom efforts in the American mainland. This is reminiscent of the alliances the enslaved made with the Spanish and French colonial powers in resistance to the colonial enterprise in the North American mainland, a resistance the English colonists wanted so desperately to stop by separating from the British Crown. International alliances hinted at throughout history, and emerging present-day solidarity efforts like the one between Black Lives Matter and Palestine, may serve as roadmaps to the graveyard where the afterlives of slavery (more on this later), and the American exceptionalist ideology that protects them, are buried once and for all.

CHAPTER 4

"Did the United States Really Save the World? Remembering and Misremembering World War II"

"[The] construct of American exceptionalism was invoked to justify the settlement and expansion of English colonies in North America, the creation of the United States as an independent country, its territorial expansion across the continent, and the extension of American military and political power around the globe. In the wake of World War II . . . its increasingly hegemonic power is proffered as evidence of its inherent superiority, its evolutionary 'fitness' to remake the world in its image."

—Natsu Taylor Saito[1]

"This is the crime of which I accuse my country and countrymen, and for which neither I nor time nor history will ever forgive them, that they have destroyed and are destroying hundreds of thousands of lives and do not know it and do not want to know it."

—James Baldwin[2]

By 1840, the American capitalist economy was a burgeoning world power. Rapid industrial development was enabled by the enormous profit reaped from the genocide of the Native and the enslavement of the African. Profit under capitalism is never equally distributed, for this would negate the purpose of the system itself. This was no less true in the American republic. The spoils of land theft and slavery went primarily to land speculators, bankers, industrialists, and whichever political party served their interests at the time. Whatever profit wasn't pocketed by the opulent robber barons of the American republic was used for further industrial expansion both in North America and around the world.

The world was a very different place by the time it became engulfed in military conflict that characterized much of the early to mid-20th century. Capitalist development in the Western world fueled even more intense drives for colonial expansion. Imperialism became much more than a mere quest for empire. It became a social system where the division of the world among imperialist nations was critical toward the continued profits of cartels, banks, and monopolies. Competing interests among Western capitalist nations in Europe, Africa, and Asia led to World War I. The American capitalist class benefited from the imperial division of the world by laying the foundations for its own empire. While Europe scrambled to colonize Asia and Africa, American enterprise invaded lands East, West, and South of its border. Large territories of French Louisiana, Mexico, and South America came under the economic and political dominion of the U.S. empire as it awaited the time where it could compete with the older European empires.

And like the genocide of Indigenous nations and the enslavement of Africans that created the foundations of European empire, the American ascent into the realm of imperialist power relied on state violence. Untold numbers of people were killed under the same banner of "Manifest Destiny" that presupposed American civilization superior to that of "backward" people residing in Mexico, Puerto Rico, and the Philippines. The Monroe Doctrine declared South America an extension of the American Republic and thus gave the U.S. government the right to "defend" South American nations and peoples from European colonization. American exceptionalism was thus adjusted to fit the global vision of American politicians and businessmen who saw expansion as a necessary precondition to the preservation of the American way of life.

The savior complex inherent to the ideology of American exceptionalism was altered to justify the assumption of control over nations and regions of the world thought of as European colonial domain. American influence abroad would not only protect the interests of the American people but also people living in all corners of the globe. American democracy, according to the American political and economic establishment, was a civilizing order destined for world dominance. Indeed, as early as 1780, rich and prominent Americans such as Thomas Jefferson spoke of the American nation-state as an

"Empire of Liberty." This empire would spread liberty and democracy across the world in a similar manner that such virtues were brought to Africans and Indigenous people within its original colonial borders.

Perhaps no other historical event has been so tied to this notion of an American "Empire of Liberty" as World War II. The Second World War made the U.S. the world's lone superpower. U.S. imperialism spent most of the war developing the most technologically feared military in the world while American capitalism became the most prosperous economy in terms of total Gross Domestic Product (GDP). The American dollar became the dominant currency of global exchange under the Bretton Woods Agreement. European powers such as France, Britain, and Germany relinquished many of their colonies to anti-colonial forces. However, many of these nations fell under de facto colonial rule with a new master: the United States. Superpower status allowed the American establishment to take credit for the defeat of both the "Great Depression" and the march of "Fascism," lending much credence to the narrative of American exceptionalism.

The image of U.S. imperialism's supposedly heroic role in the Second World War has endured for more than a half a century after the war's end. Over this period, the great conflict between capitalist empires has been framed by prominent historians, academics, and elite class figures as a struggle between "good" and "evil." On one side stood the arbiters of "democracy" led by the U.S. military. On the other stood the arbiters of "fascism" led by Germany, Italy, and Japan. Democracy prevailed, the argument goes, making the war not only necessary but also "good." The United States' decisive entrance into the war supposedly made it the force that saved the world from the spectre of fascism and barbarity.

American virtuosity during the Second World War instilled a deep sense of patriotism in the populace. Patriotism, a key pillar of American exceptionalism, was bolstered by the hegemonic economic and military position that the nation now occupied in the world. Unquestioned American dominance was heralded as a Golden Age brought about by military superiority and "New Deal" policy. American workers saw wages increase and living standards rise as a result of the global dominance of the American capitalist economy. However, while the conditions of poverty experienced by Black, Native, and immigrant sectors of society persisted, they were whitewashed in the frenzy of patriotism and conservatism that gripped the nation.

The Second World War is a prime example of the ways in which American exceptionalism has shaped historical memory by divorcing it from material reality. Said differently, American exceptionalism and innocence are not merely ideas, but also weapons. The notion of American superiority masks the realities of U.S. policy and thus detracts us from a true understanding of the system that designs such policy. American exceptionalism and innocence are connected in that the presumption of the U.S. as an "Empire of Liberty" and arbiter of "democracy" deifies its existence and absolves the U.S. of its crimes. As Lisa Yonemaya argues, such narratives play a critical role to the making of American wars in the present:

> During the U.S. military invasion and occupation of Iraq, I argued that the reason why so many U.S. war crimes, especially those in Asia, remain unredressed might be found in what can be most appropriately called the American imperialist myth of "liberation and rehabilitiation." According to this myth, the losses and damages brought on by U.S. military violence are deemed "prepaid debts" incurred by those liberated by American intervention. This myth, which presents both violence and liberation as "gifts for the liberated," has serious implications for the redressability of U.S. military violence. The injured and violated bodies of the liberated . . . do not seem to require redress according to this discourse of indebtedness, for *their liberation has already served as the payment/reparation* that supposedly precedes the violence inflicted upon them. This economy of debt . . . is what sustains the regime of unredressability pertaining to colonial injustices.[3]

Thus, the ideas of freedom, democracy, and liberty attributed to American national identity are a formidable barrier to lifting the veil of innocence and nobility that surrounds American involvement in the Second World War.

Just like all American wars, U.S. involvement in the Second World War is far more complex than what is generally taught in schools and the media. Readers might be a little uneasy with the way World War II is remembered outside of dominant circles. After all, when asked to defend the "greatness" of their country, American exceptionalists seem to always circle back to World War II. So why do so many Americans still cling to the idea that the United States saved the world? Perhaps it reflects the fact that the United States cannot claim any positive role in any other war. In addition, the U.S. had the advantage of becoming the most prosperous capitalist economy shortly after. This excites people. It gets them thinking it could happen again. Plus, it's a lot easier to believe that your country is a benevolent and liberating force for good in the world, rather than as an imperial nation that enters (and wages) war to further its strategic and economic interests. Of course, this is not to deny that individual soldiers in the battlefields may have had virtuous motives for fighting in the war. But it is to say that the United States may not be as benevolent, exceptional, or innocent as we once thought.

To begin, we'd be wise to remember Aimé Césaire's famous observation that the West never wanted Germany as an enemy and only waged war against the Nazi regime after Hitler "applied to Europe colonialist procedures which until then had been reserved exclusively for the Arabs of Algeria, the 'coolies' of India, and the 'niggers' of Africa."[4] In other words, it didn't bother the United States and its Western allies to see such evil perpetrated against the slave and the colonized—especially when the U.S. was the one committing the violence. Rather, it only became a problem when imperial violence was perpetrated against their own "family" of white-ruled, Western nations.

And while we might like to think that the United States' "land of the free" represents a stark contrast to Hitler's racist regime, the truth is more troubling. Ideologically, the white supremacist roots of America's legal system provided great inspiration to the rise of Nazism in Germany. In his book *Hitler's American Model: The United States and the Making of Nazi Race Law*, Yale legal historian James Whitman notes:

> In the 1930s the United States, as the Nazis frequently noted, stood at the forefront of race-based lawmaking. American immigration and naturalization law, in the shape of a series of laws culminating in the Immigration Act of 1924, conditioned entry into the United States on race-based tables of "national origins." It was America's race-based immigration law that Hitler praised in Mein Kampf . . . and leading Nazi legal thinkers did the same after him, repeatedly and volubly. The United States also stood at the forefront in the creation of forms of de jure and de facto second-class citizenship for blacks, Filipinos, Chinese, and others; this too was of great interest to the Nazis, engaged as they were in creating their own forms of second-class citizenship for Germany's Jews.[5]

The fascist Nazi movement in Germany thus found great inspiration in the ability of the United States to codify racism into law through policies such as the segregation of Black and white American institutions, the forced removal of Indigenous Americans from their land, and the nation's discriminatory treatment toward immigrant populations.

White supremacy was but one bond that connected the so-called democratic America to fascist Germany. Attracted to Adolf Hitler's suppression of German labor unions and communists, as well as his overarching goal of destroying the Soviet Union, many of America's most powerful corporate interests gave critical support to the German fascist regime. General Motors, Ford, and Standard Oil of New Jersey (Exxon) were just a few of the major American monopolies to invest in Nazi Germany's economic and military development. By the time of the strike on Pearl Harbor, American investments in Nazi Germany were estimated at $475 million dollars.[6] And it was none other than Prescott Bush, banker and grandfather to George W. Bush, and famed industrialist Henry Ford who provided decisive financial support for Hitler's rise.[7] Until 1941, Nazism was seen as not only a profitable investment but also a bulwark against the Soviet Union.

The United States entered the Second World War in 1941. Popular mythology holds that the U.S. entered the war in response to Japan's attack on Pearl Harbor and Germany's subsequent declaration of war with America. There are a number of problems with this assertion. For one, American monopolies had already been supporting Germany and Great Britain, two of the biggest players in the war, since its inception. While American economic investment in Germany gradually decreased just prior to 1941, there was a rapid increase in economic activity with Great Britain through the Lend-Lease program. This government program lended subsidized contracts to American monopolies in their efforts to fortify Great Britain's military. By 1945, military expenditures to Great Britain amounted to 45 billion USD.[8]

U.S. imperialism did not begin to break its ties with Germany out of some yearning to preserve "the free world" from fascism. In fact, much of the U.S. elite supported Germany early on in the hopes that Nazism, as *TIME* magazine put it, would be "an antidote against Bolshevism."[9] Prominent American elites such as Herbert Hoover, Henry Ford, and James Mooney of General Motors supported Hitler with the hopes that his leadership would destroy the Soviet model. The Soviet Union was established in 1917 in a popular revolution against Tsarist rule. Its socialist model presented a nightmare to the owners of private property in the American and European world and their monopolies and corporations that controlled production in the West. They feared that this model would spread and that the rule of private profit would come under growing danger. When Hitler's Nazi regime appeared incapable of destroying the Soviet Union by 1941, American businesses sought to diversify their portfolio with Great Britain, which was embattled in war with Germany.

Furthermore, U.S. imperialism played a major role in provoking the strike on Pearl Harbor. Not only did American officials have knowledge of Japan's plan to strike, but the U.S. government had also been escalating tensions with Japan through economic sanctions and naval provocations in the Pacific. The Roosevelt Administration hoped Japan would bite and it eventually did. As Yonemaya observes, "[T]he 'good war' narrative produced during Cold War years remembers that the United States fought a just war for the liberation of the people of Asia and the Pacific region, including the Japanese themselves, from Japan's barbaric militarism and racial backwardness."[10] But the United States sought a war not to *liberate* Japan but to prevent it from colonizing East Asia in hopes that the valuable resources there would come under American possession soon after. Only the appearance of being attacked would allow the American military to intervene without being forced to give up its supposedly "neutral" position in the war.

However, the American elite miscalculated and was dragged into Eurasia when Hitler desperately declared war on the U.S. on December 11th, 1941. Hitler hoped that declaring war on the U.S. would convince Japan to join Germany in the fight to destroy the Soviet Union. Suddenly, the U.S. found itself alongside its arch enemy, the Soviet Union, and the allied powers. This was not an alliance of principle but rather of convenience. U.S. imperialism hoped that Germany and the Soviet Union would destroy each other. By the time the U.S. entered the war full steam, only one goal mattered: to redesign the world in the interests of American monopolies, with Great Britain by its side.

Two major events during the war underscore U.S. imperialism's true motivations. First, the British Royal Air Force firebombing of Dresden, Germany, in 1945 primarily utilized American bombers to kill over 300,000 people.[11] While Dresden was not an important strategic location in the war, the bombing was meant as a show of force to the Soviet Union of American and British military capabilities. The firebombing of Dresden is a quintessential example of how U.S. imperialism utilized its participation in the war for aims other than the preservation of "democracy" against nascent fascism.

Second, the United States is often credited for ending the Second World War for good following its use of the atomic bomb on the Japanese cities of Hiroshima and Nagasaki. America's nuclear bombing of these cities incinerated over 100,000 people. The nuclear bombs inflicted long-term damage on the population. The U.S. establishment deemed the bombing necessary to force a Japanese surrender. Several members of the military establishment at the time felt differently. In his 1949 memoirs, commanding general of the U.S. Army Air Forces Henry "Hap" Arnold wrote, "it always appeared to us that, atomic bomb or no atomic bomb, the Japanese were already on the verge of collapse." President Roosevelt's Chief of Staff Admiral William Leahy confirmed Arnold's assessment, stating, "[T]he use of this barbarous weapon at Hiroshima and Nagasaki was of no material assistance in our war against Japan. The Japanese were already defeated and ready to surrender." Still, the bombs were dropped and to this day not one American president has apologized for the damage that the bombs or the war caused. Not to the people of Hiroshima. Not to the people of Nagasaki. And it wasn't until 1988 when the federal government formally apologized for the Japanese Americans imprisoned in U.S. internment camps during the war.[12]

American exceptionalism and American innocence have rendered the reality behind the use of nuclear bombs in Japan a "necessary evil" that brought lasting peace to a brutal world war. The dominant narrative presumes that the United States was an exceptional player in the Second World War and thus was justified in its use of biological warfare against the authoritarian "Jap" government. However, even mainstream historians have called into question the heroic justification for America's use of nuclear weapons against Japan. Many historians have cited that the U.S. used the bombs to intimidate the Soviet Union in preparation for the Cold War.[13] This is especially relevant since a Japanese surrender was likely without the bombings. Historians have recently concluded that the Soviet Union's decision to break neutrality with Japan ultimately forced surrender, not two nuclear bombs which only added more damage to a country that had been ravaged far worse by conventional warfare.[14] The use of nuclear weapons ultimately did more to support U.S. imperialism's broader strategic interests than to end the war.

The realities of the Second World War reveal the extent to which American exceptionalism has influenced the way history is taught and remembered. Few in the U.S. have been allowed to learn about the connections between American business and German Nazism or see American-bred white supremacy as linked to the rise of fascism in Europe. And even fewer can recall the hundreds of thousands that were killed in places like Dresden and Hiroshima in the prelude to the Cold War. The rulers of American society benefited mightily from its participation in the war and used American exceptionalist ethos to hide their imperial ambitions. The United States imposed itself as the hero of the Second World War despite the leading role that *the Soviet Union* played in defeating Nazi Germany at the cost of 27 million Soviet lives. The illusion of American heroism in the Second World War helped prepare the way for a permanent American war agenda against both foreign and domestic challenges to imperialism while at the same time strengthening the notion that America was in fact an exceptional, democratic nation. This is all that the myth of the "good war" has ever been good for.

CHAPTER 5

"The Korean War: An Endless War Forgotten in the Haze of American Exceptionalism"

"We know we can't stand for peace on one foot and war on the other."

—Eslanda Robeson[1]

". . . we have killed, maimed and rendered homeless a million Koreans, all in the name of preserving western civilization. U.S. troops have acted like beasts, as do all aggressive, invading, imperialist armies. North and South of the 38th parallel, they have looked upon the Korean people with contempt, called them filthy names, raped their women, lorded it over old women and children, and shot prisoners in the back . . ."

—Paul Robeson[2]

Not long after his inauguration as the 45th president of the United States, Donald Trump wasted no time in racheting up tensions with the Democratic Republic of Korea (DPRK), known to many Americans as North Korea. The DPRK was accused by American media, military, and political officials of testing intercontinental ballistic missiles (ICBM) that possessed the capabilities of reaching American shores. Trump hurled insults at DPRK leader Kim-Jong Un, calling the head of state a "madman" and a "Rocket Man." Kim Jong-Un lashed back by labeling Trump a "deranged" leader. The new administration's war of words over the DPRK's missile tests facilitated war provocations in the form of increased sanctions and military exercises directed at the "rogue regime."

The DPRK and neighboring South Korea responded to Trump's

belligerence with manuevers toward peace. It started during the Winter Olympics when the leaders of the two countries agreed to form a joint women's hockey team. Numerous talks between the heads of state of the DPRK, South Korea, and China ensued over the following months. The DPRK invited Donald Trump to meet with Kim Jong-Un in March of 2018. In a stunning reversal of policy, Trump accepted the invitation. When the summit finally occurred in June of that year, Trump agreed to halt joint military exercises between the U.S. and South Korea in exchange for the denuclearization of the DPRK. A step toward peace was made.

However, the corporate media and the entire ruling class saw the summit differently. Democrats and Republicans alike expressed distrust in the DPRK's willingness to comply with the agreement. The corporate media slammed Trump for meeting with Kim Jong-Un, a sworn enemy of the American nation-state. Jong-Un was depicted as a crazed dictator that didn't deserve a pass from an American president. Such coverage proved that the corporate media and the mainstream of both parties were just as hawkish toward the DPRK if not more so than Trump.

The American ruling establishment's hostilities toward Kim Jong-Un are an extension of a long-standing trend in American folklore that has positioned American leaders and leaders of the DPRK on opposite ends of sanity. On one side sits the exceptional American nation-state responsible for promoting democracy around the world. On the other is the DPRK, the antithesis of American-style democracy. The DPRK is described as an impoverished and increasingly dangerous nuclear-armed "regime" with an abysmal human rights record while the United States and its South Korean ally are depicted as success stories that the DPRK must emulate, or else. Every American president since Harry Truman has upheld this narrative to some degree, whether it was George W. Bush including the DPRK in his "Axis of evil" or Barack Obama threatening the DPRK with "consequences" for its "reckless pursuit of nuclear weapons."[3]

The role of American exceptionalism in the hostilities between the DPRK and the U.S. cannot be fully understood without remembering "the Forgotten War," otherwise known as the Korean War of 1950–1953. This war really began in the aftermath of the Second World War. It was World War II that brought the defeat of Japan at the hands of American and Soviet forces. Japanese defeat led to a reconfiguration of the world order in East Asia. The decimated Japanese empire was forced to relinquish many of its colonial possessions, including Korea. The Second World War also precipitated the rapid expansion of arms production led by U.S. imperialism and its wartime allies. Incendiary and nuclear weapons were just some of the military advances made during the Second World War that would play a role in the American invasion of Korea. "In the case of "Korea", writes Nayoung Aimee Kwon, "there was no time in its history in which actual domination did not come in the name of 'sovereignty' and 'liberation' promised either presently or 'in due course'—often in the name of 'freedom' from a past hegemon from which it was supposedly being liberated by the new force."[4]

As one colonial power was forced to leave Korea, another one came storming in with guns ablaze. And as one global war came to a close, another one opened. The Second World War's finale gave way to the opening act of the "Cold War." The Cold War was born from U.S. imperialism's obsessive disdain for communism. The Soviet Union, then the only nation founded upon communist principles, was an impediment to the unfettered spread of American enterprise. However, the rulers of U.S. imperialism faced a major problem despite its new status as economic and military superpower in the world. That problem was the Soviet Union's rapid economic and military development based on the collectivization of feudal agriculture, the elimination of unemployment, and the socialization of private production in service of human need. The Soviet "workers state" played a decisive role in the defeat of fascism during the Second World War and could not be ignored in the new world order that emerged after 1945. To compound the problem, one of the largest populations in the world—China—waged its own victorious revolution under the banner of communism in 1949.

Fear of losing East Asia to communism compelled the rulers of U.S. imperialism to wage war in the Korean Peninsula. Prior to the Chinese Revolution of 1949, the United States had negotiated a "trusteeship" in Korea with the Soviet Union to ensure that the Red Army would not march alongside Korean communists and nationalists to totally liberate the country from Japanese colonialism. Korea was divided along the 38th parallel in the summer of 1945, with communist committees in control of the north and Korean landlords, Japanese operatives, and American military advisors in control of the South. Independence was to be achieved within five years of the division along the 38th parallel despite the fact that the ROK, formed in 1948 as the South

Korean government, restricted voting to landlords and large taxpayers. What transpired instead was an American-led war to prevent Korean independence.

The Korean War began officially on June 25th, 1950. American involvement was sanctioned by the United Nations (UN) as an American-led "police" operation to rescue South Korea from a communist takeover. Korean communists and nationalists both north and south of the 38th parallel (known commonly as the Demilitarized Zone or DMZ) had in fact marched on Seoul in 1950, precipitating the American invasion. However, narratives of American exceptionalism and innocence have played a dominant role in how the Korean War has been depicted from the very beginning. Those who know anything about the war have been led to believe that American military forces entered in response to an evil, communist uprising. The origins myth of the Korean war has been contradicted in recent years, with new research claiming that American-supported guerillas in the South invaded Northern villages as early as 1949.[5] This evidence supports claims that the American-backed regime in the South was wildly unpopular and often resorted to repression in the face of popular insurgency. As Tim Beal notes in regard to the Cheju Island uprising against Republic of Korea (South Korean) forces in 1948, up to "20 percent of the population were killed or fled to Japan and more than half the villages on the island were destroyed. Even the army was not immune to the rebellion, and the 14th regiment . . . mutinied in the Port City of Yosu in October 1948."[6]

Joint American-ROK atrocities would only intensify in the three years of armed conflict that ensued in Korea prior to the July 1953 armistice agreement. What was alleged by President Harry Truman to be a "limited conflict" turned into an all out American-led massacre as China's entry into the war in the fall of 1950 raised the spectre of a fully independent, and communist, Korea. And the massacres of the war have been erased from American memory. As Bruce Cumings suggests,

> The forgotten war—the Korean war of 1950–53—might better be called the unknown war. What was indelible about it was the extraordinary destructiveness of the United States' air campaigns against North Korea, from the widespread and continuous use of firebombing (mainly with napalm), to threats to use nuclear and chemical weapons, and the destruction of huge North Korean dams in the final stages of the war.[7]

American exceptionalism and innocence have a large part to play in keeping the American invasion of Korea an unknown war. The relevance of these ideologies can be broken into two parts. The first is the erasure of U.S. imperialism's ambitions and actions during the three year invasion. Second is the narrative that was devised by the American ruling class to dehumanize the Korean people. These components share equal importance as one cannot exist without the other.

The horrors imposed on the Korean people and the ambitions behind them are now a matter of public record even if most Americans are unaware of them. The United States' combined air campaign and occupation killed three million Koreans, mostly from napalm bombs and indiscriminate killings. The damage was far-reaching, Cumings writes, drawing on his co-authored book (with Jon Halliday), *Korea: The Unknown War*, and the work of Conrad Crane:

> Over the course of the war . . . the US air force "had wreaked terrible destruction all across North Korea. Bomb damage assessment at the armistice revealed that 18 of 22 major cities had been at least half obliterated." A table [Crane] provided showed that the big industrial cities of Hamhung and Hungnam were 80–85% destroyed, Sariwon 95%, Sinanju 100%, the port of Chinnampo 80% and Pyongyang 75%. A British reporter described one of the thousands of obliterated villages as "a low, wide mound of violet ashes." General William Dean, who was captured after the battle of Taejon in July 1950 and taken to the North, later said that most of the towns and villages he saw were just "rubble or snowy open spaces." Just about every Korean he met, Dean wrote, had had a relative killed in a bombing raid. Even Winston Churchill, late in the war, was moved to tell Washington that when napalm was invented, no one contemplated that it would be "splashed" all over a civilian population.[8]

Air Force General Curtis Lemay reinforced this assessment in an interview decades later when he said "over a period of three years or so . . . we burned down every town in North Korea and South Korea, too."[9] The American air campaign dropped 635,000 tons of bombs on Korea and over 30,000 tons of napalm while threatening to use nuclear weapons on numerous occasions.[10] On the ground, American military forces supervised South Korean forces responsible for their own kind of atrocities. Dong-Choon Kim writes that between the fall of 1950 to the spring of 1951, about 10,000 civilians were killed by ROK soldiers.[11] ROK divisions often tortured and buried political prisoners in mass graves under the South's national security law that labeled the North as a "non-state" entity with no rights the South was bound to respect.

Despite being literally forced to live underground, the Korean people waged a heroic resistance against the heavily armed American invasion and forced a stalemate in July of 1953. This brings us to the question of how the Korean War was forgotten amid the massive destruction it left in its wake. The answer has driven American foreign policy ever since and is rooted in the race-based logic of U.S. imperialism. For by 1950, the United States' superiority on the world stage following the Second World War had already become deeply ingrained in the American psyche. This entailed the belief that the U.S. was synonymous with "good" while communism was an "evil" that must be eradicated from the world. Growing competition from the Soviet Union, China's infant revolution in 1949, and massive upheaval in Korea threatened American hegemony and gave the ruling class plenty of targets in its anticommunist policy of containment both at home and abroad, popularly known as the "Red Scare."

While radical labor organizers and Black freedom organizers were being labeled communists to justify racist and class-based repression from the FBI or the Ku Klux Klan, Koreans were subject to a similar anticommunist racism. Cumings explains that anti-Korean sentiment was pervasive in all spheres of American life, especially in the media and the military. Prominent publications such as the *New York Times* and Marshall Plan officials such as Edgar Johnson described Koreans as "fanatics," "barbarians," and "wild."[12] American military officials were trained to think of Koreans as "gooks," giving fertile ground for the mass extermination campaigns that characterized American military policy during the war. Anticommunist racism followed an old formula in new clothes. It stemmed from the white supremacist and capitalist roots of the American nation-state that depended on the dehumanization of enslaved Africans and displaced Indigenous nations to develop the economic infrastructure capable of invading Korea.

The dehumanization of the Korean people rendered the true purpose of the war invisible. Anticommunist racism cloaked in American exceptionalist garb united Americans around the U.S. military and the corporate interests it served. The American ruling class wanted to stop the march of communism in East Asia so that the region would remain an "Open Door" to the profits of American monopolies and corporations. Japan was a key player in this arrangement. Its defeat in the Second World War led to the American occupation of the country, with U.S. officials guiding both its military and economic policy. In 1947, Secretary of State George Marshall pressed his successor, Dean Acheson, to have a "plan drafted of policy to organize a definite government of [South] Korea and connect . . . its economy with that of Japan."[13] The Korean War was thus a necessary precondition to securing Japan's economic and military progress as a bulwark against the independent predations of communism spreading in the region like wildfire.

Korea remains in the crosshairs of American warfare nearly seven decades after the Republic of Korea and the DPRK agreed to an armistice. The DPRK has been economically strangled with American-imposed sanctions. Over 40,000 American military personnel conduct regular military exercises in South Korea along the demilitarized zone (DMZ).[14] Japan, Guam, and Hawaii are also occupied with over 100,000 American troops stationed in military bases equipped with deadly war armaments such as B-52 bombers. Since a peace treaty has not been signed despite the progress made at the "Trump-Kim summit," the Korean War continues on today as a "hot conflict." The persistence of this particular war in the context of a generalized American-led project of endless warfare around the entire globe has meant that Korea continues to be mischaracterized and forgotten in the haze of the "Cold War," decades after the fall of the socialist bloc in 1991.

And because U.S. imperialism possesses the same interests now as it did during the rise of the socialist bloc in the 20th century, the DPRK finds itself the target of an ideological war not unlike the one that existed during the Korean conflict. North Korean leadership and society has been described as a totalitarian police state. Racist tropes from the Korean war such as the term "gook" and the mockery of citizens of the DPRK as "brainwashed" and submissive are pervasive in American media and politics. Americans possess few channels in which to unmask the Korean war's "unknown" character. This is readily seen in the difference between how the Korean War is memorialized in Korea as opposed to the American mainland. As Tessa Morris-Suzuki shows, while the Korean War National Museum in Illinois depicts American participation in the war as a triumph against communism and a victory for "democracy," museums in the North and South of Korea tell a different story. Memorials in the DPRK portray the war as a great victory for Korean independence despite the hardship suffered, while the ROK's status as a protectorate of America has meant that memorials in the South reinforce the largely false image of the ROK as a nation that bravely fought off the foreign threat to the North. For example, an image found in Seoul's War Memorial "shows a large and muscular South Korean soldier embracing and looking down upon his smaller and frailer North Korean kinsman—thus simultaneously embodying messages of triumph and of reconciliation."[15] Such imagery reveals the deep influence of American power on the political system in South Korea.

The manipulation of memory is critical toward the normalization of American exceptionalism and innocence as the ideological bedrocks that justify the real-life consequences of U.S. imperialist plunder. Indeed, a close relationship exists between the inculcation of American superiority as the law of the land and the racist tropes that continue to fuel American war crimes in East Asia and the world at large. The depiction of the DPRK as a wild country ruled by insane children keen on developing nuclear weaponry in a vendetta against American democracy strips away the humanity from the Korean people both south and north of the DMZ. Without having to recognize the humanity of its "enemy," the United States' past war crimes against the Korean people are not only forgotten, but its current war crimes are also exonerated in the court of ruling class opinion.[16] They've become reasonable responses to crazed dictatorships.

One of these "reasonable responses" involves threatening the DPRK with nuclear annihilation. After all, what scares so many Americans is the thought of a crazed and fanatical DPRK acquiring a nuclear bomb. As Shane Maddock notes in his book, *Nuclear Apartheid: The Quest for American Atomic Supremacy From World War II to the Present*, superpowers like the United States have "remained so convinced of the correctness of their respective privileged positions in the world system that they refused to make mutual concessions to achieve arms control."[17] Thus, ideologies of national superiority and exceptionalism are impossible to disentangle from popular discourses about nuclear proliferation. "Even U.S. leaders who sincerely desired to stem proliferation," Maddock writes:

> could not break free from the presumptions of national superiority that fostered nuclear discrimination. At its heart rested a variant of American exceptionalism that envisioned the United States as outside the normal constraints of a combative world system, therefore exempting Washington from most of the arguments used to dissuade other countries from acquiring nuclear arms.[18]

Rhetoric of an irrational enemy with whom the "rational" West cannot negotiate makes it hard for us to understand why North Korea seeks nuclear capabilities.[19] And while media pundits assert that the DPRK cannot be trusted with a nuclear weapon or to uphold a joint agreement, rarely is the question ever asked: Why should the *United States* be trusted with a nuclear weapon, let alone 9,600 of them? Or, to take it one step further, why is the DPRK expected to "demilitarize" but the United States is not? As offensive as these questions might sound to many Americans, such sensitivity only exposes the historical amnesia and sense of moral superiority one must have to find these questions offensive in the first place.

The Korean war is but one of the first examples of how American exceptionalism creates a dialectical relationship between "national" superiority and the targeting of racialized "others" in the service of imperial aims. This phenomenon was not lost on early Black radical thinkers like Eslanda Robeson, her husband Paul, W.E.B. Du Bois, and Lorraine Hansberry who fiercely opposed the Korean War.[20] "Big business wants war to keep your mind off social reform; it would rather spend your taxes for atom bombs than for schools because in this way it makes more money," Du Bois famously remarked. "[It] would rather have your sons dying in Korea than studying in America and asking awkward questions. The system which it advocates depends on war and more war."[21] Later wars in Vietnam, Cambodia, Grenada, Iraq, Afghanistan, and the remaining fifty foreign governments that the U.S. would overthrow followed a similar model, with American values extolled, corporate profits pursued, and the people of the targeted nations dehumanized as "terrorists," "towel heads," and "dinks." Whatever public opposition to these wars existed would morph into forgetfulness or outright support, even though the American people would have as little say in their implementation as they do in domestic policies like mass incarceration or the rise of poverty. This is the real legacy of the Korean War, a legacy that the Korean people and the majority of people all over the world do not have the privilege of forgetting.

CHAPTER 6

"Charlottesville and the Real Monuments to White Supremacy"

"There is simply no getting around it, a myth of Anglo-Saxon 'exceptionalism' has shaped America's sense of self. It and the culture of whiteness that sustains it runs deep within the DNA of this country."

—Kelly Brown Douglas[1]

"Whiteness is a problem of being shaped to think that other people are the problem."

—Alexis Shotwell[2]

"[Race] is, to try another phrasing, a 'division of species' effected and maintained by the technologies of violence and sexuality that underwrite the social formation, not a discriminatory manipulation of already existing bodily marks."

—Jared Sexton[3]

The ideologies of American exceptionalism and innocence rest on the foundations of white supremacy. Theodore Allen described white supremacy in two volumes of works that explored the "invention of the white race."[4] He argued that "white race" privileges conferred on European Americans were created by the ruling class as a system of social control that led to racial slavery and oppression for "free" Black Americans. White supremacy has been a critical component of American capitalist development. It formed the glue that held together policies such as slavery, land theft, and imperial expansion. In other words, white supremacy has historically rallied white Americans—and non-Black people of color[5]—of all classes to the side of the oppressor with the promise that, if compliant, they too will bear the fruits of the system. Whether it was the slave patrols in the early colonies or the recruitment of Army volunteers to commit mass murder in Korea, U.S. imperialism has privileged the condition of white America at the expense of the darker masses, which made American exceptionalism synonymous with *white* exceptionalism and *white* innocence.

If the systems of American capitalism and imperialism possess white supremacy at the root, then every branch of the American nation-state is a monument to white supremacy. Mainstream discourse in the U.S. has fallen well short of this analysis. Few, if any, institutions condemn white supremacy as a pillar in the architecture of the American way of life. To do so would be to question, if not fully condemn, the creed of American exceptionalism. This is why episodes of racial violence by KKK members bring with them chants from people exclaiming, "This isn't who we are!" When acknowledged at all by Americans, white supremacy is mostly depicted as a relic of the past or an individual behavior, both of which have long been reformed by the self-correcting nature of American "democracy."

The Trump presidency has only heightened the contradictions apparent in the American discourse on white supremacy. Donald Trump has been credited with emboldening white supremacist forces in America, forces that were thought to have been buried by an increasingly "color-blind" society. Events in Charlottesville and cities across the country confirmed fears of a white supremacist "backlash." In August of 2017, white Americans under the banner of "Unite the Right" marched in protest of the removal of a Confederate monument to Robert E. Lee. Counter protesters descended in opposition to the right-wing mob, leading to an eruption of violence that left one counter protester dead and many more injured.

The spotlight that Charlottesville placed on monuments to the Confederacy led to the removal of statues and monuments across the country. In Durham, North Carolina, anti-racist activists pulled down a memorial to Confederate soldiers just days after the protest in Charlottesville. President Donald Trump opposed the removal of statues as a dangerous precedent, claiming that removing Robert E. Lee because of outrage to slavery meant that monuments to George Washington and Thomas Jefferson would also need to be taken down. Trump's comments sparked a renewed conversation about the character of white supremacy in the American mainland. On one side, protesters rightfully pointed to Confederate statues as symbolic celebrations of Black enslavement and racism that continue to hold ramifications for the present. On the other hand, the American corporate media, Democratic Party officials, and even some Republicans in Washington utilized mass opposition to Confederate symbols to clamor for "national unity" and strengthen American exceptionalism. As one *Atlantic* piece argued, Americans will continue to remove Confederate monuments because "America is still working on the project of constructing a more equal society, and reinvesting in the experiment of a multi-ethnic democracy."[6]

This narrative of American exceptionalism and innocence views the United States as a gradual project in perfecting "democracy" and "equality." The structural roots of white supremacy are effectively erased. To be sure, there is nothing wrong with opposing the Confederacy on the basis that its development was a military response to preserve an agricultural capitalist order based largely on the immense profits plantation owners derived from the enslavement of Blacks. To paint the Confederacy as an *aberration*, however, turns opposition to white supremacy into a mere clean up crew for the American nation-state. The enormous influence of American exceptionalism ensured that the debate over Confederate monuments was directed in a way so that "the spectacular actually camouflages the routine;" namely, "the normal operation of the law against blacks in all its everyday terror and contempt, its misbehavior, and broken ethicality."[7]

Genuine opposition to white supremacy requires that the laws that govern the United States are torn down, root and branch. Law in this context cannot be limited to the enforcement of legislation passed by the ruling class. Law is a fundamental expression of the economic, political, and cultural oppression enforced by the system of white supremacy and American capitalism. It's true that colonial powers in Europe practiced their own version of racial animus to justify the plunder of African, Asian, and Latin American civilizations. But it was only in the English colonies that would later form the U.S. where "whiteness" would provide the guiding framework for capitalist development and thus seep into each and every institution erected thereafter.

A great challenge exists, then, to expose just how pervasive white supremacy remains in the structure of American society. The structural role white supremacy played in the development of the U.S. has left nothing untouched by the laws of whiteness. White Americans are often oblivious to the manifestations of white supremacy because the institutions of society operate in their favor. Racially "innocent" white people might admit that they *benefit* from white supremacy, or even that they might be *complicit* in white supremacy—perhaps in an unintentional, unconscious, passive manner—but they rarely admit all the ways they *actively*, *consciously*, and even *proudly* participate in it. As Katie Grimes notes,

> they figure white supremacy more like a shady friend from high school who comes around every now and then and lures you into committing various acts of mischief, or like a slightly unsavory businesswoman with whom you occasionally collaborate and from whose questionable ethics you frequently reap profits. In truth, whites do not simply collaborate with and benefit from racial evil; it lives within them, and they enact it directly with their bodies and not just through their interactions with structures.[8]

Kirstine Taylor similarly argues that "racial innocence" operates as a way for wealthy Americans to point the finger at a certain class or geographic region—namely "the poor" and "the South"—for the country's racism.[9] In other words, it's the "white trash" using racial slurs and burning crosses who represents white supremacy, not the owner of my favorite football team, my financial adviser, or that suburban neighbor who runs my homeowner association. Even more troubling, here, *racism* is still largely perceived as an individual's attitude or belief and not, as Ruth Wilson Gilmore more accurately describes, "the state-sanctioned or extralegal production and exploitation of group-differentiated vulnerability to premature death."[10] Whiteness and American exceptionalism are thus deeply interrelated. American exceptionalism consumes whiteness under the banner of the state. It ensures that even as poor white Americans are labeled "white trash" by their elite counterparts, the crimes against peoples of color embedded in the fabric of American society remain broadly unchallenged.

If American society itself is a monument to white supremacy, then the economic, cultural, and legal manifestations of white supremacy must take precedence over individual attitudes. No better example exists of a legal and political monument to white supremacy than the U.S. prison regime. As of 2017, the United States possessed twenty-five percent of the world's prisoners despite having only five percent of the world's total population. According to the Prison Policy Initiative, 40 percent of all prisoners are Black American despite Black Americans making up just 13 percent of the U.S. population.[11] Black Americans make up over fifty percent of those serving life sentences. Nearly one-third of all young Black males are either incarcerated or under criminal justice supervision while Black women represent one of the fastest growing prison populations in the nation.[12] Outside of prison, another 840,000 are serving parole and 3.7 million are serving probation, with these numbers reflecting the same racial disparities that exist in the prison system.

Both Angela Davis and Stephen Dillion agree that the prison regime, often termed the "prison industrial complex," serves to reimpose slavery in the context of present day American political economy. "The spirit of slavery animated the bars of prison cells and the coldness that surrounded captured black bodies," Dillion writes as he chronicles the experience of formerly incarcerated Black liberation activist Assata Shakur. "[It] seeped past the razor wire and the concrete walls of the prison, structuring poverty on the street, regulatory violence in the welfare office and the unfreedom that governs an antiblack world."[13] The U.S. carceral state has its roots in the Thirteenth Amendment of the American Constitution, which outlawed slavery *except* as a means of criminal punishment. [14] Wealthy planters and capitalists were thus legally empowered to enforce a prison regime of terror in the post-Reconstruction period. Between 1882 and 1946, there were at least 5,000 recorded cases of lynchings involving the killing of Black Americans by white Americans. Many more freed Black Americans were forced to work for little to nothing in the "convict-lease" system enforced by Black Codes. Today, prisoners, many of whom are Black, are similarly forced to work for slave wages while behind bars. It would be a mistake, however, to reduce slavery to a practice that was merely reshaped or adopted by the criminal legal system during the postbellum period. This would entail that the state's system of anti-Black domination *narrowed*—rather than *expanded*—as a result of so-called emancipation. "What we're dealing with," writes Tryon Woods, " is not the winnowing of slavery to the purview of criminal justice, but rather the socialization of slavery—no plantations, no auction blocks, no prisons, no laws necessary."[15]

In a neoliberal era characterized by the increasing disposability of Black labor, the United States has placed high importance on the criminalization of Black life to fill prison beds. The proliferation of Blacks and people of color (19 percent of the prison population is identified as "Hispanic") behind the prison walls is a consequence of multiple, interrelated developments.[16] Neoliberal policies such as "welfare reform," the North Atlantic Free Trade Agreement (NAFTA), and harsh sentencing laws included in bills like the Violent Crime Control Act of 1994, placed an increasingly deadly target on Black lives. The rise in Black poverty and unemployment was complemented by the racist demonization of Black Americans as "welfare queens" and "super predators," all of which justified the enormous increase in the number of prisoners in America.

It is from these conditions that the U.S. prison regime became a monument to white supremacy and the police became the armed body that filled prison beds. The disposability of Black life under American neoliberal capitalism helped spark the formation of the Black Lives Matter movement and its protest of the daily murder and terror which police departments impose on Black Americans. Without the momentum of the Black Lives Matter movement, the protests in the U.S. against racist symbols such as Confederate statues may not have proven to be so significant. However, conversation about the structural foundations of white supremacy during these protests has been limited. American capitalism, founded upon enslavement and genocide, has developed into an imperial powerhouse dominated by finance capital. And finance capital is no less a monument to white supremacy than the country's Confederate statues.

Finance capital is most commonly referred to as FIRE or Finance and Real Estate, much of which is controlled and administered on Wall Street. Finance capital was also the backbone of the nascent slave trade in the early years of the American Republic. Slave traders faced great challenges accessing credit to finance their long-distance expeditions in the sale of enslaved labor. Traders demanded liquid assets and buyers wanted financing to help lower the costs of the trade. As Calvin Schermerhorn explains, "In the Chesapeake, slave traders routinely advertised 'CASH FOR NEGROES.' But buyers demanded financing. When selling bondspersons in the lower Mississippi Valley, traders were forced to extend credit and accept bills or promissory notes that had little interregional mobility." Thus, slave-trading firms required external financing to maximize the profitability of the sale of enslaved Black labor.[17]

Bank capital was dependent upon the enslavement of Blacks as much as slave traders were dependent on bank capital to ensure profitability from the enterprise. Wall Street itself formed out of the enormous growth of the slave trade experienced in the American nation-state in the 18th and 19th centuries. In fact, New York's first slave market was established on what is now Wall Street in 1711.[18] The founder of what is now Citibank, Moses Taylor, became the richest man of his century through the illegal trade of slaves from New York to Cuba.[19]

Captive slaves brought in enormous profits for all parties involved, not least because the total dehumanization of Black Africans made them useful financial instruments. As Zenia Kish and Justin Leroy show,

> Through a process of financialization, masters and investors transformed slaves from subjects excluded from market activity because of their legal status into mitigators of risk absolutely essential to the functioning of such markets. Yet their status also obscured this central importance. Planters alternately considered them the ultimate risk, in the form of potential rebellion, or the most prudent investment, because the natural increase of enslaved property created what Jefferson termed a "silent profit", as slaves were a self-reproducing form of capital.[20]

Bank capital thus took advantage of slavery's profitability. It made Black captives the very instruments that underwrote additional credit to slave masters and traders looking to maximize their investment. This history places in clear view how Wall Street is one of the most prominent monuments to white supremacy that exists today. Wall Street benefited mightily from white supremacy, as the bondage of Black slaves and the relative freedoms bestowed upon whites of all classes helped secure the fortunes of early Wall Street financiers. Not coincidentally, whites were made to believe that they rightfully created the most exceptional nation to have ever been birthed. Wall Street has laughed all the way to the bank ever since, monopolizing into six mega corporations responsible for the great fleecing of Black Americans during the 2008 financial crisis. More to come on this in the next chapter.

And finally, many monuments to white supremacy exist in U.S. popular culture. American schools and sporting events regularly play the "Star-Spangled Banner" despite the fact that its author, Francis Scott Keyes, was an avowed racist who owned slaves and referenced his contempt for Africans in the third verse of the song.[21] White supremacy is present in everything deemed exceptional about American "culture," which is really an amalgam of stolen cultures re-prescribed to the people through the levers of power and profit. It is rooted in the corporate food we eat, the corporate clothing we buy, and the corporate music we consume. American exceptionalism and white supremacy are not only deeply connected but also stand as the driving forces of American cultural life.

The broadway musical *Hamilton,* which premiered on Broadway in 2015 and has since shattered records in recording sales, is a case in point. *Hamilton* sports a Black cast that places a spotlight on Alexander Hamilton's experience as a "Founding Father" of the U.S. The musical has garnered critical acclaim but little criticism as an entertaining monument to white supremacy. However, according to Rutgers historian Lyra Monteiro, the musical downplays the Founding Fathers' involvement with slavery by dressing up Black actors in their garb and painting Alexander Hamilton as the abolitionist-minded father of the nation.[22] In the hilariously titled article, "'Hamilton: the Musical:' Black Actors Dress Up like Slave Traders . . . and It's Not Halloween," Ishmael Reed argues that such representations obscures how Hamilton not only married into a slave holding family, but also conducted transactions in the sale of slaves for them during his tenure in the Continental Army.[23] None of this was mentioned in the *Hamilton* musical, making it another monument to white supremacy, rather than a critique of it.

Hamilton is a pitch perfect example of how practices of diversity, inclusion, and multiculturalism often reinforce the ideologies of American exceptionalism and American innocence. Consider how Lin-Manuel Miranda explained his rationale for casting black actors in the roles of people like George Washington and Thomas Jefferson. Such casting, he said, "allow[s] you to leave whatever cultural baggage you have about the founding fathers at the door."[24] Oskar Eustis, artistic director of the Public Theatre that hosted *Hamilton* added his take. "It has liberated a lot of people who might feel ambivalent about the American experiment to feel patriotic," he said. "I can feel it in myself—it makes me cheer to be reminded of everything great about America and to have the story reappropriated for the immigrant population."[25] To make matters even worse, in an advertisement deceptively disguised as a journalistic interview, Lin-Manuel Miranda spoke with Wall Street giant Morgan Stanley to promote the importance of personal financial planning.[26] It should come as no surprise that Morgan Stanley would try to exploit *Hamilton*'s success, and given the pro-capitalist ideology that permeates the musical, it *definitely* should come as no surprise that Miranda would welcome the bank with open arms.[27]

Claims of *Hamilton* being "revolutionary" are quite laughable once we consider the kinds of people who have fallen in love with it. In his article, "You Should be Terrified That People Who Like 'Hamilton' Run Our Country," journalist Alex Nichols says fans should feel rather skeptical whenever people like Dick Cheney, Barack Obama, Rupert Murdoch, and the rest of the D.C. and Wall Street elite unanimously praise a show like *Hamilton*. Sarcastically drawing from a line in a positive review featured in the *New Yorker*, Nichols argues *Hamilton* really *is* the "musical of the Obama era":

> We might call it a kind of, well, "blackwashing," making something that was heinous seem somehow palatable by retroactively injecting diversity into it [. . .] Contemporary progressivism has come to mean papering over material inequality with representational diversity. The president will continue to expand the national security state at the same rate as his predecessor, but at least he will be black. Predatory lending will drain the wealth from African American communities, but the board of Goldman Sachs will have several black members. Inequality will be rampant and worsening, but the 1% will at least "look like America." The actual racial injustices of our time will continue unabated, but the power structure will be diversified so that nobody feels quite so bad about it. *Hamilton* is simply this tendency's cultural-historical equivalent; instead of worrying ourselves about the brutal origins of the American state, and the lasting economic effects of those early inequities, we can simply turn the Founding Fathers black and enjoy the show.[28]

Like Lin-Manuel Miranda, bankers and other ruling class elites view condemnation of the nation's genocidal and slaveholding origins as "cultural baggage." And one's refusal to either venerate or celebrate America's anti-Black and anti-Indigenous Founding Fathers is a condition from which one must be "liberated." No wonder both conservatives and liberals are enamored with *Hamilton*. "The musical flatters both right and left sensibilities," Nichols concludes. "Conservatives get to see their beloved Founding Fathers exonerated for their horrendous crimes, and liberals get to have nationalism packaged in a feel-good multicultural form." So as it turns out, in addition to the NFL, the *New York Times*, CNN, NPR, Hollywood studio executives, and America's public schools, we now have another chief propaganda tool for the U.S. state: *Hamilton*, a musical where "[t]he more troubling questions about the country's origins are instantly vanished, as an era built on racist forced labor is transformed into a colorful, culturally progressive, and politically unobjectionable extravaganza."[29]

The veneration of the "Founding Fathers" is a crucial aspect of American exceptionalism. Hamilton, Washington, Jefferson, and the like have been canonized as the foremost representatives of the values of democracy, freedom, and liberty so often ascribed to the United States. Their critical role in the maintenance and expansion of white supremacy is rarely taught or remembered. The erasure of historical memory under the guide of American exceptionalism has created a hierarchy of slave owners that represent divergent yet related trends in American politics. This was evident in a *Saturday Night Live* sketch that awkwardly tried to contest Donald Trump's sarcastic statement that perhaps statues of Washington and Jefferson should be removed as well. In the contemporary context of Charlottesville, Washington and Jefferson are "good" while Robert E. Lee and his Confederate allies are "bad." More specifically, Washington and Jefferson are venerated as representatives of noble and sophisticated liberalism in contrast to the barbaric conservatism of the Confederacy.

The tendency to defend the Founding Fathers' racism by calling Washington, Jefferson, and Hamilton mere "products of their time" is a paramount example of anti-Blackness. By suggesting that "everyone believed slavery was okay back then," we equate *everyone* with *every white elite person*. But not only were there plenty of white abolitionists (both rich and poor), there were—much more importantly—*all of the slaves who were against slavery*, slaves that waged numerous rebellions throughout the history of their enslavement. The typical "product of their time" argument totally erases slaves from our imagination, as if they themselves had no moral agency. They are—once again—pushed into what Frantz Fanon called the zone of nonbeing, or what Saidiya Hartman calls "the position of the unthought."[30]

Again, this is one of the perplexing things about *Hamilton*. If the goal is to let people of color know that this is their country too, and that the American story is also *their* story, the question must be asked: Were you simply unable to find *any* person of color in the history of this country—from its inception to today—that could have driven this point home? Before we too quickly judge the creators of the musical, however, we must confront our own sinister practices of spreading the U.S. "Founding Fathers" propaganda. Why are these slave owners and white elite bankers presented as the nation's heroes which children are raised to emulate? Are our imaginations *that* limited? Is our knowledge of history so whitewashed and our aspirations for social justice so contaminated that we have students celebrate the people who *perpetrated* state violence and oppression, not those who actively *resisted* it? What if we stopped telling children that they, too, can be president of the United States? What if instead we taught them that they, too, can be like Ella Baker, Eslanda Robeson, or her husband Paul Robeson. They can be like Ida B. Wells, Anna Julia Cooper, W.E.B. Du Bois, Octavia Butler, Toni Morrison, George Washington's runaway slave Ona Judge, or even the 18th-century revolutionary quaker dwarf Benjamin Lay.[31] What does it say about *us*—and the stories we believe about our "exceptional" and "innocent" nation—that we think it noble to pursue a job as head of an imperial state? Indeed, if we're talking about monuments to white supremacy, we can add the office of the presidency to that list. As both the domestic and foreign policies of Barack Obama have shown, the office can serve as a monument to and enforcer of white supremacy even with a person of color running it.

White supremacy laid the foundations for the development of the U.S. and its subsequent growth into the largest capitalist and imperialist power the world has known. The ideology of American innocence has us admit, deceptively, that our country might be racist, but that our founding values and ideals will carry us forward. Ideas such as liberalism and conservatism, and the Americans that uphold them, are reflections of the dominant system of a given society. Such people, especially in the liberal spheres, are deceived into naively and innocently thinking that we can move past our brutal racism with the structures and ideologies put in place by our nation's rulers. But "America" itself is a monument to white supremacy. As Jodi Byrd points out, "We can take down all the Lee, Jackson, Jefferson, Washington, Cook, and Columbus monuments that litter the cities and towns of this nation, but the structural intent behind putting them up in the first place remains written onto the land." "Those monuments," Byrd continues, "order space, naturalize possession and dispossession, and even in their absence continue to produce the ownership of land as the only path to freedom."[32] White supremacy thus remains alive and well in the genesis of Wall Street, the prison industrial complex, and numerous channels of cultural reproduction such as the musical *Hamilton*. Those who have torn down Confederate monuments to white supremacy have hopefully begun a process where these monuments can be torn down, too.

CHAPTER 7

"The American Dream versus American Reality: Black Wealth and the Myth of Meritocracy"

"The ability to distinguish between the ideology of the American Dream and the experience of the American nightmare requires political analysis, history, and often struggle."

—Keeanga-Yamahtta Taylor[1]

"Indeed, white Americans' historied penchant for both knowing that racial inequality exists but construing that inequality as separable from their own racial advantages, their habit of interpreting economic privilege as a matter of individual merit or virtue, and their studied denouncement of the worst southern crimes while ignoring the presence of other forms of racial domination indicate that our national condition has long been marked by a severe disconnection from reality. In this sense, racial innocence is the alchemy by which Americans turn enduring and otherwise visible inequality into redemptive stories of rights, equal protection, individualism, and progress. It is America's belief in their own blamelessness for the material realities of racism."

—Kirstine Taylor[2]

"Some people are born on third base and go through life thinking they hit a triple."

—Barry Switzer[3]

A core principle of American exceptionalism is the myth of meritocracy. The myth presumes that the United States is the only place in the world where great fortunes can be derived from hard work and perseverance. The achievement of wealth and private property forms the essence of the "American Dream." Horatio Alger, a 19th-century author, is often credited with first promoting the myth in his own story about being a "self-made" man who rose from "rags to riches" through hard work. Much of his personal story was a lie, but the myth has become forever useful to an American ruling class that depends on the "American Dream" to obscure the source of its opulent wealth. The narrative firmly reduces race and class position in American society to mere obstacles that can be overcome with diligent participation in the capitalist system.

We are constantly reminded about this supposedly unique condition by American presidents, media pundits, and representatives of the capitalist elite who use the "American Dream" to paint the U.S. as the best country in the world. The "American Dream" legitimizes the wealth of the American ruling class. American capitalism, after all, is about winning and losing. Winners obtain riches while losers must continue to play the game. Yet as Daniel Smith points out,

> when you hear someone refer to their professionalism, merit or hard work, it's generally an attempt to divert attention from their inherited privilege. They are saying they deserve their position because of their individual performance—despite the reality that individual accomplishment almost always lags behind inheritance, accumulated wealth or contacts, and educational credentials.[4]

Accumulated wealth is a staple of American national identity, which has always been rooted in the relationship between whiteness and property.[5] The so-called leaders of American "independence" were not just white, but wealthy property owners, many of whom traded and exploited African slaves. Whiteness purified the American colonial system of inheritance and theft. It altered class relations to ensure that poor whites sought property and not allegiance with property-less slaves. So, when Malcolm X stated that he didn't see any "American Dream," just an "American Nightmare," he was speaking to the actual conditions that Black people have been forced to endure in America throughout the nation's history.

The "American Dream" has never been achievable for most Black Americans due to the legacies of white supremacy and mass enslavement. To obscure this reality, American exceptionalism has explained American history through the prism of progress. The American Dream narrative tells us that Black Americans are no longer enslaved and have been participating in the capitalist economy as "free labor" for over a century. They've had the same opportunities to enrich themselves as anyone else, the story goes, and a small few indeed have become rich. The general economic condition of Black America, however, is far from exceptional.[6]

Numerous studies have been conducted on the state of Black wealth in America following the 2007–2008 capitalist economic crash. According to the Institute for Policy Studies (IPS), Black wealth in America will hit zero by 2053 if current trends persist. Black median wealth has dropped from $6800 in 1983 to just $1700 in 2013, a decrease of 75 percent. White American wealth has increased by 14 percent, from $102,200 per family household to $116,800 over the same period. The economic pain inflicted by the foreclosure crisis explains the steep loss of wealth experienced by Black Americans. Home equity for Black Americans was $16,700 less in 2017 than it was in 2007.[7] Even more damning to American exceptionalism's altar of progress are recent studies by the Economic Policy Institute which show *no* progress for African Americans in areas of incarceration, homeownership, or unemployment since 1965, with over 21 percent of Black men finding themselves unemployed in 2016.[8]

The 2007–2008 economic crisis hit Black America particularly hard because the American capitalist system was always predicated upon the super exploitation of Black people. As another study points out,

> Sworn testimony from former Wells Fargo employees alleged that the bank deliberately tricked middle-class black families they called "mud people" into subprime "ghetto loans." They were certainly not the only originator doing this, as the overall differences were extremely significant. A Center for Responsible Lending study found that from 2004–2008, 6.2 percent of white borrowers with a credit score of 660 and up got subprime mortgages, while 19.3 percent of such Latino borrowers and 21.4 percent of black borrowers did.[9]

American finance capitalists motivated by profit and racism had already segregated Black neighborhoods, devalued Black homes, and pushed millions of Black families to the economic margins characterized by low-wage work, unemployment, and poverty. Schools in Black America have been deliberately segregated and underfunded while welfare programs have been significantly scaled back since former President Bill Clinton ended "welfare as we know it" in 1996.[10] In fact, ten million of a total of fourteen million Black households fall into the bottom fifty percent of households in America that control just one percent of the national wealth. Overall, White Americans control over ninety percent of the national wealth. It would take the average Black family 228 years to amass the wealth of the average white American family.[11]

These numbers reflect a racialized poverty that the American ruling class refuses to publicly acknowledge. To do so would cast a light on the reality that the "American Dream" was never meant for Black America. In fact, America's leadership in the global enterprise of racialized capitalism has driven down conditions for poor people generally both inside and outside of the American nation-state. In 2017, the richest 1 percent of the world's population usurped 82 percent of all global wealth created, while the bottom 50 percent of the world's population saw no increase in wealth.[12] By 2021, only 1 percent of the population will own 70 percent of the wealth in the U.S. while 80 percent of the American population is on the brink of poverty or worse.

The Black condition thus reflects the common adage that one would have to be asleep to truly believe in the "American Dream." There are many reasons why these conditions have not caused massive upheaval. Most American workers are not in labor unions and few organizations exist to collectively demand redress for worsening inequality. The displacement and chaos that poverty causes in the lives of working people is mainly to blame. However, a less visible reason is the belief among many Americans that the U.S. remains the most "exceptional" country in the world regardless of hardship.

This widely held sentiment is supported by the optics of the United States' political and media apparatuses. Critical to the optics of the "American Dream" is the heavy promotion of individualism as the means to economic and cultural progress. In her book *Myths that Made America*, Heike Paul traces the centrality of individualism in the historical development of the American nation-state. Tales of individual striving toward personal economic glory trace back to the days of Benjamin Franklin and run a thread through American history. The notion of the "self-made" man has long become one of America's strongest cultural values. As Paul further explains,

> The term . . . is deeply intertwined with various aspects of American exceptionalism. There are contradictory forces at work in this notion, as it includes both aspects of self-denial (education, hard work, and discipline) and self-realization based on an ethic of self-interest that aims at the sheer accumulation of property, recognition, prestige, and personal gain without any concern for others.[13]

Unsurprisingly, today's most ardent promoters of "self-made" individualism and the "American Dream" often describe themselves as modern day Horatio Algers. The post–Civil Rights era in particular has seen the advent of a politics of representation that fuels a "hero mentality." Black politicians and celebrities are advertised as role models and proof that the "American Dream" does in fact exist. When Barack Obama became president in 2008, posters went up of a popular Jay-Z lyric in schools around the country that read, "Rosa sat so Martin could walk, Martin walked so Obama could run, Obama ran so all our children can fly!" This perversion of history equates the aims of the Black Freedom movement with those of Obama, obscuring the fact that the former Black president is credited for instituting economic policies that decimated Black wealth during his tenure.[14]

The "hero mentality" thus bestows innocence upon the U.S. by fetishizing the wealth and personal success of American celebrities, politicians, and business elites. That the accumulation of wealth is predicated upon exploitation or that the safety of wealthy suburbs is dependent upon homelessness and racist policing are effectively obscured. Poor Black Americans are supposed to "dream big." Dreaming big means becoming NBA players, rappers, or entrepreneurs rather than fighting for social and economic justice. Social uplift is defined as whatever the elite class says it is, namely, the desire to achieve the status possessed by the very people responsible for poverty.

Lisa Guerrero places a spotlight on the role the National Basketball Association (NBA) plays in defining Black economic success. The NBA, she writes, is "marketing (and manipulating) the [American] dream better than almost anybody in the pop culture game today."[15] The NBA achieves such success by iconicizing players like Michael Jordan and LeBron James and attaching "American Dream" tropes to their personal success. The message corporate enterprises like the NBA send to Black America is often riddled with conflict. Black NBA players are expected to both reject their Black identity and embrace it at the same time as a key marketing tool for advertisements and product promotions. A duality is created where some players, like Michael Jordan, embody the rejection of racist, anti-Black stereotypes while others like Allen Iverson are encouraged yet chastised for representing the "street" life (i.e., poor Black communities) to maximize and diversify sales to white and Black fans alike. Whatever the case, the NBA and sports leagues generally are some of the biggest distributors of the American Dream ideology that exist today.

In the realm of the corporate media, however, perhaps no one embodies how steeped American culture is in the myth of the "American Dream" than Oprah Winfrey. Known to many as Oprah, the Black woman turned billionaire rose to stardom during the neoliberal era of American capitalism. Oprah's show became immensely popular for the host's ability to sell the "American Dream" by connecting her early life struggles to the personal struggles of "ordinary people" and advising her viewers to strive for personal self-help and well-being. In his book, *Fabricating the Absolute Fake: America in Contemporary Pop Culture*, Jaap Kooijman aptly summarizes Oprah's neoliberal philosophy:

> Oprah Winfrey herself, as a formerly overweight African-American woman who became one of the most powerful individuals in the American media industry, embodies an American success story, whose star myth (Oprah's American Dream) is reinforced by each episode of her talk show [. . .] The Oprah Winfrey Show regularly employs American celebrities, who appear on the show to promote themselves and their recent products by revealing a glimpse of their personal lives, suggesting that they too are just ordinary people, encountering the same problems as the *Oprah!* viewers do.[16]

Oprah has accumulated a billion-dollar fortune by prescribing individualist solutions for systemic problems. Through hard work, perseverance, and Oprah's "self-help" tools, we too can become billionaires. Yet in the age of neoliberal capitalism, Oprah and the celebrity class represent mere proxies for American exceptionalism and innocence. Their fortunes tell the mythical story of racial progress and the development of a more exceptional society despite the reality that wealth distribution is highly skewed to a tiny minority of the population; that a wealthy minority keeps Black America without wealth; and that even Black celebrities such as Kanye West and Tisha Campbell-Martin have revealed their own struggles with debt, making their public image as wealthy millionaires a mere illusion.[17]

Wealth concentration and the explosive growth of debt and poverty in the United States have called the "American Dream"—and thus the whole notion of American economic exceptionalism—into question. The narrative that one can achieve prosperity on the basis of individual effort and hard work has given way to the reality that American capitalism has always been a racialized inheritance system. And the wealth of the 1 percent has never come about primarily because of merit, effort, or "small government." Rather, history shows that banks, businesses, and corporations—far from letting "the free market do its thing"—actually *depend* on government intervention to maximize profits. As Matt Taibbi argues, "nobody, be he rich or poor, wants his government services cut."[18] Such government handouts to the wealthy and powerful include: military contracts from the Pentagon; Quantitative Easing programs from the Federal Reserve; strict government regulation and protections from competition for pharmaceutical companies; and, finally, spending "twice the amount of the annual federal budget" to bail out and preserve bonuses for the thousands of Wall Street bankers "who nearly blew up the world economy."[19] It might be more accurate, then, to call our system a "trickle up" economy, one where the earnings of the poor, working, and middle class subsidize the wealthy and the powerful. Capitalism *does* indeed involve a redistribution of wealth, just not in the way a just society is supposed to.

Wealth is privately accumulated through the exploitation of workers, especially Black workers, and then passed down to future generations. Every lever of American capitalism reinforces inheritance, whether it is in the low taxes that corporations and wealthy individuals pay on capital gains or the tax code's deductions on donations to the nonprofit sector. Nonprofits, often seen as the benevolent hand of private enterprise, help reify wealth disparity by providing tax shelters to rich donors who receive a tax deduction for their contribution. Most nonprofits are under the direct control of their wealthy donors. According to Christine Ahn,

> In 2000, 66 percent of foundation board members were men and 90 percent were white. Although a handful of liberal foundations may employ some program officers that are people of color or progressive, it is ultimately

> foundation trustees who have the final say in the grantmaking process. And with few exceptions, foundation trustees are extensions of America's banks, brokerage houses, law firms, universities and businesses.[20]

With the amount of bracelets, marathons, and free concerts promoted by and for charity groups, the average American may not feel comfortable critiquing what has been coined the nonprofit industrial complex. After all, who could be against giving money to charity? But as Heike Paul observes, "Giving away one's wealth, of course, retrospectively affirms once more that one had earned and owned it legitimately." So the problem with many forms of charity, she continues, is that it "seeks to close the gap between self-interest and the common good by 'returning' to the general public what had previously been extracted from it through often exploitative practices."[21]

Nonprofits are not the only example of how American capitalism is based more on inheritance than meritocracy. The institution of marriage is another example of American capitalism's veracious system of racialized wealth inheritance. Historically, marriage has organized the family into a monogamous pair in order to facilitate the patriarchal control of women as the private property of men. Today, this institution has served as an important social control mechanism in many respects, including the state's privileging of the romantic couple (either straight or gay) as the ideal form of relationship. In addition, the institution of marriage reserves certain health and immigration benefits exclusively to monogamous couples, while at the same time creating the rather crude categories of "legitimate" and "illegitimate" children. Finally, and more importantly for our discussion here, scholars like Morgan Bassichis and Dean Spade have shown that marriage has historically been weaponized to reproduce the accumulation of white wealth at the expense of Black America, mainly by demonizing the Black poor as incapable of the stable marriages necessary to achieve economic uplift.[22] This is why imagining a way forward out of capitalism must include the abolition of inheritance. After all, it's not just wealth that is inherited in American society, but poverty as well.

"American Dream" mythology is embedded in every fiber of the U.S. power structure to prevent Americans from seeing capitalist inheritance and the inequality it produces. Corporate media such as the *Oprah!* show, the sports industry, marriage, and even the nonprofit sector reinforce the sanctity of individualism and the notion that the U.S. is a meritocratic society.

Material conditions, however, beg to differ. Black Americans, and indeed most Americans (as well as most the world's people generally) have seen a dramatic decline in their share of total wealth in recent years. Of course, this doesn't stop many white people—who naively believe that their wealth is *earned*—from blaming Black people for their dire economic situation. Katie Grimes argues that this sentiment is nothing new, and places such racial animus in historical context:

> Federal spending practices . . . accorded white power much-needed ideological camouflage. In the Cold War era, whites needed to believe themselves not only not "racist" but also not "communist." Authorities assured them that federal meddling in the mortgage market represented not a violation of free market principle but their illumination. Rather than the gift that enabled their affluence, whites considered government housing subsidies a type of reward they earned by being hard-working winners. As if recapitulating the ideology that animated racialized slave mastership, whites believed both that they deserved these interventions but that they did not need them. They conversely imagined black people as those who did not deserve but greatly needed federal aid. As whites, they had rights and well-earned rewards while slave-descended black folks had already been given more than they deserved. Black people were owed nothing; white people had been given nothing and deserved everything they had.[23]

To give another example, as Ira Katznelson shows in his book, *When Affirmative Action Was White*, the GI Bill played a significant role in "widening an already huge racial gap in postwar America."[24] Such are the material realities produced by racial and American innocence when applied to the framework of the "American Dream." Innocence has us assume the United States offers equal opportunity for *all* to flourish. If you do succeed, it's because you took advantage of the greatness America has to offer. But if you don't succeed, then it's your fault, not the state's.

The time is coming when the narratives of American exceptionalism and American innocence will no longer be able to sustain the country's meritocratic image. Wealth disparities will eventually give way to popular frustration. We have already seen signs of such frustration in the rise of the Occupy Wall Street movement in 2011, the Wisconsin labor protests that same year, and the Bernie Sanders presidential campaign of 2016. It is time to build on these efforts and develop a new model of social organization based on Martin Luther King Jr.'s idea of a "Beloved Community"—"a global vision, in which all people can share in the wealth of the earth" and where "poverty, hunger and homelessness will not be tolerated because international standards of human decency will not allow it."[25]

To begin this process, future social movements will have to rejuvenate the political ideas of Martin Luther King, ideas that had developed radically in the last years of his life. By the time of his assassination, King was organizing a "Poor People's Campaign" to aid the strike effort of sanitation workers in Memphis while simultaneously denouncing the triple evils of militarism, racism, and materialism (capitalism). The complete evaporation of Black wealth in America should lead to similar visions and drive us toward a society where dreams of true economic justice for working and poor people are in fact a reality. This will require a system of wealth *redistribution* that rids of the many mechanisms that loot Black wealth under American capitalism's system of profit and inheritance, thereby eliminating the conditions that allow the "American Dream" ideology to fester and thrive.

Yet because of the economic impact that the system of slavery and capitalism has produced for Black Americans, we must not stop at a call for radical redistribution or even reparations. As Saidiya Hartman points out:

> The reparations movement puts itself in this contradictory or impossible position, because reparations are not going to solve the systemic ongoing production of racial inequality, in material or any other terms. And like inequality, racial domination and racial abjection are produced across generations. In that sense, reparations seem like a very limited reform: a liberal scheme . . . that reinscribe[s] the power of the law and of the state to make right a certain situation, when, clearly, it cannot. I think too that such thinking reveals an idealist trap; it's as if once Americans know how the wealth of the country was acquired, they'll decide that black people are owed something. My God! Why would you assume that? Like housing segregation is an accident![26]

Racial capitalism is no "accident." It is deeply entrenched in the American political, economic, and social structure. We cannot rely on reform alone to remedy such a grave, structural injustice. We must move beyond debates about a universal basic income, a higher minimum wage, what a fairer tax policy might look like, and how to punish the big banks. We need to expand on these important demands further and try to imagine a world without capitalism, without private property, without the sale of labor to property owners, and without the American Dream. We need to admit that we're unable to imagine what exactly this will look like because our conception of what is possible has been so contaminated by capitalism and its ideologies of American exceptionalism and innocence in the first place. Yes, it is hard for us to imagine otherwise, to imagine a world without capitalism. But if Claudia Jones taught us anything, it is that we *must* dream of a different kind of politics—one that, as her biographer writes, is even "more radical than communism."[27]

CHAPTER 8

"Should U.S. Imperialism Matter to Black Lives Matter?"

"American women bear a heavy responsibility to the millions of our anti-fascist sisters in the world camp of peace, precisely because the threat to world peace stems from the imperialists of our land."

—Claudia Jones[1]

". . . the people of the Congo refuse to mine the uranium for the atom bombs made in Jim Crow factories in the United States."

—Paul Robeson[2]

"Black Lives Matter" has become a familiar slogan in American political discourse. The Black Lives Matter movement was born in Ferguson in 2014 when protests erupted in the city after police officer Darren Wilson was not indicted for the murder of 18-year old Michael Brown. Slogans such as "Hands Up, Don't Shoot" and "Black Lives Matter" encapsulated the outrage of Black communities sick and tired of decades, if not centuries, of life-threatening police harassment, terror, and abuse. When police units armed with military grade weaponry occupied the streets of Ferguson, some concluded that American police shared many similarities to military occupation forces deployed in Iraq or Afghanistan. Yet as activists Tamara Nopper and Mariame Kaba observed, "For blacks, the 'war on terror' hasn't come home. It's always been here."[3] The Black Lives Matter movement provided an opportunity to connect police violence against Black Americans in cities across the country to struggles against U.S. imperialism and militarism around the world.

The connection between Black America and Palestine, for example, flowed organically from the American nation-state's long support for Israel's existence as a settler colonial state in the Middle East. In 2016, the Obama Administration agreed to lend Israel $38 billion in military aid over the next decade.[4] This was the largest deal ever reached between the two nations despite the fact that much of the world considers Israel in gross violation of the Palestinian people's right to self-determination. The Center for Constitutional Rights (CCR) calls Israel's decades-long colonial policy of displacement, military occupation, and terror a violation of international law that meets and the UN's definition of genocide.[5] CCR cites the hundreds of thousands of Palestinians killed and displaced by Israeli military forces following the UN mandate of 1948 and the subsequent invasions of Gaza in the 21st century as examples of Israel's crimes against humanity.

Similar to Israeli forces, American police departments act as an occupation army in Black communities. Police murder Black Americans at a near daily rate while subjecting many more to constant terror and violence.[6] The connection between Israel and American police is multifaceted. According to one report, the Obama Administration increased Pentagon transfers of battlefield weapons to police by 2400 percent by 2014.[7] Not only are police departments armed with the same military grade weaponry provided to Israeli soldiers, but many American police departments send their officers to Israel for training in methods of brutality rebranded as "counter-terror" measures.[8]

These connections were not lost on Black Lives Matter activists in the movement's initial stages. Black activists in Ferguson immediately began making links between the Israeli occupation of Palestine and the occupation of Black Americans by police. Palestinians communicated with Black activists in Ferguson staring down militarized police in the aftermath of the non-indictment of Darren Wilson through Twitter. They advised Ferguson activists on the proper method of throwing back tear gas canisters so commonly used by the Israeli Defense Forces (IDF). Later, the Movement for Black Lives, a coalition of Black Lives Matter organizations, made solidarity with Palestine and the divestment of resources from the American military a key demand in their platform.[9] In addition, several delegates from the Movement for Black Lives coalition traveled to the West Bank in 2016 to participate in protests against the Israeli occupation.[10] These examples of solidarity across borders left little doubt about whether the Black Lives Matter Movement also believed that

U.S. imperialism mattered, too. The Black Lives Matter movement appeared well on its way toward developing an internationalist movement capable of transforming American society.

Such optimism was challenged after National Football League (NFL) player Colin Kaepernick decided to sit during the pre-game "Star Spangled Banner" in August of 2016. Kaepernick's protest of the anthem has precipitated a years-long worth of political debate that the Black Lives Matter movement has largely been absent from. Kaepernick linked his protests to police brutality and the oppresses of Black America. He stated that he would not "stand up to show pride in a flag for a country that oppressed Black people and people of color." NFL owners, and indeed much of the American ruling elite, saw Kaepernick's actions as something much larger than a mere protest against police brutality. Kaepernick has been forced into exile from the NFL. By linking the national anthem to Black oppression, his actions questioned the very legitimacy of American exceptionalism as it related to the never ending wars conducted by U.S. imperialism in all corners of the globe.

The veneration of the National Anthem is a racist cultural tradition that is intimately connected to the intense militarization of U.S. imperialism that has occurred in recent years. Kaepernick's protest struck a nerve in vested military and corporate interests that heavily invest in sporting leagues to spread propaganda for the American military.[11] The NFL in particular has partaken in a form of "paid patriotism" with the Department of Defense. It wasn't until 2009 that NFL players were mandated by the league to stand as a team for the National Anthem. The change came after the Pentagon agreed to transfer over $11 million from the Department of Defense to the National Guard and the NFL to stage on-field displays of "patriotism" as a means to fuel military recruitment.[12] Kaepernick was banned from the NFL in a coordinated effort by owners to ensure that no aspect of the NFL's profitability—especially the millions of federal dollars accumulated from the glorification of the military as an extension of American superiority—would be disrupted.

The NFL's institution of "paid patriotism" reveals the broad relationship between the military and U.S. imperialism. U.S. imperialism is a global system that depends on the military to keep the profits of monopoly corporations "safe" from the people who the military so ruthlessly occupies and terrorizes. With a budget of $700 billion dollars, the U.S. military is larger than the military budget of the next ten countries combined. Over 800 American military bases are scattered across the world.[13] This figure does not include American Special Operations forces, which are deployed to 149 countries around the world fully equipped with high tech weaponry and trained in torture techniques.[14]

Since 1945, the American war machine has been estimated to have killed between 20–30 million people in nations such as Vietnam, Iraq, Afghanistan, Guatemala, and Libya. Such an enormous number does not count the thousands that have been killed by drone strikes since 2001. Also not counted are the casualties of the ongoing American proxy wars in nations such as Syria. Perhaps even more relevant to our discussion, the U.S. currently has a military presence in 50 of the 54 nations in Africa.[15] The expansion of the American military apparatus has not only provided reinforcement for the ideology of American exceptionalism through the threat of arms but has also created the necessary economic, political, and cultural conditions for American dominance abroad. "U.S. has Special Operations forces in 70 percent of the world's nations and has active duty troops in over 150 nations in the world. Due to the endless character of U.S. wars in the 21st century, it has become increasingly difficult to measure the enormous scope of the U.S. military's global reach."

The further militarization of U.S. imperialism has in effect intensified the militarization of American exceptionalism. American exceptionalism is dependent on American military projection and power. Both President Donald Trump and former President Barack Obama have repeatedly linked the strength of the American military with the so-called American values of "democracy" and "freedom." While the United States has historically claimed civilizational superiority through the military conquest and dehumanization of African and Indigenous people, the contemporary militarization of American society has built on this framework to justify a more expansive form of global empire. David Theo Goldberg argues that race is an essential component in the militarization of society:

> Militarizing societies accordingly are those in which anyone (characterized as not belonging and threatening, as beastly, along with those considered their associates, their bidders) is available for being killed or letting die. They may just be forgotten while rotting away in Guantánamo or Supermax solitary confinement. It is a society in which anyone deemed trustworthy on behalf of the state or its nominal interests can be licensed to kill. There is a

> litany, for instance, of unindicted police officers killing unarmed black people in the United States. It is a society as well in which the ordained increasingly can authorize unmanned killing via distance destroying technologies such as drones. They are licensed by the order of sovereignty to identify who can be killed or let die and who not, who is beast and who is human.[16]

Race forms the skeleton that directs the American military to perform the role of armed protector of so-called "white" and exceptional values such as "prosperity," "national security," and "democracy."[17] Nations and peoples who stand in the way of American interests are deemed savages. Those who carry out the atrocities of American warfare are deemed human. Instead of focusing on how American military corporations such as Boeing make enormous profits from government contracts to develop drones, or the connection between corporate access to mineral resources and the war in Afghanistan, the American public is led to believe that the U.S. war machine is coming to the aid of nations around the world. The reality is that it is keeping much of the planet in a state of perpetual violence, poverty, and terror.

The racist foundations of U.S. militarism explain why this condition can exist alongside the worship of American troops and police officers. American troops, despite high rates of poverty, suicide, and addiction after service, are glorified as heroes in nearly every speech given by acting presidents. The treatment for police officers injured or killed on the job (a rare occasion) is similar. Humanizing the soldiers of war comes at the expense of their victims. The more that police and military officers are positioned as guardians of American exceptionalism, the more difficult it is to criticize them for their atrocities. Kaepernick can thus be scorned and banned from the NFL for speaking out against the hundreds of police murders of Black Americans that occur each year, while police and military units deployed to oppressed communities commit unspeakable numbers of atrocities with impunity.

These conditions have placed an immense amount of pressure on Black Lives Matter–affiliated organizations and movements to remain silent about the full spectrum dominance of the American military. Protests against the symbol of the American military—the American flag—carry material consequences, as Kaepernick's case suggests. Anti-war activity does not bring lavish careers, nonprofit opportunities, or personal gains of any type. While police brutality in the U.S. is reflective of the total war imposed by U.S. imperialism, the ruling class has attempted to make it a single-issue reform project. Corporations such as Google have donated millions to particular Black Lives Matter organizations to make information about "racial bias "more "available."[18] Meanwhile, no such funding exists to imprison cops that have killed Black Americans or make information about American wars abroad more available to the public.

The responsibility thus falls on courageous individuals such as Colin Kaepernick or movements such as Black Lives Matter to connect the struggle against white supremacy and police brutality with wars waged abroad by the American nation-state. The term "war" does not merely reflect a relationship between nations. It reflects a relationship to oppression more broadly and points to a vital bond that the majority of humanity shares with each other. Christina Sharpe notes how officers of the New York Police Department (NYPD) often described "furtive movements" as the reason for stopping and frisking over 700,000 Black and Latino youth in 2011.[19] The description painted racialized youth as sexualized beasts, which is not unlike how the Obama Administration painted the Libyan people prior to the North Atlantic Treaty Organization (NATO) bombing of the African country that same year. Libya's leader Muammar Gaddafi was deemed a "murderer of his own people" by American leadership and the army stood accused of using Viagra to rape women and children. None of these claims were verified yet the American-led NATO invasion of Libya still bombed the most prosperous country on the African continent over 60,000 times over a six-month period. The NATO war on Libya left upward of 50,000 dead, which is a conservative estimate given that NATO has been accused of covering up the full extent of the damage.

U.S. imperialism possesses such a large body count, both within its own colonial borders and beyond them, that the system must exert exhaustive effort to cover up the damage. American exceptionalism places a veneer of innocence over American economic and political domination. The racist policing of Black Americans is forgiven because police officers supposedly "serve and protect" American interests on the home front.[20] Over 26,000 American bombs can be dropped on the world in a year (2016) yet the American military is forgiven for allegedly protecting American interests abroad. American political officials—and the corporate media outlets that serve them—describe these interests as universal moral principles when in reality they reflect the political and economic objectives of the ruling elite.

The bullet and the bomb—the American military occupation and the police occupation—are the bonds that link the condition of Black Americans to oppressed nations around the world. Barbara Ransby says of Eslanda Robeson that "in speech after speech, and article after article, she insisted that the relationships among capitalism, sexism, colonialism, racism, and empire were symbiotic."[21] Thus, as Claudia Jones also showed, the point isn't just that Black Americans should care about oppression at home *and* oppression abroad, as if to suggest that the two are separate, isolated actions perpetrated by the U.S. Rather, Black internationalists were able to *connect* oppression abroad with oppression at home. As Claudia Jones's biographer puts it, "unity becomes a radical strategy against both masculinity, racism, and imperialism. This is what the government recognized as dangerous—the linking of these disparate struggles into a unified movement for social justice."[22]

U.S. imperialism has grown larger and deadlier because American corporations must protect private property to fully maximize profit. U.S. imperialism must therefore render Black Americans sexual beasts, Libyans sexual mercenaries, and Koreans in the North brainwashed slaves to explain why American police and military forces should exercise political power over their wealth and labor. American exceptionalism makes the U.S. military takeover of nearly every African nation under the banner of AFRICOM a matter of spreading "democracy" even as the continent loses tens of billions of dollars worth of expatriated profits per year to American and Western corporations. Black Americans, on the other hand, have seen their wealth fall dramatically in conjunction with the intense policing, surveillance, and mass incarceration that characterizes Black daily life.[23]

Black internationalist critiques "of American foreign policy revealed not only the contradiction of preaching 'freedom' abroad while maintaining Jim Crow violence at home," writes Robeson biographer Tony Perruci, "but also the attempt by 'American Big Business,' as the *Chicago Defender* protested, 'to carry abroad the system that prevails in South Carolina.'" "In other words," Perucci continues, "by subsidizing transnational capitalism, the American government was supporting the exportation of its own brutal labor practices in countries throughout Africa."[24] Thus, as Robeson and countless other Black internationalists exemplified, the conditions produced by American exceptionalism have the potential to strengthen supposedly separate movements against police brutality and war into a broad effort to imagine alternatives to the entire system of U.S. imperialism.

A collective consciousness connecting the Black condition at home and American warfare abroad is exactly what the ruling class hopes to render invisible. The response to Kaepernick's protest of the national anthem is case in point. When the protest began to inspire actions from NFL and other sports players across the country, the ruling class seized the moment to narrow their focus. This became much easier to accomplish after President Donald Trump suggested that an NFL player was a "son of a bitch" for protesting the anthem and should be fired accordingly. Suddenly, all one could hear was how protests against the anthem were a matter of American "national unity." Rapper Eminem produced a freestyle denouncing Trump's comment while at the same time proclaiming that "we love our military, and we love our country." Eminem received a popular response from the corporate media, the Democratic Party, and a significant portion of the American public, including Black Americans. The power of American exceptionalism, then, is in its ability to mold opposition to the overt racism of Donald Trump or the murders of Black Americans by the police into politically acceptable responses that reinforce the legitimacy of the American nation-state. In this case, Eminem's celebration of the U.S. military responsible for the oppressive conditions around the world is able to masquerade as a stand against anti-Black racism despite the intimate connection between the two.

Black internationalism has been the historic antidote to the political confusion caused by American exceptionalism and its power brokers. Internationalism, and Black internationalism in particular, is an ideology that presumes that the freedom of Black Americans is completely intertwined with the freedom of oppressed nations around the world.[25] The Black Lives Matter movement and actions like Kaepernick's have been unable to revive the spirit of Black internationalism that peaked in the mid to late 20th century. The dominant tendency has been for Black Lives Matter organizations to appeal to the American criminal "justice" system for redress or to form nonprofits to serve the Black community. While good work has come from these efforts, American exceptionalism remains a powerful ideological barrier in the development of an internationalist consciousness consistent with the historic legacy of the Black Radical Tradition in America. Historian Robyn Spencer highlights one of these intellectual heroes of the movement,

Connie Matthews, who served as the International Coordinator of the Black Panther Party:

> In an interview with Angela Davis, Matthews outlined the Panther internationalist agenda. The party, she declared, sought to educate black people "to the importance of internationalism. To get them to understand that we are in the belly of the whale here and that imperialism, manifested in the U.S., is a monster with tentacles and the other oppressed peoples of the world are trying to cut off the tentacles but that we here have to get the monster from inside."[26]

Thus, rather than repeating the mistakes of some Black movement leaders who understood the importance of critiquing American foreign policy yet "felt compelled to prove their American loyalties above all else," Black Lives Matter can find inspiration from internationalists like Connie Matthews.[27]

The seeds of internationalism were first planted in the American mainland by African slaves who allied themselves with rival colonial powers to win freedom.[28] Internationalism took on even more concrete meaning, however, when anti-colonial and socialist revolutions began sweeping the world following the Russian Revolution of 1917. Ella Baker, Paul Robeson, and his wife Eslanda Robeson are but a few stalwarts of the Black radical tradition who proudly espoused internationalism as an indispensable aspect of the Black Freedom movement. Ella Baker is often remembered for her leadership role in the formation of the Mississippi Freedom Democratic Party as an alternative vehicle to pressure Civil Rights reforms. However, Baker was also a staunch internationalist who campaigned against Italy's 1934–35 invasion of Ethiopia and spoke out against Eurocentric depictions of Africa that drove support for the war. As her biographer Barbara Ransby reminds us, Baker's activities "were framed by a much larger internationalist perspective and included a particular concern with the issues of African colonialism and independence." Later in her life, Baker would extend her internationalist support to Puerto Rican independence and join Peace organizations such as the Third World Women's Alliance.[29]

Paul Robeson was an actor and singer who, along with Eslanda, presented the *We Charge Genocide* petition to the United Nations (UN) in 1951. The document, which was also signed by W.E.B. Du Bois, Claudia Jones, and numerous other Black freedom activists, sought redress for Black Americans from the UN on the basis that their treatment in America met the internationally recognized definition for genocide. Robeson supplemented calls for international redress of Black oppression in America with staunch opposition to American wars abroad, particularly America's so-called "Cold War" against the Soviet Union. His actions compelled the U.S. to revoke his passport and "blacklist" him for sympathizing with communism. As Tony Perucci explains, Robeson was punished for his

> promotion of African American rights, but also his linking of the cold war crisis with capitalist investments in colonialism . . . For Robeson, the possibility of African Americans going to war against the Soviet Union was "unthinkable" because the adverse material effects of war on blacks throughout the black diaspora rendered the very notion of fighting in such a war in direct conflict with the movement toward substantive redress and the realization of freedom. Blacks' participation in such a war amounted to fighting for their own disenfranchisement and to their own disadvantage.[30]

Paul's wife Eslanda was another leader of the Black Freedom movement who opposed U.S. warfare for similar reasons. Eslanda often connected her opposition to the Korean war and the American arms race with the Soviet Union to efforts to improve Black life in America. Ransby argues that Eslanda, or "Essie," was an "advocate for internationalizing the Black Freedom struggle in the United States and for drawing parallels with socialist, communist, and anti-colonial movements abroad." Essie "would expand greatly on this idea in her later writings," Ransby continues, "where she would emphasize the importance of being part of a global political family and developing a global Black identity."[31]

Black internationalism was not merely an idea, but a movement informed by and organized around the everyday struggles of Black Americans. Activists such as Paul Robeson and W.E.B. Du Bois visited the Soviet Union and China to learn from anti-colonial revolutions abroad and to build support for the Black Freedom movement. As Lisa Lowe notes, "Du Bois situated the African American freedom struggle within a world historical struggle of laborers of color and implied that the struggle of Black labor did not depend on recognition by white Americans or the U.S. state, but on recognition by other laborers of color in the colonized world."[32] Such support helped place pressure on the U.S. imperialist establishment, which saw Jim Crow racism as a potential public relations hurdle in the establishment of economic and political hegemony abroad. "The push to frame America's civil rights and economic justice movements . . . to the larger anti-colonial and anti-imperialist movements abroad," writes Barbara Ransby, "might actually have strengthened and accelerated, rather than derailed, the push for racial equality had the Black leadership at the time adopted that stance." Indeed, by the end of the Second World War, U.S. imperialism was worried about how Jim Crow white supremacy would impact its newfound hegemony abroad. The worry was so intense that the United States not only revoked the passports of Robeson, Du Bois, and other Black Freedom activists but also sent jazz musicians to Africa and Asia to offset bad international press about American racism.[33]

Black internationalism would continue to develop into the era of Black Power and Black liberation. Malcolm X reignited the claims of the *We Charge Genocide* petition of a decade prior to petition African countries to prosecute the U.S. government at the UN for genocidal crimes against Black Americans.[34] The Black Panther Party, which formed in part because of Malcolm X's legacy, possessed chapters in dozens of countries around the world including in the DPRK and Algeria. The organization offered Black Panther members to fight U.S. imperialism's war in Vietnam on the side of the Vietnamese. Huey P. Newton, founder of the Party, was invited to visit China in September of 1971, months prior to President Nixon's supposedly historic visit in 1972.[35] The Black Panther Party arguably led the most significant peace movement that has ever existed in America. This movement placed significant pressure on the U.S. to withdraw from its invasion of Vietnam.

U.S. imperialism should matter to Black Lives Matter, then, because Black internationalism has always mattered to the development of a path toward Black freedom. Recognizing, like W.E.B. Du Bois, "that the pursuit of political enfranchisement for a single group within an imperial United States could contribute to the subordination of others, both inside and outside of the American capitalist empire," Black internationalism envisions a world where white supremacy and empire are replaced by a new, global system of relationships based in solidarity and mutual cooperation.[36] Black internationalism imagines a world where Colin Kaepernick is not blacklisted from the NFL for standing up against the wanton murder of Black Americans by the police. It imagines a world where the U.S. military is no longer able to invade, sanction, and bomb nations into submission. Racial oppression in America has reached a climatic intensity, as has U.S. imperialism's ceaseless profit-driven wars on the planet. Conditions exist, as they did in the 20th century, for Black internationalism to make a revival. This makes the remembrance of Black internationalism a critical tool toward deconstructing American exceptionalism and its cacophonous cries for more war at Black America's expense.

There are contemporary efforts that are attempting to revive Black internationalism. In 2016, after numerous testimonies were given by individuals and organizations impacted by the practice, a UN working group concluded that police killings of Black Americans were reminiscent of lynching.[37] China has produced an annual report on the United States' human rights record since at least 2014, highlighting racism and police brutality as hallmarks of American society.[38] And in the U.S., the Black Alliance for Peace (BAP) is leading the way in the development of a new anti-war movement. According to their website, BAP "seeks to recapture and redevelop the historic anti-war, anti-imperialist, and pro-peace positions of the radical black movement."[39] These particular developments indicate that Black internationalism has not been forgotten, just arrested by the influence of American exceptionalism. This is an important lesson that was articulated by Martin Luther King Jr. in his final years. "Like the anti-colonial activists of the 1940's," writes Penny M. Von Eschen, King "connected the possibility of change—a genuine transformation of American society and global power relations—to an ongoing struggle of memory against forgetting. The moral imagination to create a genuinely democratic world depended on remembering and bearing witness to the enslavement of Africans, the exploitation of colonial peoples, and the development of racial capitalism."[40]

American exceptionalism and its attendant ideology of American innocence have helped the U.S. cover up its atrocities abroad and disconnect them from its racialized atrocities at home. The American military is widely seen as protecting our nation from savage peoples and their inferior ways of life. Police brutality sparked the Black Lives Matter movement because it reminded us that American exceptionalism has never applied to Black people. To the oppressed, the United States has never been a force for good. The Black Lives Matter phenomenon, however, has not yet led to the emergence of a serious anti-imperialist movement. Black Lives Matter organizations cannot be blamed for the overall lack of such a movement. But American exceptionalism *can* be blamed, as the narrative is intertwined with the justifications the American ruling class uses to promote its military ventures abroad. With U.S. imperialism risking the possibility of nuclear war with nations such as Russia, China, Iran, and the DPRK, and with the Black condition in America in decline, we cannot miss another opportunity like what Colin Kaepernick's anthem protest afforded. That is, to ensure that peace becomes integrated in the movement to imagine a future that is free from U.S. imperialism and white supremacy. This will require that anti-racist and social justice movements publicly break from U.S. imperialism's fantasies about the U.S. military's role in the world without hesitation or exception.

CHAPTER 9

"Protecting Whose Speech? Protecting Whose Assembly?"

"The imprisonment of those seeking social and political change in the United States is as old as its elite-based democracy rooted in slavery, anti-Indian genocidal wars, and 'manifest destiny.'"

—Joy James[1]

"We help each other inhabit what is an otherwise uninhabitable and brutal social context."

—Saidiya Hartman[2]

"We were never meant to survive."

—Audre Lorde[3]

Most students educated in the United States learn at an early age that the right to free speech and assembly are protected rights under the First Amendment of the American Constitution. These rights are heralded as hallmarks of American "democracy" that exist nowhere else in the world. American exceptionalism has been the dominant framework from which to understand these rights, whether they are discussed in the Oval Office, the corporate media, or the American education system. The dominant narrative holds that Americans are the only people in the world who have a "free press" and the right to vocalize their beliefs without persecution, despite the fact that the U.S. ranks 41st in the recent World Press Freedom Index.[4] Just like other aspects of American exceptionalism, the free speech and assembly debate has been guided by the economic and political interests of U.S.

imperialism rather than the amorphous and abstract ideals of the American democratic project.

American discourse over free speech and assembly has been challenged in the era of the Trump presidency. The U.S. has found it increasingly difficult to justify its claim to "free speech" when the majority of Americans have little trust in a media landscape where just six corporations control ninety percent of all media in America. Some have concluded that Trump's victory in the 2016 presidential elections reflected a loss of trust in American ruling institutions, like the media, to produce favorable economic and political conditions for an increasingly impoverished, policed, and misinformed population.[5] Meanwhile, American progressives have credited the racist ideology of Donald Trump for the emergence of the "Alt-Right," a supposedly new, more chic, right-wing ideology with roots in neo-Nazi and Ku Klux Klan formations. Figures such as Richard Spencer and Milo Yiannopoulos have sparked large protests at universities across the country. Spencer and Yiannopoulos have claimed leadership in what is coined the "Free Speech Movement" while their opposition has viewed the "Free Speech Movement" as nothing but a cover for neo-fascist tendencies.

The American ruling class has used American exceptionalism to contain the discourse of the "free speech" debate within acceptable parameters. Yiannopoulos and Spencer are indeed white supremacists. They avidly support movements that claim that "white rights" are under attack.[6] While the extension of university speaking invitations to Spencer and Yiannopoulos have sparked understandable antiracist sentiment, the American Civil Liberties Union (ACLU) and others have mainly responded by focusing on the application of First Amendment rights, even to the point of defending Yiannopoulos for his right to speak about topics regardless of their racist or bigoted nature. This has created a false dichotomy not uncharacteristic of American exceptionalism. On the one hand, the ACLU has fought diligently against the erosion of civil liberties and sees the persecution of whistleblowers such as Edward Snowden and Chelsea Manning as indicative of a political environment that picks and chooses what is acceptable speech and what isn't. On the other hand, protesters have drawn a line in the sand over what speech is acceptable, and the Alt-Right's brand of white supremacy has clearly crossed it.

Both sides of the "free speech" debate have subtly given legitimacy to the notion that the U.S. is designed to protect the freedoms of speech and assembly for all people living within its borders. Antiracist protesters have clearly asserted that "hate" speech should not be considered "free" given the county's history of white supremacy. This positions the American populace as the primary force that determines what speech and assembly are protected by the U.S. The ACLU has taken the side that the U.S. should defend *all* speech and assembly due to the dangerous precedent set when certain forms are banned. American exceptionalism remains at the center of both sides of the debate. The American nation-state's hostile treatment of social movements throughout history has been largely ignored in place of a debate that focuses on how to "fix" the government's treatment of free speech. However, it is precisely this history that exposes how the First Amendment has never applied to those who have challenged U.S. imperialism in their efforts to build a better world.

Social movements have challenged key narratives that give legitimacy to American exceptionalism, and as an extension, U.S. imperialism as well. To provide context, legal theorist and activist Dean Spade is worth quoting in full:

> Social movements engaged in resistance have given us a very different portrayal of the United States than what is taught in most elementary school classrooms and textbooks. The patriotic narrative delivered at school tells us a few key lies about US law and politics: that the United States is a democracy in which law and policy derive from what a majority of people think is best, that the United States used to be racist and sexist but is now fair and neutral thanks to changes in the law, and that if particular groups experience harm, they can appeal to the law for protection [. . .] [But social movements] have shown that the United States has always had laws that arrange people through categories of indigeneity, race, gender, ability, and national origin to produce populations with different levels of vulnerability to economic exploitation, violence, and poverty. These counter narratives have challenged the notion that violence is a result of private individuals with bad ideas and that the state is where we should look for protection from such violence. Conversely, resistant political theorists and social movements have helped us understand the concept of "state violence," which has been essential for exposing the central harms faced by Native people, women, people of color, people with disabilities, and immigrants. They have exposed that

state programs and law enforcement are not the arbiters of justice, protection, and safety but are instead sponsors and sites of violence.[7]

Two movements that have consistently challenged such patriotic narratives of social change—Black radicalism and labor radicalism—have seen their rights to the freedom of speech and assembly suppressed throughout American history. Co-founder of the Black Panther Party, Huey P. Newton, discussed this history in his doctoral dissertation. Newton outlined the historical context for the suppression of Black radicalism and more specifically the Black Panther Party. "Clear-cut superiority in things social and economic—by whatever means—has been a scruples-free premise of American ruling class authority from the society's inception to the present," he writes. "The initial socioeconomic advantage, begotten by chattel slavery," he continues, "was enforced by undaunted violence and the constant threat of more violence."[8] Whether it be actual or threatened, the state violence that repressed the political speech of the government's most ardent critics continued well beyond so-called emancipation. The United States' supposed support of all citizens courageous enough to "speak their mind" appears to be just one more exceptionalist myth. This myth of "free" speech, like so many other myths discussed in this book, obscures the state's systematic categorization of those who are or are not *American*, as well as those who are and are not *human*.

Political repression of certain forms of "free speech" took on new forms during the rise of industrial capitalism in America. Facing immense pressure from labor unrest, the United States began to lay the basis for the development of a secret political police, now known as the "intelligence community." American intelligence has its roots in the suppression of factory workers in Chicago on strike for an 8-hour workday. After a dynamite bomb was thrown in a labor rally on May 4th, 1886, police forces opened fire on the crowd. An untold number of people were killed or wounded. Socialists and anarchists had their homes raided and searched without warrants. Thirty-one were indicted and four were hanged.[9]

The First World War, and the Russian Revolution, led the U.S. to formalize its secret police into the General Intelligence Division (GID). By 1919, workers all over the country were engaged in strikes and labor actions for improved working conditions. Black Americans also rebelled over precarious working conditions and the constant threat of violence from white lynch mobs. The American ruling class feared that such "industrial disturbances" would lead to popular sympathy for the socialist character of the Russian Revolution. In a diary entry, Woodrow Wilson made this clear by stating "the American Negro returning from abroad [WWI] would be our greatest medium for conveying Bolshevism in America."[10] The GID collaborated with the Bureau of Investigation to collect information on radical organizations such as the African Blood Brotherhood and the Industrial Workers of the World, which culminated in the infamous Palmer Raids of 1919. Intelligence raids were given legal justification through the passage of the Espionage and Sedition Act of 1917 and 1918. Thousands of "foreign radicals" were arrested around the country and many of them were deported or placed in federal prison on the basis of alleged disloyalty to America's participation in the First World War. Others, like Emma Goldman and Marcus Garvey, were accused of advocating the overthrow of the U.S. government.

U.S. suppression of domestic radicalism was not only a response to the growth of socialism in the USSR and China but also to the fact that the Communist Party USA and the Black Freedom movement worked together to achieve their common visions for US society. The Communist Party USA established itself as a leader in the fight against Jim Crow racism, especially in their defense of nine young Black men sentenced to death in Scottsboro, Alabama, in 1931 after being wrongfully accused of raping two white women. Six years later, the combined efforts of communists and Black organizations helped reverse their death sentence. Black Americans would swell the ranks of the Community Party as they jointly organized against Jim Crow and the economic discrimination and exploitation of the post-emancipation and post-war eras. In his dissertation, Newton correctly identifies that racial and class cleavages have always hindered the establishment of "democracy" in America.[11] These cleavages explain why the United States has claimed to hold a monopoly on the rights to "freedom of speech and assembly" even as it waged a campaign of suppression against both Black and communist organizations. The U.S. state, in the words of Chandan Reddy, is "defined by its *freedom with violence*."[12]

State repression of domestic radicalism based on the manufactured fear of the "Red Menace" continued in the period following the Second World War. The U.S.'s campaign of suppression against communist and Black radicals during this period is generally known as "McCarthyism," in reference to

Senator Joseph McCarthy's leadership in the Special Committee to investigate un-American activities and propaganda in the United States. This committee, established by Congress, galvanized legal and intelligence resources toward the registration, surveillance (especially through wiretapping communications), deportation, and execution of presumed communists. Two Acts passed during this period, the Smith Act of 1940 and the McCarran Internal Security Act of 1950, provided the legal basis for such severe repression. In her biography of Claudia Jones, Carole Boyce Davies directly traces the genesis of these laws to the deportation of the Black Trinidadian woman who also happened to be a leader in the Communist Party.[13] The laws forced communists to register with the Attorney General and broadly interpreted what it meant to advocate, distribute, and organize the "overthrowing or destroying of any government of the United States." Unfortunately for Claudia Jones, she fell victim to this witch hunt which was a clear and "deliberate attempt by the U.S. government to erase her from U.S. history."[14]

Atrocities such as the deportation of Jones and the execution of Jewish communists Ethel and Julius Rosenberg were no aberrations but rather part and parcel of a general policy of repression that characterized the U.S. at the time. Cyril Briggs, another Black communist and founder of the African Blood Brotherhood, found himself subpoenaed to testify in front of the House of Un-American Activities Committee, or HUAC. His testimony summarized the truly abhorrent and bankrupt character of the repression that was so ardently defended by the U.S.:

> Like numerous others hauled before HUAC, Briggs refused the role assigned him in what amounted to little more than a congressional show trial. Rather than play the hapless Negro seduced by a foreign ideology that he could neither fully comprehend nor resist, or cower before HUAC as so many others had, Briggs expressed his outrage at "being interrogated by a committee whose members include out-and-out white supremacists and . . . that during its 20 years has never once investigated the Ku Klux Klan."[15]

Briggs used the public hearing to expose the illusion of American exceptionalism and the reality of U.S. imperialism. Cyril's testimony to HUAC was a damning critique of American exceptionalism and innocence. He essentially revealed that the reason white supremacists were never brought before the committee is that *there's nothing un-American about the KKK.* The U.S. has proved itself exceptional in granting white nationalist terror groups such as the KKK legal immunity while bearing the full weight of American imperial repression down on Black Freedom activists.

Such hypocrisy only became more apparent after the McCarthy period formally ended in the late 1950s. The intense repression of radical political activity continued into the 1960s and 1970s. With the Communist Party severely weakened, the FBI, led by J. Edgar Hoover, waged a brutal war of suppression against the Black Freedom movement and its allies. The war came under the auspices of the FBI's Counterintelligence Program (COINTELPRO) and brought local police departments, federal intelligence agencies, and the executive branch of the U.S. together in a coordinated effort to "expose, disrupt, misdirect, discredit, or otherwise neutralize the activities of black nationalist hate-type organizations and groupings."[16]

It is important here to note that COINTELPRO often described "black nationalist" leaders and groups as criminals, terrorists, and a threat to the security of society. This allowed the various arms of the COINTELPRO apparatus to repress the Black Freedom movement in a similar manner that "McCarthyism" criminalized any association with the Soviet Union or communism as a pretext for the suppression of the Communist Party USA. The FBI wiretapped and collected information from people like subversive cartoonist Jackie Ormes,[17] noteable so-called "pacifist" civil rights leaders like Ella Baker,[18] W.E.B. Du Bois,[19] Martin Luther King Jr., and their affiliated organizations such as the Southern Christian Leadership Conference (SCLC). It is quite telling that in 1999, a Memphis jury concluded that Martin Luther King's assassination was a conspiracy that implicated many American governmental agencies.[20] The FBI's willingness to suppress so-called nonviolent Civil Rights leaders and organizations reveals that "free speech" and "assembly" can only come at the expense of the Black Freedom movement, regardless of the peaceful means the movement employs. Sadly, Black radical activists had to learn the hard way what American liberty *truly* means; namely "that the degree of freedom they enjoy is exactly proportional to the actual threat they represent."[21]

It was the socialist-oriented Black liberation movement in general and the Black Panther Party in particular that faced the harshest repression from COINTELPRO. This prompts some scholars to describe COINTELPRO as the "state's record of terror with impunity against black people, and the accompanying changing performative dynamic of whiteness whereby the self-image of civil society comes to require a repression of its sadistic antiblackness in favor of an ostensible race neutrality."[22] Mainstream and ruling class observers, especially liberal ones, often equate the Black Panther Party with the Ku Klux Klan. Despite lynching thousands of Black Americans on the basis of racial animus since the late 19th century, Klan leaders and members have never faced persecution by the American nation-state in any significant way. The Black Panther Party, on the other hand, was a radical Black organization that formed Black community patrols of the police and free breakfast programs for Black children. Black Panther leaders such as Huey Newton were inspired by Malcolm X and wanted to organize the energy of the Black rebellions that erupted in cities across the country into a movement for full Black emancipation. They were inspired by the anti-colonial and socialist revolutions in Vietnam, China, and Mozambique and actively worked to make the Black Panther Party an anti-imperialist organization. While the Party called for the restructuring of American society toward these ends, never once did it call for violence unless it was required for self-defense.

The FBI saw things differently. It employed the full force of COINTELPRO to destroy the Black Panther Party. In 1969, J. Edgar Hoover described the Black Panther Party as the "greatest threat to the internal security of the country," citing its affiliations with Marxism and so-called violent confrontations with police officers as the primary reason.[23] Yet Hoover's own internal FBI memo reveals that it was really the Black Panther's Free Breakfast Program for Children that so threatened the security of the country.[24] Because the program helped increase the influence of the Panthers in the Black community, it was harder for the government to neutralize them. As a result, the FBI declared war. Dozens of Black Panther Party leaders were assassinated, including John Huggins and Alprentice Bunchy Carter in Los Angeles, Fred Hampton and Mark Clarke in Chicago, and Bobby Hutton in Oakland. Numerous others served lengthy prison sentences. Police and intelligence operations were organized to raid Party offices, including the infamous 6-plus-hour shootout on 41st and Central, Los Angeles, in 1969. The history of U.S. repression against the Black Panther Party is now available to the public, thanks to publications like *Black Against Empire* and Huey P. Newton's doctoral dissertation.[25]

The pervasiveness of American exceptionalism in all aspects of American political, economic, and cultural life has set the stage for the virtual disappearance of this history from public memory. Indeed, many Americans believe that the nation they live in presents the only example around the globe where one can "speak their mind" and pursue their interests without repercussions. Few are aware of the severe repression that radical political organizations—especially Black organizations—faced when they attempted to exercise their right to "free speech" and "assembly" in America. Even when knowledge of such repression exists, it is usually narrated as something unfortunate or tragic that happened *back then*. Yet sixteen Black Panther Party members remain in prison for political purposes, and Assata Shakur, a member of the Black Panther Party and Black Liberation Army, lives in exile in Cuba with a $2 million bounty on her head. The Jericho Movement lists dozens of political prisoners who face long-term sentences due to COINTELPRO, including American Indian Movement leader Leonard Peltier. COINTELPRO may no longer be in operation but its violent legacy lives on in the present day.

That is to say that the narrow debate about "free speech" characteristic of the Trump era has reinforced the erasure of this legacy by conforming to the logic of American exceptionalism and innocence. The terms of the debate are set by the presumption that the U.S. was designed to protect the right to "free speech and assembly" of all. Just exactly *what* and *who* defines these rights is often missing from the conversation. The United States is the most powerful imperialist state in history, ruled over by a capitalist class that has sought to maximize profit, power, and pleasure from the infrastructure of the state and economy. Policing and surveillance are tools of state power wielded in the interests of this class. As Nikhil Pal Singh explains:

> The specific importance of police power revolves around its ongoing links to colonial and settler colonial methods and relationships including extermination and population transfer, but as importantly its conservation within and utility for the machineries of value creation, capital accumulation, and the economies of violence that these machineries require and develop.[26]

State repression of the communist movement and the Black Freedom movement, as well as any movement that aligned with them, was thus of utmost importance toward the conservation and subsequent expansion of the

American imperial system.[27] A distinction must be made, then, between rights granted to the rulers of American society and those granted to the oppressed. The ruling class and its white American supporters never granted Black America any rights it was bound to respect. Singh argues this when he quotes "Founding Father" Benjamin Franklin: "The majority of Negroes are of a plotting disposition, dark, sullen, malicious, revengeful, and cruel in the highest degree," Franklin wrote. And although he is more famously remembered for sympathizing with the abolitionist movement, "Franklin doubted," in his own words, "that 'mild laws could govern such a people.'"[28]

Criminalizing Black existence has justified racial and economic oppression since the country's inception. Black *resistance* has equally been criminalized. The notion that Black Americans can neither rule nor exist without white supremacist state force has guided the development of U.S. imperialism throughout history. In his book, *American Inquisition: The Hunt for Japanese American Disloyalty in World War II*, Eric Muller discusses how policing and surveillance practices seek to enforce a particular kind of patriotism and attachment to the nation-state. "The government's various loyalty screening programs in World War II bequeathed us many lessons," he writes. "Their most important lesson, however, is also their most basic: Loyalty is too ephemeral and ambiguous a criterion to support a national security program, especially in a racially or ethnically charged setting. When government officials on a loyalty inquest screen citizens for hidden biases and motivations, they are likeliest to find their own."[29] This has become all the more salient in the current era of American economic decline and crisis. The technologies of repression once reserved for racially oppressed and insurgent radical movements have been transformed into worldwide instruments of war that affect the entire population. In the words of P. Khalil Saucier and Tryon Woods, "the only law is the law of racial elimination."[30]

Barack Obama's presidency was a byproduct of the desperate need for the American ruling class to both conceal and intensify the policies that produced such a condition. The Obama Administration raided Occupy Wall Street Movement encampments and used the FBI to conduct surveillance on the Black Lives Matter movement. American intelligence agencies, most notably the National Security Agency (NSA), were given free rein to expand their surveillance dragnet to include every call, text message, and digital communication made by as many people worldwide as possible, including leaders of the "free world" such as Angela Merkel. The Obama Administration presided over a full-scale erosion of civil liberties through a record shattering use of the Espionage Act to prosecute whistleblowers of government misconduct.[31] Legal precedent was given to the presidency to indefinitely detain and even murder U.S. citizens anywhere in the world, culminating in the drone strikes that killed two American citizens in Yemen in 2011. Moreover, under Obama, a record number of "illegal" immigrants were deported, despite the administration's patently false pretenses that it was targeting "felons, not families."[32]

Black Americans remained the inheritors of the harshest forms of repression from prison and police departments during the Obama era. Yet, the country saw to it that Obama erect a police state that labeled almost every person and nation a potential "terrorist." The U.S. developed a massive wall of repression as a means of self-preservation amid the deteriorating conditions of not only Black Americans but also working Americans generally. It is from such a vantage point that the questions of "free speech" and "assembly" must be approached. Far from a land of tolerance and "free speech," the U.S. has developed into the most formidable police state in human history. It doesn't matter what politicians, the corporate media, and most law schools teach us about the police and judges working to "serve and protect." As Claudia Rankine cautions us, "the justice system has other plans."[33]

American exceptionalism and American innocence tell us that the U.S. is neither a police-state nor an imperial system, but rather a nation that delivers "democracy" and "free speech" regardless of its flaws. Police state measures such as mass surveillance,[34] incarceration, and the repression of social movements are advertised as necessary for the preservation of "national security." Yet poor Americans, Black Americans, "illegal" immigrants, and global "terrorist threats" are sections of the population, or classes, that Lisa Marie Cacho refers to as those deemed "ineligible for personhood."[35] Such populations, she writes, "are excluded from the ostensibly democratic processes that legitimate U.S. law, yet they are expected to unambiguously accept and unequivocally uphold a legal and political system that depends on the unquestioned permanency of their rightlessness."[36] The rights to "free speech and assembly," then, are not "universal" but rather the exclusive property of the white and the rich, and are only respected so long as one fits the right profile and accepts the system as it is currently constituted. In other words, the simultaneous "ascent of rights and U.S. global power has given rise to a fundamental contradiction: the United States champions the rights of all and simultaneously renders people rightless."[37]

Debate over the questions of just *whose* speech and *whose* assembly are protected by the U.S. should not fall entirely into the hands of right-wing white supremacists or liberal gatekeepers of American exceptionalism. Many white nationalist groupings want a "free speech" movement to ensure the primacy of whiteness in American discourse in a period where white racial superiority is already firmly implanted in state policy. Liberal gatekeepers of American exceptionalism seek to counter this movement by upholding the sanctity of "free speech and assembly." The promoters of the ideology, mainly establishment liberals and conservatives, say nothing about how the system of U.S. imperialism is designed to suppress free speech and assembly rights for radical social movements or how such suppression is rooted in the white supremacist and imperialist character of the American nation-state itself.

So while it is important to condemn "hate speech" and racist rhetoric, perhaps it is more important to begin imagining a world without the police state, a state that the U.S. has fortified.[38] As Kristian Williams shows in his book, *Our Enemies in Blue: Police and Power in America*:

> Laws have been passed, and interpreted, and enforced in ways designed to maximize the control White people exercise over people of color. But they have also been broken, and ignored, and under-enforced with the same aim in mind. When the demands of White supremacy and the requirements of the law have conflicted, the maintenance of White supremacy has almost always appeared higher on the police agenda. Police illegality and complicity in White terror continue in an unbroken sequence from Reconstruction to today.[39]

The American police state has become normalized in a system where repression, ironically, is often framed as necessary to preserve the very rights that the majority of the population—especially Black America—is being asked to sacrifice. The history of U.S. state repression of social movements and its current manifestations in the form of political prisoners, deportations, and reductions in civil liberties show that the U.S. cannot and will not protect the "free speech" of those on the margins of society. We must imagine a new social order that protects the political *and* economic rights of the exploited and oppressed.[40] This will require that more Americans understand the function of the American police state. That function is to protect the property and wealth of elites at the expense of the poor, the oppressed, and the movements that point toward a different, more egalitarian path for humanity.

CHAPTER 10

"Am I an Ungrateful Son of a Bitch?"

". . . so we get King Leopold masking his atrocities in the Congo in the discourse of anti-slavery, or British colonial figures in Ghana effectively saying, 'Well, we saved you from the slave raider so you should be grateful.' In both cases, it's the same notion: 'We've given you your freedom, so now you're in our debt.'"

—Saidiya Hartman[1]

". . . in what sort of account and under what conditions of forgetting does one in the present understand slaveowner and slave to have had the same absence of choice?"

—Christina Sharpe[2]

Eight months had passed since his inauguration yet President Trump was still on the campaign trail making speeches to his voting bloc. At the time, the 45th president of the United States found himself in a myriad of crises. Russia, prominent Democrats and Republicans claimed, interfered in the 2016 elections to secure Trump's victory. When the media wasn't discussing the unverified Trump-Russia connection, it was speculating on his failure to pass meaningful legislation in the areas of immigration and health care. It was this context that Trump decided to address a different set of detractors based in the National Football League (NFL).

No particular aspect of the game itself caught the president's attention. Trump used his rally and his Twitter handle to condemn quarterback Colin Kaepernick and the players that followed his lead for protesting white supremacy and police brutality during the pregame national anthem. At the rally,

Trump asked, "Wouldn't you love to see one of these NFL owners, when somebody disrespects our flag, to say, 'Get that son of a bitch off the field right now. Out! He's fired. He's fired.'" Later, Trump would elaborate on his comments in a Twitter post about how NFL players who make millions of dollars should not be allowed to "disrespect" the "great" American flag and keep their jobs. The president's comments propelled the NFL anthem protests into the realm of "official" politics.

"Official" political discourse in the U.S. did not react kindly. NFL owners and many of Trump's political detractors in Washington used the comments to wage a campaign for "national unity" with the anthem protests at the center. Political opposition denounced Trump for the racist connotations inherent in his comments and how they distracted from more pressing matters. NFL owners and entire teams began linking arms and kneeling during the anthem in protest of the president. In effect, Trump had successfully shifted the focus of the anthem protests away from racist policing. The American ruling class exploited his comments to make the protests center around Trump's failure to respect the sacred values of American exceptionalism.

As is expected whenever a professional athlete decides to speak out against injustice, NFL players were accused of being "ungrateful," presumably to the country that allows them to make millions of dollars to play with a ball. The veterans group The American Legion were quick to play this card, as was former Speaker of the House of Representatives Newt Gingrich, who thought any NFL player who feels oppressed must be crazy.[3] These players "need a therapist," Gingrich said, "not a publicity stunt." One Fox News commentator even stated that it was *Donald Trump* who needed to be thanked for starting this "national conversation" about race. But as comedian Samantha Bee quipped, "Hey, wow, and what a conversation we're having." "Talking about black people and their owners and how they should be grateful for the privilege of working on a field," she added. "Who says Trump is taking us backward?"[4]

Trump's comments had inadvertently placed American exceptionalism on trial and the NFL and its political partners came staunchly to its rescue. "National unity" and the "right" to stand up for what one believes became synonymous with the anthem protests. NFL owners, many of whom had opposed Kaepernick's stand against police brutality and conspired to keep him unsigned because of it, began protesting with players. The American ruling class required that the U.S. be viewed as the arbiter of "national unity" and "democratic values." This is in keeping with the dominant interpretation of American history which presumes that the U.S. is exceptional to all other past and present state formations.

What such a narrative fails to consider, however, is that Trump's comments are rooted in the suppressed history of white supremacy in America. White supremacy is often narrowly promoted in the American mainstream as a symptom of individual hatred toward people who fit non-white racial categories. Acts of racial violence and discrimination are seen as individualized aberrations in a historical context characterized by progress toward the country's founding ideals. American exceptionalism and innocence help to conceal the more subtle (and violent) manifestations of how white supremacy is built into American political economy.

Throughout the controversy that surrounded Trump's "son of a bitch" moment, few observers pointed out that Trump's and his supporters' reference to ungratefulness is a relatively common theme in American history. American exceptionalism and innocence are inherently white supremacist ideologies. The former presumes that American national superiority should be appreciated by racially oppressed people regardless of their circumstances and the latter assumes that past racist crimes have been rectified by the benevolence of institutions dominated by white America. White Americans commonly react to the grievances of Black America with "a love it or leave it attitude" toward the U.S., which few if any acknowledge is rooted in the benevolence narrative often attached to the period of slavery.

White supremacy could not justify the enslavement of an entire people through violence alone. It needed to create a variety of narratives that reinforced the inferiority of the slave and the superiority of the slave master. During the antebellum period in the American South, Frederick Douglass described gratitude as one of the educational methods slave masters employed to push slaves toward subjugation and away from freedom. Brian Warnick describes the use of gratitude during slavery this way:

> The slaveholders, for instance, highlighted the slaves' dependency by linking rewards of position and comfort to faithful service. The will of the master and slave were linked by these offers of positions and rewards within the oppressive system [. . .] The overseer thus becomes the bestower of reward

> and office, the slave the grateful and dependent recipient. The slaves see all good things as contingent on pleasing the master.[5]

Warnick places the rhetoric of gratitude in the context of Frederick Douglass's observations that slave masters would give certain privileges to slaves that showed gratefulness *to* and *for* their masters. Enslaved Blacks were taught that they were inferior to their white masters, meaning any benefits derived from the slave system could only be won from the generosity of their overseer. The assumption was not necessarily grounded in historical reality. From the beginning of the enterprise of African enslavement, the enslaved organized rebellions that changed the course of history many times over. The perceived gratitude of the slave master strips the enslaved of their independent strivings for freedom, making the slave master the sole maker of history.

Historians have contributed to the perception that slavery produced a relationship marked by paternalism between the master and the slave. Eugene Genovese is one such historian. His work argued, from a Marxist perspective, that slavery in the American South was a paternal relationship.[6] Josh Cole, however, explains the limitations of Genovese's work by emphasizing that while he understood slavery as a cruel institution,

> he believed that extreme forms of mistreatment were very minor. Genovese introduced slave-owner "paternalism," not a good, painless, or benign slavery, but a slavery in which masters took personal interest in the lives of their slaves. Genovese believes that paternalism "brought white and black together and welded them into one people with genuine elements of affection and intimacy." It was a compromise between master and slave—the master would provide for the slave as long as the slave produced for him. Genovese fails to distinguish between paternalism as an ideology and as a way of life. This sense of paternalism that Genovese mentions was a self-justifying ideology and, with a few exceptions, not a very visible practice in the slaveholding South. The institution of slavery was meant to fully exploit the slaves, while the ideology allowed whites to exercise their "superior" status with relatively no guilty conscience.[7]

Cole contrasts Genovese's assertions with the realities of slavery. He explains that slave masters "whipped slaves for various and often-insignificant reasons, branded them to reaffirm their domination over them and sometimes had their ears cut off if they disobeyed direct orders." It was also customary, he writes, for slaveholders to find ways "to trim the costs of feeding their slaves and threatened to sell them if they did not produce enough for their masters."[8] Rather than a "fringe benefit" or a material privilege, the benevolence of slave masters was more often than not utilized as a weapon to further exploit and pacify the enslaved.

The social relations that dictated slavery in the American South exist today. These relations have changed in form, not substance. Trump's comments expose how paternalism continues to shape the narrative of white supremacy in the context of American exceptionalism. Trump's reaction to the NFL protests is indicative of the hegemonic view in the U.S. that Black athletes should appreciate the "privileges," real or observed, at the expense of the community as a whole. It is an expectation of both the American power structure and many white Americans that Black Americans worship the nation that enslaved them.

Saidiya Hartman, in reference to slavery, asks "How do we mourn something that is still going on?"[9] The assertion that Black Americans—and Black athletes in particular—should forget about slavery, "get over it," "stop dwelling on the past," and "appreciate" what the U.S. has given them reinforces the master and slave relationship, and at the same time sweeps the afterlives of slavery into the dustbin of history. But as Lisa Lowe writes, many "contemporary critics asks if one can even consider slavery a past condition." Given "the continuing captivity, expropriation, disposability, and fungibility of black communities," she argues, "they ask if slavery can be treated as a historical object that is completed or overcome, from which recovery would be possible."[10] Black resistance disrupts the comfort that paternalism affords. It reminds the American ruling class and those who benefit from white supremacy of the imminent danger posed by Black resistance to the continued existence of the system. This elicits many different responses from the contemporary slave masters of American society, one of which is the demand that the enslaved be grateful for the "freedom" bestowed upon them by the slave-owning power structure.

The NFL protests of the national anthem invoked this response. League rosters have become increasingly occupied by Black players. White America's initial reaction to Kaepernick's anthem protest largely mirrored that of the corporate media and later Donald Trump. Kaepernick was described as selfish, unpatriotic, and unappreciative of the glamour that his career provides. When other NFL players joined in, they too were painted in a manner similar to Kaepernick. Not even coach Mike Tomlin's refusal to choose a side in the debate could satisfy White America. After Tomlin's Steelers decided not to take the field during the anthem in an act of team "unity," a local fire chief 20 miles outside of Pittsburgh named Paul Smith announced via Facebook that Tomlin had "added himself to [his] list of no-good niggers."[11] It's curious that two other coaches who made their teams stay in the locker room for the national anthem—Pete Carroll of the Seattle Seahawks and Mike Mularkey of the Tennessee Titans—did not make the list. Or if they did, writes journalist Shaun King, "Smith simply forgot to write a Facebook status about it." "We're not quite clear on how exhaustive a list Smith has built over the years," King added, but we do know that Mike Tomlin made the cut. And let us not forget "that Smith didn't put Tomlin on his 'list of no-good niggers'—instead, Tomlin put himself on that list."[12]

In her cringe-worthy article, "I Used to Lead Tours at a Plantation. You Won't Believe the Questions I Got About Slavery," Margaret Biser reveals how common it is to find people like fire chief Paul Smith all across America.[13] When her job required that she chronicle the brutality of slavery to the site's visitors, many white people responded with the narrative of "appreciation" as a defensive posture. During a tour, for example, a visitor asked Biser whether "the slaves here *appreciate* the care they got from their mistress?" Many of the questions she would receive in her day-to-day work revolved around whether slave masters were *benevolent* or *kind* to their slaves. One visitor in particular demanded that she answer this question affirmatively. The visitor asked, "Were they loyal?" He elaborated on his question by claiming that slave masters "gave 'em food. Gave 'em a place to live." Such logic insinuates that Black Americans had much to appreciate for their enslavement prior to formal emancipation. Furthermore, it reinforces the division of oppressed people into "deserving" and "undeserving" categories with the measure being one's appreciation of their oppression. Much was at stake for these white visitors in getting the history right, or forgetting it altogether. As one guest reminded Biser, "Listen, I just wanted to say that dragging all this slavery stuff up again is bringing down America." When Biser began to protest, he interrupted her. "You didn't know," he said. "You're young. But America is the greatest country in the world, and these people out there, they'd do anything to make America less great."[14]

The list of "no-good niggers" and the narrative of appreciation both stem from the social conditions that make American exceptionalism and American innocence such dominant ideologies. American exceptionalism reads from the lens of the American ruling class, which has a vested interest in telling the developmental story of the U.S. in the most positive light. This class owns the major media outlets, influences school curriculum through its control of the state, and enforces conditions of poverty and repression. The ruling class not only profits from these conditions but also establishes powerful material and ideological disincentives to those who may deviate from its false narratives. American exceptionalism thus becomes common sense in an environment where no other narrative is allowed to thrive.

It is important, then, to place into proper context the phenomena such as the list of "no-good niggers" and the expectation that the oppressed "appreciate" the nation that oppresses them. In light of the fire chief's "list" of who is "good" and who is "no good," along with the questions Margaret Biser received during her time as a tour guide, one can't help but think of Thavolia Glymph's groundbreaking work on black women's domestic labor in the plantation household.[15] Ideologies of making "good," "better," and "decent" girls played a fundamental role in slavery and its many afterlives. "The tight market for household help did not dissuade former mistresses from their mission to find the kind of black servant they imagined they had once owned," Glymph observes of the racial and gendered economics of domestic labor in the postbellum period. "They wanted a 'good one,' a black woman who would stand in awe of them, and wash, cook, and clean for them with a smile and a grateful attitude, a black woman who would understand that black women were best constituted for the kind of work they were expected to do."[16]

American exceptionalism demands that Black Americans remain silent about injustice and appreciate what the American nation-state has "given" them. Consider how most Americans are taught about the history of social change. For example, it was Lincoln who freed the slaves to move us toward a more perfect union.[17] It was Brad Pitt's character who "freed" Solomon Northup in the film *12 Years a Slave*. Civil Rights legislation, the argument goes, was granted to Black Americans because the U.S. government repudiated the excesses of racial segregation. In short, Americans are consistently taught that social justice comes as a result of a benevolent CEO, president, senator, supreme court justice, or white abolitionist. But as Calvin Warren points out about the irony of "giving" freedom to a population already damned to social death: "What philosophy of becoming sustains this romantic narrative? What type of life, given by the master, can transform the dead thing?"[18]

Overlooked are the movements, organizations, and rebellions that Black America has led over the course of American history that forced change from below. This applies to workers movements and other social insurgencies that sought to dismantle U.S. racial domination and imperialism. For the oppressed and exploited, gratitude is a vow of silence. It means acceptance of the conditions that lead to abject poverty in the face of plenty, racist police murders amid a system incapable of stopping them, and endless war in the face of a system that disdains peace. Connie Wun, in her research on the policing of black girls in American schools, examines one of the most violent ways that the state expects gratitude from its most vulnerable groups. "The girl of color can be perceived as too angry, defiant, despondent, and critical," Wun writes. "She is also imagined as a subject that illegitimately takes from society, its institutions, and good people. At the same time as she extracts resources from society, she is ungrateful for its generosity."[19]

The reality is that the American nation-state's "no good niggers list" is a rather long one. It includes the over 2.3 million people in prison, the millions of people that have perished from its endless wars, poor women of color who are left uninsured or underinsured by the corporate health sector, and the wide number of political prisoners in danger of dying behind bars. Colin Kaepernick has been told many times to appreciate what the NFL—and the U.S. by extension—has given him, namely, a large income compared to most. Yet Kaepernick has been exiled from the NFL for his actions with a high likelihood that he will never be able to play another game. As Dave Zirin notes, NFL executives "hate the idea of a freethinking, openly anti-racist player more than they love the idea of winning a Super Bowl." The NFL's decision to tank its season rather than give Kaepernick a job leads Zirin to conclude that "the league's moral compass points in one direction: It's not toward money and it's not toward winning." Instead, he writes, "It's toward remaking this country in their political image: An image where billionaires make the decisions and the rest of us just shut up, work, and salute on demand."[20]

The message is clear: no job is safe, and no status is too comfortable if one fails to appreciate the United States' exceptional character. American exceptionalism has only been truly exceptional for a minority. The ideology relies on the fear imposed by the system and the comfort gained from adhering to it. However, if we are to truly dismantle American exceptionalism and develop a social movement strong enough to force transformative change, it will require more "no-good niggers" and ungrateful "sons of bitches" to emerge in the weeks, months, and years to come.

CHAPTER 11

"A Rising Tide or a Sinking Ship? American Economic Decline and the rise of the Unexceptional Majority"

"You cannot have untold, obscene wealth unless you have untold, obscene poverty. That is the law of capitalism."

—Keeanga-Yamahtta Taylor

"Today, we witness renewed projects of 'democratization' carried out through a civilizing globalizing war against terrorism as well as projects of political emancipation through the broadening of the 'rule of law' of liberal democracies, which naturalize the violence of dominant everyday protocols of being human embedded in increasingly neoliberal, capitalist ways of life."

—Neferti X. M. Tadiar[1]

"The claim of innocence . . . is a double-edged sword: it contains not-knowing, but also not wanting to know."

—Gloria Wekker[2]

For the last several decades, American economists and politicians have declared that a "rising tide lifts all boats." The slogan assumes that if the American capitalist economy is prosperous, then so, too, is the American worker. It has been most commonly used alongside other popular neoliberal dogmas such as "trickle down economics." This is no coincidence. The "rising tide" ideology cannot be separated from the deteriorating conditions of the working class and poor in America. Both are a byproduct of American capitalism's economic decline. Economic decline has left American capitalism vulnerable by exposing the growing fissure between American exceptionalism and the economic reality of the masses.

Most Americans find the economic reality of the United States difficult to confront. The ruling classes of the American nation-state, which also happen to be the captains of enterprise, have spread a narrative of American economic supremacy. American exceptionalism rears its head in nearly every mainstream discussion of the American capitalist economy. We are told American capitalism is a "global force for good" rather than a system driven by profit maximization. Rather than serving as capitalism's economic engines, conditions such as slavery, poverty, and war are considered "unintended consequences" of what it takes to develop a prosperous society. Yet despite the pride Americans hold for their capitalist economy, "capitalism" remains a taboo word, often spoken of instead as "the economy." This amorphous "economy" is the largest, most prosperous on the planet. Why should anyone want to change it?

Because many Americans are kept in the dark about how the American capitalist economy actually *works*, it is commonplace to hear platitudes such as "America is the best place to become successful" or "there is nowhere else I'd rather live." A central tenet of American capitalism is the veracious worship of private enterprise and individualism. Individualism renders the collective punishment distributed by capitalist economics invisible. It also ignores how such punishment is itself built into the infrastructure of capitalism. Americans are too busy figuring out how to "get ahead" in a society that stifles social solidarity. Indeed, every worker and family is pit against each other for the promise of individual enrichment so much so that the language of capitalism has become normalized in day to day life in America. As Scott Sandage describes in his book, *Born Losers: A History of Failure in America*:

> Ours is an ideology of achieved identity; obligatory striving is its method, and failure and success are its outcomes. We reckon our incomes once a year but audit ourselves daily, by standards of long-forgotten origin. Who thinks of the old counting house when we "take stock" of how we "spend" our lives, take "credit" for our gains, or try not to end up "third rate" or "good for nothing"? Someday, we hope, "the bottom line" will show that we

> "amount to something." By this kind of talk we "balance" our whole lives, not just our accounts.[3]

For many Americans it is difficult to see the violence of American capitalism because it is cloaked in the ideologies of American exceptionalism and individualism. American capitalism is a system based on the exploitation of labor to advance the accumulation of profit. Competition among capitalist enterprises for the prize of surplus value, or unpaid labor, is the lifeline of capitalism. Only by usurping a greater share of the "market" (monopoly), intensifying the exploitation of labor, and investing in technologies that accomplish both can capitalist enterprises achieve their main objective of profit maximization.

A combination of ideological and material factors have facilitated the hegemony of American capitalism worldwide. The U.S. became home to the most dominant capitalist system in the world, first through the mass enslavement of African people in the 17th and 18th centuries. While other colonial powers abolished the slave trade by the beginning of the 19th century, American capitalists gained a significant competitive advantage from the super profits of slavery well into the late 19th century. Enslaved Black labor and captured Indigenous land insulated the impact of the boom and bust cycles inherent to capitalism and gave the U.S. relief in periods when the capitalist economies of Europe began to falter. White supremacy also proved to be a useful buffer against labor solidarity as investments in whiteness made it difficult for impoverished white workers to find common ground with enslaved Africans or free Black Americans in the decades that followed formal emancipation. Social scientist Toby Miller muses on the unique character of American capitalist domination and why it has been more difficult for its colonized subjects to overturn the system:

> It's much harder to gain independence from the United States than it ever was from European colonists, because US imperialism is often indirect and mediated. It produces few dramatic moments of resistive nation building, unlike the painful but well-defined struggles towards sovereignty that threw off conventional colonial yokes across the twentieth century. This is because Yanqui imperialism began at a well-developed stage of industrial capitalism and developed—in fact led into—the post-industrial age, seeking to break down colonialism in order to gain access to labor and consumption on a

> global scale. Its mature form coincided with the Cold War, which favored imperial proxies over possessions, owing to both prevailing ideology and the desire to avoid direct nuclear conflict with an equal.[4]

However, when it comes to the American capitalist system, American exceptionalism is designed to disconnect many of the topics already covered in prior essays. The ideology neither openly celebrates the centrality of slavery to the development of American capitalism nor the settler colonial warfare against Indigenous peoples which formed the economic base for rapid industrialization and monopoly. American exceptionalism would never dare cast a light on the United States' true intentions during the Second World War, nor its criminal behavior in Korea and dozens of countries thereafter. To do so would expose the historical thread that binds these developments together and lay bare the pernicious economic and political motivations behind them.

Narratives of American exceptionalism have therefore diverted popular attention toward the so-called "Golden Age" of American capitalism. The "Golden Age" occurred after the end of the Second World War, which also happened to be the same period that the world's most cataclysmic economic crisis came to a close. During the "Great Depression," (1929–1941) American capitalism experienced its longest bout of stagnation and crisis. Unemployment was rampant, wages dropped significantly, and popular confidence in capitalism around the world waned significantly. A great war had emerged between capitalism and socialism around the world. Conventional American wisdom holds that the U.S. recovered from the "Great Depression" by its own merit. Superior military strategy and progressive New Deal policy birthed the exceptionally prosperous American capitalist economy. After all, many more workers entered the so-called "middle class" of relative economic comfort after World War II, and the American capitalist economy became a superpower that now possessed nearly half of the world's resources and the largest Gross Domestic Product (GDP) relative to other countries.

The overall picture of the "Golden Age" was more complicated than what American exceptionalists have us believe. Jim Crow white supremacy largely excluded Black Americans from New Deal reforms such as the G.I. bill. Residential segregation and outright discrimination ensured that the emerging "middle class" would be mostly white.[5] Then there was the fact that American capitalism did not grant concessions based on "goodwill" or because it possessed an inherently prosperous model of development. The U.S. was in fierce competition with the Soviet Union's rapid economic growth and sought to "save capitalism" by gaining control of Europe's colonial possessions to gain advantage. Franklin Roosevelt's Administration made its objectives clear in this regard. In his book, *A People's History of the United States*, Howard Zinn quotes two government officials. The first, a spokesperson for the U.S. State Department said "a review of the diplomatic history of the past 35 years will show that petroleum has historically played a larger part in the external relations of the United States than any other commodity."[6] In 1944, a second official from the State Department was quoted as saying: "As you know, we've got to plan on enormously increased production in this country after the war, and the American domestic market can't absorb all that production indefinitely. There won't be any question about our needing greatly increased foreign markets."[7]

The "Golden Age" was thus marked by the expansion of American capitalism around the world, laying the basis for American wars across Latin America, Africa, and Asia. These wars allowed the system to spread the spoils of plunder to an increased number of workers. Yet workers themselves often had to force American monopolies to spread their share of the wealth. According to Zinn, fourteen thousand labor strikes occurred during the Second World War in the automotive, steel, and transport industries while a record three million workers went on strike in 1946, just one year after the war ended.[8] Strikes and labor actions were necessary to ensure that corporations abided by collective bargaining agreements codified into law by the National Labor Relations Act (1935). They also demanded that corporations raise wages, provide health care, and ensure decent working conditions during negotiations for union contracts.

The broader "social contract" struck between the American working class and American capital is the economic bedrock of American exceptionalism. In the three decades after the Second World War, labor unions became increasingly conservative in their dealings with employers. A "middle class" sentimentality guided by the "American Dream" became dominant in a domestic environment where anticommunism and war polluted the political air of the "Golden Age." Labor leaders outside of the Communist Party often failed to oppose wars such as the invasion of Korea and often opposed any sort of unity with Black workers affected by racist state terror. During the 1960s, the divide between labor union leadership and social movement politics only grew. Few unions supported the anti-war efforts to end the American invasion of Vietnam or were willing to endorse Black Power and Black liberation. So while American capitalism celebrates the "Golden Age" for the super profits it brought to American enterprise, the conditions of the period left American workers politically unprepared for the assault that was to come.

The reversal of American capitalism's "social contract" is often called the age of "neoliberalism." Neoliberalism is defined as the reemergence of "free-market" ideology and the privileging of private enterprise over state regulation in all spheres of economic life. Many view President Ronald Reagan's decision to break the Professional Air Traffic Controllers Organization (PATCO) strike in 1981 as the genesis of neoliberalism, though Black feminists and other radical thinkers trace its origins back even earlier.[9] "Although it produces the neutral discourses of equality, diversity, freedom, and opportunity," writes Stephen Dillon, "neoliberalism necessitates force, punishment, warfare, immobilization through incarceration, and the uneven distribution of social and biological death." And despite what narratives of American innocence might suggest, state violence has never been "the exception to neoliberalism, but rather, is its condition of possibility. Simply, the neoliberal state requires the management, regulation, and immobilization of surplus or expendable populations."[10] By the Reagan years, the shift toward an all-out assault on organized labor and the social welfare system by American capitalism led to a steep decline in living conditions for all workers. The "Golden Age" had officially ended.

The reasons for the abrupt end to American capitalism's " Golden Age" are particularly important since they lead directly to the unexceptional condition that characterizes economic life for the majority of Americans today. Beginning in the 1970s, Germany and Japan had begun to recover from post-war wreckage to compete on the capitalist stage with the United States. The tendency of capitalist enterprises to monopolize began to take a toll on the purchasing power of workers and poor people all around the world. It did not help that a strong socialist bloc existed to limit the complete division of the world by the imperialist powers. American capitalism saw its share of the world economy begin to steadily decrease alongside a decline in the rate of American capitalist profit. Steady decline led to a new wave of American investment in automation, privatization, and credit that helped maintain American capitalist hegemony. This only intensified after the disintegration of the socialist bloc and the advancement of "globalization," but at great cost. A weakened socialist movement abroad left millions of workers in America even more vulnerable to capital's incessant drive to weaken organized labor and the welfare state.

Americans have become much poorer and economic crises have lasted a lot longer as a result of the hegemony of American capitalism. These developments are not unrelated. The poorer that workers become, the more difficult it is for investments in technology and production to yield profit from labor's surplus. That is, most Americans and indeed much of the world are unable to purchase what is being sold in the global market. This inevitable outcome of capitalist production produces periodic economic crises. What was once periodic, however, has become a permanent condition carrying dire consequences for the majority of Americans. The numbers do not lie. More than half of Americans make under $30,000 per year.[11] A similar percentage can't pay for a five-hundred dollar emergency should it arise.[12] Wages in the American nation have been stagnant for nearly four decades.[13] Wealth disparities have widened significantly over the same period to the point where the bottom 90 percent of income earners in America hold just 23 percent of the nation's wealth.[14]

Such immense poverty has left American workers out to dry, sometimes literally. Philip Alston, the UN's special rapporteur on extreme poverty and human rights, spent two weeks touring the United States to get a sense of the economic conditions that make up the "greatest nation on earth." The results were damning.[15] Around 18.5 million Americans live in "deep poverty," or one-half of the federal poverty line, which itself has historically been seen as an underestimation of poverty.[16] Over 3,000 counties have water systems with lead counts higher than Flint, Michigan, the majority-Black city where dangerous levels of lead in the water system led to international attention and scrutiny in 2014. Many impoverished communities that Alston visited possessed yards filled with sewage because residents could not afford septic systems. Nearly 45,000 Americans die each year from a lack of health care. The number of homeless Americans is estimated to be over 500,000 in 2017, which, as Philip Alston reported, is a number "widely considered to be an undercount, as illustrated by estimates of 21,000 in San Francisco [alone] provided by various experts with whom I met."[17]

To buttress the empty pockets of American workers, debt has become an extremely important mechanism for economic survival. Students in the U.S.

are mired in a $1.3 trillion student loan debt bubble that will never be paid. One in five Americans cannot afford their medical bills, with hundreds of thousands declaring bankruptcy as a result. The biggest debts that Wall Street banks lend, however, are mortgage debts. These debts caused the American capitalist economy to crash in 2008 when the inability of Americans to pay off their fraudulent loans caused a tidal wave of layoffs and foreclosures across the country. As journalist Jon Jeter notes, the 43.8 trillion additional dollars that households, businesses, and governments have taken out in credit since 2008 is proof that the American capitalist economy has yet to recover from the crash.[18] If that doesn't convince readers, then a 2018 ACLU report about thousands of Americans currently serving time in "debtors prisons" should.[19]

American exceptionalism and innocence have played critical roles in erasing the unexceptional economic situation that the 2007–2008 crash created. During both terms of the Obama Administration, a narrative of "recovery" was promoted non-stop by the U.S. corporate media. The narrative reinforced the myth that the crash was less about the structural character of the economic system and more about poor individual choices. This was especially true in the mainstream narrative that framed the crisis as a "subprime" lending crisis. As Paula Chakravartty and Denise Ferreira da Silva argue:

> References to law and morality, expectedly, prevail in condemnations of those served with "subprime" loans, who are construed as intellectually (illiterate) and morally (greedy) unfit if measured against any existing descriptors of the modern economic subject: the (liberal) rational self-interested, the (historical-materialist) productive-creative laborer, and the (neoliberal) obligation-bound debtor/creditor. The "immanent risk of foreclosure" and ultimately loss of home for millions in the United States overwhelmingly affected Black and Latino/a borrowers and communities. Lacking property and stocks passed down through generations and burdened by greater reliance on consumer credit, Black and Latino/a borrowers were less able to weather the sudden decline in home values. Foregrounding their predicament, the incomprehensible task of affording the consequences of not-paying what the lenders knew were unpayable debts allows questions that challenge the assumption that the failure to meet an obligation should necessarily lead to punishment when the lender's profits are secured by betting and spreading the risk globally, against the "high-risk" borrower.[20]

Laying the problems of American capitalism on the poor is a staple of neoliberalism that protects American exceptionalist mythology. Blaming the increasingly impoverished working class shielded the Obama Administration from accountability for bailing out the banks responsible for the crisis with trillions of dollars worth of "stimulus" funds. Problems such as homelessness that were exacerbated because of the economic crash have received little attention, especially since many Americans are told that it was the fault of fleeced American workers trying to maintain "Golden Age" living standards. No matter that nearly 18 million vacant homes are scattered across the country waiting to be occupied by the nation's homeless, or that the Reagan Administration's reduction of the Housing and Urban Development (HUD) budget by 77 percent marked the genesis of modern homelessness.[21] American exceptionalism tells us that it is the "high-risk borrower," the individual who failed to "make it," who is responsible for whatever economic ailments plague the United States. Rarely is blame placed on the inherently exploitative and oppressive conditions that form the very structure of "America" itself.

Neoliberal ideology has not only placed blame for poverty on individuals but has also sought to medicalize and essentialize conditions that cannot be explained by individual failure alone. Craig Willse uses the example of "chronic homelessness" and how the term has shaped housing policy in the U.S. for the last several decades. The term "chronic" served to medicalize homelessness by centering policy on problematic individuals such as the addicted or mentally ill, rather than the structural causes of housing disparities. Federal funds and organizational programming have since focused on getting these populations out of sight and out of mind, mainly through programs that enforce discipline and promote "efficient" use of resources. As Willse explains,

> . . . chronic homelessness programmes are part of neo-liberal economies, and thus they enable rather than challenge the very conditions and systems that produce housing insecurity and deprivation. As proponents of the programmes note, 10-year plans come into being through the support of police and local business organizations, both of which eagerly endorse the effort to remove unsheltered individuals from public view. In this way, 10-year plans function as the second phase of the neo-liberal reorganization of the city begun in the 1950s with the destruction of Skid Rows. These 10-year plans attempt to clean up the mess made by the evaporation of SROs and other

> forms of low-cost housing by removing the individuals left behind. They do nothing to alter the structural conditions that reproduce and distribute housing insecurity and deprivation. In this sense, the plans preserve an earlier medicalized conception of housing insecurity, as if removing 'problem individuals' from 'the streets' is an adequate solution. The fact remains that 'the streets'—here we can substitute labour markets, privatized housing, police/prison systems and inadequate public assistance programmes—will continue to produce unsheltered populations.[22]

Homelessness is but one symptom of the decline of American capitalism. The decline shows no signs of letting up. It is the working class and poor in America who are paying the price. American exceptionalism has laid the foundations of anti-worker, anti-poor, and anti-Black neoliberal policies attempting to restore the capitalist system to stability. The ideology is what made Hillary Clinton call poor Black youth in America "super predators" that needed to be "brought to heel" through racist policing and incarceration. A politics of disposability has emerged where trillions can be spent abroad eliminating people of other nations while it is the homeless, the Black, and the poor who are most feared and criminalized in America. Meanwhile, American politicians and media analysts speak of the U.S. economy as completely capable of reviving the post-war "Golden Age" of nearly seventy years ago.

The hold that American exceptionalism has over the American people, however, appears to be waning. The political party that takes the most credit for the "Golden Age" of American capitalism, the Democratic Party, also happens to be the chief organ of subversion of progressive and radical politics. That is, the Democratic Party has often credited itself as the party of American exceptionalism because of its supposed ability to preach multiracial political pluralism and neoliberal economic dogma. But the Democratic Party's popularity waned in the 2016 elections. Wall Street's favored candidate, Democrat Hillary Clinton, campaigned on the platform that America was "already great" and in the midst of an economic recovery. The Clinton campaign was forced to use its influence to sabotage the campaign of the more popular and economically critical Bernie Sanders to secure the nomination, only to lose to a billionaire business mogul whose slogan was "Make America Great Again" in a general election where a larger percentage of voting-age Americans preferred not to vote than to choose between the nominees.

Bernie Sanders remains the most popular politician in America because of his economic program for single-payer health care, living-wage employment, and student loan forgiveness. However, he too beckons the call of American exceptionalism by supporting American imperialist war policies. Sanders voted for the largest military budget in recorded history in 2017. Sanders shows that the proliferation of the unexceptional majority is a problem inherent to the American capitalist system. No politician can reform it. This system is an imperialist system dominated by the war dictates of monopoly corporations and financiers. These entities want to make "America Great Again" and accumulate more profit at the expense of the poor everywhere, including America. They adhere to the three "P's" of war: policing, prison, and profit. To make America "great," we must figure out how to put an end to the disastrous capitalist system that has made much of America, and indeed the world, unbearable to live in. There will be no rising tide or lifting of boats under American capitalism. Its anchor of exploitation has sunk the working class in a sea of misery, making it more than time to begin thinking about building a new boat all together.

CHAPTER 12

"'We can't have the inmates running the prison': Black Labor, White Enjoyment, and the Billionaire Capitalist Class"

"What concerns me here is the diffusion of terror and the violence perpetrated under the rubric of pleasure, paternalism, and property."

—Saidiya Hartman[1]

"The only difference between here and the streets is that one is maximum security and the other is minimum security. The police patrol our streets just like guards patrol here. I don't have the faintest idea how it feels to be free."

—Assata Shakur[2]

"That's what America means: prison."

—Malcolm X[3]

It would be hard to refute that billionaires control American society or that the majority of American workers struggle to make ends meet. It is also public record that the United States possesses the largest prison population in the world, by a lot. Not often, however, do billionaires themselves expose all three of these "taboo" developments in one metaphorical statement. In October 2017, Houston Texans owner and billionaire Bob McNair said in reference to NFL players protesting racism and police brutality that "we can't have the inmates running the prison." McNair was forced to apologize for what he later called a "figure of speech." However, his Freudian slip exposed the ways in which Black labor, pleasure, and profit are vital to the transmission of American exceptionalism through the venue of American sports monopolies.

One central pillar of American exceptionalism is the presence of billionaires who provide living proof of the American Dream. Worship of the rich is what rapper and partial Brooklyn Nets owner Jay-Z encouraged when he responded to criticisms from Black Freedom activist and singer Harry Belafonte by saying that his very "presence was charity." In other words, the potential to become a billionaire should, by itself, motivate the American populace and uplift the poor. Billionaire worship is especially evident in American sports. After all, American sports are institutions of American culture. American culture emerged from the political economy of a nation-state founded on imperial theft, slavery, and genocide. And if cultural institutions find their basis in the genealogy of the political and economic system from which they emerge, then the pleasure and profit derived from American sports must necessarily reflect the genealogy of the racist, imperialist American nation-state.[4]

Black labor has always been central to white American pleasure and profit. The Black worker built the infrastructure of American enterprise as an enslaved class. Its position in American society was justified by the white supremacist logic that Black people were not workers or humans at all. An often overlooked and earliest form of domination did not occur at the plantation, the prison, or the auction block, but in the home. In her book, *Out of the House of Bondage: The Transformation of the Plantation Household*, Thavolia Glymph examines how enslaved black women were seen as "uncooperative" with their white mistresses demands.[5] "Their manners had to be perfect, and their households had to demonstrate attention to order, punctuality, and economy," Glymph writes. "Failure threatened their status as ladies and the institution of slavery [. . .] Success, in turn, depended on the cooperation of black women who notoriously refused to play their part."[6] It was common for mistresses to interpret Black women's refusal to cooperate "as a refusal to be 'better girls,' in terms that suggested innate backwardness" and "made them unalterably inefficient, slothful, and dirty."[7] Glymph's work on the violence of domesticity and "black women's noncooperation" is essential for contextualizing the demand that Black athletes today should know their "place," keep their political beliefs private, or simply "shut up and dribble." What allows such demands to take center stage is the assumption that Blacks were inferior to whites and thus predestined for super exploitation by way of enslavement. Slavery created the economic conditions necessary to enrich a small portion of propertied elites. These elites, America's ruling class, then developed an ideology of "exceptionalism" which justified enslavement, teaching black workers to stay in their place for the good of the "nation."

What makes something exceptional in America is defined by its proximity to white supremacy and economic power. Modern sports are a cultural filter for American exceptionalism. The afterlives of slavery continue to haunt the legitimacy of American exceptionalism in an age where mass incarceration, poverty, health disparity, and militarized policing place Black life in danger every single day. "Even as slavery's afterlife is crushing, visible, and pervasive, it also looks like dust floating in the air," writes Stephen Dillon. The study of Americans' fascination with—and investment in—sport can help illuminate what Dillon calls "slavery's mark on the now."[8] Not only does this "mark" manifest "as the prison, as poverty, as policing technologies," he writes, but the mark also "emerges in insurance ledgers and in the organization of urban space. It also appears in the space cleared by so much death. Slavery's afterlife surfaces in the gaps between the recorded, the forgotten, and the never will be."[9] Sporting leagues have received large corporate investments not so much to mitigate the afterlives of slavery, but to provide an avenue of pleasure. Pleasure serves as a form of repression of Black resistance that fully maximizes white enjoyment and (white) profit at the same time. Colin Kaepernick and the other NFL players who used their platform to protest white supremacy disrupted the primary function of modern corporate sports.[10] This is what prompted Bob McNair to liken them to modern day slaves (prisoners) who were threatening to run the plantation (prison).

Sports, especially the NFL and the NBA, have taken on a significant role in the regulation of Black life, especially that of Black males, in the age of mass incarceration and neoliberalism. For many poor Black men, sports are an avenue for upward mobility. Sports provide an opportunity to make a generous income from endorsements and team salaries. American disinvestment in public education, welfare, and employment and its overinvestment in policing, prison, and military weaponry has shortened the pathways to the mythical "American Dream." Corporate sports have thus been given ample opportunity to pose as an economic pathway for Black life in a period where few exist. But as Ruth Wilson Gilmore reminds us, "prison is not a building 'over there' but a set of relationships that undermine rather than stabilize everyday lives everywhere."[11]

The NFL, for example, could be considered a multibillion dollar prison industry dominated by Black players (inmates). Yet the economic conditions for prospective Black NFL players are more precarious than what is advertised in the American corporate media. Black labor in the NFL is exclusively found on the field. Numerous authors have shown that the NFL has been falsely advertised as Black America's ticket to the "American Dream" when the reality is "best understood by the example of the plantation and its exploitation of black bodies for white profit."[12] One need only consider the nauseating optics of the NFL draft, where white owners are seen bidding on black bodies. Journalist Matt Taibbi famously described the NFL draft as possessing a "creepy slave-auction vibe and armies of drooling, flesh-peddling scouts . . . looking for raw gladiatorial muscle whose sweat-drenched faces will be hidden under helmets as coaches drive them to be rapidly ground into hamburger." The NFL, Taibbi continues, is made up of "bloodless corporate enterprises using advanced scientific and economic metrics to measure the material worth of human flesh down to the half-pound, the 16th of an inch."[13]

White enjoyment and billionaire profit masquerade as Black opportunity, even though sports leagues like the NFL resemble more so the relations of slavery. Black males provide the labor while white audiences and billionaire capitalists with the means to invest big dollars in sports shape the cultural terrain. Nearly two-thirds of players in the NFL are Black yet Black Americans only hold 28 percent of the assistant coaching positions. The situation fares no better for Black Americans the farther up the NFL ladder one goes. White Americans currently occupy 30 of the 32 head coaching positions in the NFL. Meanwhile, every majority owner of an NFL franchise is white.[14] Black males therefore not only produce *profit* from their labor exclusively for white Americans but *pleasure* as well. The Bob McNair's of the world simultaneously enrich themselves while disseminating images of Black males that ascribe to the designs of white supremacy. These images make the games especially enjoyable for white consumption. And, as Steven Thrasher explains in his article, "Super Slaves," all aspects of the NFL enterprise are geared toward this purpose:

> The NFL draft allows audiences to see physically strong black men bought, sold, and traded much as in a slave auction. The NCAA collegiate sports

> league allows students and fans to watch big, strong black men wrestling on mats and battling on fields, while claiming to educate them. Both allow spectators to watch one of their biggest fears—large black men—in a controlled setting. Both the NCAA and the NFL condition sports fans to see large black men as physically intimidating but also as controllable under the right conditions. These actions are examples of the theory of mandingoism, which can be applied to black athletes but also to [Michael] Brown. American consciousness of mandingoism, such as it is, is rooted in the misguided belief that slaves once fought to the death, which never happened. But that specific fantasy . . . fuels the aspect of mandingoism that looks the most like watching black football players tackle each other or wrestlers pin each other.[15]

When Thrasher describes how images of Black males in sports have been tailored toward white supremacist desire, he juxtaposes American sports culture with the police sanctioned murder of Michael Brown. Officer Darren Wilson was quoted as saying that Michael Brown looked like a "demon," prompting him to shoot him in cold blood. Thrasher says that this language isn't uncommon among "white parties in power . . . with charge over black bodies," including many team owners, sports recruiters, and the corporate media at large.[16] Whether "off the field or out of the ring," Thrasher writes, "when a black male with a similarly 'menacing' large body is seen outside the confines that white team owners and spectators alike have been conditioned to expect, white men freak out."[17]

Far from arguing that professional and collegiate sports merely *reflect* ideological culture struggles, Thrasher argues that narratives of intimidation and control found in the NFL and other sports leagues play a critical role in *shaping* white American perceptions of Black males, helping justify and even cement institutional white supremacy. According to Thrasher, "the link between black bodies as slaves and black bodies as carceral subjects—the link between how black bodies have been commodified in America's most nascent and most recent days—has been bridged through sports." Some of the largest sports enterprises like the the NCAA and NFL, he continues, "have monetized black bodies as 'beasts of burden' that are property, not human, kept in line for profit through the social control of sports."[18]

Colin Kaepernick and allied players disrupted the disconnect between the perception of the Black condition on the field and reality off the field. By taking a stand against the racist police murders of Michael Brown, Trayvon Martin, and the many underreported acts of state violence against women of color, Kaepernick and WNBA players like Maya Moore exposed how American exceptionalism positions the sanctity of the American nation-state and power structure against Black existence. As Andrea Ritchie argues, the "racially gendered and sexualized myths conjured to justify the brutal social control used to maintain racially gendered hierarchies" in the past "persist to this day, having transformed, solidified, and mutated over time to fit shifting realities."[19] For this reason, NFL owners like Bob McNair "freak out" over the undisciplined Black body. "This is the body that has been constructed in stark opposition to cherished white property," writes Kelly Brown Douglas. "It is the most threatening to America's narrative of exceptionalism and, thus, to the success of its Manifest Destiny mission."[20] As of this writing, Kaepernick remains unemployed. That Kaepernick missed the entire 2017 and 2018 regular seasons should not be seen as a coincidence, but rather the surest example of the lengths the American ruling class will go when Black athletes challenge their control over Black labor.

Some casual observers might object and say, "But didn't Redskins owner Dan Snyder and Cowboys owner Jerry Jones lock arms with their teams during the protests?" Still others might say, "How dare you call my favorite players slaves! I love them!" But if history is any indication, it would be a mistake to view an owner's "pat on the back" or a fan's "high five" as anything even closely resembling love or care for the oppressed. In fact, such actions instead only mask another form of racial violence, what Robin Bernstein calls "racial innocence." In her book, *Racial Innocence: Performing American Childhood from Slavery to Civil Rights*, Bernstein joins a host of cultural historians who have shown that "physical tenderness can function as a necessary component of racial domination and violence."[21] Providing a history of various "performances of play in everyday life," Bernstein highlights the many ways in which "they stealthily reconfigured slaveholding and enslavement as racially innocent fun."[22] A careful engagement with Bernstein's work helps us understand not just supposedly innocent calls to "protect our children" but also the seemingly innocuous calls heard around the sporting world to "Relax, it's just a game!" This discourse, according to Bernstein, "reanimates, disguises, and draws power from old, half-forgotten contests over love and pain and fun, over the racial limits of innocence, and over the American question of who is a person and who is a thing."[23]

A number of examples have surfaced that demonstrate how white enjoyment and capitalist profit are predicated upon the social control over Black athletes as "things." Celtics forward Jaylen Brown was subtly criticized by an anonymous NBA executive for being "too smart for his own good" after deciding to enter the NBA draft without an agent or manager.[24] Brown's story, however, did not make headlines as much as LeBron James's recent encounter with Fox News analyst Laura Ingraham. Ingraham directed James to "shut up and dribble" in response to his claim that President Donald Trump neither understands nor cares for people. In her rant, Ingraham falsely claimed that James made $100 million per year. She also discouraged youth from following the example of someone like LeBron James who left school too early. And more recently, the NCAA—a multibillion dollar industry—recently used the Thirteenth Amendment to justify why college athletes, many of whom are Black, should not be paid.[25] These examples show how the American ruling class interprets any level of independence exercised by Black athletes as a significant threat to its social control over their bodies and labor, a fear similarly held by slave masters over their slaves. As Saidiya Hartman writes, "to take delight in, to use, and to possess are inextricably linked."[26]

The American ruling class uses American exceptionalism as the framework to justify the demand that athletes like Jaylen Brown and LeBron James appreciate their status in society and remain silent about injustice.[27] White enjoyment, then, is merely a show of mastery from the rulers of society. Black labor in America has historically been oppressed as both a commodity *and* the property of slave masters—now the modern day ruling class. Institutions of pleasure and leisure in American society thus reflect the longstanding need for the American ruling class to show mastery over their subjects as a means to legitimate its rule over them. Saidiya Hartman explains that during the period of chattel bondage, stupendous profits were not the only benefits that slave owners and white Americans accumulated from the institution. The Black identity ascribed to the enslaved served also as the marker from which white settlers indebted to the slave economy negotiated their power and the philosophical truths supposedly inherent to this power:

> The owner's display of mastery was just as important as the legal title to slave property. In other words, representing power was essential to reproducing domination [. . .] The innocent amusements and spectacles

> of mastery orchestrated by members of the slaveholding class to establish their dominion and regulate the little leisure allowed the enslaved were significant components of slave performance. Consequently, it is difficult, if not impossible, to establish an absolute and definitive definition between 'going before the master' and other amusements [. . .] Such performances confirmed the slaveholder's dominion and made the captive body the vehicle of the master's power and truth.[28]

Hartman's analysis places American sports in the context of the reproduction of capitalist and racist domination over Black labor. U.S. popular culture has changed in form, but not in substance, since the period of chattel bondage. No longer are Black American athletes or performers the exclusive property of a slave-owning class. However, the social relations that made slavery such a pernicious system of domination—and not merely an economic arrangement—remain firmly intact. Sports owners and the corporate media continue to exercise exclusive control over the labor of Black Americans for the purpose of extracting profit and fueling white enjoyment, even if that labor is paid. Indeed, our nation's repeated denials about the ways anti-Black domination persists today—even after so-called emancipation—merely illustrate what Kimberly Juanita Brown describes as the "the world that slavery made: haunting, hybrid, and completely invested in memorial amnesia."[29]

American exceptionalism has obscured the legacies of enslavement by focusing attention solely on those conditions of Black oppression that have been deceptively presented as opportunities to achieve the American Dream. This is why it seems crazy to most Americans to liken the treatment of professional athletes to slaves. After all, as the argument goes, look at all the money they're making! Or, if they're college athletes, look at the millions of fans cheering their name!! If anything, this is what makes America great! But such a reaction allows the American ruling class to assume the identity of a charitable, paternal caretaker rather than a brutal oppressor class that makes billions from the exploitation of labor and land. The work of Lisa Lowe is important here, for her use of Cedric Robinson's term "racial capitalism" exposes the fact that the American political and economic system "expands not through rendering all labor, resources, and markets across the world identical, but by precisely seizing upon colonial divisions, identifying particular regions for production and others for neglect, certain populations for exploitation and still others for disposal."[30] U.S. imperialism is one of the most formidable and deadly forms of of racial capitalism to date. Black labor, and more specifically, the Black working class, has been the central target of its exploitative, global apparatus.

It is thus no coincidence that Texans owner Bob McNair likened Black NFL players to inmates in a prison. U.S. imperialism is indeed obsessed with incarcerating people of color. Black Americans make up roughly half of the 2.3 million prisoners despite being a mere 12 percent of the population. And as popular knowledge about mass incarceration has evolved in recent years, prisons have more and more been likened to slavery. "Prison is the modern day manifestation of the plantation," writes Joy James. "The antebellum plantation ethos of dehumanization," she continues, "was marked by master-slave relations revolving about sexual terror and domination, beatings, regimentation of bodies, exploited labor, denial of religious and cultural practices, substandard food, health care, and housing, forced migration, isolation in 'lockdown' for punishment and control, denial of birth family and kin."[31]

The Thirteenth Amendment of the U.S. Constitution, famous for leaving imprisoned individuals outside the realm of "freedom" from slavery, sparked a "Millions for Prisoners Human Rights March" in August of 2017. Activists who organized the march condemned the Thirteenth Amendment as the political weight behind the continuation of slavery. Marchers connected the Amendment to the super exploitation of Black prisoners and prisoners generally, many of whom work for wages of no more than forty cents per hour. Prison labor services the massive profits of corporations like the Correctional Corporation of America (CCA), Starbucks, Whole Foods, and Verizon. However, as Beth Richie notes, these corporations would not possess such an abundant Black labor force were it not for "the political process whereby enforcement strategies, criminal justice policy, the creation of new laws, and mass incarceration are used strategically as part of a larger social agenda aimed at maintaining the power of economic elites through the control of marginalized groups."[32]

American exceptionalism and white enjoyment have historically helped justify the conditions that lead to mass Black incarceration. While President Bill Clinton passed harsh drug policies targeting Black Americans, American corporate record labels such as Universal Music Group distributed "gangster" rap music that portrayed Black American communities as criminally inclined. The passage of the 1996 Telecommunications Act, also by Clinton, gave corporate record labels the ability to conduct unlimited mergers and purchases of radio stations. One study found that a large reason why corporate record labels promoted "gangster rap" was due to the fact that it was wildly popular among white suburban males.[33] Corporate record labels thus possessed a vested interest in promoting images of Black life that justified the "Tough on Crime" policies of their political backers.

Of course, it would be a mistake to think that Hip Hop artists, football players, and people in prison are the only targets of the state's "Tough on Crime" policies. To this day, the policing, punishing, and disciplining of black girls underscore another afterlife of slavery—one that occurs every day in our nation's school system. Connie Wun, in her article, "Anti-Blackness as Mundane: Black Girls and Punishment beyond School Discipline," chronicles the stories of many young Black girls getting dismissed from the classroom for innocent "violations" like chewing gum or walking over to the trash can to throw something away. While the tendency is to focus on racial disparities in school arrests, expulsions, and suspensions, she argues, such studies shift attention away from how Black school-aged girls are vulnerable to more common forms of policing and disciplining, ones that are executed by teachers, administrators, and peers alike.[34] "These practices are not generally traced within school discipline research in large part because they are not exceptional forms of discipline," Wun writes. "Instead they are commonplace and embedded within the fabric of the girls' everyday lives, a condition of schooling."[35] To learn of yet another "burdened subject no longer enslaved, but not yet free," requires that we examine how exceptionalist myths of meritocracy and the American Dream ignore how even children in the nation's public school system are not immune to the afterlives of slavery.[36] As Wun concludes about one of the students featured in her article, "despite her academic achievements, Simone's narrative demonstrated that a black female student who succeeds in school can also be subject to gratuitous punishment."[37]

With one statement, Bob McNair burst asunder the illusion of Black upward mobility so critical to the promotion of white enjoyment and capitalist profit as "exceptional" characteristics of the American nation-state. Black American NFL athletes and "gangster" rappers have been heavily promoted symbols of the American Dream without any regard to the many forms of racial domination that plague the daily lives of most Black Americans. Exceptionalist narratives that construct slavery as an unfortunate—but overcome—event of the past helps maintain the entrenched power of an

American racial capitalism ruled over by an overwhelmingly white elite class. The realities of American racial capitalism should prompt us to respond to Bob McNair's statement that "we can't have the inmates running the prison" with a strong rebuttal: Prisoners indeed will *not* run the prison; they will abolish it.[38] Or, as Fred Moten puts it, the prisoners of American capitalism will need to focus "not so much [on] the abolition of prisons but the abolition of a society that could have prisons."[39] NFL owners, corporate media, the police, and public school administrators consistently remind us that the problem is much larger than what the abolition of one particular institution can alleviate. As Tryon Woods observes, "The house of antiblackness can withstand renovations to its architecture as long as its fundamental design remains intact."[40]

CHAPTER 13

"Is American 'Aid' Assistance or Theft? The Case of Africa"

"American exceptionalism operates as a mythology of convenience that does a tremendous amount of work to simplify the contradiction between the apparent creed of US society and its much more complicated reality."

—Keeanga-Yamahtta Taylor[1]

"In fact, empires are not innocent, absent-minded, accidental accretions. They are given purposive direction by rulers who consciously mobilize vast amounts of personnel and materials in order to plunder other lands and peoples."

—Michael Parenti[2]

"We know that we, the Blacks, and not only we, the Blacks, have been, and are, the victims of a system whose only fuel is greed, whose only god is profit."

—James Baldwin[3]

U.S. imperialism's staggering military footprint abroad has already been emphasized in prior essays. A lengthy historical record exists of American-led wars of aggression conducted on nearly every continent since the end of the Second World War, especially in the darker nations of Africa, Asia, and Latin America. The United States spends its annual $700 billion-plus war budget on weapons of mass destruction and military operations that have cost the lives of millions and left dozens of countries in near total ruin. It seems unlikely that the U.S. could possess such a record and simultaneously project itself not only as an innocent bystander to the evils of *other* countries, but also as the world's humanitarian saving grace. In the next three chapters, we examine the various ideological tools that the U.S. employs to promote itself as an exceptional force for "good" in the world.

Beginning with the United States' proclaimed desire to build an "Empire of Liberty" in the late 18th century and into the 19th century, western liberalism fundamentally shaped American efforts to develop an empire under the guise of spreading freedom around the world. Yet, as discussed in earlier chapters, liberal ideology has always possessed an inherent contradiction. Proclamations of individual liberty depend upon the oppression of those deemed incapable of realizing the fruits of this promise. As Lisa Lowe explains, liberalism's contradiction only "resolves in 'freedom' within the modern Western political sphere through displacement and elision of the coeval conditions of settler dispossession, slavery, and indentureship in the Americas."[4] In other words, freedom—as defined by modern liberalism—is not only *reserved for* the civilized over the "savage" and the human over the nonhuman; it is *acquired by* and *dependent upon* the oppression of the other.[5]

When U.S. imperialism eclipsed the power of its European rivals in the mid-20th century, the world was sick and weary of war. Competition between Western imperial powers not only devastated European economies during two World Wars, but also kept nations under their colonial possession in a brutal state of subservience and starvation. Moreover, an American-led alignment emerged between the imperial powers after the Second World War. This meant that post-war prosperity for countries like the U.S. continued to rely on the super exploitation of formerly colonized nations that had just freed themselves from European bondage by using the division of the colonial powers to lay a path toward independence. The United States' need to preserve its reputation as an exceptional "civilization" while dominating the former colonial possessions of its Western allies made "foreign aid" an important mechanism for securing American power abroad.

It is this backdrop that explains why the U.S. possesses a disproportionate influence over international institutions that distribute so-called "aid" abroad. Many Americans are unaware of the extensive mechanisms used by the U.S. to leverage "aid" as a means for dominance. Common misconceptions about American "aid" abroad came up during the 2016 presidential elections. Supporters of Donald Trump found his "America First" slogan enticing since it reflected their long-held belief that American political and economic activity abroad has privileged foreign nations at the expense of American national prosperity. The slogan positioned countries like China into enemy territory for benefiting from American economic power at the expense of white Americans. "Free Trade" agreements like NAFTA were rightly seen as anathema to the interests of the American worker, but only because they allowed non-white nations to steal American jobs. On the other hand, Hillary Clinton supporters opposed Trump's "America First" position on the basis that the United States' global influence provided economic and humanitarian benefits to both the American people and the world at large.

Neither position reflected the realities of American imperial power around the world. The impact of American foreign aid abroad is more damning than what Trump and Clinton suggested. Trump's "America First" position reinforced the racial animus inherent in the exercise of American imperial power by suggesting that the U.S should not waste precious resources on those who use it at the expense of Americans. On the other hand, Clinton's firm belief that U.S. influence abroad is a positive force for Americans and peoples around the world alike completely erased the devastating conditions that American foreign policy produces at home and abroad. Amid such confusion, it is imperative to deconstruct American influence abroad as neither beneficial for the majority of Americans nor for the nations around the world that have been on the receiving end of American "foreign aid."

"Foreign aid" cannot be defined as one particular policy, but a multitude of policies meant to secure the interests of U.S. imperialism. "Foreign aid" takes the form of military and political "assistance." Other types of "aid" include loans and financial assistance from international financial institutions dominated by the U.S. The United States is also home to a number of "civil society" groups or Non-Governmental Organizations (NGOs) that receive public and private funds to create favorable political conditions for American domination. Few Americans, however, look at these policies critically because they are framed as "aid." After all, how could poor, underdeveloped countries *not* benefit from assistance that comes from the most exceptional nation on the planet? This rhetorical question plays over and over in the discourse about American "aid" to remind the world that the U.S. can be counted on to attend to the needs of the global poor.

For many, "aid" is the same as "help" and the "distributor of aid"—in this case the U.S.—the same as the "helper". But "aid" and empire cannot exist together in an abstract sense.[6] Since it became the chief imperialist power after the Second World War, the United States has primarily been motivated by the interrelated desires to maximize the profit, scale, and influence of its multinational corporations, financial monopolies, and military industries. Imperial motivations are very clearly outlined in the actual operative frameworks of U.S. "foreign aid" institutions. When the American dollar became the global exchange rate in 1944 and then replaced gold as the reserve currency in the early 1970s, American financiers were given free reign over the Bretton Woods institutions of the World Bank and the International Monetary Fund (IMF). These institutions were originally advertised as agents of "assistance" and "development" in a post-World War planet, but became nothing more than agents of American empire.[7]

It is important to note that the U.S. has historically held disproportionate influence over the IMF and World Bank. The U.S. has by far the largest vote at nearly 18 percent in both institutions. U.S. influence is reflected in IMF and World Bank policy, especially in the Structural Adjustment Programs (SAP) that have ravaged nations in Africa, Latin America, and Asia. These programs began in 1980 as measures of assistance to relieve poor and formerly colonized countries from debts imposed on them from their colonizers during the post-war period. Instead of lending assistance, however, SAPs have only increased the economic burden imposed by U.S. imperialism by forcing indebted countries to privatize state industries, open up their economies for corporate investment, and restructure their political systems to benefit American and Western monopolies.

Nowhere is this burden more apparent than on the resource-rich African continent. The imposition of American "aid" in the form of SAPs was not embraced but rather imposed with the help of military "aid." In the mid-20th century, Africa was ablaze with the spirit of independence and Pan-Africanism. Nations such as Algeria, Ghana, and Zaire (now Congo) waged heroic anticolonial struggles, often with success. However, such success was consistently met with the force of U.S. imperialism and its interests in the resource-rich continent. Revolutionary leaders like Patrice Lumumba of Zaire and Kwame Nkrumah of Ghana were assassinated in coups organized by the Central Intelligence Agency (CIA). What were their crimes? They had decided to organize the national economies of their respective countries around the needs of the African people and not those of European and American corporations.

This, in the CIA's estimation, made them potential breeding grounds for 20th-century socialist arrangements like those that existed in Russia and China. Thus, early military "aid" to independent African nations—a.k.a. violent overthrows of revolutionary leaders—created the political conditions necessary for "economic" aid in the form of SAPs.

SAPs have been disastrous for Africa ever since they became the continent's dominant economic arrangement. According to Asad Ismi, SAPs have dramatically increased foreign investment and trade with Africa at the expense of a number of social indicators. Nearly 350 million Africans lived in extreme poverty as of 2003 and over a dozen countries possessed incomes in 1999 that were below 1975 figures.[8] SAP mandates forced African countries to pay off debts with the receipt of more debt in exchange for austerity and privatization measures. These measures have led to a scarcity in clean drinking water and medical care in many African nations, which has ensured that life expectancy remains low while deaths from diseases such as HIV remain high. Meanwhile, African nations have paid over four times the amount of their original debt to World Bank and IMF lenders since 1980.

The IMF is the American-led face of what Ghanian revolutionary leader Kwame Nkrumah called "neocolonialism."[9] Neocolonialism accurately describes the continued foreign plunder of African nations despite formal recognition of their independence. American imperial dominance on the world stage has facilitated the conditions of neocolonialism. Because of SAPs, American and Western corporations have made enormous profits from the debt forced upon the African continent. New research from a coalition of UK and African development campaigners shows that in a given year, more wealth leaves Africa than enters it, by a figure of more than 40 billions dollars.[10] The coalition found that $18 billion of the $32 billion in "aid" given to African countries in 2015 was used to pay outstanding interest to lenders. African countries have been deeply impoverished by American-led "foreign aid" arrangements despite the enormous wealth in their possession. The Democratic Republic of Congo alone possesses over $24 trillion worth of mineral wealth yet is one of the most underdeveloped nations worldwide.[11] What the coalition does not mention is the role of the American-led IMF and World Bank in fostering these conditions.

The U.S. avoids explicit mention of the role it plays in the plunder of African wealth. It instead has deployed NGOs to resolve the problems that result from it. SAPs, for example, create the poverty necessary for American NGOs to operate as the philanthropic arm of U.S. imperialism. NGOs are "nonprofit" institutions, meaning that donors receive generous tax benefits for their contributions. NGOs, however, do not operate outside of the imperial exploitation of African wealth. Their philanthropic mission statements which purport to alleviate poverty and suffering in Africa are nothing but smoke-screens that mask the underlying motivations of NGO donors and directors who, more often than not, are the very executives of the monopolies plundering the continent.

The Bill and Melinda Gates Foundation (BMGF) is one of the most prominent American NGOs on the African continent. Bill Gates is the owner of the Microsoft corporation and the second richest person in the world. The Gates family possesses lucrative investments in Africa, including in the volatile mining of minerals in the Democratic Republic of Congo spurred a U.S.-backed genocide led by Rwanda and Uganda which has killed over 6 million Congolese people since 1996. The fortunes of Microsoft and other tech monopolies are aided by the philanthropic influence of the BMGF. It is the second largest funder of the World Health Organization (WHO) behind the U.S. itself.

According to a 2016 study by Global Justice Now, the BMGF has an extensive record of promoting corporate interests in Africa.[12] The foundation has lucrative shares in corporations such as Coca-Cola and Monsanto. After the fall of the Soviet Union, the Gates Foundation used its influence to lobby for Public-Private Partnerships (P3s) in Mozambique that effectively imploded the nation's public health system and placed it in the control of private operators, some of which were overseen by the Gates Foundation.[13] Many of its board members and directors in the foundation's agricultural and medical programs are current or former advisors for these monopolies. Sam Dryden, the Director of Agricultural Development at the foundation, previously worked for Monsanto, and the Director of HIV was a former senior researcher at the pharmaceutical giant, Pfizer. Global Justice Now links the corporate governance of the foundation to the policies it promotes on the African continent. For example, the Gates Foundation has long pushed for exclusive corporate ownership of seed and land titles throughout Africa. According to a summary of the study:

> . . . the foundation is working with US trader Cargill in an $8 million

> project to "develop the soya value chain" in southern Africa. Cargill is the biggest global player in the production of and trade in soya with heavy investments in South America where GM soya mono-crops have displaced rural populations and caused great environmental damage. According to Global Justice Now, the BMGF-funded project will likely enable Cargill to capture a hitherto untapped African soya market and eventually introduce GM soya onto the continent.[14]

NGOs are thus many things, including tax-havens for the rich and humanitarian proxies for corporate profit. But they also provide a valuable ideological tool that U.S. imperialism could not do without. Endless poverty in Africa requires justification, especially to an American population largely cut out from the super profits that derive from it. NGOs promote subjection with a human face and reinforce the white supremacist logics of the American nation-state. U.S.-based NGOs promote a philanthropic image that effectively strips Africans of agency and places it firmly in the hands of American profiteers and their mainly white supporters. NGOs depict Africans as poor, helpless nonhumans compared to Americans who supposedly live in a prosperous and generous nation. NGOs regularly enlist the talents of celebrities such as Bono to advertise the "private sector" as a solution to "Africa's problems."

NGOs give a human face to U.S. imperialism's plunder of Africa. However, in the last few decades, American economic influence in Africa has eroded despite the presence of American NGOs and American-led IMF financial arrangements. African nations indebted to the IMF and plundered by corporations with the support of NGOs have looked to China for an alternative model of development. Chinese trade with Africa currently dwarfs the United States by more than double at $220 billion dollars.[15] Western leaders like Hillary Clinton accuse China of practicing a "new colonialism," "as if China was an invader in a zone that 'naturally' belongs to Europeans and Americans."[16] Yet while American and Western nations have focused on repatriating profitable raw materials from Africa to feed the production cycles of monopoly corporations, leaving African countries in debt, China has focused on providing technical support and infrastructure development to African countries in exchange for access to their natural resources. As Zambian economist Dambisa Moyo points out, it also helps that China treats Africans not as charity cases but business partners.[17]

China's economic partnership with Africa has caused the American ruling class to panic and shift their focus in the continent. Rather than presenting Africans as poor and helpless, the U.S. has casted the continent as a "security" threat that requires American military "aid" to eradicate. "Africa as a zone of risk, cast as a source of looming threats," writes Maximilian Forte, "has been one of the central tenets of U.S. policy statements, refurbishing the colonial 'Dark Continent' narrative."[18] Many observers, including the U.S. armed forces establishment itself, have openly admitted that the explosive growth of the American military is a direct response to Chinese economic growth. The Council on Foreign Relations, an influential U.S. foreign policy think-tank, warned about China's rise in Africa as far back as 2006: "U.S. policy has not responded to the implications of intensifying activity in Africa by China along with other Asian countries. This activity may have consequences not only for access to resources but perhaps more importantly for the pursuit of important U.S. objectives of good governance, protection of human rights, and sound economic policies."[19] Lest we forget, however, by "good governance" they mean "regimes that are supportive of U.S. policy and that model their political systems in some fashion on the American one." And by "human rights" they mean a particular notion of "freedom," one tied directly to "free" markets, "free" trade, and "the relatively unrestrained ability of wealthy private interests to operate and act to maximize their gains."[20]

Concerns over restricted access to Africa's wealth prompted an increase in American military "aid" to Africa, which was institutionalized in 2008 with the formation of the US Africa Command (AFRICOM).[21] According to Khaled Al-Kassimi, AFRICOM placed American military operations in Africa under one institutional umbrella for the first time in history as a response to the post-9/11 narrative that posited the continent as an emerging threat to American national security.[22] American military expansion is therefore framed as a humanitarian mission in Africa. As Al-Kassimi observes, drawing from the work of Maximilian Forte, "humanitarianism is always brought about by the West, the 'self-appointed messiah that has the right to determine which is the right side of history [using] the American military as savior.'" "These myths," he continues, "create further opposing binaries such as the US being the helper because it is independent while Africans are helpless because they are dependent."[23] AFRICOM's role as the rightful savior of African problems, without permission or consultation from African nations themselves, has been assumed from the outset of the institution's development. American foreign policy advisors, however, have claimed that AFRICOM is a collaborative institution that "partners" with African militaries to resolve their own problems.[24]

Yet it isn't too difficult to see that AFRICOM has reinforced American hegemony in Africa by recolonizing the militaries of "partner" African countries. Under the Obama Administration, AFRICOM grew exponentially. It currently has a presence in nearly every African country. In 2015 alone, the American military carried out 674 operations, a nearly 300 percent increase from the period of AFRICOM's formation in 2008. AFRICOM's security experts do not hesitate to justify its expanding presence as a necessary response to a number of so-called "security" threats. The largest threat often cited is that posed by transnational terror groups. Describing Africa as a "battlefield" for the defense of American "national security" interests has given cover to the real motivations that underlie American military presence in Africa.

These motivations were exposed by AFRICOM's first full-scale military invasion of Libya in 2011.[25] Prior to the invasion, AFRICOM maintained a relatively light footprint in Africa. The Libyan Jamahiriya led by Muammar Gaddafi strongly opposed AFRICOM's presence and presented to the African Union (AU) a plan for a continental military and gold currency independent of the American dollar. In fact, the WikiLeaks dump of Hillary Clinton's emails revealed that such plans formed the basis for the U.S.-NATO invasion.[26] Moreover, writes Maximilian Forte, "Gaddafi's power and influence on the continent had also been increasing, through aid, investment, and a range of projects designed to lessen African dependency on the West and to challenge Western multilateral institutions by building African unity."[27] Beginning in March of 2011—after positioning himself as a significant rival to U.S. economic and strategic interests—the U.S.-NATO alliance led by AFRICOM dropped over 30,000 bombs in six months, killing at least 60,000 Libyans.[28] AFRICOM played a central role in the implementation of the "no-fly zone" established by the UN Security Council enactment of Article 1973. This article declared that the U.S.-NATO alliance had the Responsibility to Protect (R2P) Libyan citizens from what they declared was an oppressive regime that was murdering "its own people."[29]

By October 2011, AFRICOM-NATO backed "rebels," many of whom

shared affiliations with terrorist groups such as Al-Qaeda and openly called for the genocide of Black Libyans, had successfully overthrown the Libyan government. As Forte observes:

> . . . while "genocide" was quickly proffered by some as the way to characterize the suppression of the revolt by the government, a term especially popular within the small circle of Western liberal imperialists whose banner is the "responsibility to protect," the term "genocide" was never used by the same people, nor by the UN or Western leaders, to describe actual facts on the ground that involved "ignited public anger" in a "battle against black people." If this was "humanitarianism," it could only be so by disqualifying Africans as members of humanity. The actual practice of intervention did just that.[30]

The most prosperous nation on the African continent was turned to rubble. Muammar Gaddafi was brutally assassinated without trial. The socialist-oriented system in Libya that provided free health care, affordable housing, and free education was dismantled and replaced by the corrupt rule of competing "rebel" militias. These "rebels," in turn, took their arms across Africa and even into nations such as Syria to wreak similar destruction, giving AFRICOM more opportunities to justify the 5,000 to 8,000 military personnel it had deployed to Africa by 2014.[31]

AFRICOM achieved its mission in Libya, which was to secure the conditions necessary for American corporate penetration of the continent. Indeed, David Hamod, CEO of the US-Arab Chamber of Commerce, declared a "gold rush" for American and Western corporations in the wake of Libya's demise.[32] Hamod's remarks confirmed the true intentions of the American war in Libya. AFRICOM was created to serve as military arm of American "aid' to the African continent. Yet military "aid" has helped American economic interests while providing Africa with nothing in return. This, of course, should come as no surprise to those privy to AFRICOM's initial design. As Forte shows:

> Opportunities for U.S. expansion have been at the forefront of planning for AFRICOM, which as an idea began to be articulated for a decade prior to its establishment. The plan to establish such a program came as a result "of a 1-year thought process within the U.S. government" that saw the "growing

> strategic importance of Africa" [. . .] In fact, the idea first took shape in the plans of lobbyists for the oil industry, joined by a select group of members of Congress, and military officers who issued a white paper titled, "African Oil: A Priority for U.S. National Security and African Development" in 2002.[33]

Even Vice Admiral Robert Moeller admitted that AFRICOM's true purpose is to maintain "the free flow of natural resources from Africa to the global market."[34] Of course, by "free" flowing he meant that U.S. policy "aims to ensure that African resources flow in the 'right' direction."[35] We need not guess where this "right" direction points.

By examining American "aid" to Africa, it becomes increasingly clear that the concept further justifies imperialist policy at the expense of the sovereignty and self-determination of African nations. American "aid," whether in the economic form of IMF and World Bank loans, the political form of NGOs, or the military form of AFRICOM, serves to reinforce the ideology of American exceptionalism. American exceptionalism takes after the Western capitalist world's toxic, anti-African racism that justified colonial plunder and enslavement as early as the 17th century. American exceptionalism has relegated Africa to an inferior status to the American nation-state and its Western allies. Africa's presumed inferiority to the "white" imperialist countries is precisely why the imposition of poverty and war can be framed as "aid" with little criticism emanating from the majority of Americans. "Western liberalism's multiple myths of humanitarianism, which include the benevolent spread of democracy, the protection of innocent civilians, the benign building of nations, and the liberation of peoples suffering under dictators," Maximilian Forte writes, "are myths that fabricate a world where there are rightful actors and those acted upon."[36] AFRICOM thus reinforces the Eurocentric nature of American foreign policy by justifying expansion with "the belief that the world should be engineered in its image and that the destiny of the US is to civilize and democratize the world over."[37] African countries never asked for AFRICOM's presence in Libya or elsewhere.

To ask African countries permission to intervene in their affairs would be to affirm the humanity of African people. However, American innocence and American exceptionalism have worked together in Africa to erase African existence. When Africa does exist, it is viewed through the prism of inhumanity where uncivilized Africans require American "humanitarianism" to advance their societies. American "aid" is dependent on the legitimation of "humanitarianism," which occurs in all channels of American society. White billionaires such as Bill Gates are promoted as stalwarts of humanitarianism in Africa for their generous charity in the form of NGOs with little mention of their negative impact on the continent. IMF and World Bank loans are disguised as "development" aid to provide economic "opportunity" to poor Africans. And AFRICOM's main operation in Libya was described as a "humanitarian intervention" to save Africans from their allegedly brutal government. Indeed, these institutions have mastered what Deborah Elizabeth Whaley calls "the language of imperialism": "moralistic crusaders" with "a divine right to conquer, civilize, and tame the wild."[38]

The very notion of American "aid" implies that the U.S. empire is capable of providing assistance to other nations on a benevolent and mutual basis. However, each and every form of American "aid" has merely reproduced conditions of inequality, instability, and oppression for recipient nations in Africa. "Aid" has been used as an instrument to reinforce the social relations of American superiority and African inferiority. Africa proves that there is no exceptionalism under the dictates of American empire. The conditions of empire are mirrored throughout the world, whether in the American-led war on Syria where "aid" takes the form of weapons to "rebels" and "coalition" airstrike, or in the hostile sanctions on Latin American countries such as Venezuela and Cuba. American foreign policy is much larger than its "aid" structures, of which only a small number have been covered in this essay. In the following essays, we explore further the relationship between U.S. foreign policy and the ideology of "humanitarianism" so critical in the promotion of American exceptionalism and, by extension, American expansion.

CHAPTER 14

"Does the U.S. Really Care about Human Rights?"

"Few speak of U.S. policies as genocidal because the dominant tendency is to analyze national policies as the byproduct of specific administrations or political parties not as the consequence of a state apparatus built on and seeped in racial animus."

—Joy James[1]

". . . any serious interrogation of the history of Black life in the United States upends all notions of American exceptionalism."

—Keeanga-Yamahtta Taylor[2]

"The difference between what U.S. citizens think their rulers are doing in the world and what these rulers actually are doing is one of the great propaganda achievements of history."

—Michael Parenti[3]

Countries vying to host the Olympic Games face a number of challenges. One of them is convincing the International Olympic Committee (IOC) that their government's human rights record does not violate the Olympic Charter's fundamental principles of Olympism. In past bids, Americans had no problem pointing to Russia's anti-LGBT laws and China's practices of imprisoning journalists as grounds for breaching the IOC's commitment to "social responsibility and respect for universal ethics." Rarely, however, do Americans question their own human rights record. Sportswriters Dave Zirin and Jules Boycoff are refreshing exceptions, pointing out what millions around the world already knew. Just as Los Angeles was submitting its bid to host the 2024 summer olympics, Zirin and Boycoff argued the following: "It's easy to single out Russia and China as major human rights violators that do not merit hosting the world's top-flight Olympic athletes. But the United States deserves similar condemnation. Americans should not allow historical amnesia and the tendency to root for the home team to cloud their vision. It's time to face facts: The U.S. is a human rights outlier."[4]

If the IOC really does care about a country's human rights record—which is doubtful—then how has the United States managed to win bids to host *eight* Olympics games? Perhaps even more perplexing is the offense most Americans take to such a question. In the previous essay, we analyzed how U.S. imperialism employs a number of "aid" structures to facilitate the corporate robbery of Africa's immense wealth. American imperial plunder is consistently masked behind a discourse of "human rights" that dominates American foreign policy discussions in Africa. The United States has taken it upon itself to rid the continent of "terrorist threats" in the form of Boko Haram and Al Qaeda. Yet as U.S. strategy in Africa reveals, "humanitarian" concerns are merely justifications for American political, economic, and military expansion at the expense of African nations. The sham of U.S. "human rights" discourse, however, is not restricted to Africa. For the rest of the world, American concern over "human rights" is synonymous with war.

Americans tend not to see what the world sees because "human rights" is often described in U.S. foreign policy circles as a righteous motivation for global action. Such "action" is driven by urgent calls for American military and political officials to "do something" about human rights violations around the world. American expansionism has become buried by a "human rights" discourse which assumes the well-being of people around the world is the primary concern of American foreign policy. Exceptionalist assumptions about human rights have rendered the U.S. not only an innocent global actor, but a benevolent and just one as well.[5] After all, how many times have we heard politicians call the U.S. the "leader of the free world" with special responsibilities to protect it?

The point is not to grade the U.S. on how well it has lived up to expectations that it has defined for itself. Where the real problem lies is in the ideological framework of American exceptionalism and American innocence. These ideologies have prevented too many Americans from understanding just how much damage U.S. imperialism has spread around the world. Few Americans question U.S. foreign policy abroad since it is assumed that the U.S. upholds "human rights" around the world. When the U.S. *does* mess up, then it is simply that—a "mess up." If people die along the way, then it must have been for good reason. If the country that the U.S. invaded is worse off than before, then at least it was done with good intentions. Whatever the result, America is always on the right side of history. The question of whether the U.S. really cares about human rights not only prompts further study into its record on the subject, but also leads directly to the urgent need to envision a new human rights framework independent of American imperial ideology.

A proper examination of the United States' human rights record must take into account its imperial roots. American society has always been organized along the principles of racial oppression and class exploitation. "Racial genocide has been a historical fixture in Western democracies as citizens amassed existential wealth (white privileges) and material wealth (capital and militarism) through antiblack policies," writes Joy James. "But those realities tend to be muted in public discourse, where blacks and other people of color are invited to sit at the table of accumulation as national and global narratives note progress."[6] The rulers of this society have from the outset sought global domination to achieve these ends. This explains why the Black Freedom movement, for example, has often placed human rights in the context of global politics. Black internationalism is an enduring theme of the 20th century. The dozens of Black Freedom activists who submitted the "We Charge Genocide" petition to the United Nations in 1951 did so on the basis that racist oppression violated international law. Malcolm X would echo these sentiments a decade and a half later in his call for the UN to recognize an independent plebiscite for Blacks in America. The demand was inspired in part by Malcolm's visit to a number of African countries such as Ghana where he saw firsthand the benefits of genuine independence from American influence. The Black Panther Party even took after Malcolm X to openly call for the end of the American war machine, going to such lengths as to offer Black Panther Party members to fight alongside anti-colonial and anti-imperialist movements abroad.

The fact that the Black Freedom movement has led the majority of domestic critiques of U.S. foreign policy should come as no surprise. Human rights have never applied to Black people in America. The U.S. has dehumanized Black people from the outset, beginning with mass enslavement and followed by segregation, Jim Crow terror, racist policing, and state repression. Human rights have only applied to white Americans because "white" has been the definition of "humanity" in America. White Americans were given the "privilege" of humanity, regardless of the degree of their labor exploitation, to ensure that they would comply with the super exploitation of the Black worker. Moreover, as Maximilian Forte shows, the U.S. has appropriated the concept of dignity—which serves as the moral grounds of human rights discourse—for its own imperial agenda. "U.S. national security documents seem to essentially equate dignity with having modern conveniences and cash," he writes. "[I] n other words, an instrumentalist or transactionalist view of dignity that sits well with capitalist values, and makes for easy policy options."[7] Those who do not subscribe to this capitalistic view of dignity inevitably find themselves outside the protection of the capitalist state. Concepts "such as national dignity, and black dignity," Forte continues, "speak of dignity as the possession of large collectivities, nor are they reducible to pragmatic calculations and the quest for monetary gain."[8] Human rights have been flexibly defined by the U.S. to fit its domestic and international agenda in stark opposition to collectivist definitions of dignity.[9]

A number of scholars have commented about the selective way that U.S. imperialism defines human rights. The politics of genocide are case in point. Acts of genocide—or "the deliberate killing of a large group of people, especially those of a particular ethnic group or nation"—committed or aided by the U.S. are rarely questioned and often times ignored. Yet the term "genocide" has been used selectively to justify "humanitarian" interventions abroad while absolving imperial powers like the U.S. of their own crimes against humanity. As Edward S. Herman and David Peterson note, "The path from the 'White Man's Burden' to the regimes of selective 'human rights' and 'international justice' has been a lot more direct than its current-day travelers like to believe."[10] Or, as Maximilian Forte puts it:

> It's also interesting to reflect on the contradictory and bifurcated image created of ourselves by the humanitarian imperialists. On the one hand, as civilized Westerners we are something akin to angels. Our actions and thoughts reign high above history, residing in an altostratus of unimpeachable rectitude. In our teleological view of our own progress, we are at the highest point of human cultural evolution, ours being the highest stage of

> human achievement. We are the standard by which others are measured. We are what the future of all humanity looks like. The absence of our institutions and values in other societies is a measure of their inferiority. We should help them. We should help them to become more like us. These various "savage" others can be raised to our level of dignity, if we help them to acquire "prosperity" through the advance of "opportunity." Fixated on providence and destiny, we of course resent history, because history carries the inevitability of change, and of the decline of empire. As much as we resent history, we find cultural particularity loathsome: some differences simply defy polite tolerance, and demand our corrective intervention. High up in the clouds, perched on the wings of our stealth bombers, we preach the ideology of universal, individual human rights.[11]

In other words, American foreign policy still operates under the assumption that the U.S., deemed a white state, must come to the rescue of darker, less civilized nations.

Few individuals embody the "White Man's Burden" syndrome in U.S. foreign policy more than Samantha Power, the former U.S. Ambassador to the UN under the Obama Administration. Power has been one of the most vocal architects of the doctrine of "humanitarian intervention" throughout her career in politics, media, and foreign policy think tanks. Her book, *A Problem from Hell: America and the Age of Genocide*, illustrates the central problem with the United States' doctrine of human rights. It also serves as a welcome case study for how easy it is to be deceived and seduced by ideologies of American exceptionalism and American innocence. The book, which won a Pulitzer Prize in 2003, characterizes America's foreign policy toward genocide in the 20th century as that of bystander. Power details countless examples of when the U.S. knew that genocide was happening but decided to do nothing about it. The U.S. had the opportunity to stop genocide, she argues, but chose not to intervene. This is, according to Power, *our* "problem from hell."

But is this *our* problem at all? Power attempts to pass as a courageous citizen-journalist speaking truth to power about the country's many sins of omission when nothing could be further from the truth. There are many problems with her book, a few of which are exposed by Edward Herman and David Peterson. The book, they write, "devotes only one sentence to Indonesia, ignoring entirely the mass killings of 1965–1966, mentioning only its invasion-occupation of East Timor in 1975 and after."[12] Power then argues that America "looked away" during the quarter-century long genocide in Indonesia from 1975–1999, failing to mention that the U.S. and its Western allies generously supported what she called a "monstrous regime" during that period. Power also left out the fact that U.S. imperialism created the conditions for the genocide when it supported a coup a decade earlier which killed over a million so-called "communist sympathizers." As Herman and Peterson conclude, "Notice that in Power's hands, the 'monstrous regime' is the one that arose after the other regime's bombers 'killed tens of thousands of civilians'—but no negative adjectives are applied to the regime that sent along those bombers from the other side of the planet."[13]

The doctrine of American humanitarianism disguises American innocence as guilt to mask the direct role that U.S. imperialism plays in the most heinous war crimes around the world. In other words, by painting the U.S. as bystanders to genocide, Power deceptively covers up America's long history of *perpetrating* genocide. Power's problem, argues Dan Kovalik, is "her refusal to acknowledge the incontrovertible fact that the U.S . . . is in reality the world leader in war crimes commission, and an active facilitator of genocide." Power, like many of us, would like to believe that the the U.S. has been "a force for halting such evils." Her book invites readers to embrace the seductive myth that Americans should have known better by pressuring the government to live up to what America is *really* about; namely, the business of protecting human rights. "Power has done an impressive job in advancing this myth," Kovalik concludes, as well as "in perpetuating the false belief that the world would be better off if only the U.S. were more active militarily throughout the world."[14]

The idea that the U.S. is a bystander to genocide further perpetuates the myth of American innocence. When it comes to genocide, American innocence compels a national admission to the sin or mistake of "looking away," but never of perpetrating it. Recall that one of the ways this myth functions is by painting the U.S. as a victim of other countries' aggression. The U.S. is never the aggressor. It is either retaliating for something that was (supposedly) done *to* Americans or something it anticipates *will be* done to them. Either way, the U.S. is, as Captain America's shield suggests, always on the defensive. The deceptive nature of this ideology makes it much easier to buy into Samantha Power's argument. Power's logic describes the U.S. as a nation-state showing *too much restraint* in the realm of foreign policy—we did *nothing* when we should have done *something.* But this fantasy becomes much harder to believe when we take into account just how involved the U.S. military is in the world. The U.S. is constantly playing the role of aggressor. Its war-apparatus is constantly "doing something." But Power would have us all believe that the U.S. is in the habit of *not acting* and only acts when acted upon. This narrative is incredibly convenient for the U.S. war machine. After all, it becomes much easier for the U.S. to dismiss charges of imperialism if it is perceived as a mere passive bystander to global events.

Urgent calls from the likes of Power for humanitarian intervention have justified many atrocities, including American-led sanctions on Iraq in 1991. The U.S. and its allies had already invaded Iraq for using its oil wealth to modernize domestic infrastructure and fortify its national borders in a conflict with Kuwait. However, the U.S. expressed concern for human rights to justify the war. American foreign policy experts claimed that the war prevented Iraqi atrocities by enforcing a UN mandate for the removal of the nation's chemical and biological weapons. When Iraq was declared out of compliance with the mandate, American forces deliberately invaded Iraq and bombed vital infrastructure. Sanctions ensured that Iraq was unable to repair vital infrastructure damaged by American bombs. In 1998, these sanctions were declared a form of "genocide" by the UN coordinator of Humanitarian Affairs in Iraq.[15] The World Health Organization (WHO) found that a half million Iraqi children died because of the sanctions, a body count that U.S. Secretary of State Madeline Albright claimed was "worth it."

The mass genocide of children was "worth it" because of the supposed danger to "human rights" that Iraq's possession of chemical and biological weapons posed to the world (a danger that has long been proven a lie). What the damage of the first American venture into Iraq ultimately reveals, however, is the utter hypocrisy of "human rights" discourse in U.S. foreign policy. Human rights have historically only mattered when the U.S. has a vested interest in invading or destabilizing the nation in question. The American nation-state claims to possess a duty as "leader of the free world" to protect "democracy" and "human rights" abroad while it simultaneously violates the human rights of nations where it sends its military. This contradiction becomes all the more apparent when we compare U.S. policy toward its allies on the one hand with nations that it has deemed human rights violators on the other.

Take, for example, the United States' so-called concern for Iran's possession of nuclear capabilities and Syria's possession of chemical weapons. War in the form of sanctions and proxy invasions has been waged on both countries despite their efforts to appease the demands of U.S. imperialism. Iran signed a P5+1 agreement in 2015 to curb the development of domestic nuclear energy in exchange for an alleviation of sanctions. When Obama drew a "red line" in the sand over the Syrian government's alleged use of chemical weapons in 2013, Russia and the U.S. negotiated a deal with Syria to rid it of its stockpiles of chemical weapons. Yet both Syria and Iran remain in the crosshairs of U.S. imperialism. American foreign policy experts have said little about the human rights atrocities committed by American, NATO, and Saudi-backed "rebels" in Syria since 2011, which include extrajudicial killings and kidnappings that have been aided and abetted by the so-called "human rights" organization, the White Helmets.[16] As journalist Stephen Gowans has observed, the real reason for hostilities toward Syria and Iran is their independent political and economic posture toward the American global empire, a posture that the U.S. desperately wants to destroy as it did in Libya and Iraq.[17]

So while Iran continues to face economic sanctions and Syria continues to see death and displacement tolls rise beyond a million, U.S. imperialism maintains its "innocent" and "exceptional" position as the world's dictator of "human rights." This despite the fact that the majority of American "allies" receive American aid to commit the most heinous human rights violations around the world. Israel, for example, receives nearly $4 billion per year in military aid from the U.S. to colonize the Palestinian people. During Israel's invasion of Gaza in 2009, the U.S. stood by Israel by blocking any UN resolutions from forming in opposition to the 21-day assault that murdered over 1,300 Palestinians.[18] Israel invests heavily in American politics through the lobby organization AIPAC, which bribes American officials with campaign financing to support Israeli policies in the Middle East and Africa. Furthermore, Israel possesses over 200 nuclear warheads that have been kept secret from the public while the United States' nuclear arsenal approaches 7,000.[19] Yet the U.S. has fixed its gaze not on its own threat to humanity, but rather on those countries it has labeled a "threat." The U.S. thus succumbs to one of the earliest critiques of the "Responsibility to Protect" doctrine (R2P), namely "the issue of selectivity, of who gets to decide, and why some crises where civilians are targeted (say, Gaza) are essentially ignored, while others receive maximum concern."[20]

American exceptionalism and innocence render invisible an obvious double standard in U.S. foreign policy. When American imperial interests are at stake, the "human rights" narrative is invoked to capture enough public support to ensure that opposition to American war crimes is minimal.[21] Criminality comes to define the targets of war, whose governments are labeled "threats" to American interests and security. Michael Parenti offers a substantial list of independent, left-wing governments that the U.S. government has overthrown in service of this narrative:

> US leaders profess a dedication to democracy. Yet over the past five decades, democratically elected reformist governments—guilty of introducing redistributive economic programs—in Guatemala, Guyana, the Dominican Republic, Brazil, Chile, Uruguay, Syria, Indonesia (under Sukarno), Greece, Cyprus, Argentina, Bolivia, Haiti, the Congo, and numerous other nations were overthrown by their respective military forces funded and advised by the United States [. . .] US forces have invaded or launched aerial assaults against Vietnam, Laos, the Dominican Republic, North Korea, Cambodia, Lebanon, Grenada, Panama, Libya, Iraq, Somalia, Yugoslavia, and most recently in Afghanistan—a record of military aggression unmatched by any communist government in history. US/NATO forces delivered round-the-clock terrorist bombings upon Yugoslavia for two-and-a-half months in 1999, targeting housing projects, private homes, hospitals, schools, state-owned factories, radio and television stations, government owned hotels, municipal power stations, water supply systems, and bridges, along with hundreds of other nonmilitary targets at great loss to civilian life.[22]

U.S. imperialism continues to wage war in all forms to ensure that nations around the world are unable to exercise sovereignty and self-determination. "Intervention," writes Maximilian Forte, "is fundamentally opposed to" the respect of human dignity. "[T]he very act of intervention," he writes, "implies that there is some deficit or deficiency that requires the curative power of foreign actors." Of course, we cannot ignore the exceptionalist ideologies that underlie the United States' obsessive urge to meddle in the affairs of other nations. "With a heightened sense of their own entitlement as a people blessed by God and destined to rule the earth, their overweening estimation of their own dignity is accompanied by an equally lordly view of 'justice,'" Forte concludes. "The basic structure of belief in providence in shaping empire has changed little since the U.S. wars against Indigenous resistance in the nineteenth century and its invasions and occupations of Central American and Caribbean nations."[23]

A critical piece of American warfare is the support of brutal, oligarchic dictatorships around the world. As Glenn Greenwald explains, American foreign policy "has been predicated on overthrowing democratically elected governments and, even more so, supporting, aligning with, and propping up brutal dictators. This policy has been applied all over the world, on multiple continents, and by every administration."[24] Indeed, a significant part of the U.S.'s *modus operandi* involves propping up ruthless right-wing formations to prevent the rise of popular movements from taking power in a given country. The list of specific cases is exhaustive, spanning from Brazil's coup government led by Michel Temor, which paved the way for the election of the far right-wing Jair Bolsonaro, to the openly neo-Nazi government in Ukraine. Often, these oligarchic arrangements are satisfied with exporting national wealth to American corporations while importing dependence on U.S. military and corporate arrangements.

That the United States supports such arrangements may come as a surprise to many Americans who have been told that their government is primarily concerned with"human rights" and "democracy." Yet American support for brutal dictatorships is not incidental to American foreign policy. Such support is part and parcel of the structure of U.S. imperialism, a system where war crimes are inherent to its drive for profit and power. The U.S. provides military aid to over 70 percent of the world's dictatorships.[25] Thus, claims "of protecting civilians, preventing genocide, ending human rights abuses, putting war criminals on trial, providing humanitarian relief," writes Maximilian Forte, "are rarely even of secondary concern to the Key Western actors in practice, except as weapons."[26] As we will see, this contradiction between American imperial support for dictatorship and its purported commitment to human rights becomes even more evident in the the United States' engagement with Saudi Arabia and Cuba.

For U.S. imperialism, Saudi Arabia is a long time friend while Cuba is a long time foe. Saudi Arabia's human rights record is rarely mentioned in American corporate politics or media, while Cuba has been subject to American economic, military, and political warfare since 1959, the year of the Cuban Revolution. The discrepancy in the United States' treatment of Cuba and Saudi Arabia confirms the phenomenon that "human rights help produce a certain narration of history, which simultaneously confers . . . a highly flexible political discourse with the capacity to be constantly appropriated, translated, performed, and retooled in different political arenas."[27] Human rights discourse has been used flexibly by American political and military officials to demonize Cuba on the one hand and ignore Saudi Arabia's egregious human rights record on the other.

Since the Cuban Revolution of 1959, Cuba has charted an independent path of socialist development and separated itself from the grip of American corporations that dominated politics on the island for nearly a century prior. The U.S. has never acknowledged the legitimacy of the Cuban Revolution, instead labeling the country a pariah to "freedom" and "democracy." For almost six decades, the U.S. imposed sanctions on Cuba in an attempt to starve the country back into submission to its imperial dictates. According to a Cuban report to the UN, American sanctions have cost Cuba over $800 billion dollars worth of development generally and over $2 billion worth in health care spending alone over this period.[28]

Yet despite the devastating impact of sanctions coupled with thousands of American attempts to politically and militarily overthrow the Cuban government, Cuba in many ways is an exemplary case of a country that extends fundamental human rights to all of its citizens. The UN Educational, Scientific, and Cultural Organization (UNESCO) rates the Cuban education system the best in Latin America in terms of reaching the Education for All (EFA) indicators. Education in Cuba is free through university level. And in just six decades, Cuba has raised the standard of living for all of its citizens despite the challenges posed by a history of underdevelopment, slavery, and colonialism. The Cuban health care system is also free for all Cubans. Cuban health care has reduced the infant mortality rate to below that of the U.S., eliminated child malnutrition, and reduced the HIV transmission rate to one of the lowest in the world. Investment in universal health care has also led to achievements such as a lung cancer vaccine. Cuban society's overall dedication to human rights is also seen in its internationalist orientation toward Africa and the world at large.[29] Cuban assistance to South Africa, for example, was instrumental in the fall of apartheid from 1975–1991, and Cuban doctors and aid workers currently outnumber all other countries around the world in the provision of free health care to nations such as Venezuela, Haiti, and Pakistan.

Cuba's achievements in the field of human rights have gone unrecognized by the the United States. Imperial ambitions have compelled American political and military officials to label Cuba an "authoritarian regime." The Cuba "regime" has been repeatedly accused of violating what the U.S. defines as "democracy' and "human rights." The U.S. even invaded Grenada in 1983 under the pretext that Cuba—and the Soviets—were turning the island nation into a military base. Of course, few Americans consider their own "rogue democracy" when condemning "failed" democracies in other countries.[30] Americans are unable to see—and often refuse to see—the ways "their own democracy had been thwarted, their Constitution undermined, and their diplomacy militarized" by their so-called political "representatives."[31] And while this hasn't stopped the U.S. from punishing Cuba for its alleged human rights abuses, never has the U.S. protested the violations of its long time partner, Saudi Arabia.

Saudi Arabia possesses one of the worst human rights records in the world on the basis of its domestic policies alone. It is one of the few states left in the world that maintain a monarchy organized on the basis of religious right, in this case a variant of Sunni Islam called Wahhabism. Wahhabism is an extremely conservative strand of Sunni Islam that is reflected in all spheres of Saudi policy. Saudi women were unable to vote for political office until 2011. While American human rights doctrinaires have criticized Cuba for a lack of "free speech" in the media, Saudi Arabia possesses a long track record of imprisoning and executing dissident journalists. Public beheadings of activists and Shia minorities are an ordinary policy of the Saudi monarchy. In one day in 2016 alone, Saudi Arabia executed 47 people.[32] These human rights abuses have received little attention or scrutiny in the halls of American power.

In the case of Saudi Arabia, the U.S. has not merely "looked away" from the human rights abuses of one of its key allies in the Middle East. A deep economic and military partnership exists between U.S. imperialism and the Saudi monarchy. For over seventy years, the American ruling class has provided the Saudi Royal Family with military protection in exchange for access to Saudi Arabia's large oil reserves for American corporations such as Chevron, Exxon, and Dow. American corporations currently possess hundreds of billions of dollars worth of assets in Saudi Arabia. From 2009–2015, President Obama facilitated over $100 billion worth of arms deals to Saudi security forces.[33]

The Saudi-American oil-for-arms partnership has directly implicated the U.S. in each and every one of Saudi Arabia's domestic and foreign policies. Saudi Arabia is one of the largest state sponsors of terrorism throughout the world. Their sponsorship of terrorism has been linked to the 9/11 hijackers, which was fully exposed in a 28-page Congressional report.[34] Saudi-backed proxies can be found throughout the world but have played especially critical roles in the American-led wars in Libya and Syria. Yet perhaps the most heinous example of the United States' implication in Saudi human rights violations resides in Yemen.[35]

Since 2015, Saudi Arabia has been engaged in a bloody invasion of neighboring Yemen in an attempt to maintain hegemony over the insurgent and independent Shia-led Houthi movement. American weapons traded to Saudi Arabia are drenched in Yemeni blood. Saudi Arabia has used American-produced F-15 fighters and an array of weapons to carpet bomb Yemen's schools, hospitals, and water supply systems. Several thousands of civilians have been killed and 80 percent of the country's population needs some form of humanitarian assistance.[36] Not only has U.S. military weaponry facilitated the Saudi war on Yemen, but it has also directly participated in it. American military advisors have given extensive logistical support to Saudi Arabia and coalition forces invading Yemen in so-called opposition to unverified claims that its long-time foe, Iran, is backing the Houthi movement. This includes guidance in the facilitation of torture in United Arab Emirates (UAE–controlled prisons in southern Yemen which are reminiscent of the CIA torture program most famously exposed during the Bush-era years of the War on Terror.[37]

If the U.S. really cared about human rights, it would not condemn Cuba, an island nation that has used its meagre resources to advance human rights, and support a country like Saudi Arabia, which has used its vast riches to do the exact opposite. It would not facilitate economic warfare on Cuba in the name of "human rights" and provide military assistance to Saudi Arabia in its brutal war on Yemen. The narrative that presumes the U.S. as the global guardian and protector of human rights is soaked in the blood of American exceptionalism and American innocence. Entire nations have been disrupted, devastated, and dehumanized as a result of America's "commitment" to "human rights." These wars serve as "grim reminders of the millions of bodies upon which the audacious smugness of American hubris is built."[38] However, war crimes in the name of "human rights" are "worth it" to the American ruling class regardless of how much they obliterate the very notion of international law. The American project to bring "democracy" and "human rights" to the world defines international law in its image. More to the point, international law doesn't apply to the U.S. at all. This means that the United States' self-proclaimed exceptionalism gives it the right to intervene wherever it wants and whenever it wants with absolute impunity.

The doctrine that the U.S. cares about human rights has rendered most Americans unable to challenge the lies that justify U.S. militarism. This can be seen in the small numbers of Americans who have opposed Washington's cries to "do something" about alleged uses of chemical weapons by the Syrian government, deemed by both Obama and Trump to be a "red line" that shall not be crossed. The long record of American imperial warfare abroad shows that concern for "human rights" is a mere public relations framework that facilitates public acceptance for wars of aggression that enrich American corporations, military contractors, and financial institutions. Part of this propaganda involves drawing a sharp contrast between *their* barbaric violence and *our* benevolent attempts to keep the peace. "A US President can declare a 'red line' against the alleged use of chemical weapons in Syria," observes Maximilian Forte, "while still using white phosphorus, depleted uranium, and various cluster munitions in the US weapons stockpile. Poisoned gas becomes the weapon of the 'uncivilized,' and the cruise missile the weapon of the 'civilized.'"[39]

To envision a new framework for human rights requires that American exceptionalism and innocence be exposed as governing ideologies of the United States' "human rights"–based foreign policy. Rather than centered on American domination, human rights must be centered on the people forsaken by the American quest for global domination. Human rights must be "people's centered" along the lines articulated by the US Human Rights Network. A "people's centered" approach to human rights is not based on guilt or the "white savior's" commitment to defining the existence of oppressed peoples and nations. Rather, the approach is rooted in the internationalism and global unity of the oppressed reflected throughout the history of the Black Freedom movement and the Cuban Revolution. It is up to us, the people, to imagine what a "people's centered" approach to human rights can look like today in the American context.[40] A good start would be for more Americans to realize how the twin evils of American exceptionalism and American innocence are inevitably geared toward turning them into devoted disciples of U.S. imperialism.

CHAPTER 15

"Humanitarian Impulses: The American Corporate Media and the White Savior Mentality"

"I do not need to be rescued by anyone, whether their underlying motive is driven by oil or feminism. As such, I have only one unequivocal demand of all 'liberators': Leave me alone. The only solidarity I am interested in seeing is the kind that throws a wrench in the war machine which occupies my homeland."

—S.R.—an Iraqi living in the United States[1]

"This world exists simply to satisfy the needs—including, importantly, the sentimental needs—of white people and Oprah."

—Teju Cole[2]

". . . no one colonizes innocently."3

—Aimé Césaire

In 2010, Jason Sadler had to give up his dream. He wanted to send T-shirts to Africa. One million of them to be exact. Sadler had never been to Africa and presumably had no academic or professional background in economics, but that didn't matter. He wouldn't let this lack of expertise get in the way. It was simply enough that he *cared*. But before readers start to feel too bad about this failed "humanitarian" mission to clothe (supposedly) naked Africans, better news arrived a few months later. It was then when Blake Mycoskie of TOMS Shoes gave plenty for the White Savior Industrial Complex to celebrate, as his "socially responsible" company sent its one millionth pair of shoes to Africa.

Sadler and Mycoskie are just two of many Western do-gooders featured in Richard Stupart's article, "7 Worst International Aid Ideas."[4] Putting aside the logistical, economic, and political problems involved in their pursuits, it's hard not to reflect on T. S. Eliot's words of wisdom. "Half the harm that is done in this world is due to people who want to feel important," he wrote. "They don't mean to do harm; but the harm does not interest them. Or they do not see it, or they justify it because they are absorbed in the endless struggle to think well of themselves." While we might hesitate to assign motives to people like Sadler and Mycoskie, it is not a stretch to see these aid efforts as another arm of U.S. imperialism. Despite their popularity among American shoppers, charities, and the U.S. corporate media outlets, we cannot overlook how these movements represent some of the "worst attempts at helping others since colonialism."[5]

An important but overlooked feature of American exceptionalism is not just the idea that the U.S. economy, government, or culture is exceptional. The ideology also maintains that the U.S. is made up of exceptional *citizens*. As Inderpal Grewal writes in her book, *Saving the Security State: Exceptional Citizens in Twenty-First-Century America*, "Under advanced neoliberal conditions in which inequality has resulted in protests and critiques of state welfare rollbacks, the US nation-state's exceptionalism has now moved to its citizens." Grewal thus helps us see clearly the link between American exceptionalism and American innocence. It is not just our elected officials and military personnel who are forces for good in the world, acting with the most benevolent of intentions. *It is individual Americans too.* "Instead of an exceptional nation," Grewal concludes, "there are exceptional citizens, and one way their exceptionalism is produced is through their participation in humanitarianism."[6]

The field of journalism is often thought of as a venue of humanitarianism where citizens help other citizens understand the world around them. Yet in America, the media has been called the fourth branch of the American government. A mere five corporations control 90 percent of the U.S. media. These monopolies, which include Time Warner, Disney, and Viacom, possess close ties with the American political and military apparatus. Former and current military officials dominate news airwaves, often serving as "terrorism experts" for networks like CNN, and corporate media journalists have become embedded in the American military. This symbiotic relationship between U.S. militarism and the corporate media is no coincidence. It's a typical quid pro quo partnership. On the one hand, the U.S. military helps boost ratings for news networks that are hungry for war. On the other hand, American corporate media outlets play an essential—and reliable—role in helping the American military establishment mold popular opinion and perceptions about the world we live in. It's a win-win situation for the war-makers and the opposite for all those who have lost their lives to war as a result of the relationship between corporate media and U.S. military.

American political and military officials have a vested interest in using the corporate media to achieve their interests. Corporate media outlets benefit from favorable legislative policies, such as the Telecommunications Act of 1996, that have increased their profitability through the easing of regulatory burdens on monopolization. The ultimate winner here is U.S. imperialism. The ideologies of American exceptionalism and American innocence are filtered through the corporate media in a repetitive and predictable manner. Corporate media outlets deceptively brand their news coverage as an assortment of "balanced" and "factual" perspectives. Americans are encouraged to digest MSNBC, FOX News, CNN, the *New York Times*, the *Wall Street Journal*, and yes, even NPR and PBS as the only sources of objective information. One will rarely—if ever—find voices on these outlets that critique capitalism, U.S. militarism, settler colonialism, anti-Blackness, the police, or the idea that the U.S. is a force for good in the world. Over the years, the American corporate media has been on the front lines of interpreting the endless imperial ventures of the U.S. around the world in ways that produce favorable—and profitable—outcomes for the American ruling class.

American corporate media outlets regularly interpret imperial ventures as "humanitarian" in scope. This interpretation promotes a savior mentality that turns war, imperial violence, and racism into charitable missions. According to Inderpal Grewal, international charitable organizations have become a $10 billion a year industry with connections to the largest corporations and the most powerful governments, mainly the United States.[7] Despite their nonprofit status and purportedly community-centered mission, these institutions are wedded to the corporate media in many ways, especially in regard to ideology. The relationship between the American nation-state, the corporate media, and "charity" is more aptly called the White Savior Industrial Complex. White-savior ideology is a direct outgrowth of the pervasiveness of the White Savior Industrial Complex.

The White Savior Industrial Complex is a modernized expression of American individualism and thus a direct product of the United States' racist and capitalist roots. In an article in the *Atlantic*, Teju Cole describes the White Savior Industrial Complex as "a valve for releasing the unbearable pressures that build in a system built on pillage."[8] White saviorism recruits Americans—and white Americans in particular—to resolve the guilt inevitably produced by the unbearable conditions that U.S. imperialism has wrought on the world with individual acts of charity funded and sponsored by the very agents responsible for the destruction. Acts of "charity" not only focus on individualized action over collective response but also tend to reinforce the United States' obsessive fear of racialized "others." The White Savior Industrial Complex uses charity to absolve the U.S. of responsibility for the conditions produced by this obsession. White guilt is the escape valve. "We can participate in the economic destruction of Haiti over long years," Cole writes, "but when the earthquake strikes it feels good to send $10 each to the rescue fund."[9]

American corporate media outlets have historically promoted white savior ideology in its coverage of major events relating to U.S. foreign policy. In the process, it has produced what Grewal calls "humanitarian citizenship." Humanitarian citizenship has its basis in post-World War II politics when American leadership in the global sphere required an institutionalized basis for the promotion of "values" that justified American domination abroad. In the neoliberal area, the corporate media transformed humanitarian citizenship into a paternalistic act where Americans and Westerners perform "good works" in nations where the U.S. has a vested interest in asserting its dominance.

Take the example of Malala Yousafzai. Yousafzai was awarded the Nobel Peace Prize in 2014 for her work detailing the atrocities she experienced from the Taliban. A young Pakistani girl, Yousafzai has become the corporate media's white savior subject. She has received *New York Times* documentaries, accolades, and funds from the West to forward her goal in bringing education to young girls in Pakistan and Afghanistan.[10] Neither Yousafzai nor her white savior backers in the corporate media raise the fact that it was the U.S. and the West that funded and armed the Mujahideen, the predecessor of the Taliban, to destroy the Soviet-supported Afghan government beginning in 1979. In fact, the Soviet-supported government of Afghanistan was not only secular but also committed to eradicating illiteracy and other educational hurdles imposed on young girls in the country. These efforts were in full effect prior to the proxy war that then-National Security Advisor Zbigniew Brzezinsky hoped would give "the USSR its own Vietnam War."[11] Yousafzai's backers within the White Savior Industrial Complex hail her stance against the Taliban as a worthy humanitarian cause, but have omitted the U.S. role in enabling the Taliban's rise, all in an attempt to maintain its image as the world's saviors.

Prior to Malala's rise to stardom, Grewal analyzed the popularity of the 2007 book *Three Cups of Tea* and its alignment with American imperial objectives in Afghanistan. The book details the author, Greg Mortenson, and his co-author's efforts to build schools in Afghanistan and Pakistan as a means to counter "Islamization." The book's popularity skyrocketed at the same time the U.S. military escalated a "surge" of bombings in these countries to ostensibly fight the Taliban. Grewal describes the *New York Times*' coverage of the book as a quintessential "narrative of the bravery, deprivation, and sentimentality of the heroic white man who eschews military solutions."[12] While the book itself projects Mortenson's "humanitarian" work as a civilizing mission—dehumanizing Pakistan and Afghan locals in the process—journalist Elisabeth Bullimer reveals the deep connections between the author and the U.S. military, including direct consultations with General Stanley McChrystal, the commander of American operations in Afghanistan at the time. *Three Cups of Tea* has since been discredited, not least because of Mortenson's connections with the military. Despite revelations that Mortenson's NGO, the Central Asia Institute, was found to have pocketed its donations by exaggerating the number of schools actually built in Afghanistan and Pakistan, Bullimer's article and other corporate news outlets continue to promote *Three Cups of Tea* as an example of a modern day "missionary" who risked his life to "civilize" the Native.

Three Cups of Tea is but one example where the American corporate media and white saviorism worked together to brand American empire as benevolent in scope. Little attention has been paid to the bombs the U.S. military has reigned down on Afghanistan and Pakistan or the United States' historic role in sowing instability in the region. The ideology of white saviorism has provided cover to the real interests of imperialism. Afghanistan is a resource-rich country with trillions of dollars worth of important minerals necessary to produce advanced technology in all sectors of the capitalist economy. American military officials have even admitted to the "stunning potential" of Afghanistan's wealth.[13] However, in case after case, the White Savior Industrial Complex has buried the real motivations for war under the guise of "good intentions." It isn't that these more sinister motivations have gone completely unreported—after all, it was the *New York Times* that reported on Afghanistan's mineral riches—but that Americans often find it hard to believe that such motivations could serve as the driving force behind their country's "humanitarian" missions abroad.

The White Savior Industrial Complex is the shovel that buries American imperial warfare in the graveyard of popular consciousness. Acts of charity help sooth the craving for Americans, especially white Americans, to feel exceptional and innocent in their relationship with the historical "other," the targets of imperialism. In the age of *corporate* social media, information disseminated by the ruling class reaches consumers at rapid speed. A social media campaign in 2012 harnessed the mass appeal that the White Savior Industrial Complex has engendered toward Africa. Started by the nonprofit group Invisible Children, the campaign involved the distribution of a video that accused the Lord's Resistance Army in Uganda of recruiting child soldiers. The video received 100 million viewers, many of whom were captivated by the urgent calls to capture Lord's Resistance Army leader Joseph Kony.

Invisible Children blamed Kony for the atrocities in Uganda with no mention of the broader political context in the country or the region as a whole. Nor did the organization explain what exactly gave it the right to resolve a political conflict in an African country. Invisible Children claimed legitimacy in the shadows by exploiting the ideological tools of the white-savior industrial complex. The *Kony 2012* video clearly projected Africa as a "heart of darkness" where inhabitants are incapable of mastering the attributes of Western civilization necessary to govern themselves. As a result, Americans and Westerners generally have no other choice but to force these attributes upon them. As Nerida Chazal and Adam Pocrnic explain,

> The western world and the US in particular were depicted as the saviours of the Kony story. At the end of the video we see the US sending in military support and technology to help the 'primitive' Ugandan army track down Kony in the vast and savage Ugandan jungle. These scenes employ

> the saviour metaphor by constructing Ugandans as primitive and in need of rescue by the strong, experienced and morally superior US. Similar savior references feature throughout the documentary as US activists declare: 'we are demanding justice'; 'we are going to do everything that we can to stop them. We are going to stop them'; 'we[are]committed to stop Kony and rebuild what he has destroyed'; 'if we succeed we change the course of human history' (Invisible Children 2012a).[14]

The demands for "justice" and to "do something" ignite the imperial and colonial flame lit by the corporate media. Invisible Children is but another NGO within the White Savior Industrial Complex that strategically exploited "humanitarian" impulses through the corporate media to justify American imperial policy. The organization repeatedly called for American and Western intervention but failed to mention that the Obama Administration waived the application of the Child Soldiers Prevention Act (2008) to select countries. "In other words," writes Sverker Finnström, "Obama claimed—and Invisible Children was actively silent on the matter—that child soldiers can be warranted as long as they are allies in the US-led war on terror. One might again ask what the slogan 'Stop at nothing' really means."[15]

Nor did Invisible Children mention that its lobbying efforts had already successfully pressured the Obama Administration to send troops to Uganda, not as a means to end atrocities but to secure oil.[16] American imperial support for the brutal Ugandan government of Yoweri Museveni, which has been linked to the genocide of over six million Congolese since 1996, has not precipitated any outrage from the Invisible Children lobby. This is no accident. The white-industrial complex relies upon the recruitment of donations from white Americans and Westerners, especially those with deep pocketbooks. It is hard to solicit donations from the wealthy if *their* government is accused of facilitating genocide. It's not something that arouses "good" feelings so it is better left unsaid. Humanitarian projects must reinforce the exceptionalism and innocence of the American imperial project or they are not worth supporting. Indeed, this is what Invisible Children meant in the Kony video when it stated "don't study history, make history."

Kony 2012 ended up being the most watched documentary in history. It galvanized millions to donate their money toward a supposedly humanitarian cause that in actuality covered up the true nature of American imperial ambitions in Africa. The White Savior Industrial Complex, however, does not merely cover up the exploitation and oppression inherent under U.S. imperialism. Enormous profits are reaped not only from the wars covered up by white saviorism but from the devastation it leaves behind. Naomi Klein calls the exploitation of tragedy for profit "disaster capitalism." More specifically, disaster capitalism is "the imposition of neoliberal economic policies through the exploitation of weakened states," a condition fitting for Haiti directly after the devastating earthquake of 2010.[17] The earthquake left the already vulnerable Haitian political, economic, and social system in ruin. But what was a disaster for the Haitian people was seen by the architects of the White Savior Industrial Complex as an opportunity for U.S. economic and political expansion.

Haiti is a prime case study into the formula used by the White Savior Industrial Complex to achieve dominance in the wake of destruction. The formula has three components:

1. The use of military intervention to secure American political dominance.
2. The enforcement of neoliberal economic policy to facilitate privatization and austerity measures.
3. The deployment of NGOs to manage American hegemony permanently through the usurpation of sovereign state power.

Following the earthquake, Haiti was known as the "NGO republic" due to the presence of anywhere between 3,000 and 10,000 NGOs operating within the country. NGOs were ostensibly present in Haiti to facilitate the distribution of "foreign aid" but instead reinforced the United States' historically imperial relationship with Haiti. Aid monies donated from the U.S. for emergency and reconstruction relief were funneled into American military and corporate investments. In fact, 75 cents of every dollar of the $379 million donated after the earthquake was invested into American NGOs. After providing a detailed list of U.S. firms and organizations that benefited from American "aid" projects to Haiti, Keir Forgie concludes, "Relatively speaking, the Haitian government and local businesses were almost entirely bypassed in the reconstruction of their own country, whereas the US received substantial capital investment."[18]

In other words, the White Savior Industrial Complex has created an ideological environment where the "good intentions" of NGOs were weaponized to facilitate the plunder of Haiti. It was the plunder of Haiti that gave wealthy white actors the opportunity to volunteer for NGOs and pose as "saviors" of the impoverished country. Yet white saviorism has coincided with an American-led occupation of Haiti that saw the deployment of tens of thousands of American soldiers and UN "peacekeepers" accused of spreading cholera to nearly a million people across the country. White saviorism also went hand in hand with the privatization of Haitian agriculture, mining, and construction industries. To make matters even worse, American-backed privatization has left hundreds of thousands of Haitians living in tents and the minimum wage in Haiti suppressed to a mere 24 cents an hour.[19]

American corporate media outlets have struggled to maintain the legitimacy of white saviorism in Haiti, mainly due to the exposure of Bill and Hillary Clinton's role in the looting of the country. The Clinton's record in Haiti hurt Hillary Clinton's popularity in the 2016 presidential election. WikiLeaks found that it was Hillary Clinton's State Department that prevented a minimum wage increase in Haiti. As president, her husband Bill supported right-wing death squads that helped engineer the second coup of Haitian President Jean Paul Aristide in 2004. Through the Clinton Foundation, Bill and Hillary Clinton accumulated billions of dollars worth in donations that were then siphoned to billionaire investors who built hotels and other profitable ventures at the expense of poor Haitians. The exposure of the Clinton Foundation produced a rupture in the legitimacy of the White Savior Industrial Complex in Haiti. Even Oxfam has come under recent fire for allowing aid workers to commit sexual acts in exchange for participation in the organization's food program.[20]

Still, the corporate media has paid scant attention to the Clinton-sponsored plunder of Haiti. Corporate media inattention to U.S.-made humanitarian disasters is often complemented by incessant attention to humanitarian interventions led by the U.S. For example, when NATO bombed Yugoslavia in 1999 ostensibly to prevent "ethnic-cleansing," the *New York Times* devoted nearly 18 percent of its daily coverage to the issue to ensure that Americans were not privy to the hundreds of thousands of dead and displaced civilians caused by the NATO bombings. By the end of the bombings, Virgil Hawkins observes, "The damage had already been done . . . by the extensive and misleading media coverage, and the 'do something syndrome' came into full effect."[21] While the *Times* covered up U.S.-led NATO atrocities in Yugoslavia, it virtually ignored the burgeoning humanitarian crisis in the Democratic Republic of the Congo, devoting less than 1 percent of its international coverage to the millions that have perished due to constant war. Such a gap in media coverage demonstrates that the corporate media reflects not the welfare of nations around the world, but rather the agenda set by U.S. political and military officials serving the rich and the powerful. The White Savior Industrial Complex masks this agenda behind the veil of humanitarianism.

The United States possesses plenty of contradictions within its own borders that further call the legitimacy of the White Savior Industrial Complex into question. The devastation that Hurricane Katrina leveled on the lower 9th ward of New Orleans in 2004 is case in point.[22] Hundreds of thousands of poor Black Americans were left displaced from their home without the possibility of return and thousands of public housing units were destroyed. The conditions that Hurricane Katrina left in its wake gave the U.S. little room to espouse exceptionalism. Hurricane Katrina made it clear that the American imperial apparatus was not constructed to serve the interests of the majority Black and poor city of New Orleans. American corporate media thus had a difficult time promoting the "humanitarianism" so characteristic of the United States' responses to so-called international crises. The Bush Administration's leadership over the Federal Emergency Management Agency (FEMA) allowed media images to surface of Black families trapped on top of their homes and their drowned bodies afloat in the flooded 9th ward. American corporate media outlets interpreted the disaster in a number of ways to avoid challenging the role of the state and its capitalist infrastructure in the devastation. Many corporate journalists framed the disaster as a rare American loss in a war with "nature" while others blamed "poor government responsiveness."[23]

However, American corporate media outlets could not avoid the fact that many Americans—especially the Black community hit hardest by what had transpired—would view such emergency responses as lackluster. Not surprisingly, criticisms by media pundits emerged which centered on neoliberal logics of American exceptionalism. White reporters employed by corporate news outlets were framed as heroes going into the heart of a disaster to question how such a devastating event could ever happen in the U.S. Inderpal Grewal cites Anderson Cooper's Hurricane Katrina coverage as indicative of this phenomenon. Cooper was portrayed as a hero who took government officials to task, exclaiming that "I never thought I'd see this in America—the dead left out like trash."[24] His coverage led to a 400 percent increase in CNN's viewership. Many journalists echoed Cooper's sentiments by comparing the tragedy to something more akin to something seen in Somalia and Iraq.

By painting the scene of Hurricane Katrina as a product of villainous government officials exposed by heroic journalists of the American corporate media, the weapon of American exceptionalism was once again being drawn to make up for the complete lack of a "savior" narrative to explain the carnage. Rather than view the events of Katrina as indicative of a structural crisis, the U.S. once again addressed the issue in the context of reform. Irresponsible government officials glossed over the fact that American corporations abandoned vital telecommunications infrastructure during the storm to ensure that rescue for thousands was impossible. Militarized American police forces prevented poor Black Americans from escaping to the white, wealthier neighborhoods that were protected from Katrina's excesses. In other words, the entire apparatus of U.S. imperialism was responsible for the utter neglect and suffering imposed upon the mostly Black victims of Hurricane Katrina.[25]

That the American system of imperialism wasn't blamed by the very corporate agents responsible for its propogation is nothing new. More concerning is the effectiveness of the neoliberal narrative of heroism and faith in American reform that still exists among many Americans today. These aspects of U.S. exceptionalism help bail out the system of imperialism in moments of crises. Faith in American heroism and reform opened the door for the corporate media to criminalize Black Americans starved of resources for taking what they could from stores and businesses. Blacks were depicted as unworthy pariahs partaking in "uncivilized" behavior. Their desperate struggle to survive became a criminal act against the U.S. state. In times of crisis, faith in the U.S. state to protect "freedom" and enact reform condemns and dehumanizes the racialized "other." Katrina opened gaping wounds in society and required Black Americans to be framed as enemies of the state so that the U.S., which is built upon anti-Black racism, could maintain its hero image in a moment where it was difficult to do so. Such racialized criminalization inherent to American exceptionalism ultimately led to the permanent displacement of a large percentage of New Orleans' Black community and the complete privatization of the city's school system, a development that led President Obama's Secretary of Education Arne Duncan to declare Hurricane Katrina "the best thing that happened to the education system in New Orleans."

The humanitarian impulses of American exceptionalism serve the empire's rulers, not its victims. American exceptionalism, however, also gives the U.S. sole responsibility for civilizing the world's "darker" nations. The darker nations of the world uncoincidentally happen to be the primary centers of profit for the American ruling class. American "humanitarian" efforts in locations as close as New Orleans and as far as Uganda have thus come at the expense of poor and the oppressed people who have been dispossessed of half of the world's wealth which currently sits in the coffers of just six individuals.[26] American exceptionalism and American innocence gave birth to the White Savior Industrial Complex and represent the first line of defense against opposition to the actual impact of American "humanitarianism." They create the ideological conditions for issues like unequal wealth distribution, poverty, and war to be ignored, despite the central role the U.S. plays in their proliferation. Even worse, the widely held belief that corporate media outlets, corporations, or NGOs are primarily interested in the welfare of people around the world makes it increasingly difficult for Americans to accept the reality that in fact the opposite is true. In other words, hardly is it ever addressed that the U.S. and its "humanitarian" backers cause the very humanitarian disasters they purport to fix.

So when celebrities such as 50 Cent and Bono latch on to the latest "humanitarian" effort in Africa on behalf of some corporation or foundation, it is important to remember *who* and *what* actually benefits from what may appear on the surface as pure charity. When TOMS corporation gives a pair of shoes to African children for every pair purchased, we should remember that the corporation is profiting from—and contributing to—the impoverishment of African nations that in no way can be resolved by "dumping a pair of shoes in places where people otherwise might be employed to make them."[27] The real question that arises from American imperial "humanitarianism" is this: Why do so many American leaders and institutions consistently refuse to see that so many of the problems they're trying to solve are the problems that *they themselves created*? When corporate media darling Angelina Jolie, for example, says that "the conflict in Iraq" is "the source of so much Iraqi suffering to this day," and also claims to be "a proud American," it should raise a few eyebrows.

And when she further proclaims that "a strong nation, like a strong person, helps others to rise up and be independent," we should be even more alarmed. As journalist Belén Fernández notes in response, "Never mind that the US—a strong nation indeed—happens to have effectively destroyed Iraq, inflicting unquantifiable death and misery upon the Iraqi people."[28]

Narratives of American exceptionalism and American innocence attempt to convince "exceptional citizens" living in the U.S. that the world's crises are caused by *someone else.* And they believe that these problems are fixed by charitable donations, documentaries, celebrity-organized concerts, and bombs dropped on the "uncivilized" so that they learn to recognize the error of their ways. Furthermore, many Americans believe that simply by being born in the U.S. or by being white, or by attending an American university, that they have a unique, God's-eye perspective as to how other countries should be governed. As African feminist Ifi Amadiume describes in her story about encountering a well-meaning university student:

> I asked a young White woman why she was studying social anthropology. She replied that she was hoping to go to Zimbabwe, and felt that she could help women there by advising them how to organize. The Black women in the audience gasped in astonishment. Here was someone scarcely past girlhood, who had just started university and had never fought a war in her life. She was planning to go to Africa to teach female veterans of a liberation struggle how to organize! This is the kind of arrogant, if not absurd attitude we encounter repeatedly. It makes one think: Better the distant armchair anthropologists than these 'sisters.'[29]

Such hubris is commonly found among many U.S. college students, prompting Maximilian Forte to outline some questions he asks his students who want to change the world: "Do you really have any special skills to offer other than the ability to articulate good intentions? Has your assistance been requested by those who would presumably benefit from it? How well do you understand a different society that you can permit yourself to undertake potentially transformative action?"[30] Theologian William Cavanaugh takes this a step further and explains why he would never be invited to deliver a U.S. college commencement address. "Please *don't* go out and change the world," he would tell the graduates. "The world has had enough of well-meaning middle class university graduates from the U.S. going out and trying to change the world and the world is dying because of it . . . go home."[31]

U.S. humanitarianism is therefore not part of the *solution* to the world's problems. It is part of the *problem*. Thus, true revolutionary social change will not come from the generous donations of former presidents, poverty awareness campaigns by Hollywood celebrities, or American university graduates with a degree in international economics. As Maximiliam Forte tells his students, "It is important not to assume that others are simply waiting for a stranger to come and lead them, like a Hollywood tale of the usual white messiah who is always the hero of other people's stories." In fact, true change will not come from the U.S. ruling class at all.[32] Charity will not bring justice. Capitalism cannot bring justice. Capitalism *is* injustice. It is the *problem*.[33] Justice requires the very dismantling of the systems upon which the ruling class finds its ultimate reason for existing. This is a tough pill to swallow for Hollywood celebrities, CNN correspondents, and the board of the Clinton Foundation. After all, if their lives, emotions, perceptions, and ways of "being the world" depend on systems of capitalism, militarism, and white supremacy, then they would never wish to bring about their own demise. The ruling class depends on American exceptionalism and American innocence to paint the system it presides over as the savior of humanity, which is why any hope that this class will bring about its own demise is futile. We must place our hope in a new humanitarian impulse not guided by NGOs that take funds from the U.S. government or U.S. corporations. Oppressed people need their own self-funded institutions, including media, that offer a new vision and path toward a more equitable and just society. Deconstructing the humanitarian impulses of the deadly ideologies of American exceptionalism and American innocence is a necessary starting point toward these ends.

CHAPTER 16

"If It's Bad, Blame Russia"

"Governments and societies of exceptionalist states develop a need to have external enemies; for this reason, threats are often concocted or, where minor, are inflated to extreme proportions."

—K. J. Holsti[1]

"We will never escape the material underpinnings of historical knowledge production. But by investigating the marketplaces of remembering that give shape and meaning to American cultural memory of the past, we can deconstruct the narratives with which Americans have made and remade identity as fundamentally innocent."

—Boyd Cothran[2]

"Brutality, torture, and excess should be understood as an essential element of American statecraft, not its corruption or deviation."

—Dylan Rodriguez[3]

Our chapters up until this point have analyzed the ways in which American exceptionalism and innocence have legitimated the American capitalist empire at every stage of its development. American exceptionalism has formed the backbone of the white supremacist and capitalist ideology of the U.S. imperial project. American innocence is a trusted ideological partner to exceptionalist ethos that washes away all guilt and accountability for the project's massive crimes. Ideologies of exceptionalism and innocence bestow upon the U.S. imperial project a sense of "goodness" that Americans, especially white Americans, can be proud of. Because of the American way of life's essential "goodness," many Americans feel they do not have to concern themselves with the terror and havoc that their government has spread all around the globe. More than a few Americans even claim ignorance to the endless wars the U.S. wages worldwide or the ubiquity of racism within American borders. After all, it is difficult to name such evils when these wars are popularly framed as "humanitarian" interventions, "revolutions," or just plain "forgotten." You cannot fight what you cannot name.

However, the American imperial project is not an invincible force. Prior systems of societal organization have collapsed and been replaced. American exceptionalism and innocence have sought to render this reality invisible. While these ideologies reify the imperial project, they cannot resolve the inherent contradictions of the system and the crises these contradictions produce. Maybe no other development exemplifies this more than the ongoing hysteria about Russia that has captured the full attention of the American imperial project.

Since the inauguration of Donald Trump, one of the most talked about stories in the American corporate media and the Washington political establishment has been Russia's alleged interference in the 2016 elections. The allegations came at a tumultuous period for the American imperial project. On the international front, American imperial power has been most starkly challenged by Russia and China. Chinese economic activity in Africa, Asia, and Latin America has threatened U.S. economic dominance and prompted a massive buildup of American military power in Africa and the Asia Pacific through the "pivot to Asia" and AFRICOM. Russia has also experienced a political and economic revival of late. Its intervention to protect the integrity of the Syrian government from the machinations of U.S. warfare in 2015 sent a strong message to the U.S. that Russia will no longer tolerate the instability and subservience imposed on the country after the fall of the Soviet Union in 1991. Putin's tenure as Russian head of state has also led to a more independent Russian economy. Russia has grown closer to China and further away from the American and European orders that celebrated the fall of the Soviet Union, an event that Putin has called the "greatest political catastrophe" of the 20th century.

Concern about the newfound political and economic independence of the Russian Federation has been discussed openly by the American ruling class. An array of studies from the RAND corporation and the Pentagon have warned of the dangers presented by the rise of Russia and China to American hegemony.

Former Secretary of Defense for the Trump Administration James Mattis cited "great power confrontation" with Russia and China as the primary challenge to American interests in the United States' latest National Security Strategy.[4] However, it was Obama's Administration that dramatically escalated tensions with Russia. His two terms saw the immense expansion of the North Atlantic Treaty Organization (NATO) along Russia's borders despite the United States' promise not to expand NATO's presence in Eastern Europe during negotiations with Russia in 1990. These imperial maneuvers on the part of Obama culminated in the 2014 coup in Ukraine that brought a Nazi-aligned government to the Russian border and the world to the brink of war.

On the domestic front, the American imperial project faced a similar level of turmoil. This turmoil rose to the surface all at once during the 2016 presidential race. Billionaire arch-racist Donald Trump defeated each and every establishment Republican candidate by a wide margin by ramping up right-wing, racist American orthodoxy combined with hardline positions against corporate free-trade agreements and "regime-change" wars. Hillary Clinton, the presumed favorite to become the first woman president of the U.S., struggled to defeat the wildly popular Bernie Sanders in the Democratic primary while exercising her connections in the Democratic National Committee (DNC) to ensure that the Vermont Senator's popular policy positions of single-payer health care, student loan forgiveness, and living wage employment would not have a chance to face up against the politics of Donald Trump in the general election.

Many Democrats and Republicans believed that Hillary Clinton was the most likely candidate to defeat Donald Trump despite polls that showed Sanders winning a general election by a wider margin than Clinton. Analysts of the ruling class instead depended on polls that suggested Clinton was a shoo-in for president. These polls ignored several inconvenient truths about the 2016 election, such as the fact that WikiLeaks had done irreparable damage to Clinton's reputation by releasing information from her email server that revealed her role in the DNC conspiracy against Bernie Sanders and her long list of high-paid speeches for Wall Street. Clinton increasingly looked like a candidate for war and Wall Street while the American corporate media gave her opponent Donald Trump billions of dollars worth of coverage in an attempt to paint the billionaire as an outsider with little credentials to hold presidential office.

Little could the American imperial project predict that these conditions would push voters to view the Clinton versus Trump option as no option at all.[5] Non-voters in the 2016 general election represented the largest voting bloc.[6] This gave the Republican Party and Donald Trump the edge necessary to win the electoral college and, as a result, the presidency. The loss sent shockwaves through the entire U.S. imperial apparatus, not just the Democratic Party. Trump embarrassed a large portion of the ruling class, with many corporate media outlets comparing him to Hitler or calling him America's own Hugo Chavez. A calculated decision was made to rid of the embarrassment by portraying Trump as a dupe of Russia, first to exonerate Clinton of accountability in her electoral loss and then to achieve broader bipartisan objectives with Trump in office.

The Trump-Russia connection story began with Trump's campaign promise to ease relations with Russia. When WikiLeaks dumped private emails written by Clinton on an unsecure server in July of 2016, Trump applauded the whistleblower organization. A plethora of Clinton supporters in the U.S. intelligence departments began to question whether Trump, WikiLeaks, and Russia were working together to undermine American "democracy," defined here as Clinton's surefire victory. This alone should have caused outrage among Americans struggling to survive under a political system that even former President Jimmy Carter has called an oligarchy.[7] That such outrage never occurred demonstrates how deeply the ideology of American innocence has penetrated the American psyche. Sure, a good number of Americans were disillusioned by the trajectory of the 2016 elections up until this point. Severe damage had been done to the Clinton campaign for stealing the Democratic primary from Bernie Sanders. And Sanders gained popularity in large part because the "billionaire class" (as Sanders puts it) had been exposed for using its fortunes to buy politicians and control the policies of all three branches of government. Still, few if any Americans mustered open condemnation of the emerging narrative that placed Russia at the forefront of a conspiracy to undermine an American "democracy" that worked only for the rich.

Clinton's campaign was thus afforded the political space to masquerade as the embodiment of democracy. It followed up on the simmering suspicions of Russian subversion by incorporating the allegations into her campaign talking points. Clinton posted questions on her website such as "Why is Trump encouraging Russia to interfere in our election?"[8] The FBI, CIA, and the NSA responded to Clinton's questions of Russian interference with the launch of an investigation into whether Russia interfered in the election to Trump's benefit. The investigation remains ongoing.

So much has happened since the investigation was set into motion that negates the claim of Russia's responsibility for Trump's victory. What we know is that as early as April 2016, the Clinton campaign had paid Fusion GPS, the corporation responsible for the "Steele Dossier," to find links between Russia and Trump.[9] Former intelligence agent Christopher Steele was a paid Clinton informant. Using his connections to American intelligence agencies, Steele paid sources to concoct the unverified narrative that Putin had "blackmailed" Trump by videotaping his salacious activities in Russia. Trump's foreign policy advisor Carter Page was then accused of collaborating with Russian diplomats by promising to ease sanctions in exchange for the "Russian hack" of the DNC. These allegations have been promoted as fact by American intelligence and corporate media channels despite the complete absence of evidence.

Allegations of Russia "hacking" or "interfering" in the 2016 elections have become a criminal indictment in and of themselves. The CIA and its allies claim Trump was blackmailed by Russia, but evidence seems to suggest the opposite. As Dan Kovalik explains,

> . . . it was not the Russians who came to Trump to tell him that they had incriminating evidence on him, as any blackmailer would do. No, it was the CIA—who we know wants to pressure Trump into staying on the path toward confrontation with Russia—that not only went to Trump about the allegedly incriminating evidence on him, but also went to a number of other government officials and the public to let them know about this "evidence."[10]

Obama's CIA director John Brennan led the charge in "warning" Trump to withdraw his campaign promise to ease relations with Russia. Brennan's CIA then became the chief distributor of the "Russia interference" story to the the media, Trump, and the general public. Heads of the other sixteen American intelligence agencies joined the chorus, including Obama's Director of National Intelligence James Clapper. That Clapper, Brennan, or the CIA could be considered trustworthy sources of information speaks to the level of credibility of the Russia investigation. Clapper has consistently lied under oath about the illegal spying conducted by the NSA on American citizens.[11] Brennan has defended torture as useful "harsh interrogation techniques."[12] And the CIA's long record of lying to the American public about the dangers of "communism" helped the agency facilitate deadly wars and coups in Asia, Africa, and Latin America, including the assassination of Salvador Allende in Chile in 1973. This coup alone led to the death and disappearance of tens of thousands of Chileans and the full privatization of the economy.

Chile is not the only victim of U.S. foreign meddling, particularly in Latin America. Billions of American tax dollars have been poured into "soft power" NGOs such as the National Endowment for Democracy (NED). NED has a long history of using its influence to stop democracy in its tracks. It helped undermine the democratic Sandinista movement in Nicaragua in 1990 after the CIA had for years sponsored "contra" mercenaries to sow violent discord throughout the country.[13] NED also provided millions of dollars to the right-wing opposition in Venezuela responsible for the short-lived 2002 coup of democratically elected Hugo Chavez.[14] Indeed, as Stephen Kinzer notes, NED labeled Russia a "priority country" in 2013, meaning that it topped the list of nations that the U.S. wants to overthrow by way of its electoral process. Despite no shortage of evidence, American liberals and Democratic Party faithfuls are often ignorant of the United States' long history of subverting democracy around the world. And when they are aware, their conclusions are steeped in the ideology of American innocence that presumes their government's destruction of democratic movements and elections abroad is paved with "good intentions."

"Good intentions" are almost never coupled with the evidence necessary to justify the disastrous conditions produced by American meddling. In the case of Russia, the U.S. is supposedly defending democracy through its investigation of Putin's alleged role in Trump's victory. However, the hardly reliable intelligence sources leading the Russia investigation have admitted that little evidence exists to prove their claims of Russian interference in the 2016 election. A "National Intelligence Estimate" report devised mainly by the CIA, FBI, and NSA directly after Trump's inauguration in January of 2017 began to backtrack from the story that Russia "hacked" the DNC and pivoted to a narrative that blamed Russian media such as *Russia Today* (*RT*) for contributing to "the [2016 election] campaign by serving as a platform for Kremlin messaging to Russian and international audiences."[15] This report, widely claimed as the most irrefutable evidence of Russian interference, states that "the types of systems Russian actors targeted or compromised were not involved in vote tallying."[16] Even when U.S. security officials testified in June of 2017 that unverified "Russians" backed by the Russian government hacked election systems in 21 states, no evidence was found to suggest that their actions affected the final results.[17]

So if Trump's supposed collusion with Russia is based on unproven allegations that ultimately had no effect on the outcome of the 2016 elections, then why has such a large section of the American ruling class continued its nonstop investigation of the matter? Between February 20th and March 31st, 2017, MSNBC's Rachel Maddow spoke of Russian "collusion" with Trump for 53 percent of her broadcasts.[18] It could be argued that even a cursory study of the American corporate news media generally may yield an even larger percentage focused on the Russia election story. The cacophonous obsession with Russia on the part of the American ruling class has continued ultimately because of its contemporary usefulness. In the absence of its preferred presidential candidate, the U.S. imperial project has successfully carried out its domestic and foreign policy objectives while Americans set their gaze on an unverified Russian "threat" to American "democracy."

Blaming Russia for undermining so-called American democracy has given the U.S. a convenient foe to justify its military expansion worldwide. If everything "bad" is Russia's fault, then the U.S. is the only force of "good" available in the world. Russia has been labeled a "bad country" not only for its alleged interference in the 2016 U.S. presidential elections. Americans are also repeatedly told that Russia is "bad" because it imprisons journalists, oppresses the LGBTQ community, and poisons former intelligence operatives in other countries (see the Skripal case). These accusations have either gone unverified or exaggerated for political aims; and even if they were true, their impact would pale in comparison to the war crimes that the U.S. has committed in Iraq alone. Since 2004, it is estimated that 2.4 million Iraqis have been killed as a result of the U.S. invasion of Iraq in 2003. Yet we are told that "bad" Russian meddling is the reason why Trump was forced by Congress in 2017 to sign a "good" military budget larger than the one even he proposed, with billions added in military operations along the Russian border to "deter Russian aggression." "Bad" Russian meddling also led to a unanimous Congressional vote to renew "good" sanctions, forcing Trump to renew sanctions against

Russia and North Korea and impose new ones on Iran. American military encroachments, whether in the form of murdering Russian pilots in Syria or moving American military installations closer and closer to the Russian border, are thus "good policies" seeking to punish a "bad" Russia regardless of the fact that such an orientation threatens human existence with a new world war of nuclear proportions.

What is important to realize, however, is that when it comes to war, there really is no contest between the U.S. and Russia (or China). The U.S. is hands down the most violent war-maker in human history. This means that punishing Russia is not the only consequence of the Russia blame game. Some authors and activists such as the late William Blum have characterized the United States' obsession with Russia as a new Cold War. The war has two fronts. The first is international in scope. Demonizing Russia prepares the American public for another war abroad, this time with a foe in possession of an equal if not greater nuclear capacity than the American military. The second front of the new Cold War is domestic. Casting blame on Russia for what transpired during the 2016 presidential election has also led to a counterinsurgency war against dissent similar to the first Cold War.

Unlike the first Cold War, which targeted the very real threat of communist movements replacing the capitalist order worldwide, the new Cold War has been brought about by a crisis in American exceptionalism. The Democratic Party has led the charge against Russia and used the Putin-led menace to blame everyone but itself for Hillary Clinton's embarrassing loss to Trump. Russians have been accused of buying $50,000 in social media ads to spur the Black Lives Matter and environmental movements. *Sputnik News* and *Russia Today* (*RT*) have been forced to register as "foreign agents." Thirteen anonymous Russians have been blamed for "sowing discord" in the U.S. political system, mainly through social media. Radical voices and formations such as the Green Party have been censored and silenced as a result, with Google and Facebook promptly changing their algorithms to make left-wing media increasingly difficult for internet users to find. All of this has been done in the name of countering Russian-backed "fake news." As Matt Taibbi writes of the January 2017 National Intelligence Estimate report on Russian interference, the report

> "assessed" that Russians were behind the hacks of the Democratic National Committee. The conclusion among other things was based upon the

> security agencies' interpretation of programming on the Russian-backed channel RT. RT stories about 100% American protests against fracking, surveillance abuses, and "alleged Wall Street greed," were part of "Russian strategic messaging" campaigns, the intelligence analysts insisted.[19]

These claims successfully demonized WikiLeaks as an agent of Russia and blamed Hillary Clinton's loss on progressive and radical voices, including Bernie Sanders. Forget that WikiLeaks uncovered the Clinton campaign's attacks on Sanders through its connections with the DNC, or that WikiLeaks revealed that the CIA has copied the cyber techniques of hackers all over the world and has the capabilities of using these techniques against targeted individual or state entities.[20] We should also forget that Clinton has a long history of supporting racism and austerity, calling Black American males "super predators" in her defense of Bill Clinton's massive escalation of mass Black imprisonment and playing an instrumental role in gutting welfare in the mid-1990s. Finally, forget that Clinton received millions of dollars from despotic dictators in Saudi Arabia and financiers on Wall Street in exchange for peddling wars abroad and supporting Wall Street–friendly policies. Accusations of a Putin plot successfully influencing the 2016 elections in Trump's favor to "embarrass" the American political system on the world stage have effectively shifted blame for Clinton's loss and the crisis of the American political system onto a foreign actor. The truth is that our nation's "democracy" has always been a cleverly hidden embarrassment as far as humanity is concerned.

The crisis of the American political system is really a crisis of American exceptionalism. Trump did not win the popular vote, yet the Clinton campaign refused to criticize the undemocratic electoral college system and Republican Party-led voter fraud for its loss. Nor did it reflect on the reasons for low voter turnout. Trump's occupation of the oval office signaled a deep loss of popular faith in the American political system that the American ruling class could not afford to question. The American imperial project relies on projections of exceptionalism to justify its rule but has nothing to offer the great majority of people around the world. Trump's opponents in Washington have scantily criticized the billionaire for his overt racism and xenophobia that has understandably sparked outrage among millions of Americans. These attributes are less worthy of condemnation and impeachment than Trump's expressed closeness to Russia. Administrative appointments such as Michael

Flynn have found themselves quickly ousted due to alleged conversations with Russian diplomats yet Trump's opposition in Washington have failed to muster the same excitement when it comes to the president's assault on people of color.

It isn't as if there aren't innumerable qualities about Trump that understandably prompt mass outrage. His racist demagoguery toward immigrants, his dangerous provocations toward the DPRK, and his heinous comments about women are all reasons to condemn the rule of the billionaire real estate magnate who has made his fortune exploiting workers. While superficial commentary has been made by the American ruling class on these issues, Trump has received the embrace of his elite opponents when he has fallen in line with the American establishment. For example, following one of his first speeches to Congress that saw Trump pay tribute to the family of a Navy SEAL who died in a raid in Yemen, CNN's liberal darling Van Jones commented that Trump "became President of the United States in that moment, period." When Trump ordered missile strikes on a Syrian airbase in April of 2017, MSNBC's Brian Williams praised Trump for using his "beautiful weapons" while others called the act of war his most "presidential" moment since winning the election. The American ruling class has thus created a path for Trump to escape the torrent of criticism he has received since taking office. As long as Trump keeps fueling the U.S. war machine, everyone in the establishment is happy. Even still, the American ruling class refuses to drop the Russia story lest it be forced to confront the dwindling faith in the American political system among the masses. Avoiding such a confrontation is something every millionaire politician in Washington can agree on.

The more the so-called Russia scandal distracts from the real issues affecting Americans, the less Americans trust the U.S. political system. Russia has become the object of elite opposition to Trump as a last ditch effort to reinforce the worldview that America's inherent exceptionalism is in fact under attack from an external foe that has placed a "Manchurian candidate" in the White House. For example, scapegoating Russia helps justify the consolidation of the American imperial project under the leadership of its military and intelligence apparatuses. The World Socialist Website recently conducted a study of Democratic Party candidates in the 2018 midterm elections and found that former State Department, military, and national security intelligence operatives made up one quarter of all Democratic Party challengers for

Congress.[21] The gradual takeover of the U.S. apparatus by military and intelligence elites ostensibly points to the continuation of American hysteria over Russia for years to come. This has become all the more necessary in a political context where the Democratic Party is unable to offer poor and oppressed people any alternatives to corporate and imperial rule. Ruthless austerity, endless war, and draconian state repression have become staples of Democratic Party policy, leaving it with nothing but the tools of the old Cold War to maintain legitimacy with American voters.

Democratic Party-led attempts to revive American exceptionalism at the expense of Russia have relied on the ideology of American innocence as an escape route from accountability. "Evil" Russians lurk in every corner of American life in the new Cold War, similar to the "evil" communists of the old Cold War. Russians undermine American elections, spark social unrest and instability, and aggressively wage war on American institutions. They are to blame for the decline of American exceptionalism, even if the specific "evils" Russia is accused of perpetrating are staples of American domestic and foreign policy. The U.S. has undermined countless elections around the world, including the 1996 presidential election in Russia. It has caused instability both domestically and around the world through the levers of free market capitalist economics and military invasion. U.S. liberals tend to be the most offended by this claim, accusing such "defenders of the Kremlin" of engaging in a distracting game of "what-about-ism." When media pundits are forced to entertain this objection, the nation's long history of meddling in other countries' elections is justified in a number of ways. The U.S. meddled for that country's own good, they say. Or, if the devastating conditions produced by U.S. meddling become public, then the operation was nothing but a mistake made with the best of intentions. It is impossible, though, for Russia to have good intentions. If *they* meddle, it's to execute some sinister plan. Yet the U.S. has aggressively waged war, whether on undocumented immigrants, Black Americans, its own Indigenous populations, or nations around the world (like Russia) to secure economic and political dominance worldwide for centuries. When it comes to the "evil" Russia narrative, the ideology of American innocence functions to reinforce the sanctity of American citizenship whereby identifying as "American" means that the U.S. could never be blamed for the embarassing results of the 2016 elections or the historical conditions that precipitated them.

The new and old Cold wars have promoted American citizenship as the leading force for "good" on the political stage. "Evil" is defined by imperial script writers. Russians play the "evil" role in the new Cold War, replacing the communists of the old Cold War. According to Tony Perruci, "The Communist was always seen to be acting, while the anti-Communist American was transparently truthful. The American citizen, constituted in noble sincerity, refused mimesis and instead inhabited an authentic citizenship. So strong was the belief in the anti-Communist honesty, that the fictionalized film adaptation of professional informer Matt Cvetic's memoir, *I Was a Communist for the FBI* (1951), was nominated for a Best Documentary Oscar in 1951."[22] The equation of anti-communism with "authentic" American citizenship allowed the U.S. to villainize Black freedom fighters, Communist Party leaders, and just about anyone who challenged American imperial domestic and foreign policy in the mid-20th century. Deportations, arrests, and executions for alleged communist sympathies were commonplace. In the mid-20th century, U.S. imperialism was on a rampage of expansion around the world. Communism was depicted as an even greater evil than imperialism, thus rendering the criminally racist structures of Jim Crow and imperial warfare invisible at best or critically important anti-communist crusades at worst. The replacement of communists with Russians beginning in 2016 comes at a time when the American ruling class needs an "inauthentic" non-citizen to blame for the misery it has imposed on the planet. And like the first Cold War, this has led to the suppression of radical political alternatives and the expansion of dangerous wars that masquerade as crusades against the great Russian "threat" to American civilization.

The new Cold War has indeed captured the consciousness of many progressives and even those who consider themselves radicals. Corporate media headlines regularly include terms like "Putin's Russia" and "authoritarian Russia." Social movements such as Black Lives Matter have been portrayed as dupes of Russia just as the Black Freedom and Labor movements were seen as dupes of the Soviet Union in the 20th century. Thus, the development of a radical imagination that can chart a course out of the desperate attempts to revive American exceptionalism is of critical importance. We need look no further than Paul Robeson for guidance as to how to begin the process.

Paul Robeson was a member of the Communist Party USA. A widely popular Black actor and singer, Robeson came under severe attack from the anti-communist House Committee of Un-American Activities (HUAC). What FBI Director J. Edgar Hoover described as Robeson's "extreme advocacy of the independence movements of the colonial peoples of Africa" led to the State Department revocation of his passport and his exclusion from the music/film industry. However, such repression only reaffirmed Robeson's internationalist and anti-racist principles rather than alter them. Gerald Horne recounts Robeson's testimony in a 1948 hearing accusing the Black radical of "communist subversion" of the United States:

> Robeson admitted what could not be denied. He had travelled to Moscow: "I was there for over a period say between '34 and '37, two weeks, three weeks, three months . . ." And he refused to back down from his bedrock opinion: "I found in Russia," he maintained, "complete absence of racial prejudice." This was "the first time in my life, Senator," he argued, "that I was able to walk the earth with complete dignity as a human being."[23]

Indeed, Robeson had not only traveled to the Soviet Union, but he had also enrolled his children to attend school in the "evil" communist country.[24] His principled stance in defense of the Soviet Union and against the American racist and imperial state was not received well. Robeson was called the "Black Stalin" by the Truman Administration. While the Russia of today is not the Soviet Union, Robeson's example remains relevant. Robeson asked the American working class and poor, especially Black Americans, why the Soviet Union should be their enemy when America's own version of apartheid and war was creating desperate conditions all around the world. He also refused to answer questions regarding his affiliations with communists or the Communist Party, seeing them as illegitimate attempts to criminalize the righteous resistance of the people. The context of U.S. imperialism in 2016 may differ in form from the period of 1948, but the underlying structure is the same. Both Paul Robeson and his wife Eslanda's courage and commitment to transnational solidarity provide important lessons for those wanting to resist the new Cold War of the present.[25]

Like the Robesons, we should challenge the American imperial project's obsession with labeling Russia as "evil" when it is the "evils" of the U.S. system that created the need to blame Russia in the first place. And like Robeson, we should defend Russia from American imperial provocations, the scope of which threaten all of humanity. To embrace the Russia hysteria plaguing Washington means to defend American exceptionalism and innocence in a moment of crisis unseen in American history. It is to embrace the same class of Americans that accused Saddam Hussein of having "weapons of mass destruction" in order to justify the invasion of Iraq and the massive reduction of civil liberties within our borders. U.S. imperialism requires the creation of new enemies when old ones are no longer able to help it maintain legitimacy in the eyes of many Americans and people around the world. The dwindling legitimacy of the American political and economic system, not Russia, is to blame for the ascendancy of Trump. The scapegoating of Russia is an act of desperation that seeks to preserve America's exceptional and innocent identity. Those who truly want to see progressive and radical changes in this country must understand that America's exceptional and innocent identity is one of the most troublesome obstacles standing in the way.

CHAPTER 17

"Saving American Exceptionalism: Barack Obama, Hillary Clinton, and the Politics of Inclusion"

"The actual state of the country has never been measured or determined by the wealthiest and most powerful—even in those few instances when those people are Black or Brown. A more accurate view of the United States comes from the ground, not the perch of the White House. When we judge this country by the life of Charleena Lyles, a thirty-year-old, single Black mother, who was shot seven times and killed by Seattle police officers in June 2017, the picture comes into sharper focus."

—Keeanga-Yamahtta Taylor[1]

"We tend to continuously allow negotiations in our feminism or support of women: we forgive multi-billion dollar exploitative corporations as fast as they can put a headscarf on a model or imperialism as fast as it can put on a pink pantsuit."

—Hoda Katebi[2]

"If feminism only concerns itself with the women at the very top of our society, it's not feminism at all. It's just elitism."

—Liza Featherstone[3]

The United States' obsession with Russia may signal the beginning of the end for American exceptionalism. That the U.S. and the corporate media have relied so heavily on fears of Russian subversion says very little about the so-called strength of American "democracy" in the current period. Not only does Russia have an economy and military a fraction the size of America's, but everything that Russia has been accused of doing are proven staples of American imperial policy. U.S. imperialism overthrows democracies abroad, possesses the most advanced surveillance and police-state ever developed, and is ruled by corporate oligarchs that have used their money and influence to control all three branches of Washington. Hysteria over Russia covers up the fact that American imperial dominance has become a drag on the political, economic, and cultural advancement of humanity. The 2016 elections and the Russia hysteria that developed from them were a sign that times have changed. Millions of Americans are fed up with the dramatic difference between how the American nation-state presents itself to the world and the misery that it has imposed on many people both within and beyond its borders.

To imagine and then develop a new society and a new world, it is important to understand why American exceptionalism appears worn out from overuse. This is not an easy question to answer. Most would retort that American exceptionalism is not worn out at all, and that it remains in daily operation in all spheres of American society. Such an assertion is correct, but not entirely. It is possible for two opposing trends to exist at the same time. American exceptionalism and its partner American innocence are durable ideologies, but U.S. imperialism is in crisis. The system these narratives rely on is struggling to maintain legitimacy on a global scale. As the system of U.S. imperialism has decayed, the system's ideological influence has decayed as well.

The decaying influence of American exceptionalism and American innocence was at a low point in 2007. President George W. Bush had led disastrous invasions of Afghanistan and Iraq based on lies. The indefinite detention of hundreds of people—many charged with nothing other than suspicions of terrorist links—at Guantanamo Bay quickly became a national embarrassment. Legislation such as the Patriot Act represented a vast extension of the U.S.'s ability to conduct surveillance on anyone it pleased. To make matters worse, the American capitalist economy crashed just prior to the 2008 presidential elections. At this juncture, America looked neither exceptional nor innocent. Something had to be done to take American exceptionalism off life support, lest anger over war, surveillance, immigration, and the financial crash boil over into an open rebellion.

It is precisely at this point where the Democratic Party became the political engine of American exceptionalism. For decades, the Democratic Party had played the role of "lesser evil" to the increasingly conservative and Reagan-leaning Republicans. It was the party most credited as the champion for civil rights, women's rights, and labor unions in Washington. This took a marked policy shift during the Presidency of Bill Clinton. Clinton used his corporate backing to deregulate the banks, destroy welfare, sign the North Atlantic Free Trade Agreement (NAFTA), and wage international wars of "humanitarian intervention," all of which decimated living conditions for workers and the poor wherever they resided. Clinton also passed legislation that led to a dramatic increase in the number of Black Americans put behind prison walls and undocumented migrants detained and deported. His Administration represented the first Presidency of the Democratic Leadership Council (DLC), a prominent nonprofit made up of Democratic leaders often credited with shifting the party's politics rightward to appeal to a more conservative and wealthy base. The Democratic Party engine of American exceptionalism, then, was constructed to forward the agenda of the ruling class.

A total assault on working people and poor people occurred as a result, with Republican Party politicians openly espousing policies that their Democratic Party counterparts carried forward more effectively. The Democratic Party's political shift to the right was not without complexity. As the engine of American exceptionalism, it maintained its political appeal to women, Black, LGBTQ, and union voters while globbling up funds from wealthy donors on Wall Street and inside of the military industrial complex. Republicans shared in the spoils of these funds but appealed instead to white, conservative voters. These voters defined American exceptionalism in terms of white male advancement in stark contrast to the more "inclusive" image promoted by Democrats.

The politics of inclusivity reached their high point of success with the ascendancy of Barack Obama to the Presidency in 2008. The politics of inclusivity emerged from the ashes of the Black freedom, feminist, and working class LGBTQ struggles of the 20th century. Obama came at a most convenient period for the American imperial system. With the system in economic crisis and political turmoil, the first Obama campaign raised a record-setting $750 million from the likes of Goldman Sachs and JP Morgan Chase to save American exceptionalism. His popularity with the American ruling class grew as it became clear that his candidacy personified the politics of inclusivity.

The Obama campaign masterfully used its support from the U.S. ruling class to appeal to millions of people sick and tired of "business as usual" politics in Washington.

Indeed, as the first identifiably "Black president," Obama branded himself as the quintessential "hope" and "change" that people could believe in. His personal story held the promise of a mythical restoration of American exceptionalism through the possibility of entrance into the channels of American power. The Obama campaign was advertised as a "movement" to develop a more inclusive imperial system, one that allowed more Black, Latino, and other oppressed people to co-manage the American imperialist project alongside the largely white ruling class. This "movement," Donald Pease explains, exploited the "pervasive fantasy of dispossession—of citizens stripped of their constitutional rights by the Patriot Act, of parents separated from their children by war, of families forced from their homes by the subprime mortgage crisis—that was already inscribed and awaiting enactment in the script responsible for the production of the Bush Homeland Security State."[4] In other words, Obama inspired a form of hope, a hope rooted in the restoration of "citizenship" and American exceptionalism, that allowed the campaign to promise sweeping changes while failing to address the structural causes of targeted problems.

Obama was thus the "trojan horse" of the American imperial system. Armed with the politics of inclusion, Obama's charming personality and crafty campaign rhetoric to "change" all that had gone awry with the U.S. invaded the hearts and minds of progressive Americans. Indeed, as Pease remarks, Obama used his life story to curry favor with a large number of Americans yearning for solutions to the crumbling conditions of the American imperial system:

> Obama represented his life as itself the outcome of the confluence of three heterogeneous American lineages—the immigrant's dream of escape from economic poverty and political persecution, the minoritized American's endlessly deferred dream of "one day" being included within the American dream, and the white middle-class Americans' dream of future prosperity—and he promised to open up a future for all three of them.[5]

In other words, Obama's very presence in the White House held promise for the revival of American exceptionalism. This version of American exceptionalism vowed to "include" the most oppressed communities in the spoils of prosperity, superiority, and democracy. But Obama's promises were merely an exercise in public relations. His fame and celebrity were made possible not only because he represented the realization of the "deferred dream" of inclusion into the American project, but also because there was no question about his loyalty to U.S. imperialism. Once in office, Obama led a full assault on the progressive and radical principles that elected him in the first place.

His administration carried out this assault under very favorable conditions. The politics of inclusion ensured that criticisms of Obama's policies were neatly associated with the racist attacks hurled at him by his Republican Party opponents. His mere presence in office sent the thousands of American liberals who took to the streets against Bush's wars in Afghanistan and Iraq back quietly into the comfort of their homes. Obama also silenced the American corporate media's criticisms of his predecessor's efforts to privatize public education, bail out bankers responsible for the economic crash, and develop a draconian police-state under the guise of the War on Terror. However, Obama didn't silence opposition to Bush policies because the Obama Administration had any plans to reverse them. Rather, silence came amid the Obama Administration's *escalation* of the very policies he promised to "change" during his campaign.

Obama's two terms in office did indeed bring "change," but it was the type that benefitted U.S. imperialism at the expense of oppressed and exploited people. Obama chanted "Si, Se Puede" (yes, we can) during his campaign, then deported 2.7 million undocumented immigrants, many of them at the heavily militarized border shared with Mexico. His solution to the 2007–2008 economic crisis was not to punish the finance capitalists responsible (as promised), but to feed them trillions of dollars worth of public "bailout" money that only enhanced wealth and income inequality. Under his administration, Obama would massively expand the War on Terror surveillance apparatus to the extent that the National Security Agency possessed the phone, email, and online communications of every American citizen. He also prosecuted a record number of whistleblowers under the Espionage Act of 1917. By 2014, the Obama Administration had transferred three quarters of a billion dollars worth of military weaponry to police departments. This twenty-four fold increase from the Bush Administration was heavily criticized after it was revealed that Black Americans were being murdered by police at a near daily rate.

Obama's foreign policy was equally destructive. Obama won the Nobel Peace Prize in 2009 only to tell his aids in 2012 that he was "good at killing people." He wasn't lying. In contrast to just 52 drone strikes under George W. Bush, the Obama Administration conducted several hundred drone strikes and murdered over 4,000 people, including several American citizens, in countries such as Yemen, Pakistan, Somalia, and Afghanistan. Obama's method of "signature strikes" chose targets based upon "suspicious behavior," which to the administration was defined as all military aged men in the aforementioned countries. Covert warfare, such as Special Operations forces trained in strike-and-kill missions, expanded greatly under Obama to the point where they were deployed in over 70 percent of the world's countries. American Special Operations Forces carried out 674 operations in African in 2014 alone.

The Obama Administration was also no stranger to the expansion of overt war operations. Obama's expanded the theater of American war into Libya, Syria, Ukraine, and across Eastern Europe and the Asia-Pacific. The U.S. occupation in Afghanistan "surged" forward in 2009 and continued indefinitely, while the Iraq war was formally "ended" in 2011 despite the continued presence of American military forces. While the Obama Administration planned a "Grand Bargain" to cut Social Security and Medicare, it was arming the terrorists that successfully overthrew the Libyan government in 2011. That same year, it started a similar, protracted proxy war in Syria. Both wars have led to the displacement and death of millions. This is not to mention the devastation wrought by Obama's coup in Honduras in 2009, which handed power to oligarchs and paramilitary groups responsible for the murders of Berta Caceres and thousands of other Indigenous and environmental activists.

The Obama Administration's commitment to U.S. imperialism brought about an unprecedented expansion of Wall Street and the Pentagon's hegemony over American political life. In doing so, Obama succeeded in convincing some of the most radical and politically militant sections of the population to buy into the myth of American exceptionalism. According to Pierre Orelus,

> Obama led the American people—a good number of them—and the world to believe that, with him as president, the United States would be a force of good, not a warmonger, not a human-rights violator, not a destroyer of the environment, not a racist society, not a society based on injustice and

> hatred but one that was naturally superior, one that embraced the almost incomprehensible notion of "American exceptionalism.[6]

This is why so few Americans protested the subsequent decline in living standards that accompanied the Obama era. Or why no massive worker uprisings occurred during his presidency despite the fact that over 95 percent of the jobs created on Obama's watch were part-time or low wage. Despite the Chicago Teachers Union (CTU) strike in 2013, the privatization of education led by Obama's Race to the Top Initiative closed hundreds of public schools around the country and fired thousands of mostly Black teachers without significant opposition. Black Americans lost significant economic ground and remained the most incarcerated segment of the American population under Obama, yet studies have shown that the same demographic was the most optimistic about its economic prospects.

The Obama Administration was particularly devastating to the left-leaning politics of Black America. As Aziz Rana explains, the vote of Black Americans and other so-called "minority" groups became increasingly important on the eve of the 2012 elections:

> When Reagan's victory over Carter put the final nail in the coffin of the left dream of a class-rooted progressive political base, 65 percent of the voting public were whites without a college degree. In 2012 exit polls, that percentage was cut nearly in half, to 36 percent. As long as Obama's repackaged liberalism could hold minority voters, it seemed, a new Democratic majority would not need a majority or near majority of working-class whites at election time. And with the rise of white nationalism and ethnic xenophobia on the right, it was inconceivable that minorities would go anywhere else.

The importance of Black and "minority" groups to Obama's electoral success cannot be understated since their near unanimous 100 percent support for him proved decisive in both general elections. Obama was advertised as the first "Black president" but not the president of Black America, a reality that Obama would often repeat during his tenure. This contradiction was often confused in a period where Black politicians, Congressmen, and other political elites became more prominent in all spheres of U.S. imperialism. As Keeanga-Yamahtta Taylor explains in her article, "Black Faces in

High Places," the increase in Black politicians has not changed the fact that "Black elected officials have largely governed in the same way as their white counterparts, reflecting all of the racism, corruption, and policies favoring the wealthy seen throughout mainstream politics."[7] Baltimore's Black mayor from 2010–2016, Stephanie Rawlings-Blake, for example, did nothing to hold the Baltimore police accountable for its brutal murder of Freddie Gray in 2015. In fact, Mayor Rawlings had taken a page out of the Obama playbook in calling Black Americans "thugs" while forwarding the agenda of the ruling class. What passes for Black leadership in the era of Obama effectively neutralized the Black radical tradition and its long history of anti-war, pro-peace politics. In fact, a 2013 poll revealed that Black Americans supported the proposed bombing of Syria that summer more than white Americans or Latinos. Another poll showed that Black Americans favored NSA-spying more than any other racial group.

Obama's two-term Presidency was a devastatingly successful project in counterinsurgency warfare. The politics of inclusion was the weapon the U.S. ruling class used to repair the damage done to American exceptionalism and American innocence in years prior. Obama's significance was likened in the media to Martin Luther King Jr. and even Malcolm X. His presence created a virtual industry dedicated to managing the discontent of the masses with the proliferation of a more "diverse" empire. Obama confirmed to many, especially in Black America, that the achievement of the "American Dream" was indeed possible. He gave legitimacy to a formidable class of collaborators with imperialism, with figures such as Melissa Harris-Perry and Al Sharpton benefiting mightily from their defense of Obama and the Congressional Black Caucus's imperial policies. That this class was fully indebted to Wall Street and the U.S. war machine mattered less than the careers it occupied. Careerism and opportunism replaced principles, leading many to vigorously defend Obama from any criticism of his policies. Criticism of Obama often provoked allegations of racism, an accusation that rendered Obama's most heinous crimes invisible or exonerated Obama altogether.

The Obama Administration's expansion of war, privatization, and state repression was fully protected by American exceptionalism and innocence personified by Obama himself. While the right-wing contemplated racist questions of his immigration status or whether he was a Marxist, his administration could do no wrong in the eyes of most liberals and even many progressives and radicals in the Black community. It was assumed that the stability Obama brought to the American imperial project would continue under Hillary Clinton. After all, Clinton was the favorite to succeed Barack Obama as the first woman president of the U.S. Her pockets were full of Wall Street donations and her career in politics was well established. The inauguration of a woman to the Oval office was a logical extension of the politics of inclusion that proved so effective in misleading its class enemies below to ignore or support the most egregious yet profitable ventures of U.S. imperialism.

Like Obama, Clinton was a war hawk and a champion of neoliberal capitalism. She was the presumed face of a neoliberal version of women's empowerment in the U.S., similar to how Obama was the face of Black empowerment. And like Obama in 2012, she had the backing of over one billion dollars' worth in campaign donations, by far and away more than any Republican could raise in the 2016 race. What Clinton lacked was the shrewd and stealth charisma Obama possessed. Unlike Obama, Clinton had decades of experience at the highest level of American politics. While Obama also possessed years of experience in ruling class legal and economic institutions such as the International Business Corporation, Clinton's record in service of U.S. imperialism as First Lady, Senator, and Secretary of State under Obama could not be as easily hidden from the public eye.

In many ways Hillary Clinton's inability to win the 2016 election falls on the growing popular disillusionment with the politics of inclusion. For eight years, millions of people, many of them workers, Black Americans, and poor people, hoped that the presence of a Black president would resolve the misery caused by U.S. imperialism. What they received instead was an even more miserable condition than the one inherited under Bush. Yet Clinton promised to repeat what she assumed Obama already delivered; that is, an exceptional America defined by the uplift of a few at the expense of the many. Her candidacy forcefully opposed both Bernie Sanders on the left and Donald Trump on the right for their audacity to question American exceptionalism. For Clinton, the American nation-state was already exceptional, and her candidacy as a woman proved it most of all.

Hillary Clinton's second run for president was an exemplary case of the relationship between the politics of inclusion and American exceptionalism. Clinton was not hesitant to stake her rightful place as president with the claim that it was "her turn." Her defense of the claim was based on her identity as a woman with years of political experience. However, as Liza Featherstone explains, Clinton and her supporters were forced to rely on the politics of inclusion in the form of "faux feminism" because her candidacy offered little of benefit to struggling Americans. "It's understandable that Clinton supporters are only happy when they find sexists to attack," Liza Featherstone writes. "What else could give this campaign a righteous fervor. After all, her record shows that in her many decades in public life, Hillary Clinton has done an excellent job of advancing the Clintons, and an abysmal job of fighting for women less powerful than herself."[8]

There is no shortage of examples pointing to Clinton's abysmal record fighting for women—or anyone not in the ruling class for that matter. Clinton's foreign policy has been a disaster for women all over the world. As Secretary of State, Clinton helped engineer the coup in Honduras, the overthrow in Libya, and the ongoing war in Syria. When Libyan leader Muammar Gaddafi was illegally murdered by American-backed terrorists, Clinton cackled to the media "we came, we saw, he died." As Senator, Clinton supported the Iraq war that killed over a million Iraqis. Clinton's hawkish foreign policy translated directly to her 2016 campaign. Her repeated calls to "stand up to Putin" and institute a no-fly zone over Syria a la Libya made it clear that a Clinton Presidency was committed to expanding the murderous theater of American warfare abroad.

Hillary Clinton's record as First Lady most starkly highlighted her unpopular domestic policies in all spheres of imperial governance. Her fervent support of Bill Clinton's elimination of welfare led to the further impoverishment of the most vulnerable women in America, especially Black women. Clinton also championed the North Atlantic Free Trade Agreement (NAFTA), which lowered barriers for corporations to invest in Mexico and Canada at the expense of millions of industrial jobs. This increased unemployment, pushed workers into low-wage service sector employment, and placed downward pressure on wages, especially for women. And when Hillary Clinton called Black youth "super predators" who needed to be "brought to heel," she backed up her remarks with support for her husband's 1994 and 1996 crime bills that dramatically increased the Black prison population. Black women are currently the fastest growing prison population due to criminal justice policies that disproportionately criminalize Black Americans as a whole.[9]

Clinton's record certainly should not undermine the importance of sexism.

U.S. imperialism and male domination are intimately connected and have been for centuries. However, this is a new period, one where the politics of inclusion have effectively shrouded the structural character of the U.S. imperial system. Women such as Hillary Clinton personify the ways in which the politics of inclusion have led to the uplift of a select few women at the expense of the rest. Her illustrious career is filled with deep connections to the ruling class, all of which have made her a willful champion of the worst machinations of the system. And it was her attempt to avoid her political record by latching onto the ideology of American exceptionalism that ultimately gave the fractured Republican Party under Trump the electoral edge.

Clinton evoked American exceptionalism during the campaign whenever she could. The hope was that American exceptionalism would protect her from criticisms coming from the Sanders faction of the Democratic Party as well as Trump. American exceptionalism had never failed Hillary Clinton at any other point in her life. Her career defending American exceptionalism from naysayers helped her move up the class ladder first as a lawyer, second as a board member of Walmart, and third as a politician who defended the interests of the likes of Walmart. This is why, as Diana Johnstone explains, "Hillary Clinton personifies the hubris of American exceptionalism. She seems incapable of doubting that America is 'the last hope of mankind.' Above all, she certainly believes that the American people believe in American exceptionalism and want to hear it confirmed and celebrated."[10] It was Clinton's strong belief in American exceptionalism which led her to believe that the U.S. was ready for a woman president, regardless of the cost.

Clinton's adherence to American exceptionalism was demonstrated throughout her 2016 campaign, especially in opposition to Trump's call to "Make America Great Again." Clinton's response to Trump was that America was already great. In a speech to the American Legion in August of 2016, she outlined her case against Trump as follows:

> If there's one core belief that has guided and inspired me every step of the way, it is this. The United States is an exceptional nation. I believe we are still Lincoln's last, best hope of Earth. We're still Reagan's shining city on a hill. We're still Robert Kennedy's great, unselfish, compassionate country. And it's not just that we have the greatest military or that our economy is larger than any on Earth. It's also the strength of our values, the strength

> of the American people. Everyone who works harder, dreams bigger and never, ever stops trying to make our country and the world a better place. And part of what makes America an exceptional nation, is that we are also an indispensable nation.[11]

Yet what Clinton saw as indispensable many others saw as reprehensible. As Clinton spoke of an infallible America, she went on to criminalize whistleblowers such as Chelsea Manning and Edward Snowden for supposedly leaking secrets that endangered "national security." When WikiLeaks revealed a treasure trove of Clinton's secrets such as her use of the Clinton Foundation as a slush fund for political favors from the likes of Saudi Arabia, she criminalized the source of the information as mere dupes of Russia. Her campaign refused to endorse single payer health care, a $15 dollar an hour minimum wage, or any other progressive recommendation that came from her primary opponent, Bernie Sanders, even after it was found that her influence over the Democratic Party had played a decisive role in his loss. To make matters worse, Clinton spent much of her campaign courting traditionally Republican ruling class interests while insulting Republican voters as a "basket of deplorables." Under Clinton's "Big Tent" of billionaires and national security mercenaries sat over fifty GOP officials, national security hawks such as the CIA's Michael Morell, and a host of billionaires such as Mark Cuban, Warren Buffett, and Michael Bloomberg. With friends like these, Clinton thought, who needs voters?

Hillary Clinton's 2016 presidential campaign highlighted the arrogance of American exceptionalism. It also laid bare the stark reality that the American nation-state was exceptional for increasing the profits of the billionaires supporting her campaign but little else. After eight years under the Obama Administration, the politics of inclusion had proven to be an extremely effective but violent weapon in the hands of the ruling class. American wars continued to devastate the planet and finance capital continued to plunder it. Workers and poor people all over the world, especially Black workers, saw their income and wealth plummet as a result. Politicians in Washington, especially Obama and Clinton, showed little concern.

Yet these were the politicians that were supposed to represent the most oppressed segments of American society. Hillary Clinton and Barack Obama certainly diversified the rule of U.S. imperialism. However, their reign both stoked right-wing white supremacy and curtailed the independent strength of the American left. The right-wing hated Obama for soiling the white nation under Black rule, while the ruling class loved Obama for his service to their profit and hegemony. All that was left was resentment on both sides of the political aisle when Clinton declared that it was "her turn."

The American ruling class refuses to look at the growing resentment of large sections of the U.S. population because that would mean placing a mirror in front of the ideologies of American exceptionalism and American innocence. This is something the ruling class cannot do publicly. Such an admission would strip the oppressive and exploitative relations of the system down to their most naked form. The politics of inclusion was a saving grace for U.S. imperialism in the era of Obama, but not in the period that has followed. And it is not as if many Black Americans or women remember how Obama used racist language to describe Black American men or how Hillary Clinton shamed women who didn't vote for her as being controlled by their male counterparts. However, the contradiction between the false hope that inclusion politics brought to Americans and the actual policies implemented by the representatives of inclusion ultimately led many to equate "diversity" with violence.

What resulted was one of the most surprising electoral defeats in U.S. history. A mounting campaign to "blame Russia" for Trump's win has dominated mainstream explanations for Clinton's loss. Trump has become the scapegoat for, well, Trump himself. The militarists, financiers, corporate media analysts, and political officials refuse to acknowledge the political reality behind Trump. Many of them call him "unfit" for president, "mentally ill," "stupid," or Putin's ace in the hole. Others, like *New York Times* columnist Nicholas Kristof, explain what readers can learn from the book *How Democracies Die*, by Steven Levitsky and Daniel Ziblatt. Kristof warns us that under the authors' definition, Trump is a "dangerous authoritarian" leader. The criteria includes:

> 1. The leader shows only a weak commitment to democratic rules. 2. He or she denies the legitimacy of opponents. 3. He or she tolerates violence. 4. He or she shows some willingness to curb civil liberties or the media [. . .] "With the exception of Richard Nixon, no major-party presidential candidate met even one of these four criteria over the last century," [the authors] say, which sounds reassuring. Unfortunately, they have one update: "Donald Trump met them all."[12]

Such an analysis unveils a fundamental flaw with American exceptionalism and American innocence in relation to Trump. It ignores the fact that every former president *easily* meets all four of the above criteria. After all, do people really believe that Trump is the first U.S. president to "tolerate violence"? Bush seemed to have "tolerated" (i.e., unleashed) quite a bit of violence in Iraq. As did Obama with his militarized police forces and drone wars. In fact, one wonders what kind of state propaganda is necessary to brainwash so many people to think that *any* U.S. president has ever demonstrated a strong "commitment to democratic rules." If history is any indication—and if we place U.S. state violence at the center of our analysis—then it's quite a tough pill to swallow: We do not live in a democracy. And we never have.[13]

There are indeed many reasons to criticize or oppose the Republican Party. The Republican Party is the party of the rich, like the Democratic Party. And regardless of how far to the right the Democratic Party reaches, the Republican Party reaches further to demonize immigrants, steal votes from Black communities, and propose the elimination of all public subsidies. Yet to make Trump an exceptional blunder in an otherwise exceptional America is to intentionally ignore the crisis set into motion not by Trump, but the entire class that he is a part of. That crisis is defined by the agreement shared by both parties on the fundamental policies that cause misery to so many, an agreement brokered by the ruling class that administers them.

Beneath the political crisis exists the crumbling economic structure of U.S. imperialism. Trump emerged from an economic infrastructure rooted in "pure" capitalism, one that was unbothered by the fetters of feudalism in Europe. The U.S. government was structured in "pure" capitalism's image. While Europe's colonial empires had to contend not only with the colonized populations but also the communal property relations left behind by previous epochs, the American ruling class was able to focus full attention on profit accumulation. This only hastened the pace by which capitalism developed in a country already buttressed by the unique American antagonisms of racialized African bondage and Native slaughter. Herein is why the U.S. government is structured to "check and balance" the interests of the ruling class against the interests of the majority, or why the electoral college, and not the popular vote, remains the most vital aspect of American presidential elections. As a recent study by a Princeton and Northwestern University professor found, elections in the U.S. are more indicative of an oligarchy than a democracy.[14]

In other words, the American nation-state operates as a government for the rich and controlled by the rich.

Talib Kweli describes the American oligarchy succinctly in "Ghetto Afterlife" when he remarks that "the real thugs is the government, doesn't matter if you independent, Democrat, or Republican." This lyric describes in simple terms why the politics of inclusion has gradually become an ineffective tool of social and ideological control. The American political system is suffering from a crisis of legitimacy driven by the disillusionment of the voting and nonvoting sectors of America, a clear majority of the total population. Neither Democrats nor Republicans can be trusted to offer anything of benefit to poor people, workers, and oppressed people more generally. Experience has demonstrated that electing a Black American or a woman only provides a cosmetic change to empire while leaving the violent imperial apparatus intact.

Obama and Clinton were supposed to revive American exceptionalism and save U.S. imperialism from its multifaceted crisis. They succeeded for a time. However, their efforts to save the illusion of American superiority in the face of mass misery quickly turned into its opposite. The declining belief in American exceptionalist discourse, above all, is what led to the rise of Donald Trump. A high-tech capitalist empire capable of nothing but austerity and war has attempted to include a select few of its most vulnerable to help run the state machinery. These attempts led to one of the most politically stagnant periods (as far as left politics goes) in U.S. history under Obama, only to become undone when millions of Americans decided they didn't want to be included in the imperial apparatus but rather run from it.

American exceptionalism and innocence, however, will not vanish from the planet on their own. U.S. imperialism requires that the American nation-state is viewed as the only "indispensable" nation on earth regardless if such a descriptor fails to reflect the reality of millions, if not billions, of people. The truth is that U.S. imperialism can never truly "include" the oppressed into the ranks of the elite because the elite depends on oppression to maintain political power and accumulate profit and wealth. So American exceptionalism continues to be promoted nonstop by each and every American institution. It will be embraced by many in the absence of a viable ideological and political alternative. And Americans will continue to run from American exceptionalism as its arbiters become less trustworthy, making it painstakingly clear that the task from here is to give them something to run to.

CHAPTER 18

"The Violence of Inclusion"

"The belief that marginalized and hated populations can find freedom by being recognized by law, allowed to serve in the military, allowed to marry, and protected by anti-discrimination law and hate crime statutes is a central narrative of the United States [. . .] Social movements must abandon the widely held belief that oppressed people can be freed by legal recognition and inclusion if we are to truly address and transform the conditions of premature death facing impoverished and criminalized populations in this period."

—Dean Spade[1]

"Black women saw themselves not as isolated within the United States but as part of a global movement of Black and Brown people united in struggle against the colonial, imperialist, and capitalist domination of the West, led by the United States. One can see the importance of international solidarity and identification especially today, when the United States so readily uses the abuse of women in other countries, such as Afghanistan, as a pretext for military intervention."

—Keeanga-Yamahtta Taylor[2]

The ruling class failed in its attempt to use the politics of inclusion in the 2016 elections to elect Hillary Clinton. However, this by no means reduces the significance of the "inclusion" narrative in the current political moment. Issues of inclusion and diversity have dominated political debates in Washington in place of questions about structural change. Neither the Democratic nor Republican Party even attempt to address structural oppression when it comes to U.S. imperialism. Universities and corporate media outlets responsible for reproducing the ideology of the ruling class rarely, if ever, discuss the root causes of poverty, war, racism, and patriarchy. To do so would raise questions about the privileged position that the politics of inclusion has occupied in American discourse and the violence that has come with it.

The politics of inclusion is not without context. It emerged in the neoliberal era of U.S. imperialism. Following the women's movement, Black Freedom movement, and gay liberation movement of the 1960s and 1970s, developments in the American capitalist system rapidly changed. Important victories in these movements coincided with a downward turn in the U.S. capitalist economy. Worldwide competition between socialist and capitalist competitors led to the crisis of overproduction in 1973.

This crisis marked the beginning of a general downward trend in the world capitalist economy. The downward trend was fueled by the intense consolidation and speed-up of production. Technological advances simultaneously brought enormous short-term profits at the long-term cost of making overproduction a permanent fixture of the system. The waning influence of social movements of the Vietnam war-era came in a period where U.S. imperialism was gearing up to roll back social welfare in all forms and expand its war machine to protect hegemony in the face of economic decline. However, because of the movements of the mid-20th century, this could not be done in the old way.

It is no coincidence that narratives of inclusion have gained strength alongside the neoliberal assault on poor and working class people in the U.S., especially Black Americans. The ascendance of women, people of color, and LGBTQ communities into positions of imperial leadership is the product of reforms in American society. These reforms are dual in character. Social movements for Black liberation, women's liberation, and sexual liberation forced the American nation-state to grant concessions in the realm of access (inclusion) but were unable to change the relations of power in society. The American imperial apparatus remained firmly in place, which inevitably led to the escalation of violence against oppressed groups under new, neoliberal circumstances.

The concept of inclusion has fit nicely into the neoliberal framework of individualism and meritocracy. Individual women such as Hillary Clinton have been heralded examples of the fruits of feminism. Former President Barack Obama's victory in 2008 has been popularly described as a reflection of Martin Luther King's "dream" of a more equal society. In other words,

Clinton and Obama's existence in high political office made the U.S. a more exceptional, perfect union. Meanwhile, as individuals such as Clinton and Obama made lucrative political careers as the faces of inclusion, millions of women and people of color fell into poverty, incarceration, displacement, and death in record numbers at the hands of the American neoliberal state.

What Lisa Lowe calls the violence of inclusion[3] has been especially pronounced for the LGBTQ movement, especially for the transgender community. Trans people experience disproportionate rates of discrimination, joblessness, and criminalization because of their failure to accept their assigned gender at birth. The movement for the recognition of transgender issues has made significant gains in recent years, but not without cost. Neoliberal movements emphasizing access and inclusion have dominated the political discourse of the mainstream trans movement. The emphasis on visibility has often come at the expense of a sober analysis of the very institutions where access is being sought.

In the summer of 2017, for example, transgender inclusion in the military received mainstream attention after Donald Trump reversed an Obama Administration initiative to allow trans people to enlist. Outrage poured from Democrats and mainstream LGBTQ organizations accusing Trump of bigotry and discrimination against trans people. To be sure, it is worth condemning Trump's assertion that the military could not afford the "extra" cost required to service their health care needs. However, outrage over Trump's bigotry confined the issue in the narrow, neoliberal box of inclusion. As Eli Massey and Yasmin Nair explain in their article, "Inclusion in the Atrocious," while CEO of GLAAD Sarah Kate Ellis was correct to condemn Trump for issuing a direct attack on trans people, she failed to account how the issue can't simply be framed as a matter of "inclusion" versus "discrimination." That's because,

> given the brutal history of United States military action, we also have to ask important questions about the meaning of participating in unjust institutions. Singling out the issue of inclusion without examining the institution itself produces morally incoherent stances. It can be akin to asking "Should women be allowed to serve in death squads?" or "Is the Mafia unfairly ethnocentric?" or "How can we racially diversify the board of Goldman Sachs?" In each instance, discussing the question requires one to accept the institution itself.[4]

Inclusion thus enhances public acceptance of oppressive, imperialist institutions, whether by facilitating silence about their crimes or prompting overt celebration of their democratic or humanitarian nature. Acceptance of the military is especially important to framing the U.S. as exceptional. The U.S. military is arguably the most dominant institution of U.S. imperialism. There are over 800 military bases spread across the world. The U.S. not only spends trillions of dollars on its war machinery[5] but also regularly celebrates the military in a number of holidays. This makes American military power perhaps the most powerful signifier of American exceptionalism.

LGBTQ inclusion, especially the question of transgender participation in the military, has been wielded by the American ruling class to demonstrate the military's exceptional character in the realm of human rights. Some of former President Barack Obama's signature policies targeted the issue of LGBTQ inclusion. Obama set the precedent for the legalization of gay marriage, the eradication of the "Don't Ask, Don't Tell" policy in the military, and the inclusion of trans people in its ranks. This led Secretary of State Hillary Clinton to declare that "gay rights are human rights" and President Obama to lecture Kenya and other African states in 2015 over their anti-gay discriminatory policies. Such imperial hubris, Dean Spade explains, "uses lesbian and gay rights to bolster the notion that the U.S. is the world's policing arm, forcing democracy and equality globally on purportedly backward and cruel governments."[6] No mention is made of the U.S. military's support of anti-LGBTQ and anti-Black mercenaries in Libya to overthrow the most prosperous African country in 2011. Nor does the narrative that the military brings forth LGBTQ inclusion say anything about the fact that American bombs and security forces prop up murderous regimes completely hostile to women and LGBTQ communities in Saudi Arabia, Honduras, and Ukraine.

A more relaxed policy of inclusion in the U.S. military has allowed the imperial apparatus to "pinkwash" its image as a means to justify its war aims. Pinkwashing is the act of marketing oppressive institutions as LGBTQ-friendly to distract from the exploitation and war inherent to them. As journalist Glenn Greenwald explains, the CIA and other intelligence apparatus regularly decry Russia and Iran's anti-gay policies as reasons to promote regime change in those countries.[7] Allegedly exclusionary policies toward LGBTQ people have been used as signifiers that reinforce a targeted nation's backwardness and barbarity. For example, NGOs have clamored over the violation of human rights in Russia and Iran, two nations that the U.S. military has openly pursued war against. The American nation-state, and indeed the American military, is thus painted as a legitimate force of progress in the realm of LGBTQ liberation.

This exposes the violence inherent to the cause of inclusion. Big NGO and nonprofit organizations such as the Human Rights Campaign lead the way in the promotion of U.S. militarism as a noble path for transgender Americans. However, they have few solutions to the mass unemployment, homelessness, policing, and trauma that trans people face every day. One won't find mainstream LGBTQ organizations, or what Dean Spade calls "Gay Inc.," fighting the chronic withholding of health care from trans people inside of American prisons or the violence they face behind bars and in the ranks of the military. Instead, these organizations pinkwash the U.S. military by promoting trans inclusion in the military as the primary issue concerning trans people while at the same time casting their gaze abroad in service of U.S. imperialism's war agenda.

Pinkwashing is also a popular policy of the Israeli government. Israel happens to be the United States' closest military partner. Prominent intellectuals such as Noam Chomsky have called the Israeli government an apartheid state. Israeli-enforced apartheid is what prompted the formation of the Boycott, Divestment, and Sanctions (BDS) movement. The BDS movement views Israel's military, political, and economic oppression of Palestine as a form of settler colonialism. Indeed, the reality of Israeli colonialism has come under a closer microscope for its expansion of illegal settlements that continue to displace Palestinians from their homes and its periodic wars on Gaza that have left thousands of Palestinians dead in the last decade alone. Israel's long history of genocide and colonial plunder of the Palestinian people has thus given the proclaimed "Jewish State" several reasons to pinkwash its image as "LGBTQ" friendly.

The pinkwashing of Israel has emulated similar attempts by the U.S., minus the emphasis of inclusion in the military. NGOs and nonprofits such as StandWithUS have spent innumerable resources portraying Israel as the standard bearer of LGBTQ rights in the region. The influential StandWithUS organization labels Israel a "sanctuary for the LGBTQ community."[8] Dean Spade describes the broader context of StandWithUs:

> For StandWithUs, pinkwashing—the practice of promoting Israel as "gay friendly" in an effort to divert attention from the brutal colonization of Palestine—is not new. For at least seven years, the organization has been putting on events aimed at portraying Israel as an LGBT-friendly country. StandWithUs did not come up with this strategy on its own. The Israeli government developed it as part of its "Brand Israel" campaign, launched more than a decade ago to help improve Israel's public image. The Israeli Consulate, StandWithUs and other Israel advocacy groups fund international tours of LGBT activists from Israel aimed at promoting an image of Israel as progressive, diverse and inclusive.[9]

And like the pinkwashing of the U.S. military, Israel's advocacy of LGBTQ rights both diverts attention away from Israel's crimes and criminalizes the targeted "other." StandWithUS and other Israel advocacy groups reinforce the settler colonial narrative of civilized and uncivilized. According to StandWithUS, Islamic extremism and other "cultural factors" promote intolerance toward LGBTQ communities across the Middle East. The organization accuses Palestinians of seeking to "harm gay members of their communities by accusing them of collaborating with Israel, a crime often punishable by death."[10]

Yet while little, if any, evidence exists of these crimes, there is plenty of evidence of Israeli settler colonial crimes and its expansionist dreams. All one has to do is take a sober look at the history of Israel, study the Nakba, and read the Oded Yinon Plan of 1982 calling for the creation of a Greater Israel to confirm the colonial and imperialist character of Israel.[11] Not only has Israel usurped Palestinian land, but it has also taken part in a number of wars against Syria, Egypt, and Iran. Israel uses billions in American military aid to pressure these countries into the chaos and instability necessary for the "Jewish State" to achieve its imperial dreams. The promotion of Israel as an LGBTQ–"friendly" partner to the American imperial apparatus thus gives cover to the criminal violence against the Palestinians and peoples of the region by shoring up the exceptionalist narrative Israel has imitated so well from its American partner.

Where exactly, then, does the violence of inclusion take the LGBTQ movement and movements for liberation generally? We know that questions of inclusion for trans people and the LGBTQ community in the apparatus of U.S. and Israeli militarism bring more war and oppression for the people of the world. Perhaps more important, however, is how a focus on inclusion normalizes the violence of U.S. imperialism by diverting movements into acceptable forms of protest. The legalization of gay marriage, for example, reinforced private property rights and ensured that poor members of the LGBTQ community would rely on receiving health care through marital relations rather than through a universal health care system. Trans inclusion in the U.S. military and hate crime legislation also use the oppressors' tools to achieve liberation for the oppressed. Rather than focus on the question of economic and political powerlessness for the vast majority, inclusion focuses on legalistic methods of reform to "improve" the function of the imperial state for its oppressed subjects.

Social movements focused on legal reform assume that the U.S. imperial apparatus is designed to serve the most vulnerable sectors of society. The assumption is a staple of American exceptionalism and innocence. Rather than structural change, all that is needed are minor alterations to the state to make it more inclusive to LGBTQ communities and other oppressed groups. Alterations or tweaks to the U.S. imperial state, however, have left the social relations of exploitation, incarceration, and war unchanged. In many cases, they have exacerbated them. Take the passage of the Matthew Shepard, James Byrd Jr. Hate Crimes Prevention Act in 2009. The bill was celebrated for adding "gender identity or expression" and "sexual orientation" to the federal hate crimes statute. At the same time, it was attached to the National Defense Authorization Act of 2010 (NDAA), which, according to Dean Spade

> set aside the highest amount of money ever provided to the Department of Defense in U.S. history. The increase in funding to the Department was made to cover the expense of Obama's 100,000-person troop surge in Afghanistan. Chandan Reddy has described the attachment of the hate crimes bill to the NDAA as "an act of genius" on the part of Congressional Democrats. Tying the federal LGBT hate crime legislation to a bill that raised military spending to its highest level in U.S. history brought Republican support needed to pass the hate crime law, since Republicans would favor the military expansion, and helped provide cover from attacks from the left on the military spending.[12]

Hate crime legislation was thus used as a political chip to sell war and ensure that the state-based "protection" of LGBTQ communities would lead to the further militarization of the American nation-state. Top down reforms, or reforms that are dictated by the American ruling class, reflect the interests of those at the top. War, policing, prison, and economic exploitation are the weapons used to achieve these interests. They are embedded in the very structure of the U.S. imperial state. That is why the political and economic well-being of LGBTQ communities is secondary to the priority of inclusion. The concept of inclusion can be manipulated into policies that serve the ruling class, while genuine demands for an end to poverty, homelessness, policing, and discrimination cannot.

Legal institutions in the U.S. are incapable of transforming the condition of LGBTQ communities, especially those communities that are poor, Black and Brown. Reform efforts such as the struggle for hate crime legislation or inclusion in the military completely ignore the structural causes for anti-LGBTQ bigotry and ignore the demands of grassroots organizations. Not only do they often come with the promise of more war abroad, but these reforms also expand the war apparatus on the domestic front. According to Spade, the Prison Rape Elimination Act of 2003 (PREA) is a perfect example of this phenomenon. PREA was ostensibly passed to address the rampant sexual abuse that occurs within U.S. prisons, especially for LGBTQ prisoners. However, the Act has been used to discipline those who defy gender norms. Prison authorities are less likely to believe LGBTQ prisoners who complain of sexual assault yet punish consensual sex to supposedly reduce the risk of rape inside of prisons. Furthermore, prisons also use PREA "as a reason to ban and punish gender-nonconforming behavior such as wearing a hairstyle considered too masculine for women prisoners or too feminine for male prisoners."[13]

PREA is a quintessential example of why "their laws won't save us." It is "their" laws, the laws of the ruling class, which are designed to manage the exploitation of the oppressed. More LGBTQ prison guards, politicians, or military officers cannot change the reality that the American nation-state rests on a foundation of racism, patriarchy, and capitalism. Laws that imprison "hate" and reward a tiny few to the ranks of the oppressor class does not change the fact that the "people who violently destroy and end the most lives, are still on the outside—they are the people that run banks, governments, and courtrooms, and they are the people wearing police and military uniforms."[14] Inclusion offers an escape valve for those who wield power, but it doesn't offer an escape from oppression. Rather, inclusion efforts make U.S. imperialism more effective in its oppression by pushing movements for social change toward goals that are acceptable, indeed desired, by the ruling class of the system.

The effectiveness of inclusion lies in the way it brands American exceptionalism and innocence in a fresh way. Inclusion has taken on a new level of importance in the 21st century as radical social movements have been replaced by the rapacious movement of U.S. imperialism. With nothing to offer increasing numbers of poor, oppressed, and struggling people, inclusion strengthens the illusory image that the U.S. is the most "democratic" and "free" society on the planet. The rise of Black and Latino politicians and celebrities or the passage of hate crime legislation creates the illusion that the U.S. is on a path toward progress. Whatever crimes the American nation-state commits at home and abroad are accepted as long as they are carried out by Black or queer representatives of the ruling class. "Diversity" and inclusion have thus become smokescreens that make it difficult for Americans to acknowledge that representation does not necessarily lead to a more just and equitable society for oppressed people. In fact, inclusion narratives have too often failed to accentuate the worsening conditions of Black people in America, even with their celebrations of "diversity" in political and corporate offices.

This does not mean that Trump's right-wing attacks on women or LGBTQ people are acceptable or that bigotry should not be opposed at every turn. Defending oppressed people from attack is categorically different than pushing an agenda of inclusion at their expense. As Spade argues, it is time to look toward the grassroots for real solutions to the conditions before us. What is happening in the Black community in America? What is the state of trans people, especially trans people of color? Who is organizing to change these conditions and what do they seek? Are they seeking to make U.S. imperialism more inclusive or to dismantle it all together?

The narrators of American exceptionalism and innocence have made inclusion a central focus to ensure that these questions are never asked. Those who dare to ask are drowned out by well-funded efforts to diversify the American empire. A diversified empire, however, is still a dangerous empire. It is more dangerous now more than ever, with competing factions of the Trump camp and his opposition arguing over the most effective means to exploit and oppress the masses. Trump's bigotry should not be tolerated, but neither should the violence that a more "inclusive" empire has wrought on the people and planet.

CHAPTER 19

"Flags, Flyovers, and Rituals: On Giving Your Body to the State"

"I understand the good intentions, but my liberation will not come from framing my body with a flag that has flown every time my people have fallen [. . .] And I hope yours will not either."

—Hoda Katebi, "Please Keep Your American Flags off my Hijab"[1]

"Race and racism have not been exceptions; instead, they have been the glue that holds the United States together."

—Keeanga-Yamahtta Taylor[2]

Some people have described President Donald Trump as a symbol of what America looks like "unrestrained." In other words, Trump says and does out in the open what many in the American ruling class think and practice in relative secrecy. While the assumption that U.S. imperialism is less "restrained" under Trump is debatable, there is no doubt that the words and actions of the billionaire service industry magnate have raised a few eyebrows. When Trump proposed a military parade in late February of 2018, for example, many representatives of the U.S. military and intelligence sectors derided the suggestion as a waste of military resources. Yet what American military and intelligence representatives were really mad about was not the celebration of the military, but how the celebration was being conducted.

In fact, the U.S. celebrates war and militarism constantly. Ritual celebration of militarism is fundamental to American exceptionalism. The idea that the American nation-state is supreme to all others has become "common sense." Americans are told so every day. Yet it is not enough to tell Americans over and over again that the U.S. is an exceptional entity. Ideology must be grounded in reality or no one would adhere to it. Frantz Fanon used the term "cognitive dissonance" to explain the power of ideology when it is viewed from the societal conditions from which it sprouts. The anti-colonial theorist showed that under colonialism, it was not uncommon for many to hold on to core beliefs about the sanctity of the system even when presented with evidence to the contrary. As the most developed settler colonial system to date, the U.S. has produced a society where cognitive dissonance is widespread.

Cognitive dissonance is widespread because Americans are regularly coerced into giving their bodies to the nation-state. As Carolyn Marvin and David Ingle explain, those devoted to the American nation-state "must have proof of its existence, a visible body" that reifies its existence and the promises that go with it.[3] The visible body of the state reaches the realm of popular consciousness through psychological warfare and ritual practice. Psychological warfare targets the "hearts and minds" of the populace. Ritual practice complements psychological warfare by endowing people of all racial groups, classes, and nationalities living in the U.S. with the toolkit necessary to reinforce the project of American nationalism. American nationalism is defined by the focal points of American exceptionalism, whereby the borders drawn by the nation-state reflect the "democracy" and "freedom" so many are willing to die for.

The codification of American nationalism into the American psyche takes on a religious-like character. American "citizenship" is in many ways a form of American "worship." The flag is the central totem, or a symbol that possesses a spiritual significance, of the American creed. Entombed in the American flag are all the values and rituals that represent the militaristic and imperial nation-state. Some might object that it is silly to think of the American flag as something that is worshipped. But as William Cavanaugh points out, "If it walks like a duck and quacks like a duck, it is a duck. If it acts like a religion, it is a religion. If people pledge allegiance to a flag, salute it, ritually raise and lower it and are willing to kill and die for it, it does not much matter if they acknowledge it is only a piece of cloth and not a god."[4]

Worship of the flag permeates a sense of transformative power to this state that inspires many to take up the cause of militarism and imperialism.

Marvin and Ingle further comment on the religious significance of American nationalism embodied in the flag:

> In Christianity the revivified totem is the risen Christ. In American nationalism the transformed totem is the soldier resurrected in the raised flag. On the basis of his sacrifice the nation is rejuvenated. As the embodiment of sacrifice, the flag has transforming power. Certain acts cannot be performed except in its presence. Elaborate rules govern what may touch it and how devotees must behave in its presence. It must be kept whole and perfect, as holy things are, and ceremonially disposed of when it is no longer fit to perform the functions of the totem object.[5]

American militarism and nationalism, then, cannot be separated from the worship of American exceptionalism. The celebration of American warfare is indeed what defines American "citizenship." When noncitizens take the test required to gain full "citizenship" in the country, they memorize a national anthem written by a slave owner and list important wars that the U.S. has waged abroad. This is no coincidence. The most fundamental component of becoming an American is the celebration of war. War provides "substance to [a] supposedly national spirit, its character and pageantry, its performativity: something to be for, to be proud of, something real to which to commit, to fight for."[6] The celebration of war as a performance of U.S. citizenship gives the American military a universal quality. No longer is it an agent of repression, destruction, and plunder for the rich, but rather a force for American "unity" and the sense of belonging that comes with it.

No matter that American "unity" is dependent upon the exclusion, murder, and subjugation of peoples who fall outside of the borders of whiteness and wealth. American exceptionalism is reinforced as American reality through the psychological warfare inflicted by the corporate media. Indeed, the sacrifices of the U.S. military in the cause of freedom are regularly extolled, not least because the military has a significant amount of influence over the media. According to a Freedom of Information Act (FOIA) request in 2017, U.S. military and intelligence agencies have played an active role in shaping over 1,800 movies and television shows.[7] The documents revealed that the Department of Defense's (DoD) Hollywood liaison Phil Strub redacted and altered movie scripts in a number of major films to make them more palatable to the image the military wants to portray.

In all cases, this meant the removal of lines from scripts that in any way challenged or critiqued the U.S. military's role in the world, however slight. References to the Vietnam war are especially controversial. *The Hulk* (2003) and *Tomorrow Never Dies* (1997) had references to the destructive war redacted upon DoD request. But the U.S. military and intelligence apparatus does not reserve itself to edits of Hollywood scripts. Oftentimes, the military is directly involved in the making of film itself. As Tanine Allison explains,

> Film productions can often save millions of dollars by using military assets rather than recreating or renting this material elsewhere. The military charges the filmmakers for the cost of all special assistance that they provide to avoid the perception that taxpayers are on the hook for Hollywood movies, but many maneuvers performed for films are designated as training actions, reducing the cost substantially. Filmmakers also pay no location fees or salaries of military personnel involved.[8]

It is no wonder that films, especially those oriented to youth, valorize American military dominance and combat. Blockbuster films such as *Independence Day* (1996) or *Black Panther* (2018) depict the military and the CIA as protectors of freedom and human rights. These films reinforce the honor inherent to the U.S. military's so-called sacrifice for the well-being of the nation-state. In this sense, Hollywood films are some of the most effective recruitment tools for enlistment into the military. Comic superheroes have produced high grossing films for the Marvel Cinematic Universe in part because they seductively reinforce the performance of American nationalism for moviegoers. The popular Capitan America, for example, wears a red, white and blue uniform as a powerful symbol of the sacredness of the American flag. Only evil villians that seek to destroy Captain America dare ridicule his costume, which as Jason Dittmer argues, "is a marker of their villainhood and serves as an object lesson for the reader in how not to behave."[9] The American flag is naturalized as a heroic symbol of American bravery and sacrifice in the field of war. American militarism is effectively legitimized.

Hollywood is just one of the many multibillion dollar venues where loyalty and sacrifice to the American nation-state are nourished. As mentioned in prior chapters, U.S. sports are drenched in a culture of militarism. The NFL's lucrative partnership with the DoD to promote the U.S. military since 2009 is a case in point. However, celebrations of militarism were commonplace in the NFL long before it became formalized by the DoD. After President George W. Bush declared a War on Terror that led to the invasions of Afghanistan and Iraq, the rallying cry to "support our troops" was heard loudest at NFL pregame shows. As Mia Fischer explains, "the relentless 'support the troops' rhetoric rather commodifies members of the Armed Forces for the audience's pleasure and consumption and normalizes the realities of war."[10] Staged commemorations of the victims of September 11th were commonplace. Celebrities such as Robert De Niro urged fans to "honor our commitments" to those who died in the twin towers behind military aircraft flyovers and soldiers.

Perhaps the least subtle example of how U.S. imperialism invites the populace to perform American exceptionalism and militarism resides in the National Collegiate Athletics Association (NCAA). The NCAA has come under fire as of late for making billions of dollars of profit from the free labor of its college athletes in basketball and football in particular. Northwestern football players have attempted to form a union in response to labor abuses of the NCAA. Few college athletes, fans, or administrators of the NCAA, however, have challenged the promotion of militarism through the annual "Lockheed Martin Armed Forces Bowl" formed in 2004. Michael Butterworth and Stormi Moskal provide a brief outline of the significance of the game as follows:

> What is easily dismissed by many as an innocent sporting event with a "patriotic" theme is more accurately described as a mediated spectacle of militarism. Through the merging interests of the Fort Worth community, ESPN, BellHelicopter-Textron, and the game's other sponsors, football simultaneously trivializes the seriousness of war as it emphasizes the seriousness of supporting the American military. This rhetorical division offers a delimited conception of appropriate American identity, thereby sanctioning the promotion of war in general and endorsing the "war on terror" specifically.[11]

The website for the annual NCAA event does not hide its affinity for U.S. militarism. Not only is the game's primary sponsor the military contractor

Lockheed Martin, but the promoters of the bowl also provide fans and viewers ample opportunities to celebrate militarism with "fan-fest areas showcasing armed forces hardware; flyovers; [. . .] on field induction ceremonies; armed forces bands and honor guards and the awarding of the annual 'Great American Patriot Award' (GAPA) presented by Armed Forces Insurance."[12] The game's slogan, "bowl for the brave," ensures that enthusiasts of college football are also compelled to become enthusiasts for U.S. militarism. In this way, attendees of the Armed Forces Bowl legitimize the relationship between American exceptionalism and militarism through performance. The teams who participated in the 2016 game, the fans who attended, and the media and corporate sponsors who bankrolled it all played their part in legitimizing the 26,000 bombs dropped by the military that year as symbols of "freedom" and "sacrifice."

Glorified displays of U.S. militarism and nationalism are a testament to U.S. imperialism's investment in the performance of exceptionalism. Millions of Americans have bared witness to these displays and participated directly in them. Celebrations of U.S. militarism are embedded in the flag, which is saluted and pledged to an untold number of times throughout a given week, month, and year. The constant celebration of militarism has helped recruit civilians to the military and guarantee that those who don't enlist view the military as a heroic institution.

Even if one were to ignore sports and the corporate media (which is what an increasing number of Americans do), the U.S. celebrates a number of holidays in commemoration of war and militarism. In fact, nearly every federal holiday celebrates war in some form. Veterans Day honors American soldiers who have died in active combat. George Washington's birthday celebrates the life of the first president of the United States. Washington owned hundreds of slaves and made his fortune from stealing land from Indigenous people. Going further back in history, Columbus Day celebrates the accomplishments of Christopher Columbus. Those accomplishments include the extermination of Indigenous people in the Caribbean during his so-called "discovery" of the Americas in 1492.[13]

Holidays ritualize the foundational virtues of a nation-state steeped in war and militarism. They invite Americans to commemorate the "sacrifice" of American soldiers or the leaders who led them to battle. By accepting the invitation, Americans are given the opportunity to feel a sense of ownership in the making of an exceptional nation-state. The violence of war becomes normalized as attention is turned toward the great "service" that war provides the nation. Sylvester Johnson assesses the rhetorical importance of reframing war as service when he writes:

> The state has monopolized the exclusive right to take life—to kill—most commonly through military warfare. But going to battle in military service is no mere killing spree. Rather, it is immersion in the most extreme form of violence as service to the nation. This is why militarism is sacrifice and not murder (according to the rationality of state power). Military soldiers willingly place their own lives in the hands of death to ensure the well-being of the nation. So, by risking life (their own) and taking life (of state enemies), soldiers offer themselves as a blood sacrifice on behalf of the nation, the political body of their state.[14]

Of course, there a numerous economic pressures that compel poor and working class Americans to join the military and fight in American wars. The decision, however, would be undoubtedly more difficult if the American ruling class promoted the military as an institution of war, plunder, and genocide. Instead, the military represents not just a body of armed soldiers prepared to "defend" America, but a multifaceted contract between the entire population and the state. The military fights wars abroad to spread the principles of American exceptionalism in exchange for a cross-class alliance of loyalty to the American nation-state. This cross-class alliance developed under imperialism is a product of white supremacy. White supremacy unites white Americans in service of the same principles that motivate the American military: the conquest of land and labor for profit. And white supremacy is a prime component of the transactional relationship between U.S. militarism and the American "citizen."

Holidays, flags, and other commemorations to American militarism are the symbolic markers of the terms embodied in the transaction. The lofty ideals of democracy, freedom, and liberty are celebrated through these markers, but ideals alone are not enough to ensure that Americans remain silent about the atrocities that its military commits abroad. Silence and celebration are cemented by the economic and political promises embedded in the contract. In exchange for the body, the citizen receives both the honor and the prospects of more wealth and opportunity derived from the destruction of others. Alasdair MacIntyre famously highlighted the gravely disproportionate expectation the state places on its citizens. Comparing this demand to being asked to die for the telephone company, MacIntyre shows that the American nation-state is presented to us as a "bureaucratic supplier of goods and services, which is always about to, but never actually does, give its clients value for money, and on the other hand as a repository of sacred values, which from time to time invites one to lay down one's life on its behalf."[15]

The celebration of militarism and its great "sacrifices" are really celebrations of power and profit over others. Americans, especially white Americans, are made to feel superior to their so-called enemies. War and militarism provides the U.S. citizen more than simply American exceptionalist values for which to sacrifice their life. A durable military is assumed to also lead to a strong capitalist economy, which in turn means that the "American Dream," or the economic incentive of the contract, becomes much easier to reach for the American worker and "middle class."

Of course, economic reality spells something entirely different than the assumptions inherent to the celebratory inclinations of American exceptionalism. Former President Obama boasted of a median income increase in 2015 as signs of a recovering economy yet left out the most important details pertaining to prevailing conditions in the United States. Black Americans found themselves on a path to zero wealth after the 2007–08 economic crisis. White American wealth made a substantive recovery, but the numbers were skewed toward the rich. Over 40 percent of whites are considered "asset poor" in America. Death rates from suicide and drug overdose have skyrocketed for middle-aged white men, a phenomenon largely explained by an increase in joblessness and poverty. Poverty and joblessness have indeed dampered the American population's enthusiasm for war. A study in 2017 showed that voters from areas of the country that suffered the most casualties in the U.S. wars on Iraq and Afghanistan were more likely to vote for Donald Trump.[16] War fatigue may have been a decisive factor in the election of Trump and the political crisis that has wracked the nation ever since.

While war fatigue and declining living standards open more opportunity for class solidarity, the willingness to sacrifice one's body on the altar of the U.S. military state has always faced the most resistance from targets of both white supremacy and class oppression. The reasons are clear. White

Americans who experience class exploitation have historically been fed opportunities to improve their condition from racial oppression, whether in the form of joining "well regulated militias" to steal Native land or collect bounties from runaway slaves or by enlisting in the fight in World War II to receive wealth-building incentives from the GI Bill. Celebration of American exceptionalism has thus been utterly hypocritical for racially oppressed sections of the population excluded from such opportunities, especially Black Americans. Frederick Douglass famously elaborated on the hypocrisy of the Fourth of July holiday, or America's "birthday":

> What, to the American slave, is your 4th of July? I answer; a day that reveals to him, more than all other days in the year, the gross injustice and cruelty to which he is the constant victim. To him, your celebration is a sham; your boasted liberty, an unholy license; your national greatness, swelling vanity; your sound of rejoicing are empty and heartless; your denunciation of tyrants brass fronted impudence; your shout of liberty and equality, hollow mockery; your prayers and hymns, your sermons and thanks-givings, with all your religious parade and solemnity, are to him, mere bombast, fraud, deception, impiety, and hypocrisy—a thin veil to cover up crimes which would disgrace a nation of savages. There is not a nation on the earth guilty of practices more shocking and bloody than are the people of the United States, at this very hour.[17]

Douglass's words are hard to refute for those who are aware of the Black condition in America over the course of history. The hypocrisy of the American nation-state's constant glorification of its own exceptionalism has made the Black liberation movement a central pillar in the development of a new, more humane society. Racism toward Muslims in America, many of whom are Black, Arab, or from the Middle East region of the world, has also sparked resistance to the dogma of American exceptionalism and innocence in recent years. Muslims have been the target of the United States' racist and imperialist War on Terror, which has expanded the surveillance, incarceration, and murder of Black Americans to profiled Muslim and Arab "looking" populations. Developments such as the indefinite detention of hundreds of suspected "Muslim" terrorists at Guantanamo Bay, endless war on seven Muslim-majority countries, and the New York Police Department's (NYPD) surveillance of Muslim communities in New York and beyond have all been justified as "counter-terrorism" measures meant to prevent another event like 9/11 from ever happening again.

Racism toward Muslims has been mischaracterized as "Islamophobia." The motivating force is not a "phobia" of Muslims but rather a policy of racism that serves a particular political agenda. That agenda did not begin with the intensified scapegoating of Muslims after the September 11th attacks. As Zareena Grewal explains, the case of NBA player Mahmoud Abdul-Rauf anticipated the U.S.'s War on Terror policies. Rauf was an up-and-coming NBA All Star for the Denver Nuggets when, in a sixty-game span in 1995, he chose to remain in the locker room during the recital of the national anthem. But it wasn't until he called the American flag a "symbol of oppression, and of tyranny" that he was suspended from the league. After one game, the suspension was reversed when Rauf agreed to participate in the national anthem ritual (he was "allowed" to silently recite a Muslim prayer as he stood). However, the racist backlash in the corporate press toward Rauf had made him a liability to the NBA, which feared Rauf would precipitate a loss in corporate sponsorships.

Rauf was traded the subsequent year and his NBA career never recovered. In July of 2001, Rauf's home was burned down by what the FBI suspected was an act of the Ku Klux Klan. Grewal argues that Rauf's circumstances were the product of the disciplining function of the American flag against the "Other". Rauf's decision to criticize the American flag made him the target of harsh condemnations from fans and media alike who accused him of lacking "appreciation" for America. Worse still was what Grewal calls the "Arabization" of Rauf's features to depict him as a foreigner waging war on America. Rauf demonstrated that American exceptionalism is dependent on the production of a racialized enemy to reframe war and oppression as democratic governance in the interests of "the nation."[18]

The use of symbols such as the American flag to spark an extreme sense of nationalism in the population, especially in white America, helps drown resistance to American imperialist oppression in a cauldron of patriotism. And it isn't conservative or "right-wing" bigots that are solely to blame for the reproduction of racism draped in patriotism. In the aftermath of Donald Trump's election, observers in the liberal elite began to publicly critique what they called Islamophobia with appeals to American exceptionalism. America, they said, was exceptional because it "embraced" all people regardless of race, gender, or religious affiliation. The argument concluded that Trump's unwelcoming posture toward Muslims was not reflective of American society as a whole.

Liberal opposition culminated in the "We the People" series of photos that reproduced Muslim-American photographer Ridwan Adhami's photo of a woman in a hijab. The remastered photo draped the hijab in the symbol of the American flag. Liberal opposition thus used the American flag to oppose Trump's racism without recognizing the inherently racist character of the flag itself. As fashion blogger and intellectual Hoda Katebi explains, "the American flag represents oppression, torture, sexual violence, slavery, patriarchy, and military & cultural hegemony for people of color around the world whose homes and families have been destroyed and drone-striked by the very person/former president whose campaign images this one seeks to replicate."[19] Not only did the image attempt reinforce "hope" and "solidarity" through the image of the American flag, but its very formation was steeped in racism.

The image was created by a white American who used the work of a Muslim American photographer to critique Trump on the basis of his exclusionary rhetoric toward Muslims. This is a form of plunder, as the "We the People" campaign deliberately exploited the image of a Muslim-American woman toward imperial aims. The campaign never once mentioned how Trump's rhetoric has been the *modus operandi* of U.S. imperial policy for decades. "We The People" is but the other side of imperialist and racist exploitation. When white Americans and the American population as a whole are not being recruited to sacrifice their bodies in the name of patriotism and nationalism, the oppressed are being pressured to become "American" through assimilation. Being "American" means participating in its oppressive structures, whether in the form of voting for representatives of the elite, joining the military, or remaining silent about the crimes that the American nation-state commits daily. It also means extolling the values of "democracy," "freedom," and "liberty" at the expense of humanity. As Katebi quips,"Muslims are tired of having to 'prove' they are American."[20]

For many, the first step toward resistance to the "right-wing" and "liberal" sides of U.S. nationalism and imperialism will be to stop celebrating the symbols that have been codified as sacred mantles of American exceptionalism. Colin Kaepernick and Mahmoud Abdul-Rauf have learned the consequences of taking such action in the sphere of popular sports culture.

The Black liberation movement and the anti-war socialist movements of prior decades have learned on a mass scale that resistance to what the American flag represents inevitably leads to the imprisonment, murder, and slander of those who participate. Dozens of political prisoners reside in U.S. prisons across the country for their activity in organizations such as the Black Panther Party. Workers, poor people, and Indigenous people who have opposed corporate land grabs and assaults on their living standards have met a similar fate.

Yet these individuals and movements took the concept of sacrifice and applied it in a completely different way than how it is utilized by the U.S. empire. They put their devotion not toward patriotic and nationalistic symbols but in the people targeted by imperialist violence and exploitation. They recognized, as Martin Luther King Jr. did just prior to his assassination, that the American nation-state was "the greatest purveyor of violence in the world." The task, then, is to cease sacrificing our bodies and our minds for the good of "the nation." This is merely a euphemism for what is "good for the American ruling class." In order to place our minds and bodies in service of humanity as a whole and the oppressed in particular, we must reject American exceptionalism and the innocence it fosters through glorifications of "the nation." To do so is to follow in the footsteps of King and plant the seeds of a new revolutionary culture capable of addressing the damage done to our world by the suffocating footsteps of the American imperial system that preceded it.

CHAPTER 20

"Questioning Borders, Belonging, and the Nation-State"

"We live in a land where the past is always erased and America is the innocent future in which immigrants can come and start over, where the slate is clean. The past is absent or it's romanticized."

—Toni Morrison[1]

"The heroic quest, the triumph over weakness, the promises of salvation, prosperity and progress: this is the American feeling, the style of life, the ethos and spirit of being."

—Lisa Lowe[2]

". . . those committed to social justice have a formidable task: articulating the value and rights of the immigrant without relying on anti-Black and pro-capitalist tropes."

—Tamara K. Nopper[3]

What do the borders of the American nation-state represent? What does it mean to "belong" to the U.S.? Who is a "citizen" and who is not? How are conceptions of "American-ness" intricately tied to constructions of what it means to be "human"? What's at stake in asking these questions? And whose particular interests do the answers to these questions serve? We cannot begin to break down the confluence of imperialist interests behind the questions of immigration unless we fully understand how ideologies of American exceptionalism and innocence inform both immigration discourse and policy. American exceptionalism has narrowed the discourse by dividing up immigrants into categories of "good" and "bad." Moreover, as we attempt to show in this chapter, discourses from both liberal and conservative circles often rely on settler-colonial, anti-Black, capitalistic, and imperial tropes to frame the immigration debate. The U.S. has historically been in constant need of an enemy. Just like in Hollywood film, villains legitimize the hero. One cannot exist without the other.[4]

Donald Trump made the issue of immigration central to his 2016 campaign. The real estate billionaire vowed to "build a wall" on the U.S.-Mexico border to keep "illegals" from entering the country. In campaign rally after campaign rally, Trump characterized immigrants from Mexico as "criminals" and "rapists" worthy only of immediate deportation. His comments and policy promises regarding immigration were a reflection of decades of American imperial history. However, rather than discuss how Trump's anti-immigrant political orientation was a product of this history, ruling class opposition to Trump made the conscious decision to exploit the issue of immigration for its own gain.

Immigration is a complex issue best analyzed on many fronts. Forced migration is a consequence of "globalization." People travel to and from the U.S. for a host of reasons. Some are fleeing the political turmoil of war caused by the U.S. itself. Others are leaving their country of origin due to economic hardship and poverty, which is oftentimes a product of the underdevelopment imposed by American-led imperial policies. However, some migrants are given special status protections in the U.S. They are not referred to as "immigrants" at all, but rather a voting bloc or a special interest population. Take, for example, Cuban immigrants. Cubans "fleeing" the socialist state have historically opposed their government on the basis that after the revolution of 1959 they no longer could monopolize and sell off the nation's assets to the U.S. at the expense of workers and peasants. It is public record that the CIA paid and trained wealthy Cubans in the U.S. only to send them back to Cuba to commit terrorist attacks, a practice that climaxed in the failed "Bay of Pigs" invasion in 1961.

Contemporary immigration debates have largely ignored the tiered immigration system that exists in the U.S. Instead, the focus of immigration policy discussions in Washington have centered on migration from Mexico and Central America. Migration from these regions is the result of what Martin Luther King Jr. called the "triple evils" of capitalism, racism, and militarism. To avoid a public conversation about the origins of migration, two competing narratives have emerged over the course of the last several decades. These narratives are interrelated and rely heavily on American exceptionalism to reproduce the nation's white supremacist and capitalist relations.

Democratic and Republican Administrations alike have used both narratives to forward their respective agendas. And both narratives ultimately render the root causes of immigration from the Global South, particularly from Latin America, invisible. The first narrative primarily concerns the criminality and racialized inferiority of "illegal" migrants. This narrative has masqueraded as a fear that migration is eroding the long standing white majority that has existed in the country since its formation. However, what it really represents is a deep desire on the part of corporate and imperialist interests to control an exploited, racialized labor force. This ideological framework for understanding immigration has been materialized in several policies in Washington.

The second narrative directly complements the first. It presumes that since the U.S. is "a nation of immigrants" then it logically follows that any and all immigrants should be "accepted" by American society. Immigrants from Mexico and Central America take jobs that "Americans" don't want, pay taxes without benefits in the form of Social Security, and make the country a more "bilingual" and accepting place. Oftentimes, advocates of this narrative reside in the Democratic Party and support piecemeal measures that on the one hand promote "assimilation" for some, while escalating the militarized state machinery that targets millions of "illegal" immigrants on the other.

The immigration debate makes clear, then, that borders in the context of U.S. imperialism are merely demarcations of war and corporate plunder. American exceptionalism has justified the lines of demarcation on both sides of the debate. The focus on "illegal" immigrants has produced a convenient dialectic for the ruling class. Martha Escobar summarizes the dialectic of the debate as follows:

> We are fixed in a polarized debate that does little to arrive at the root causes of migration and the role the US has in creating and maintaining it. The criminality component of the debate differs little from this pattern. When immigrants are represented as criminals, the reaction is to distance immigrants from criminality and move them closer to "American"-ness by stating that immigrants are not criminals, immigrants are hard workers. However,

> this effort is framed within the context of a criminality that is mutually exclusive from the national "American" identity that is wedded to whiteness. Thus, immigrant Americanizing efforts are negotiations between racial whiteness and racial Blackness.[5]

In other words, the very attempt by the U.S. ruling class to engulf those who fall outside the scope of citizenship into the confines of "American" identity is a response to the unrest caused by oppressive immigration policy. This is partly how the ideology of American innocence creates a dangerous naïveté when it comes to the rise of the U.S. Latino population. Many well-meaning people claim that white supremacy will end once Latinos become the country's majority. As many authors have shown, however, the reality might be more complicated.[6] In fact, much of today's immigration discourse in Latino communities is rooted deeply in anti-Blackness. As Escobar notes, "when we claim that immigrants are not criminals, the fundamental message is that immigrants are not Black, or at least, that immigrants will not be 'another Black problem.'"[7]

However, representatives of both political parties in the U.S. have historically utilized the narrative of the "invading hordes" of "illegal" migrants to justify the intense militarization and exploitation of undocumented people. The immigration debate over citizenship has never fit neatly into the narrow two-party system. Democrats have historically been no better than Republicans in enforcing policies that protect "illegal" immigrants. Whether Democrat or Republican, presidential administrations in Washington have taken a similar position on "illegal" immigration. Democratic President Bill Clinton, for example, blamed "illegal aliens" for drug crime and job insecurity. His speeches often equated democracy with "secure borders." This led to the passage of both the Personal Responsibility and Work Opportunity Act and the Illegal Immigration Reform and Immigrant Responsibility Act in 1996. The former greatly restricted access to welfare benefits for "illegal" immigrants while the latter expanded the U.S. government's capacity to deport "noncitizens" with criminal records. In 1986, just 1,978 immigrants were deported for criminal violations. By 2004, that number increased to 82,802.[8]

Clinton-era policies were continued under George W. Bush. These policies sparked intense resistance to deportations, arrests, and detentions of "illegal" immigrants. In 2006, for example, millions of undocumented people around the country proclaimed "A Day Without Immigrants" and marched off their respective jobs. The protests channeled Lisa Lowe's conclusion that "the state declares the universal extension of rights to all citizens, yet U.S. history has shown that access to rights has always been unevenly distributed, requiring social movements to call upon the state to establish liberties for subjects who are guaranteed rights in theory."[9] More specifically, the protests came in response to HR-4437, a bill passed by Congress that greatly increased funding for border control and placed harsher penalties for immigration crime violations. Many believed that the bill would lead to massive deportations.

The protests were unable to reverse the bill or the broad range of policies that made mass deportations possible. Over two million immigrants would be deported under Bush during his two terms while over three million were deported under Obama during his tenure.[10] The deportation spike under Obama had much to do with his administration's decision to charge "illegal" immigrants apprehended at the border with a federal crime.[11] Obama's harsh treatment of undocumented migrants led his former Secretary of State Hillary Clinton to conclude in 2014 that tens of thousands of unaccompanied youth from Honduras, Guatemala, and El Salvador should be deported.[12] The unpopularity of these draconian immigration policies did eventually catch the interest of a section of the ruling class, compelling this class to steer immigration advocates toward acceptable means of protest. American exceptionalism was thus deployed by the U.S. ruling class to frame opposition to the criminalization of "illegal" immigrants as an assimilationist striving, or a striving for what Escobar calls "American"-ness.[13]

The Democratic Party in particular has been in the driver seat of the assimilationist narrative. Since the dissolution of the Dixiecrats in the 1960s, Republican lawmakers and administrations have appealed primarily to the anxieties produced by white supremacy. The Democratic Party stood alone at the mantle of imperial "progressivism." When immigrant rights activists marched off the job in 2006 and protested the Obama Administration over deportations in 2010, the Democratic Party and their wealthy corporate backers believed that immigrant constituencies from Mexico and Latin America represented a valuable voting bloc. Democratic lawmakers and politicians utilized American exceptionalism to create a softer narrative on immigration. Immigrant labor was valuable to the U.S. economy, they claimed, so it only made sense that immigrants were treated as "Americans" were treated.

American exceptionalism and innocence thus began to mold the issue of immigration in its image. Immigration became a debate over the moral values of American society instead of a political struggle for power. Competing views over what made the U.S. exceptional in the first place took precedence as immigrants themselves were rendered voiceless. Republicans remained outwardly hostile toward the very notion of "insecure" borders and the decline in the "white" population it facilitated. To them, America was exceptional because of its white majority. Democrats, on the other hand, attempted to appeal both to immigrant constituencies and its corporate backers. On the one hand, advocacy for the assimilation of immigrants gave the U.S. the veneer that it was an inherently welcoming society. This narrative utilized the "melting pot" framework to hide from plain sight the root causes of immigration and their impact on immigration policy.

America was exceptional, the argument goes, not because it was a "white" nation but because it was a nation that provided opportunity to diverse populations. Democrats utilized the inclusion narrative to effectively cater to both sides of the immigration debate. Because a consensus emerged from Democratic constituents that not all undocumented immigrants were criminals (i.e., as Escobar reminds us, they weren't "black" or going to be "another black problem"), piecemeal policies such as the Obama Administration's Deferred Action for Childhood Arrivals (DACA) became acceptable to the U.S. ruling class. DACA was an executive order from Obama in 2012 that protected unauthorized immigrants with a two year period of respite from the threat of deportation. The policy reflected Lowe's analysis of U.S. immigration policy, where "immigration law reproduces a racially segmented and stratified labor force for capital's needs, inasmuch as such legal disenfranchisements or restricted enfranchisements seek to resolve such inequalities by deferring them in the promise of equality on the political terrain of representation."[14] While DACA provided temporary safety for some, it did not enact a path to citizenship that many immigrant rights activists demanded. The U.S.-Mexico border remained militarized, Immigration and Customs Enforcement (ICE) continued its policy of terror and deportation of "illegal" immigrants, and multinational corporations that rely on cheap, migrant labor continued to rake in profits.

The Democratic Party has thus relegated the issue of immigration to the margins of inclusion politics. Policies such as DACA provide critical relief for some but leave the structure of U.S. imperialism intact. U.S. imperialism is reliant upon both the cheap labor of "illegal" immigrants and the militarization of the U.S.-Mexico border. It is also reliant upon "free trade" agreements such as NAFTA and CAFTA that allow American corporations free-reign in Latin America and the military domination required to enforce them. These critical aspects of the immigration question have been largely ignored in place of negotiations over whether "illegal" immigrants should be treated like all other "Americans" or not.

The truth is that no one should have to live with the state-sanctioned terror imposed on "illegal" immigrants. In order for this to happen, however, the definition of citizenship cannot be relegated to an identification with the American nation-state. Immigration policy is not merely a question of whether "illegal" immigrants are criminals or not. It is not a choice between two versions of American exceptionalist mythology that assume the nation either to be a "sanctuary" for immigrants or a strictly "white nation" that must be protected from criminal, job-stealing invaders from south of the border. Immigration policy is a question of power and always has been.

History shows that immigration is no partisan issue. Immigrants have been targeted by white supremacist terror throughout U.S. history as a means to divert attention away from the crises of American capitalism and imperialism. Kelly Lytle Hernández explains that as early as the Civil War, American capitalists took advantage of the "open door" it imposed on China to encourage Chinese contract workers to migrate to the U.S. as a replacement for African slaves.[15] The spectre of emancipation caused plantation owners and other capitalists to fear a possible labor shortage in the waning years of slavery. Chinese workers were regularly derided as "coolies," however, and racial tensions boiled over into the passage of the Anti-Coolie Act of 1862. The Act prohibited the importation of "coolies" on the basis that they represented another slave labor force. However, as Frederick Douglass retorted, the problem was not the Chinese immigrant but rather the system that forced the African and Chinese worker to be a "slave and a coveted article of merchandise."[16]

Racism and capitalist exploitation continued to shape immigration policy in the years that followed. Chinese contract workers regularly experienced violence in the form of lynching and often faced discrimination on the job. It was not uncommon for Chinese workers to be portrayed as "pollution" or "debased."[17] The U.S. fully excluded Chinese contract workers in 1882 amid hysteria that they posed a danger to "free white labor" throughout the country. The Chinese Exclusion Act of 1882 laid the basis for quotas or limitations to migration from countries in Asia and Eastern Europe. And in the early 20th century, migration from Mexico became the focus of the United States' so-called "border control" policy.

U.S. imperialism waged a brutal war of expansion against Mexico in the mid-19th century only to subject the nation to economic subservience. Mexican migrant workers became a critical contributor to the United State's southern economy, leading to the Bracero Program in 1942 which encouraged Mexican workers to contract with American corporations for low-wage work. Between 1942 and 1964, over four million Mexicans worked in the U.S under the program. Yet their presence came into direct conflict with the contradictory policy of immigration enforcement. The formation of the Border Patrol in 1924 was a direct response to the numerous laws that the state had placed on "illegal" migration. This culminated in a 1954 campaign called "Operation Wetback" to deport Mexican workers racially targeted as "wetbacks" from the country.[18]

The prevailing contradiction of immigration and "border control" has little to do with the tension between the "melting pot" theory of a welcoming, inclusive America and anti-immigrant bigotry. Anti-immigrant sentiment is a product of racism and imperialism. How racism and imperialism have been enforced has depended on the particular requirements of these systems at various points in history. Immigrant labor has provided a steady stream of low-wage labor for American monopolies and an avenue to strengthen white supremacy as a buffer from the root causes of immigration. "Citizenship" has thus been a concept defined by one's proximity to whiteness. When the U.S. saw Japan as a threat to its economic interests in East Asia in WWII, it did not hesitate to strip the citizenship of Japanese Americans by imprisoning them in brutal internment camps throughout the country.[19] The policy was enforced by President Franklin Roosevelt, revered by many as the nation's most "progressive" and "exceptional" presidents in the realms of peace and worker-friendly policies.

Recent history also proves that the benefits of "belonging" to the American nation-state are mainly conferred to white Americans, especially property owners. Joel Olson explains that:

> The democratic problem of the white citizen is that tension between the desire for equality and the desire to maintain one's racial standing results in a narrow political imagination that constrains the way white citizens understand citizenship (as status rather than participation), freedom (as negative liberty), and equality (as opportunity rather than social equality). The white imagination exhibits little incentive to expand participation in public affairs because it construes citizenship as an identity to possess rather than a power to employ.[20]

Since the U.S. was founded on the premise of white citizenship, immigration policy has utilized whiteness to reinforce the power of the ruling class at the expense of "others." The so-called "land of the free" has been anything but for undocumented migrants deemed criminals by the state. American discourse on immigration has centered on the false dichotomy between American citizenship and criminality to discourage conversation about the central issue of oppression and liberation. The criminalization of "illegal" migrants has not occurred in isolation. "Illegal" immigrants exist for the same reasons that Black Americans experience racist state terror despite having the "privilege" of citizenship conferred upon them. Citizenship narrows the parameters of the debate by burying the true reasons for the exploitation of undocumented labor in the graveyard of American exceptionalism and innocence.

American exceptionalism and innocence portray "illegal" immigration either as a clean up project or an assimilationist project.[21] Immigrants either must be assimilated into society or eliminated from it. Such a choice is little different than that which Black Americans face everyday when confronted with police terror, incarceration, and economic discrimination. And entire nations such as Syria and Iran must decide everyday whether to accept the oppression of the American nation-state or risk the threat of nuclear annihilation by fighting back. Ideologies of American exceptionalism and innocence thus operate together to create the illusion that only two options lie on the table: America must either "purify" the nation of unwanted invaders or civilize it further by including more "diverse" populations into its ranks.

Violence is endemic to the making of an exceptional America. To be a "citizen" of the U.S. is to uphold and even celebrate the oppressive structures and policies critiqued in this book. Raúl Al-qaraz Ochoa states plainly that citizenship "legitimizes the global capitalist order, as well as their borders and their nation states. So when we talk about citizenship today, we should ask who/what benefits from the exploitation of an illegal class."[22] U.S. borders have come to embody the structures and policies that facilitate the existence of U.S. imperialism. We must understand these structures and policies if we are to truly understand the root causes of migration and the subsequent criminalization of immigrants in the U.S.[23]

Over the last four decades, the structure of U.S. imperialism has altered in ways that precipitated the phenomenon of "illegal" immigration." Global capitalism has been going through a neoliberal transition where technology and monopoly have cut into the long term profitability of the system. Finance capital has leveraged debt to keep monopolies and banks profitable, but only at great cost to working people and poor people the world over. A conscious decision was made to turn everything into a potential "market," including the social welfare systems of the U.S. and its Western allies. Unions have been dismantled, social welfare policies defunded, and public sector institutions privatized. Millions of American workers have seen their wages decline sharply over this time as jobs have either been fully automated or shipped ashore to countries with lower wage scales. Homelessness, poverty, and unemployment have become permanent fixtures of an American capitalist economy wracked by constant uncertainty.

These conditions coincided with the heavy-handed response of the U.S. to domestic and global revolutionary movements for self-determination and social transformation. The Black liberation movement and movements for independence around the world forced the U.S. to greatly expand its military apparatus on all fronts. Black Americans were criminalized in a "War on Drugs" that directly followed the arming of police with military grade weaponry beginning in the 1960s to put down urban rebellions in Black cities. By defining Black Americans as criminals, the U.S. effectively found a convenient narrative to justify the dismantling of welfare and the escalation of the military state. Black Americans were "super predators," "welfare queens," and "thugs" that required incarceration to, in the words of Hillary Clinton, "bring them to heel." Hysteria over "illegal" immigration came in the context of the anti-poor, "tough on crime" policies that originated as a response to social upheaval and the subsequent degeneration of the American social order.

The criminalization of immigrants is rooted in the criminalization of the Black and the poor. But it is American imperial warfare that has sent migrants coming to the U.S. in the first place. The economic engine of American warfare has come in the form of corporate "free-trade" agreements such as NAFTA. Free trade agreements have privileged the rights of American corporations to dominate the economic organization of oppressed nations. In the case of Mexico, NAFTA devastated Mexican farm workers by removing critical state subsidies.[24] Hundreds of thousands were forced to the cities to find jobs at American factories that could not hire them. This sent a large wave of Mexican workers northward to the U.S.

American military warfare has also played a large role in migration. When Central American migrants from Honduras, Guatemala, and El Salvador came in the tens of thousands in 2014, few commentators connected the development to U.S. foreign policy. Yet it was the Reagan Administration's funding of the brutal contra mercenary forces in the 1980s in nations such as El Salvador and Guatemala that led to the instability and poverty that has sent so many fleeing their homeland.[25] The Obama Administration followed Reagan's footsteps in 2009 by sponsoring a coup in Honduras that led to the empowerment of paramilitary forces in league with American interests. These forces violently repressed social movements and forced many Hondurans to seek asylum outside of their nation of origin.

"Belonging" to the U.S., then, is to identify with the violence, oppression, and exploitation that facilitates migration. To be a "citizen" is to believe that the American nation-state is the "home of the brave" when in fact it is the home of dispossession, anti-Black terror, and imperialism. At this point, it is worth recalling Lisa Lowe's precaution against not simply the violence of *exclusion* but the violence of *inclusion* as well. U.S. immigration policies merely reinforce the "longevity of the colonial divisions of humanity in our contemporary moment," Lowe writes, "in which the human life of citizens protected by the state is bound to the denigration of populations cast in violation of human life, set outside of human society," And "while violence characterizes exclusion from the universality of the human," she continues, "it also accompanies inclusion or assimilation into it."[26] A new concept of citizenship is required to break the cycle of criminalization and racism that shapes the debate around immigration. This means that not only is it time to question the *policing* of borders but to imagine a world without borders altogether.

Andrea Smith urges activists and scholars to challenge the notion of the United States' inherent exceptionalism. "Rather than a pursuit of life, liberty, and happiness that depends on the deaths of others," she writes, "we can imagine new forms of governance based on the principles of mutuality, interdependence, and equality. When we do not presume that the United States should or will continue to exist, we can begin to imagine more than a kinder, gentler settler state founded on genocide and slavery."[27] When we question the permanency of the American nation-state, we question the legitimacy of its borders. The borders of the American nation-state were drawn from the colonization of Indigenous people, the enslavement of Black people, and the destruction of nations abroad. Borders represent the imaginary lines of plunder that have produced conditions where half of the American population makes less than $30,000 per year, with "illegal" immigrants and Black workers trailing far behind the average worker. Borders indicate exactly who and what owns the land and labor of the U.S. and who does not. They indicate who deserves to live and who deserves to die and who deserves a life of poverty, oppression, and incarceration and who doesn't. Imagining an end to these logics is what Andrea Smith means by the "Indigenous dream"; that is, imagining "a world without an America."

An alternative to the American settler colonial and imperialist arrangement cannot emerge if the preservation or reform of the American nation-state remains the framework of our social movements. Citizenship makes up a crucial piece of American innocence. Struggles to reform or alter the U.S. legal structure, for example, leave its foundation as a settler colonial and imperialist system intact. Reforms make identification with the U.S. more desirable, as if we're all banding together to form a "more perfect union." "In the classical liberal tradition," Paisley Currah writes, "the state is thought to be a neutral umpire, meting out judgment according to the rule of law [. . .] According to this tradition's contemporary script, that governments have denied rights based on distinctions of race and gender, among others, in the past is an unfortunate historical contingency, one that betrayed the principle of equality and that has now been, or soon will be, rectified."[28] The U.S. is thus seen as a nation that has "lost its way," and that can ultimately be redeemed by living up to its founding principles. Yet in pursuing mere tweaks to the system, the war, racism, and exploitation that has forever fueled our "union" remain left unaddressed, and therefore become even more deeply entrenched.

This doesn't mean that "illegal" immigrants should cease their struggle for dignity or decriminalization. It means that this struggle cannot be separated from the oppression of all people under the rule of imperialism. The U.S.-backed destruction of Yemen and Syria, for example, have facilitated refugee crises around the world. Presidents Bill Clinton, George W. Bush, and Barack Obama have relied on the neoliberal logic of "deserving" and "undeserving" poor not only to militarize their assault on undocumented people, but also to justify the privatization of schools in Black neighborhoods and their silence when twelve-year-old Black children like Tamir Rice are gunned down in the streets by police at increasing rates.

Such structures of domination lead innovative scholars like Bianca C. Williams to chronicle the lives of those involved with Girlfriends Tours International, a group of "Black women who feel they cannot experience happiness regularly within U.S. borders because of American racism and sexism." By temporarily fleeing the U.S., she writes, "they begin to search for ways to fulfill their 'inalienable right' . . . drawing on diasporic connections and imaginings, and pursuing happiness and belonging in Jamaica."[29] The questions raised by Williams and her friends highlight the urgency of rethinking borders, belonging, and the nation-state: "What about these women's lives as Black women pushes them to repeatedly leave the 'land of opportunity' to pursue happiness?" She asks. "What happens when Black American women begin to look beyond their nation's borders for happiness and fulfillment?"[30]

The interconnectedness of oppression under U.S. settler-colonialism and imperialism opens up the possibility to facilitate the "end" of the American nation-state. This should not be equated with an act of "terrorism" or reckless violence as political elites often retort. Rather, the "end" of the American nation-state would mean that the conditions of oppression and exploitation are eradicated through the formation of a new social arrangement. Under such an arrangement, solidarity replaces borders. Self-determination guides the development of nations instead of the uneven power and hegemony of one nation-state and its "citizens" over all others. Racial distinction and profit no longer represent the motivating forces of society. In its place, the needs of those dispossessed and exploited by the system determine who has control over the means of production and how that control is wielded toward the benefit of the planet.[31]

The materialization of such a society does not have to be confined to the imagination. But it must start there. We can imagine a new world only through an understanding of—and struggling against—the oppressive conditions of the system. The abolition of borders and citizenship are not mutually exclusive to the demands of undocumented people to find safety and dignity in the U.S. But such goals must redefine citizenship, not as a place of belonging or "inclusion" for oppressed populations, but as a transnational fight for a world where oppression no longer exists. As Smith further explains, "a liberatory vision for immigrant rights is based less on pathways to citizenship in a settler state, than on questioning the logics of the settler state itself."[32] This liberatory vision was demonstrated by immigrant rights activists in September 2017 when they interrupted a press conference by Democratic Party leader Nancy Pelosi with the chant, "All of us, or none of us!" Their chant, if extended to those who have been separated by borders yet united by their oppression, could signal the beginnings of a new revolutionary movement capable of dismantling imperial and settler-colonial logics. A movement capable of bringing about the Indigenous dream.

CHAPTER 21

"Conclusion: Who Exactly Does the Military Serve?"

". . . we are Black peoples in the wake with no state or nation to protect us, with no citizenship bound to be respected . . ."

—Christina Sharpe[1]

"What we recall has as much to do with the terrible things we hope to avoid as with the good life for which we yearn. But when does one decide to stop looking to the past and instead conceive of a new order? When is it time to dream of another country or to embrace other strangers as allies or to make an opening, an overture, where there is none?"

—Saidiya Hartman[2]

"Whenever we try to envision a world without war, without violence, without prisons, without capitalism, we are engaging in speculative fiction. All organizing is science fiction. Organizers and activists dedicate their lives to creating and envisioning another world, or many other worlds . . ."

—Walidah Imarisha[3]

In an article titled, "Why Do We Keep Thanking the Troops?" former army ranger Rory Fanning raises questions about a tradition celebrated everywhere from sporting events and beer commercials to church sanctuaries and airport terminals. "Since 9/11," Fanning writes, "thank yous have been aimed at veterans with the regularity of the machine gun fire that may still haunt their dreams." As one of the many U.S. soldiers around the world who has filed for conscientious objector status, Fanning has heard harsh criticisms of American foreign policy from numerous fellow veterans. "They often grasp the way in which the militarized acts of imperial America are helping to create the very enemies they are then being told to kill," he says. As for the common tendency to label members of the armed service "heroes," Fanning says that the term makes many veterans feel uneasy, which is why they often reject it. And not just out of false modesty. "Most veterans who have seen combat," he explains, or "watched babies get torn apart, or their comrades die in their arms, or the most powerful army on Earth spend trillions of dollars fighting some of the poorest people in the world for 13 years feel anything but heroic."[4]

This book has explored the narratives of American heroism, exceptionalism, and innocence and how they have influenced the way we think about the past, present, and future of U.S. empire. These interrelated ideologies have been wielded by the ruling class in a way that clouds historical memory and diffuses resistance to oppression and exploitation. In other words, ideologies of exceptionalism and innocence shift communities away from practices of solidarity, self-determination, and revolution and instead steer them toward the politics of inclusion, humanitarian intervention, and multicultural citizenship. The belief that the U.S. and its citizens are superior and serve as a force for good in the world has been promoted by the ruling class to subdue radical political thought and action. One of the biggest promoters of U.S. superiority and exceptionalism is the U.S. military.

The U.S. military is the armed body of the American state that enforces exceptionalism and innocence by way of ideological and material violence. Perhaps at no other moment has it become more important for progressive and radical scholars, activists, and organizers to come together and oppose the endless wars waged by the U.S. military. We believe this book equips a new generation of progressives and radicals to do just that. As of this writing, it not a stretch to conclude that the U.S. military is at war with nearly the entire world. At least 800 U.S. military bases are scattered across the globe and, with a budget of nearly a trillion dollars per year, there is no shortage of money to maintain its deadly arsenal of troops and weapons around the world. Continued U.S. military presence in the Korean peninsula, Syria, Ukraine, and the Baltic region threatens the existence of humanity with the potential of nuclear war.

The threat of such a war is heightened by the fact that the American military doesn't wage war randomly. Every drone strike, every invasion, and every occupation has a reason behind it. The U.S. military unleashes terror in all corners of the planet for precious resources that are required to keep the U.S.-led system of global capitalism profitable. Nations around the world must be forced to acquiesce to American economic interests, which is why the U.S. military often has as its goal the overthrow or containment of governments unwilling to allow their nations to be plundered and forced into subservience. The U.S. military has labeled Russia and China the greatest threat to "national security" at the present moment. Many of its war efforts are aimed at ensuring that these two rising powers are under the constant threat of annihilation.

The imminent threat of a nuclear global confrontation has found expression in the U.S. "pivot" to Asia as a means to "contain" China. Other flashpoints for nuclear showdown include the American use of NATO to provoke Russia and the potential clash of Russian and U.S. forces in Syria. Still, the American anti-war movement remains small and inconsequential. Actor Morgan Freeman can line up behind U.S. intelligence leaders such as James Clapper and declare "we are at war" with Russia and few in the U.S. express outrage.[5] The Trump Administration can bomb Syria like it did in April of 2017 and 2018 and the silence of the American public continues to deafen.

American exceptionalism and American innocence have been largely to blame for the widespread silence that exists in the U.S. around questions of war and peace. This book has attempted to place such silence in the context of the following questions: Who does the U.S. military serve? Does it keep us safe and protect our "national interest"? Does it "give us our freedoms"? Whose freedoms are these? Does it really fight for our rights? Who does the U.S. military protect? How we answer these questions will determine whether the U.S. remains on its current course of global destruction or is stopped by a new anti-war movement that joins the world in condemning American military aggression.

But first we need to define *we*. In a class society, the ideas of the dominant class represent the dominant ideas of society as a whole. Class society in the U.S. is also a racist society which possesses the most formidable capitalist empire in human history. The American nation-state enforces complex relations of exploitation and violence between workers and bosses, Black Americans and white Americans, and oppressor and oppressed nations, to name a few. The American capitalist class, simply by virtue of being a large chunk of the dominant class, has already answered our questions posed above. Dominant class ideologies such as American exceptionalism and American innocence have developed a solid base of support in the U.S. for the military and its wars, which is why a resurgent anti-war movement cannot develop unless these ideologies become a central focus of critique.

If we are not answering questions about U.S. military domination from the perspective of the American capitalist class, then we are answering them from the perspective of those victimized by that class. We choose to answer them from the perspective of the oppressed. Our opposition to American exceptionalism and American innocence is shaped by an intentional decision to take a stand against U.S. militarism. This isn't the norm in the U.S., where, as Trevor McCrisken writes, "it appears automatic for American public officials to conceive their policies in terms that represent some notion of the exceptional nature of the US. They do so not simply because it will be politically advantageous but because those terms form a natural part of the language they use to understand the world around them."[6] The ideologies of American exceptionalism and American innocence certainly reflect the way the dominant class understands the world around them. These ideologies purposely drown out the perspective and lived experience of the oppressed through the many mouthpieces of the ruling class: the American corporate media, the two-party political system, and the monopolies, banks, and war industries that control the state.

Consciousness of *who* and *what* is behind the dominant narratives of American exceptionalism and American innocence is a prerequisite for the development of an alternative narrative that can be popularized widely. Put simply, if state violence is at the center of one's experience, then it is more likely that state violence will be at the center of one's analysis. Likewise, if state violence is *not* at the center of one's experience, then it is highly *unlikely* that state violence will be at the center of one's analysis. As this book has tried to show, state violence is fundamental to the creation, spread, and survival of American exceptionalist logics. To be blinded by narratives of American exceptionalism and innocence is to be blind to the everyday violence perpetrated by the structures, institutions, and ideas of "America." This is why victims of U.S. state violence are uniquely positioned to critique American exceptionalism and American innocence. Over the course of history, many have refused to see such violence as a mere aberration, a deviation from who "we really are" as a nation. They have rejected any claim to benevolence—that our government, its leaders, or even some "national creed" will protect us. And they've always remained skeptical whenever legislation is passed and wars are waged under the auspices of so-called "good intentions."

Perhaps no institution embodies American exceptionalism and American innocence more than the U.S. military. According to these mythologies, there is no question about who the military serves: The U.S. military serves the interests of the American people and, even further, the good of humanity. The fact that military service is called "service" at all is a case in point. Enthusiasts of the U.S. military often portray the most heavily armed body of the state appear as a charitable organization. Maximilian Forte discusses this effective propaganda tool in his study of the Department of Defense's Flickr photostream. Although they are "tenuously emptied of political overtones," he writes, "the photographs produce a political effect, for political purposes—they do not tell the horror stories of war, of bloodshed and lives lost, of destruction and grief, but rather portray something like a birthday party. Indeed, gift giving is a central feature of most of the photographs featuring US military personnel and citizens of other nations."[7] The images represent merely one aspect of a carefully crafted public relations campaign outlined by the U.S. military in documents such as the *U.S. National Strategy for Public Diplomacy and Strategic Communication*, published in 2006. Mass distributed photos of U.S. military personnel playing with children in nations like Cambodia, Haiti, and the Philippines transform the military from the most murderous entity on the planet to an organization that innocently comes to the aid of people all over the world, bearing the gifts of "freedom" and "democracy." What most people around the world experience as a reign of terror is viewed as a birthday party by America and its allies.

The U.S. military has come under increasing pressure to maintain the illusion that it is in fact a force for good in the world. One will never catch the U.S. military discussing the one million-plus Iraqis murdered by the U.S. military over the course of the invasion that began there in 2003. U.S. military leaders will also never be caught publicly celebrating the Iraqi children who continue to be born with deformities and deadly cancers caused by the constant use of U.S. weapons stocked with toxic depleted uranium.[8] To do so would be to challenge the dominant narrative that the U.S. military keeps us safe, that it rescues poor women and children from evil tyrants, and that it is in the business of bringing peace, not wreaking havoc. The reality of American intervention abroad, however, disrupts the dominant narrative that the U.S. military keeps "us", or *anyone*, safe by protecting "our freedoms."

That the military protects "freedoms" and keeps us "safe" is laughable from the perspective of those who have always been on the receiving end of U.S. state violence. This includes Black Americans, Native Americans, and "illegal" immigrants right here inside of the U.S. The U.S. military is a direct product of the colonial origins of the state. Enslavement and genocide of Black and Indigenous people formed the core of the military and the nation at large. The U.S. military has since globalized its colonialist and imperialist system. U.S. military expansion has also ensured the militarization of American society as well. The U.S. military transfers hundreds of millions of dollars worth of weaponry to local police departments each year through the 1033 program. Local police departments stay true to their roots as former slave patrols by murdering Black Americans at an alarming rate. A Department of Justice study in 2015 found that between 2007 and 2015, Philadelphia police shot at suspects 390 times, killing 65 of them. Of the 65 killed, 55 were unarmed and 80 percent were Black.[9] This is just a snapshot of the very real military-style occupation of majority Black cities by local police departments.

Much has been made about the racial disparities produced by the mass incarceration of Blacks in America. Police departments act as the armed body of the state in much of the same way as the U.S. military does, so it should not come as any surprise that the two institutions share a special relationship. Local police departments conduct a daily reign of terror in Black cities in the U.S. to fill up body bags and prison cells in a similar manner that the U.S. military fills up body bags and imprisons entire nations under its de facto rule in Africa, Asia, and Latin America. American exceptionalism claims that the police and the U.S. military alike "protect and serve" Americans to mask the terror they inflict on humanity. American innocence claims that the military and the police provide freedom for all rather than strip a large section of the population of its freedom to live and determine its own destiny. The commonalities between the military and police as institutions of mass death become erased and replaced by the perception that they represent the pinnacle of an exceptional nation's sacrifice for the betterment of humanity. The ideology of innocence also frames incidents like the Mai Lai massacre as the U.S.

military going "off script," when it fact it is no deviation at all from the script of U.S militarism. Similarly, ideologies of innocence also frame policing as "police brutality." This renders "brutality" as antithetical to real police work when in fact "brutality" is at the very core of the job description.[10]

If the U.S. ensures mass death, incarceration, and terror for oppressed people within its own (colonial) borders, then the U.S. military cannot possibly provide freedom for nations abroad. As Lisa Lowe notes, the U.S. has been stealing the freedoms of oppressed people throughout its history, "from the destruction and dispossession of Indigenous peoples to the enslavement of Africans and the unfinished work of emancipation, from the stolen labors of indentured and immigrant workers to the losses of life as the US waged wars in Latin America, East, Northeast, and Southeast Asia, and now Central Asia and the Middle East."[11] Again, the point isn't that many Americans are unaware of these conditions and that we therefore need to teach people what *really happened*, and how history informs the present. While certainly necessary, this focus on "teaching better history" often ignores a close examination of the ideologies that inform the way we remember, excuse, or justify U.S. traditions such as enslavement, dispossession, and empire. Following Lowe, it is equally important, if not more so, to examine how these "conditions have been more often elided by an official history of American exceptionalism, the promise of freedom through citizenship, and progress through pluralism and expansion."[12]

American exceptionalism promises freedom, citizenship, and progress to render the U.S. military innocent of wrongdoing and strip it from any responsibility for its actions. U.S. forces deployed abroad are therefore granted impunity in the destruction it has leveled upon nations such as Iraq, Libya, Afghanistan, and Syria. U.S. military interventions have led to a massive wave of migration from the Middle East and North Africa. Catastrophe-induced mass migration abroad is a product of the same relations that compel Immigration and Customs Enforcement (ICE) officers to deport so-called "illegal" migrants from the U.S. The destruction caused by U.S. imperialism leaves millions uprooted and consigned to an early death, whether it is Indigenous people in the U.S. being murdered by police at a rate higher than Black Americans or in Syria where the U.S. military's arsenal has destroyed homes, hospitals, and schools.

The U.S. military and its supporters often avoid accountability by complaining about so-called dictators in places like Syria who "kill their own people." Usually these claims cannot be verified and even if they possess a shred of truth, they wouldn't make the actions of the U.S. military any less illegal under international law. Legal issues aside, it is puzzling how such an accusation can be made with a straight face, given how easy it is to find evidence of the U.S. killing "its own people." The difference between U.S. allegations of "dictators" killing "their own people" and its own actions is that when the U.S. kills, such as the hundreds of migrants who are killed crossing the U.S. Mexico border each year, it doesn't consider the victims to be people at all. The U.S. also does not consider the hundreds of Black Americans killed by police each year to be people either. America has never been "exceptional," "innocent," or a "force for good" for these populations. Yet most Americans remain blind to the state-inflicted violence perpetrated on their neighbors every day. Given the moral outrage of the American military at the Syrian or Iranian governments for "killing their own people," it makes one wonder why the same outrage isn't leveled at its own government.

Of course, to do so would threaten any claim to exceptionalism or innocence. Comparing U.S. crimes to those purportedly committed by Syria or Iran—or even admitting that the U.S. commits crimes!—is bad for PR. It is not as if there aren't other countries that kill its own citizens, like Saudi Arabia, and Egypt. Yet we would hardly ever find the U.S. military threatening to bomb their capital cities. It's almost as if the U.S. military is pointing its fingers at Syria and Iran, not because of some special, unforgivable crime they have committed, but because they happen to be two of the countries whose destruction the U.S. ruling class has deemed critical to the fulfillment of its economic and strategic interests in the region.

That Americans express outrage when their government accuses Syria, for example, of using chemical weapons to kill people is unsurprising. After all, the corporate media does not hesitate to repeatedly remind us that chemical weapons induce a painful and excruciating form of death. There is no objection to this (other than the fact that chemical weapons are highly inefficient as "mass killers" as compared to conventional weapons). What the corporate media doesn't report, however, is how unverified chemical weapons attacks pale in comparison to the excruciating and painful death that capitalism creates by way of the U.S. state. The corporate media accuses other countries of atrocities but ignores the millions of casualties that capitalism has produced within America's own borders. Perhaps it is because a death by chemical weapons is easier to see; it's easy for a CNN photojournalist to snap a picture of writhing children to invoke popular sympathy. It's much harder for a camera to capture the devastating violence wreaked slowly, painfully, and lethally by racial capitalism. Saidiya Hartman describes these often unseen "forms of structural violence" as ones that "continue to make large sectors of the population vulnerable to premature death, not as the result of frontal assault, or war, or anarchic violence but as the slow and enduring violence that allows people to die every day from poverty, neglect, incarceration, and extreme forms of exploitation and social marginality." To many Americans, "this might appear to be violence without an agent or fail to register as violence at all," Hartman concludes, "but it produces a regular death toll."[13]

One could only imagine what the American response would be to China, Iran, or even its ally Germany if one of them decided to intervene militarily in the U.S. because it was "killing its own people" and committing human rights abuses. This event sounds absurd on many fronts. For one, these countries have no interest in provoking a nuclear power like the U.S. with a proven record of bellicosity nor do they possess the capability of carrying out a first strike on U.S. borders. But we have to ask ourselves, why does the U.S. military have free reign to dictate how other nations conduct themselves, while other countries aren't allowed to critique the U.S. for the very same actions? And if the U.S. really cared about protecting our "freedom," why is nothing done to alleviate the declining living standards of ordinary Americans? The right to wage war seems to be the exclusive right of the U.S. It is easy for Americans to feel exceptional when the millions of people who die from U.S. military interventions around the world are deemed "collateral damage." It is also easier to cheer on the military as it punishes foreign leaders for (allegedly) killing their own citizens when Americans are completely disconnected from the millions of people within their own borders who succumb daily to premature death. In short, the American military's so-called mandate to "protect freedom" doesn't apply to the millions of Americans who suffer from the laws of capitalism.

The U.S. military murders millions in Afghanistan, Iraq, and Libya but pays little attention to the tens of thousands of people who die each year in the U.S. from a lack of health insurance.[14] The U.S. military receives $700 billion a year to intervene in "terrorist" states and overthrow "dictators" accused of human rights atrocities but fails to intervene on behalf of the 50 percent of the American population categorized as "near poor." The U.S. military has facilitated dozens of coups abroad in the name of "democracy" but appears disinterested in the fact that many observers have concluded that the U.S. operates more like an oligarchy than a democracy.[15] No U.S. troops have been sent to assist the residents of Flint, Michigan, who were found to be drinking poisoned drinking water in 2014. Nor have they been deployed to Lowndes County, Alabama, where a UN Special Rapporteur study in 2017 found that one in three people were infected with hookworm, a condition associated with the underdevelopment of so-called "Third World" countries.[16]

It is no wonder that most Americans have a distorted understanding of violence. U.S. capitalism forces millions of people, many of them white, to commit suicide from a combination of addiction, mental illness, and unemployment.[17] This concern is considered outside the scope of the U.S. military's job description. Still, the U.S. military is seen as the arbiter of freedom even when it collaborates with local police departments to brutalize Black Americans, sends American soldiers to fight wars abroad then brings them home to a life of homelessness, and collaborates with U.S. intelligence in the deployment of drones to spy on American citizens.[18] Ideologies of American exceptionalism and American innocence have inoculated the U.S. population from making the connection between the death imposed by modern day U.S. capitalism at home and the misery the U.S. military reigns on nations abroad.

The U.S. military does not protect "our freedoms." It might protect the freedom of *some* but definitely not the freedom of *most*. The U.S. military protects the freedoms of those who benefit from white supremacy and U.S. imperialism. A secondary beneficiary of these related systems are individuals classified as white, those who receive the nominal privilege of not being consigned to a life of imminent death just by way of their racial identity. However, many ordinary white Americans feel "war fatigue" amid a decline in living standards. The primary beneficiaries of war, then, are the rich, the owners of property, and most importantly, the owners of corporations and banks. Ideologies of American exceptionalism and American innocence have always been white supremacist ideologies at their very core, utilized in the service of the rich. And white supremacy's primary function is to universalize ruling class interests under the banner of whiteness to weaken the potential of a unified, class-based resistance to oppression and exploitation.

American exceptionalism and American innocence universalize the powerful interests behind the military. We are tricked into believing that the "prosperity" and "freedom" that the U.S. military protects around the world applies to poor people and oppressed people. The opposite is true. Wars boost the stock market numbers and profits for Raytheon and other military contractors but not the incomes or job prospects of most Americans. Wars boost the productivity of oil corporations and help leverage lending opportunities for Wall Street banks but do not liberate American students from trillions in student loan debt. The U.S. military offers nothing but poverty, misery, and violence for the majority of the world's population. It relies on the incessant marketing of its exceptional and innocent nature and the dehumanization of its targeted enemies to maintain legitimacy.

The relationship between the glorification of the U.S. military and the dehumanization of nations and peoples targeted by the U.S. military reinforces the function of white supremacy. This is especially true when it comes to the way troops are talked about in the United States. American troops are constantly thanked for their "service" while the victims of war are stripped of their humanity. Thanking U.S. troops deifies them and legitimizes the wars they fight on behalf of the ruling class. Wars are effectively sanitized as heroic operations that defend the "freedom" and "democracy" of all. Soldiers represent such heroism in the flesh and are celebrated for supposedly protecting the interests of Americans from the inferior nations and peoples seeking to harm them. As explained throughout the book, inferiority has been a mark placed on communists, nationalists, and most recently "terrorists" to justify the plunder, power, and profit that the ruling class derives from U.S. military expansionism. U.S. troops represent "whiteness" in the form of heroism as opposed to the "threat" posed by darker nations and peoples.

No other day reflects the racialization of U.S. soldiers than Veterans Day. Every year in November, a good number of Americans are given the day off from work to reflect on the heroic sacrifices of war veterans. The president or vice president makes a speech and the corporate media runs endless programming telling tall tales of bravery in the U.S. military. In 2014, the Obama Administration amplified the celebration with the help of a host of corporate partners. Starbucks, Chase bank, and HBO organized the "Concert for Valor" on the National Mall in Washington D.C. The concert featured hosts such as Oprah Winfrey and popular musicians like Bruce Springsteen.

Former Army Ranger Rory Fanning had some very important questions to ask before the concert took place. Among them were:

> Will the "Concert for Valor" mention the trillions of dollars rung up terrorizing Muslim countries for oil, the ratcheting up of the police and surveillance state in this country since 9/11, the hundreds of thousands of lives lost thanks to the wars of George W. Bush and Barack Obama? Is anyone going to dedicate a song to Chelsea Manning, or John Kiriakou, or Edward Snowden—two of them languishing in prison and one in exile—for their service to the American people? Will the Concert for Valor raise anyone's awareness when it comes to the fact that, to this day, veterans lack proper medical attention, particularly for mental health issues, or that there is a veteran suicide every 80 minutes in this country? Let's hope they find time in between drum solos, but myself, I'm not counting on it.[19]

Fanning's questions went unanswered during the concert. Such a gaudy celebration of Veterans Day teaches Americans to forget the millions of people around the world who have suffered at the hands of the U.S. military by privileging the deaths of U.S. troops. Because U.S. troops are held up to almost a divine status, it is automatically assumed that the wars they fight are "good" wars, "just" wars, and wars that benefit Americans as a whole rather than the very rich. As another Iraq War Veteran, Vincent Emanuele, puts it, Veterans Day is "one of the most hollow and absurd holidays in American society. Unless you have stock in Lockheed Martin or Goldman Sachs, there's really no reason to thank me for my 'service.' We destroyed Iraq and killed innocent people. We mutilated dead bodies and tortured prisoners. And we did it all for geopolitical and corporate interests."[20]

Testimonies from military veterans like Fanning and Emanuele show that some of the fiercest and most insightful critics of U.S. foreign policy come from those who were asked to fight its wars. It is often those that have seen the military's destruction firsthand that can best mobilize peace efforts. As Rory Fanning observes, citing the approximately 50,000 war resisters who have joined the military since 2001, "I think the potential for veterans who come back to become positive influences in the fight against exploitation and oppression is really high. Reaching out to veterans to organize and to call out injustices that they see is high. Communicating with veterans is really important."[21] Vincent Emanuele shares a more personal take from his experience in Iraq, one that serves as a powerful condemnation of the U.S. war machine. "More marines from my platoon have killed themselves since returning home than died overseas," he writes. "But vets get to go home, at least most of them. The Iraqis have to live with the legacy of Uncle Sam's madness for the rest of their lives."

However, since ideologies of American exceptionalism and innocence have largely gone unchallenged, many Americans have actually come to enjoy U.S. militarism, even as part of their entertainment consumption. As Henry Giroux explains, the Disney corporation has a long history of working with the U.S. military in projecting favorable images of U.S. political, economic, and military supremacy.[22] While Giroux focuses on the Disney corporation's promotion of films such as *The Incredibles* in the post-9/11 political climate, it is important to note that even so-called "progressive" Disney films like the box-office hit *Black Panther* reproduce dangerous glorifications of U.S. militarism. In the film, a CIA agent, played by Martin Freeman, works with the leader of a fictional African country to save it from a deadly "civil war." A Black American male is painted as the villain while the benevolent CIA agent murders and maims Africans to free them from his tyrannical rule. This film, like many other Disney productions, clearly delineates the U.S. military as heroic and villanizes its target, which in this case was the Black American antagonist, "Killmonger." This representation completely negates the fact that the CIA has historically played a significant role in sowing chaos in Africa through the repression of revolutionary independence movements from Ghana to South Africa.

Resistance to the American system of monopoly and finance capital, or imperialism for short, is currently at a low point precisely because American exceptionalism and American innocence have glorified the U.S. military as the standard bearer of everything that Americans should hold dear about their fabled nation, regardless of the oppression, exploitation, and terror it has spread throughout the planet. The subjects covered in this book were intentionally chosen to demonstrate the critical role played by American exceptionalism and American innocence in the reproduction of U.S. imperialism. Narratives of exceptionalism and innocence promote the U.S. nation-state as the most exceptional social order to have ever been born. Its imperfections, however stark, are but blemishes that stain an otherwise innocent design. Injustice and oppression are not seen as foundational to the nation's very structure, but rather unfortunate occurrences for us to ignore or discredit. An effective resistance to U.S. imperial warfare must challenge the ideologies that sustain it.

We have used this book as an opportunity to analyze the ideologies of American exceptionalism and American innocence as they apply to historical memory and contemporary questions of race, class, and empire. We focused on the American nation's roots in slavery, genocide, and corporate theft to demonstrate the ways in which the dominant narratives of American exceptionalism and innocence have caused many Americans to forget, distort, or excuse the crimes of the nation. Such distortion has led to a white-washed picture of the American nation-state and its imperial system, even when social movements that oppose racism, poverty, and other important issues come to the fore. That many Americans believe that the U.S. is inherently "democratic" and that its military spreads "freedom" around the world holds many social movements back from condemning the system of U.S. imperialism itself. This book held as its main objective the development of a broad critique of American exceptionalism and innocence that can push Americans to imagine a world without U.S. wars and without the exploitative institutions of Wall Street and white supremacy that wage them.

What should this resistance look like? It should ultimately move away from debates about narrow American nationalism or "globalization" and instead focus on the development of international solidarity. The notion of American superiority ultimately isolates Americans from the rest of the world. Past examples of movements that espoused international solidarity in the U.S. and around the world can provide fruitful lessons for the long struggle ahead. In the 1960s and 1970s, groups like the Black Panther Party made connections with the people of Vietnam struggling to free their country from U.S. aggression. Native activists in Hawaii also made common cause with the Vietnamese in the same period. Both Black Panther and Native Hawaiian activists saw their struggles against oppression as linked to the Vietnamese by a common root. That root was U.S. imperialism.[23]

These movements ultimately had to reject American exceptionalism and American innocence to differentiate themselves from the politics of the U.S. empire. The Black Panther Party saw the murder of Black people by the police as no different than the murder of Vietnamese civilians by the U.S. military. Native Hawaiian activists were similarly politicized by the theft of land at the hands of the U.S. military that was then used to help occupy and bomb Vietnam. As Simeon Man explains, it was

> liberalism and war, "paradise" and "genocide"—that radicalized the antiwar and anti-eviction struggles of the early 1970s and transformed them into a broader movement for Hawaiian sovereignty. In 1976, as Native activists occupied the island of Kaho'olawe to protest its sustained use for military bombing, they reworked the earlier call at Kalama Valley of preserving land for "local" people into a more urgent demand to protect Native land from military use and destruction. These assertions of Native claims to land and sovereignty based on Indigenous birthright continued to animate the Hawaiian Movement into the 1980s, inspiring other transpacific alliances "with American Indian activists on the mainland, antinuclear independence struggles throughout the South Pacific, and international networks in Asia and at the United Nations." Indeed, if the saga of Hawai'i's Vietnam War reveals the processes by which the US state mobilized the legacies of race and empire in the Pacific to wage war in Vietnam in the name of "liberation," then the movements it spawned would strive not only to make visible the erasures and disavowals that made the US Empire possible but to realize a different kind of liberation altogether.[24]

Resistance efforts against U.S. warfare must therefore reject the U.S. military's definition of liberation in place of its own. The Black Panther Party defined liberation as the replacement of U.S. imperialism with a new, socialist system entirely. Connections were made with the American Indian Movement (AIM) and correspondences sent to Vietnam, Mozambique, and other liberation struggles around the world that the Black Panther Party believed were fighting for the same thing. These actions would never have occurred if the Black Panther Party believed that the U.S. was an exceptional nation whose imperfections were mere aberrations that could be reformed away. The rejection of American exceptionalism and American innocence, then, are important first steps for the development of international solidarity with oppressed nations around the world.

This book is intended to be a tool to help rebuild the U.S. anti-war movement currently on life support. Heroic efforts of groups such as the Black Alliance for Peace and Veterans for Peace have kept the spirit of anti-imperialism alive in a period where it seems like American exceptionalism has won the day. These groups have emphasized the importance of solidarity regardless of the political climate. There is no shortage of reasons to support these groups as the U.S. continues to go deeper and deeper into endless war around the world. Numerous social movements have arisen in recent years that point to an increase in popular disillusionment with the status quo. More and more people are becoming dissatisfied with the miserable conditions that U.S. imperialism has produced on the homefront. Due to the centrality of race in the reproduction of U.S. imperialism, this book paid close attention to the connection between U.S. militarism and movements against racism such as Black Lives Matter. It is not often that militarism is connected to these conditions or the movements that have emerged from them.

What we have shown is that social movements cannot be relegated to a single issue if they are to be successful. More importantly, social movements that fail to fight U.S. militarism and empire will fall short in their efforts for social change. Since the 1970s, a number of social movements have attempted to enact change on important issues without a thorough examination of empire and war. The prison abolition movement has demanded alternatives to the mass caging of 2.3 million people, nearly half of whom are Black. This movement rightfully sees the prisons system as an extension of chattel slavery and a product of the political repression and disposability of Black labor. Few prison abolitionists have connected their demand to scale back the mass incarceration dragnet in the U.S. to the need to scale back U.S. military adventurism abroad as well. Yet the U.S. military and the U.S. prison system are byproducts of a broader war against oppressed people, a war that serves the interests of the same social order from which they arose. Prisons could very well be considered domestic sites of torture and prison guards domestic soldiers at times armed with the same weapons possessed by the U.S. military. [25]

The same could be said about the environmental justice movement. U.S. imperialism has indeed run the world's ecology into a state of catastrophe. Why is it that one of the biggest polluters of the world, the U.S. military, is rarely condemned by environmental justice advocates? Where is the moral outrage for its failure to acknowledge "what would appear to be obvious: that saturating the environment with toxic materials will have repercussions on both environmental and human health, including the health of the United States"?[26] The fights for $15 an hour and a union, while worthy causes, also doesn't target the U.S. military for its role in forcing other countries to enact free-market policies that emphasize low wages. Nor does the movement to preserve public education question the fact that the U.S. military budget receives over 50 percent of all discretionary federal spending and eclipses the education budget nearly ten times over. And rarely does the movement to preserve public education oppose the targeting of poverty stricken schools for military recruitment;[27] or how, as scholars like Connie Wun have shown, today's "school discipline policies help to create militarized 'prison-like' conditions for students."[28]

To question the U.S. military's inherent virtuosity is seen by the ruling elites as not only a threat to the legitimacy of war, but also to the legitimacy of the American system of profit and power that requires war. Narratives of American exceptionalism and American innocence have limited the efforts of progressive and radical forces in this country by diverting their attention away from the trillion dollar military albatross in the U.S. and its many connections to the racist, capitalist, and imperialist ambitions of the U.S. state.

So when it comes to dismantling U.S. militarism, what is to be done? First, progressives and radicals need a program that can unite a broad section of the U.S. population struggling to meet basic needs. As Aziz Rana states, such a program would "oppose American international police power—the presumptive right of intervention—and refuse to treat any community as an instrument in the service of state security ends." His demands are simple: a global commitment to social democracy as opposed to free-market capitalism, the demilitarization of the U.S. and its allies, and the institution of a "do no harm" principle where U.S. intervention no longer is debated but prohibited. Also included is the demand to transform the security state apparatus through the development of alternative institutions focused on human need rather than war and profit.[29]

However, a truly radical anti-war movement will have to go even further than this. Social democratic demands for health care, employment, and education must of course be raised to appeal to the material interests of a broad section of the U.S. population. Opposition to racism and the afterlives of slavery must also be part of the agenda due to the critical role that mass incarceration, policing, and surveillance play in American society. But war and militarism should not merely be opposed for the potential benefits that the demilitarization of U.S. society would bring to people living in the United States. Opposition to war and militarism should also be advocated out of solidarity with people all over the world who certainly are owed an immeasurable debt for the destruction of their homelands. Transnational solidarity is essential given that such destruction has its roots in the plight of Native and Black Americans who have also been robbed of their wealth and humanity through slavery, dispossession, and genocide. Of course, this does not require that we equate the oppression caused by slavery on the one hand with the U.S. military on the other. Rather, as Sara Ahmed reminds us, "Solidarity does not assume that our struggles are the same struggles, or that our pain is the same pain, or that our hope is for the same future. Solidarity involves commitment, and work, as well as the recognition that even if we do not have the same feelings, or the same lives, or the same bodies, we do live on common ground."[30]

This book is a call to imagine and fight for a new society where the U.S. military is no longer necessary. This new society requires that we dismantle ideologies of American exceptionalism and American innocence. Dismantling these ideologies isn't necessarily about learning new things or *more* things, or being taught what *really* happened in history or what *really* drives American wars abroad. Rather, it involves a long, painful process of *unlearning.* The process of unlearning is messy and unsettling. It is unsettling because there is a lot at stake in holding on to these convenient and seductive narratives. Thus, there is a lot at stake in abandoning these narratives as well. To abandon our attachment to American exceptionalism, American innocence, and to "America" itself requires transformative change. It isn't just that it would require us to relinquish all the political and economic benefits that come from one's "American-ness." It isn't just that we would have to admit to being wrong about how our country was founded or would have to relinquish political power to oppressed peoples and nations at home and abroad. More unsettling is that that it would require a totally different way of thinking, perceiving, and feeling. It would entail a radically different way of being in the world.

What makes the process of unlearning even harder is that the ideologies of American exceptionalism and American innocence are intricately tied to capitalist, imperialist, liberal, settler colonial, and anti-Black imperatives. These imperatives are backed by powerful interests in Wall Street, the Pentagon, and the instutions of the state. Again, it is not just that our minds have been shaped by these accompanying ideologies and their backers. Rather, our material way of "being in the world" has been profoundly shaped by them as well. They have restricted our ability to think "otherwise." And while it is true that dismantling ideologies of American exceptionalism and American innocence will not lead to a dismantling of injustice altogether, it is also true that our struggles for collective liberation must always reject the "fake news" of a benevolent, freedom-loving United States.

That said, our book is best read as an invitation to consider the new kinds of questions and new kinds of possibilities that might emerge once the ideologies of American exceptionalism and American innocence are debunked and discredited. To imagine a world without these ideologies requires not just an un-learning on our part, but an un-*doing* as well. Many Americans find it difficult to think and breathe otherwise,[31] to imagine a world without an exceptional and innocent America. It's even harder to imagine a world without an "America" altogether, a world where one's primary attachments and loyalties are not tied to the nation-state, its borders, and its imperialist practices. Breaking such ties would demand a rupture of the soul, an apostasy of sorts. It would require that we stop worshipping at the altar of American nationalism, that we stop praying God Bless America, and that we stop pursuing a "more perfect union." It would require us to renounce what Lincoln called the "last best hope of earth." It would require us to place our hope elsewhere, to be on the lookout for disruptive practices "that may hint at political potentials, gesture to alternative narratives, and enable an openness to multiple futures."[32] In short, renouncing our ties to "America" would force us to rethink whose lives we mourn, who is my neighbor, and what worlds are possible.

Afterword

By Glen Ford

"As has been stated by numerous legal scholars, I have the absolute right to PARDON myself . . ." So tweeted President Donald Trump, proclaiming the inherent right to absolve himself of any and all crimes, past, present and future—the quintessential "American." Trump perfectly embodies the historical personality and character of the nation over which he presides. The land huckster and child of unearned wealth had discovered yet another fact of governance and history, whose truth is self-evident, since it serves his interest: that U.S. presidents are living, breathing exceptions to the rule of law—meaning U.S. law, the only law that counts, except when it doesn't, as determined by the president. International law is a nonentity, the codified carping and whining of inferior races.

Under Trump's convenient legal construct, U.S. presidents are eternally innocent, if they choose to proclaim that they are. Half the country—the whitest half, which until relatively recently was the only part that counts—finds nothing outrageous in Trump's self-exoneration. The great bulk of whites in the U.S. reflexively absolve *all* previous presidents of any crimes egregious enough to stain the national innocence, because innocence is what these citizens cling to as their personal and collective "American" patrimony and dispensation. They are fiercely jealous of this cleansing (whitening) elixir of innocence. It's what makes them exceptional and sets them apart from the "un-Americans," who are easily recognizable by the traits that are assigned to them by white people.

Innocence is central to these Americans' identity; it's what makes them believe they are unique in the world. They are the people of good intentions: they don't commit crimes, they make "mistakes," for which they instantly forgive themselves, whether anybody else does, or not. And they are constantly under siege by those with bad intentions, and by evil inferiors, the defectives, the damnable people that can't see how innocent and good "Americans" really are.

Their American creed is a circular insanity that excretes an infinity of lies to justify the most heinous of crimes. Yes, these are "white" crimes, precisely because they are crimes that white people reserve for themselves the right to forgive—or forget, if they ever acknowledge that such things happened. Crimes of colonialism, genocide, mass chattel enslavement of human beings, culminating in the global crime of imperialism, are thus wiped clean, even before they become past. History is rewritten, even as it unfolds, converted to a lie, nicely arranged to fit the master lie mythology.

In 1776, the white settlers of the English colonies on the eastern seaboard divorced themselves from both the British Crown and the reality of their own past and present. From now on, the world would be on notice that the "Americans"—those pale people occupying a slim slice of two connected continents who reserved for themselves the designation "Americans," brandishing it like a title and deed to the whole hemisphere—were building an "Empire of Liberty" and must be judged by the advertised merit of their of their grand project, whose beneficence was Manifest and inarguable. And they would be the judges of how well the quest was going, and which facts were relevant to that assessment, or qualified as facts, at all. They would write their own history—forward and backward—and revise it as they saw fit, as a catechism for new Americans.

King George, just yesterday their beloved sovereign and protector, now stood in the way of the "liberty" project, the apex of all humanity's previous endeavors, which required that the newly transformed Americans have free rein to expand their wars against Natives beyond the Allegheny mountains so that "liberty" would have room to grow. (Another visionary would call this *lebensraum*, the eradication of millions for a higher goal, to serve a superior people.) The right to own and invest in Black chattel slavery, the primary source of wealth for the leading citizens of the lower half of the newly declared nation, must be secure beyond challenge.

The English could not be trusted on either count. King George had not the power, inclination or vision to restrain a Parliament that tolerated talk of creeping abolition, and the King ". . . has endeavored to bring on the inhabitants of our frontiers, the merciless Indian Savages whose known rule of warfare, is an undistinguished destruction of all ages, sexes and conditions."

These "rules of warfare" were well known to the "Americans," since that is how they had secured their beachhead in the "New World," the launching pad for an "Empire of Liberty" whose dimensions they could barely imagine. But theirs was the civilizing mission, and all resistance was aggression against the greater human good. The British colony to the north, which the empire builders had sought to absorb by force early in their jihad, was framed as the aggressor, compelling "the American union" to create "a barrier against the dangerous extension of the British Province of Canada and add to the Empire of Liberty an extensive and fertile Country," Thomas Jefferson told his future chief land pirate, George Rogers Clark, while the war of independence still raged.

The Americana myth holds the English as aggressors, although the settlers shot first. The Canadian Brits were scheming evil-doers for having successfully repelled a Yankee invasion the year before the Declaration of Independence. The Native Americans were monstrous impediments to the march towards liberty, refusing to succumb easily to extermination. The Black slaves, numbering one-fifth of the breakaway colonies' non-Native inhabitants, were insufficiently grateful to be in the unpaid service of the nascent Empire of Liberty. The Blacks sided overwhelmingly with the Crown, which offered actual liberty to those who would take up arms against the rebels. When the British evacuated their beaten forces from Yorktown, on the Chesapeake Bay, including 5,000 Black soldiers and their families, George Washington's men lined the shore, braying, "Give us back our niggers!"

The settlers fought for the "freedom" to enslave millions; to slaughter every people in their path; to claim and steal a continent they had not even properly mapped.

Orwell was two centuries late. In pursuit of unlimited accumulation, the Founding Ideologues turned the English language on its head, transforming every human value and aspiration into its opposite, all to serve their fevered project of unlimited accumulation.

They are still at it. Contemptuous of the restraints imposed on their imperial ambitions by international law, U.S. rulers superimpose their own pop-up, pseudo-legal doctrine of convenience: the right of strong nations to militarily intervene in the affairs of others for "humanitarian" reasons. It is, of course, a privilege the U.S. reserves for itself. Rights of national sovereignty, the inviolability of borders, and the universal right of all peoples to self-determination—the codified rules of organized human conduct that are the best evidence that something called "civilization" exists—are dismissed as impediments to the Empire of Liberty, now in deep decline.

Civilization can no more live with the 21st century American empire than the Native Americans could coexist with the 18th century white settler state. The ideology of American exceptionalism, as Danny Haiphong and Roberto Sirvent have explicated so masterfully, is the distilled and weaponized expression of white supremacy—a rationale for criminality as a birthright, with no guilt or regrets. Of course Donald Trump believes himself to be innocent. He is doing the work of America, which is the world's most virtuous project because Americans are the most virtuous people—a "self-evident truth" of the circular kind.

You can bet your Manifest Destiny on it.

Endnotes

Foreword

1 Paul Krugman, "Fall of American Empire," *New York Times*, June 18, 2018, cited in Nathan J. Robinson, "Liberalism and Empire," *Current Affairs*, July 17, 2018: https://www.currentaffairs.org/2018/07/liberalism-and-empire.

Introduction

1 Viet Thanh Nguyen, *The Sympathizer* (New York: Grove Press, 2015), 190.

2 Jasbir Puar, *Terrorist Assemblages: Homonationalism in Queer Times* (Durham: Duke University Press, 2007), xviii.

3 Mike Wendling, "The (Almost) Complete History of 'Fake News,'" *BBC*, January 22, 2018, https://www.bbc.com/news/blogs-trending-42724320 (accessed June 17, 2018).

4 Editorial Board, "Blaming America First," *New York Times*, February 7, 2017, https://www.nytimes.com/2017/02/07/opinion/blaming-america-first.html (accessed June 17, 2018) (emphasis added).

5 See Jaap Kooijman, *Fabricating the Absolute Fake: America in Contemporary Pop Culture* (Amsterdam: Amsterdam University Press, 2008), 52.

6 Tanine Allison, "How to Recognize a War Movie: The Contemporary Science-Fiction Blockbuster as Military Recruitment Film," *in A Companion to the War Film*, ed. Douglas A. Cunningham and John Nelson (Hoboken, NJ: Wiley Blackwell, 2016), 255.

7 Saidiya V. Hartman and Frank B. Wilderson III. "The Position of the Unthought," *Qui Parle* 13, no. 2 (April 1, 2003): 196.

8 Natsu Taylor Saito, *Meeting the Enemy: American Exceptionalism and International Law* (New York: New York University Press, 2010), 229.

9 Nelson Maldonado-Torres, "Fanon and Decolonial Thought," in *Encyclopedia of Educational Philosophy and Theory*, ed. Michael A. Peters (Singapore: Springer, 2017), 800.

10 Joy James, *Seeking the Beloved Community: A Feminist Race Reader* (Albany: State University of New York Press, 2013), 285.
11 Donald Pease, "Preface," in *Literary Counterhistories of US Exceptionalism*, ed. Joseph Darda, special issue, *LIT: Literature Interpretation Theory* 25.2 (2014): 74.
12 Hortense J. Spillers, "'The Little Man at Chehaw Station' Today," *boundary* 2 30, no. 2 (2003): 6.
13 Ibid., 7.
14 Aslı Bâli and Aziz Rana, "Constitutionalism and the American Imperial Imagination," *University of Chicago Law Review*, Vol. 85 Issue 2, (March 2018): 260.
15 Lisa Lowe, *The Intimacies of Four Continents* (Durham: Duke University Press, 2015), 137.
16 Ibid., 3.

Chapter 1

1 Joy James, *Seeking the Beloved Community*, 199.
2 Jasbir K. Puar, *Terrorist Assemblages*, 112.
3 Kyoo Lee, "When Fear Interferes with Freedom: Infantilization of the American Public Seen Through the Lens of Post-9/11 Literature for Children," in *Constructing the Nation: A Race and Nationalism Reader*, ed. Mariana Ortega and Linda Martín Alcoff (Albany: State University of New York Press, 2009), 49.
4 Aslı Bâli and Aziz Rana, "Constitutionalism," 259.
5 Joy James, *Seeking the Beloved Community* 198.
6 K. J. Holsti, "Exceptionalism in American Foreign Policy: Is it Exceptional?" *European Journal of International Relations* 17, no. 3 (2010): 384.
7 Jason Dittmer, "Captain America's Empire: Reflections on Identity, Popular Culture, and Post-9/11 Geopolitics," *Annals of the Association of American Geographers* 95, No. 3 (Sep., 2005): 630.
8 Ibid.
9 Robert Jewett and John Shelton Lawrence, *Captain America and the Crusade Against Evil* (Grand Rapids: Eerdmans, 2004), 34–35.
10 George W. Bush, "Address to a Joint Session of Congress and the American People," September 20, 2001, http://edition.cnn.com/2001/US/09/20/gen.bush.transcript/ (accessed June 18, 2018).
11 Donald Pease, "Preface," 75.
12 Carrie Tirado Bramen, *American Niceness: A Cultural History* (Cambridge: Harvard University Press, 2017), 7–8.

13 Holsti, "Exceptionalism," 395–396.

14 Puar, *Terrorist Assemblages*, 113.

15 Jasbir K. Puar and Amit Rai, "Monster, Terrorist, Fag: The War on Terrorism and the Production of Docile Patriots," *Social Text* 20, No. 3 (2002): 119–120.

16 Ibid., 122.

17 Nikhil Pal Singh, *Race and America's Long War* (Berkeley: University of California Press, 2017), 36.

18 Lisa Lowe, "Metaphors of Globalization," in *Interdisciplinarity and Social Justice: Revisioning Academic Accountability*, ed. Ranu Samantrai, Joe Parker, and Mary Romero (Albany: State University of New York Press, 2010), 51–52.

19 Junaid Rana, "The Racial Infrastructure of the Terror-Industrial Complex," *Social Text 34*, no. 4 (2016): 113.

20 Ibid., 122.

21 Ibid., 125–129.

22 Neferti X. M. Tadiar, "Empire," *Social Text 100*, Vol. 27, No. 3 (Fall 2009): 114.

Chapter 2

1 Sandy Grande, *Red Pedagogy: Native American Social and Political Thought* (Lanham, MD: Rowman & Littlefield, 2004), 31–32, cited in Andrea Smith, "The Indigenous Dream—A World Without an 'America,'" in *Theological Perspectives for Life, Liberty, and the Pursuit of Happiness: Public Intellectuals for the Twenty-First Century*, eds. Ada María Isasi-Díaz, Mary McClintock Fulkerson, and Rosemary P. Carbine (New York: Palgrave, 2013), 4.

2 "My Dungeon Shook: Letter to My Nephew on the One Hundredth Anniversary of the Emancipation," *The Fire Next Time*, in *James Baldwin: Collected Essays*, ed. Toni Morrison (1963; repr., New York: Library of America, 1998), 292.

3 Dave Zirin, "By Having the Washington R*dskins Host a Game on Thanksgiving, NFL Owners Show Their True Colors," *The Nation*, November 17, 2017, https://www.thenation.com/article/by-having-the-washington-rdskins-host-a-game-on-thanksgiving-nfl-owners-show-their-true-colors/ (accessed June 19, 2018).

4 DaShanne Stokes, "5 Studies That Prove Dan Snyder is Wrong About 'Redskins,'" *Indian Country Today*, April 21, 2014, http://indiancountrytodaymedianetwork.com/2014/04/21/5-studies-prove-dan-snyder-wrong-about-redskins (accessed June 19, 2018).

5 C. Richard King, *Redskins: Insult and Brand* (Lincoln, NE: University of Nebraska Press, 2016), 169.

6 Roxanne Dunbar-Ortiz and Dina Gilio-Whitaker, *"All the Real Indians Died Off": And 20 Other Myths About Native Americans* (Boston: Beacon Press, 2016), 8–9.

7 Alexis Shotwell, *Against Purity*, 38–39.

8 Christopher Hitchens, "Minority Report," *The Nation*, Oct. 19, 1995: 5.

9 See, for example, Andrea Smith, *Conquest: Sexual Violence and American Indian Genocide* (Durham: Duke University Press, 2015).

10 Saito, *Meeting the Enemy*, 63.

11 Patrick Wolfe, "Settler Colonialism and the Elimination of the Native," *Journal of Genocide Research* 8, no. 4, (December 2006): 388.

12 John Two-Hawks, "The First Thanksgiving: It Didn't Happen that Way," *Native Circle*, http://www.nativecircle.com/first-thanksgiving-myth.html (accessed June 19, 2018).

13 Saito, *Meeting the Enemy*, 69.

14 "Declaration of Independence," http://www.ushistory.org/declaration/document/index.html (accessed June 18, 2018).

15 Donald F. Tibbs and Tryon P. Woods, "The Jena Six and Black Punishment: Law and Raw Life in the Domain of Nonexistence," *Seattle Journal for Social Justice*, vol. 7, no. 1 (November 2008): 245, n. 58.

16 Ibid., 247.

17 Ibid.

18 Roxanne Dunbar-Ortiz, *An Indigenous Peoples' History of the United States* (Boston: Beacon Press, 2015), 80.

19 Ibid.

20 Ibid., 78–83.

21 Boyd Cothran, "Enduring Legacy: U.S.-Indigenous Violence and the Making of American Innocence in the Gilded Age," *The Journal of the Gilded Age and Progressive Era* 14 (2015): 567.

22 Ibid., 567–570.

23 Ibid., 570.

24 Ibid., 571.

25 Sylvia Wynter, "On How We Mistook the Map for the Territory and Reimprisoned Ourselves in Our Unbearable Wrongness of Being, of Désêtre: Black Studies Toward the Human Project," in *Not Only the Master's Tools: African American Studies in Theory and Practice*, ed. Lewis R. Gordon and Jane Anna Gordon (Boulder, CO: Paradigm, 2006), 139–140.

26 Smith, "The Indigenous Dream," 7–8.

27 "Free Leonard Peltier," www.whoisleonardpeltier.info/home/about-peltier/activist/ (acessed June 19, 2018).

28 For a detailed analysis of the process of "colonial unknowing" regarding connections between anti-Blackness and the conquest of the Americas, see Tiffany Lethabo King. "New World Grammars: The 'Unthought' Black Discourses of Conquest." *Theory & Event* 19, no. 4 (2016).

29 Kelly Lytle Hernández, *City of Inmates: Conquest, Rebellion, and the Rise of Human Caging in Los Angeles, 1771–1965* (Chapel Hill: University of North Carolina Press, 2017), 9.

30 Saito, *Meeting the Enemy*, 36.

31 Wolfe, "Settler Colonialism," 390.

32 Eve Tuck and K. Wayne Yang, "Decolonization is not a Metaphor," *Decolonization: Indigeneity, Education & Society*, Vol.1, No.1 (2012): 10.

33 Ibid.

34 Lowe, *The Intimacies of Four Continents*, 20.

35 Tuck and Yang, "Decolonization," 36.

Chapter 3

1 Saidiya Hartman, *Lose Your Mother: A Journey Along the Atlantic Slave Route* (New York: Farrar, Straus and Giroux, 2008), 6.

2 Baldwin, *The Fire Next Time*, 722.

3 Tisa Wenger, *Religious Freedom: The Contested History of an American Ideal* (Chapel Hill: University of North Carolina Press, 2017), 2.

4 "Universalizing Settler Liberty: An Interview with Aziz Rana," *Jacobin*, August 4, 2014, https://www.jacobinmag.com/2014/08/the-legacies-of-settler-empire/ (accessed June 19, 2018); see also Aziz Rana, *The Two Faces of American Freedom* (Cambridge: Harvard University Press, 2014).

5 For an in-depth account of liberalism's global narratives of "freedom overcoming slavery," see Lisa Lowe's pathbreaking *The Intimacies of Four Continents*: "My study could be considered an unlikely or unsettling genealogy of modern liberalism, which examines liberalism as a project that includes at once both the universal promises of rights, emancipation, wage labor, and free trade, as well as the global divisions and asymmetries on which the liberal tradition depends, and according to which such liberties are reserved for some and wholly denied to others. In this sense, the modern distinction between definitions of the human

and those to whom such definitions do not extend is the condition of possibility for Western liberalism, and not its particular exception. This genealogy also traces the manners in which the liberal affirmations of individualism, civility, mobility, and free enterprise simultaneously innovate new means and forms of subjection, administration, and governance," 3.

6 Lisa Lowe, "History Hesitant," *Social Text 125*, Vol. 33, no. 4 (December 2015): 89.

7 Salamishah Tillet, "Jesse Owens, a Film Hero Once Again," *New York Times*, February 12, 2016, https://www.nytimes.com/2016/02/14/movies/jesse-owens-movie-race.html (accessed June 19, 2018).

8 George Shulman, "Hope and American Politics," *Raritan* (Winter 2002): 17.

9 Hartman, *Lose Your Mother*, 40.

10 See, for example, the *Britannica* encyclopedia entry on "The Founding Fathers and Slavery," *Brittanica*, https://www.britannica.com/topic/The-Founding-Fathers-and-Slavery-1269536 (accessed June 19, 2018).

11 K. J. Holsti, "Exceptionalism," 397.

12 James, *Seeking the Beloved Community*, 120–121.

13 Tibbs and Woods, "Jena Six," 247.

14 For a brief representative sample, see: Angela Y. Davis, *Are Prisons Obsolete?* (New York: Seven Stories Press, 2003); Saidiya Hartman, *Scenes of Subjection: Terror, Slavery, and Self-Making in Nineteenth-Century America* (Oxford: Oxford University Press, 2007); Joy James, "Introduction: Democracy and Captivity," in *The New Abolitionists: (Neo)Slave Narratives and the Contemporary Prison Writing*, ed. Joy James (Albany: State University of New York Press, 2005), xxi-xlii; Sarah Haley, *No Mercy Here: Gender, Punishment, and the Making of Jim Crow Modernity* (Chapel Hill: University of North Carolina Press, 2016); Assata Shakur, "Women in Prison: How We Are," in *The New Abolitionists: (Neo)Slave Narratives and the Contemporary Prison Writing*, ed. Joy James (Albany: State University of New York Press, 2005), 79–90; Dennis Childs, *Slaves of the State: Incarceration from the Chain Gang to the Penitentiary* (Minneapolis: University of Minnesota Press, 2015); Frank B. Wilderson III, *Red, White & Black: Cinema and the Structure of U.S. Antagonisms* (Durham: Duke University Press, 2010).

15 See Michelle Alexander, *The New Jim Crow: Mass Incarceration in the Age of Colorblindness* (New York: The New Press, 2012) and Angela Davis, *Are Prisons Obsolete?*

16 David M. Oshinsky, *Worse than Slavery: Parchman Farm and the Ordeal of Jim Crow Justice* (New York: Free Press, 2016), 20.

17 Calvin L. Warren, *Ontological Terror: Blackness, Nihilism, and Emancipation* (Durham: Duke University Press, 2018), 109.

18 Gerald Horne, *The Counter-Revolution Of 1776: Slave Resistance and the Origins of the United States of America* (New York: New York University Press, 2014), 18.

19 See Danny Haiphong, "White Supremacy Continues to Provide Protection for Imperialism," *Black Agenda Report*, June 17, 2015, https://blackagendareport.com/white_supremacy_protects_imperialism (accessed: June 19, 2018).

20 "'Counter-Revolution of 1776': Was U.S. Independence War a Conservative Revolt in Favor of Slavery?" *Democracy Now* (video), June 27, 2014, https://www.democracynow.org/2014/6/27/counter_revolution_of_1776_was_us (accessed June 19, 2018).

21 Saidiya Hartman, "The Time of Slavery," *The South Atlantic Quarterly*, 101:4 (2002): 771.

22 Ibid.

23 Hartman, *Lose Your Mother*, 6.

24 Christina Sharpe, *Monstrous Intimacies: Making Post-Slavery Subjects* (Durham: Duke University Press, 2010), 26.

25 Lisa Lowe, *The Intimacies of Four Continents*, 13; See also Saidiya Hartman, *Scenes of* Subjection; James C. Scott, *Weapons of the Weak: Everyday Forms of Peasant Resistance* (New Haven: Yale University Press, 1987); and Dean Spade, *Normal Life: Administrative Violence, Critical Trans Politics, and the Limits of Law* (Durham: Duke University Press, 2015).

26 For a detailed overview of how the American Revolution led to the spread and development of revolutionary Pan-Africanism, including the significance of the understudied Ethiopian Regiment, see Sylvia Frey, "The American Revolution and the Creation of a Global African World," in *From Toussaint to Tupac The Black International Since the Age of Revolution*, eds. Michael O. West, William G. Martin, and Fanon Che Wilkins (Chapel Hill: University of North Carolina Press, 2009), 47–71.

27 Ibid., 47, 60.

Chapter 4

1 Saito, *Meeting the Enemy*, 229.

2 *The Fire Next Time*, 292.

3 Lisa Yoneyama, *Cold War Ruins: Transpacific Critique of American Justice and Japanese War Crimes* (Durham: Duke University Press, 2016), 16.

4 Aimé Césaire, *Discourse on Colonialism* (New York: Monthly Review Press, 2000), 36.

5 James Q. Whitman, *Hitler's American Model: The United States and the Making of Nazi Race Law* (Princeton University Press, 2017), 12.

6 Jacques R. Pauwels, *Myth of the Good War: The USA in World War II* (Toronto: Lorimer, 2003), 35.

7 Ibid., 35–37.

8 Ibid., 57.

9 Ibid., 47.

10 Lisa Yoneyama, *Cold War Ruins*, 20. Yoneyama reminds us of something else that is often lost in the way we remember Pearl Harbor: "Significantly, the 'surprise attack' narrative on Pearl Harbor that remains the mainstay of America's just-war narrative conveniently erases the fact that Hawai'i was an American colony at the time. Such an elision disavows the history that the Japanese attack on the U.S. colonial military outpost was an instantiation of Japan's own liberal just-war propaganda for racial and anti-colonial emancipation." Ibid.

11 Dougal Macdonald, "71st Anniversary of Dresden Fire Bombing: Allied War Crime Prelude to the Cold War," *Global Research*, https://www.globalresearch.ca/71st-anniversary-of-dresden-fire-bombing-allied-war-crime-prelude-to-the-cold-war/5507765 (accessed June 20, 2018).

12 For an excellent discussion on how the U.S. attempted to "'normalize' its confinement of Japanese Americans under the euphemistic rhetoric of 'evacuation' and 'relocation,'" as well as how ideologies of race, sexuality, and citizenship were reinforced and contested in the internment camps, see Tina Takemoto, "Looking for Jiro Onuma: A Queer Meditation on the Incarceration of Japanese Americans during World War II," *GLQ: A Journal of Lesbian and Gay Studies*, vol. 20, no. 3 (2014): 241–275.

13 Rob Edwards, "Hiroshima Bomb May Have Carried Hidden Agenda," *New Scientist*, July 21, 2005, https://www.newscientist.com/article/dn7706-hiroshima-bomb-may-have-carried-hidden-agenda/ (accessed June 20, 2018).

14 Ward Wilson, "The Bomb Didn't Beat Japan . . . Stalin Did," *Foreign Policy*, May 30, 2013, http://foreignpolicy.com/2013/05/30/the-bomb-didnt-beat-japan-stalin-did/ (accessed: June 20, 2018).

Chapter 5

1 Eslanda Robeson to Sorors in Delta Sigma Theta, Aug. 4, 1948, in "Correspondence," PERC; Eslanda Robeson, box 9, folder 17: "Notes for Progressive Party" speech, n.d., in "Writings," PERC; and series E of "Writings," PERC; cited in Barbara Ransby, *Eslanda: The Large and Unconventional Life of Mrs. Paul Robeson* (New Haven: Yale University Press, 2013), 125.

2 Paul Robeson, Speech given to Civil Rights Congress in New York City, June 28, 1950.

3 For an excellent history of U.S. imperial involvement with Korea, see Stephen Gowans, *Patriots, Traitors and Empires: The Story of Korea's Struggle for Freedom* (Montreal: Baraka Books, 2018).

4 Nayoung Aimee Kwon, *Intimate Empire: Collaboration and Colonial Modernity in Korea and Japan* (Durham: Duke University Press, 2015), 210.

5 "US and S Korea accused of war atrocities," *The Guardian*, January 17, 2000, https://www.theguardian.com/world/2000/jan/18/johngittings.martinkettle (accessed June 20, 2018).

6 Tim Beal, *North Korea: The Struggle Against American Power* (London: Pluto Press, 2005), 47.

7 Bruce Cumings, "Why Did Truman Really Fire MacArthur? . . . The Obscure History of Nuclear Weapons and the Korean War Provides the Answer," *History News Network* January 10, 2005, https://historynewsnetwork.org/article/9245 (accessed June 20, 2018).

8 Bruce Cumings, "Nuclear Threats Against North Korea: Consequences of the 'forgotten' war," *Asia Pacific Journal*, vol. 3 (1), (January 13, 2005): 5, http://www.tlaxcala-int.org/imp.asp?lg=&reference=20285 (accessed June 20, 2018). See also: Conrad Crane, *American Airpower Strategy in Korea* (Lawrence, KS: University Press of Kansas, 2000); and Jon Halliday and Bruce Cumings, *Korea: The Unknown War* (New York: Pantheon Books, 1988).

9 Bruce Cumings, Preface to I. F. Stone's *The Hidden History of the Korean War: 1950–1951* (Boston: Little, Brown & Company, 1988), Cited in Sheldon Richman, Trump's "Fire and Fury" Wouldn't Be the First for North Korea," *Counterpunch,* August 11, 2017, https://www.counterpunch.org/2017/08/11/trumps-fire-and-fury-wouldnt-be-the-first-for-north-korea/ (accessed June 20, 2018).

10 Bruce Cumings, *The Korean War: A History* (New York: Modern Library, 2011), 159.

11 Dong-Choon Kim, "Forgotten War, Forgotten Massacres: The Korean War (1950–1953) as Licensed Mass Killings," *Journal of Genocide Research*. 6:4 (2004): 533.

12 Bruce Cumings, *North Korea: Another Country* (New York: The New Press, 2004), 12–14.

13 Cumings, *The Korean* War, 112.

14 Oliver Holmes, "What is the US military's presence near North Korea?" *The Guardian*, August 9, 2017, https://www.theguardian.com/us-news/2017/aug/09/what-is-the-us-militarys-presence-in-south-east-asia (accessed June 20, 2018).

15 Tessa Morris-Suzuki, "Remembering the Unfinished Conflict: Museums and the Contested Memory of the Korean War," *The Asia-Pacific Journal*, vol. 7 (29), no. 4 (July 20 2009), https://apjjf.org/-Tessa-Morris-Suzuki/3193/article.html (accessed June 20, 2018).

16 See Gavan McCormack, "North Korea and a Rules-Based Order for the Indo-Pacific, East Asia, and the World," *The Asia-Pacific* Journal, vol. 15 (22), no. 3 (November 15, 2017): 5: "The stance of the US and its allies in threatening, denouncing, and refusing to negotiate is patently illegal and criminal."

17 Shane J. Maddock, *Nuclear Apartheid* (Chapel Hill: University of North Carolina Press, 2014), 300.

18 Ibid., 2.

19 As McCormack notes: "Utterly dwarfed in terms of conventional weapons, and increasingly inferior not only to the United States but also to South Korea (which is about double its size in terms of population and perhaps 10 times greater in terms of GDP), North Korea appears to have concluded that its only plausible defense lies in nuclear weapons and delivery systems. Such a perception can hardly be seen as irrational," ("North Korea," 2–3).

20 See Barbara Ransby, *Eslanda*, 185–187; 203; Vincent J. Intondi, *African Americans Against the Bomb: Nuclear Weapons, Colonialism, and the Black Freedom movement* (Palo Alto: Stanford University Press, 2015), 67–68; Lawrence Lamphere, "Paul Robeson, Freedom Newspaper, and the Korean War," in *Paul Robeson: Essays on His Life and Legacy*, ed. Joseph Dorinson and William Pencak (Jefferson, NC: McFarland & Company, Inc., Publishers, 2002), 133–142; W.E.B. Du Bois, "I Speak for Peace," September 24, 1950, reprinted in Pamphlets and Leaflets by W.E.B. Du Bois, ed. Herbert Aptheker (White Plains: Kraus-Thomson, 1986), cited in Vincent J Intondi, *African Americans Against the Bomb*, 41.

21 Du Bois, "I Speak for Peace."

Chapter 6

1 Kelly Brown Douglas, "Charlottesville And The Truth About America," *Black Theology Project*, August 13, 2017, https://btpbase.org/charlottesville-truth-america/ (accessed June 21, 2018).

2 Alexis Shotwell, *Against Purity: Living Ethically in Compromised Times* (Minneapolis: University of Minnesota Press, 2016), 38.

3 Jared Sexton, *Amalgamation Schemes: Antiblackness and the Critique of Multiracialism* (Minneapolis: University of Minnesota Press, 2008), 11. See: Frantz Fanon, *The Wretched of the Earth*, trans. Constance Farrington (New York: Grove, 1963); and Colette Guillaumin, *Racism, Sexism, Power, Ideology* (New York: Routledge, 1995).

4 Theodore W. Allen, *The Invention of the White Race* (New York: Verso, 2012).

5 See Jared Sexton, "People-of-Color Blindness: Notes on the Afterlives of Slavery," *Social Text* 103, vol. 28, no. 2 (Summer 2010): 31–56.

6 Yoni Applebaum, "Take the Statues Down," *The Atlantic*, August 13, 2017, https://www.theatlantic.com/politics/archive/2017/08/take-the-statues-down/536727/ (accessed June 21, 2018).

7 Tibbs and Woods, "Jena Six," 242.

8 Katie Walker Grimes, *Christ Divided: Antiblackness as Corporate Vice* (Minneapolis: Fortress Press, 2017), xxii-xxiii.

9 Kirstine Taylor, "Untimely Subjects: White Trash and the Making of Racial Innocence in the Postwar South," *American Quarterly*, vol. 67, no. 1 (March 2015): 55–79.

10 Ruth Wilson Gilmore, *Golden Gulag: Prisons, Surplus, Crisis, and Opposition in Globalizing California* (Berkeley: University of California Press, 2007), 28.

11 Peter Wagner and Bernadette Rabuy, "Mass Incarceration: The Whole Pie 2017," *Prison Policy Initiative*, March 14, 2017, https://www.prisonpolicy.org/reports/pie2017.html (accessed June 21, 2018).

12 Joy James (ed.), *The Angela Y. Davis Reader* (Malden, MA: Blackwell, 1998), 75.

13 Stephen Dillon, "Possessed by Death The Neoliberal-Carceral State, Black Feminism, and the Afterlife of Slavery," *Radical History Review*, Issue 112 (Winter 2012): 117.

14 See Tryon P. Woods' discussion of Ava DuVernay's documentary, *13th*, where he critiques the common liberal tendency to label this exception clause as a mere "loophole." "The 13th Amendment," he writes, "does not bear a 'loophole' that opportunists and racists alike have been able to exploit across the eras.

The clause in question is more accurately termed a design *feature*, not a design flaw." Tryon P. Woods, "Campaign Cover Stories & Fungible Blackness, Part 2," *Abolition Journal*, November 8, 2016, https://abolitionjournal.org/campaign-cover-stories-fungible-blackness-part-2/ (accessed June 21, 2018).

15 Ibid. See also Calvin Warren, *Ontological Terror*, 92: Referring to the emancipated slave, Warren writes, "This *new man* is the property of all whites, the universal slave. The transformation (emancipation) is really just a move from the particular (single master) to the universal (community of whites/Mitsein), a transformation that retains slavery in essence. Thus, [Orlando] Patterson's notion of *life* is not a gift of freedom for blacks at all, but a reconfiguration of antiblack mastery."

16 See Morgan Bassichis, Alexander Lee, and Dean Spade, "Building an Abolitionist Trans & Queer Movement with Everything We've Got," in *Captive Genders: Transembodiment and the Prison Industrial Complex*, ed. Eric Stanley and Nat Smith (Oakland: AK Press: 2011), 15–40.

17 Calvin Schermerhorn, "Slave Trading in a Republic of Credit: Financial Architecture of the US Slave Market, 1815–1840," *Slavery & Abolition: A Journal of Slave and Post-Slave Studies*, Volume 36, Issue 4 (2015): 586–87.

18 See "Slave Market," in *Mapping the African American Past*, http://maap.columbia.edu/place/22 (accessed June 21, 2018).

19 Alan Singer, "Wall Street Was a Slave Market Before It Was a Financial Center," *Huffington Post*, January 17, 2012, https://www.huffingtonpost.com/alan-singer/wall-street-was-a-slave-m_b_1208536.html (accessed June 21, 2018).

20 Zenia Kish and Justin Leroy, "Bonded Life: Technologies of Racial Finance From Slave Insurance to Philanthrocapital," *Cultural Studies* 29, no. 5–6 (2015): 630–651. See also Peter James Hudson, *Bankers and Empire: How Wall Street Colonized the Caribbean* (Chicago: University of Chicago Press, 2017); K-Sue Park, "Money, Mortgages, and the Conquest of America," *Law & Social Inquiry*, vol. 41, issue 4 (Fall 2016): 1006–1035; and Peter James Hudson "On the History and Historiography of Banking in the Caribbean," where he advocates "an approach that considers the history of banking as a history of racial capitalism through which the history and practices of North American banking in the region were always already embedded in and shaped by ideologies of white supremacy": *Small Axe* 18, 1(43) (2014): 37.

21 Jon Schwarz, "Colin Kaepernick Is Righter Than You Know: The National Anthem Is a Celebration of Slavery," *The Intercept*, August 28, 2016, https://

theintercept.com/2016/08/28/colin-kaepernick-is-righter-than-you-know-the-national-anthem-is-a-celebration-of-slavery/ (accessed June 21, 2018).

22 Lyra D. Monteiro, "Race-Conscious Casting and the Erasure of the Black Past in Lin-Manuel Miranda's Hamilton," *The Public Historian* Vol. 38 No. 1, (February 2016): 89–98. In one of her many poignant critiques of the musical, Monteiro writes, "every scene in the play contains an opportunity for an enslaved character—from the tavern where the revolutionaries meet in act 1, to the Winter's Ball where Hamilton meets his future wife, Eliza. In the show-stopping tune 'The Room Where It Happens,' in which Aaron Burr (played by Leslie Odom Jr.) laments his exclusion from the dinner where Hamilton, Jefferson, and Madison made secret decisions, the line 'No one else was in the room where it happened' completely erases the slaves who would have been in that room serving dinner," 94. "This pattern of erasing the presence of black bodies continues throughout the play," she observes, "as the role of people of color in the Revolution itself is silenced," 94. Thus, the musical reinforces typical anti-black discourses where the slave occupies what Saidiya Hartman calls "the position of the unthought." See Hartman and Willderson III, "Position of the Unthought."

23 Ishmael Reed, "'Hamilton: the Musical:' Black Actors Dress Up like Slave Traders . . . and It's Not Halloween," *Counterpunch*, August 21, 2015, https://www.counterpunch.org/2015/08/21/hamilton-the-musical-black-actors-dress-up-like-slave-tradersand-its-not-halloween/ (accessed June 21, 2018).

24 Alex Nichols, "You Should Be Terrified That People Who Like 'Hamilton' Run Our Country," *Current Affairs*, July 29, 2016, https://www.currentaffairs.org/2016/07/you-should-be-terrified-that-people-who-like-hamilton-run-our-country (accessed: June 21, 2018).

25 Janice Kaplan, "Why Has 'Hamilton' Become Broadway Gold?" *Daily Beast*, August 6, 2015, https://www.thedailybeast.com/why-has-hamilton-become-broadway-gold (accessed June 21, 2018).

26 "Lin-Manuel Miranda: The Power of Financial Knowledge," *Morgan Stanley*, March 15, 2017, https://www.morganstanley.com/articles/lin-manuel-miranda (accessed June 21, 2018).

27 For a perceptive critique of Miranda's attempt to portray Alexander Hamilton as a populaist, see Jason Frank and Isaac Kramnick, "What 'Hamilton' Forgets About Hamilton," *New York Times*, June 10, 2016, https://www.nytimes.com/2016/06/11/opinion/what-hamilton-forgets-about-alexander-hamilton

.html (accessed August 3, 2018): "Hamilton, with his contemptuous attitude toward the lower classes, was perfectly comfortable with the inegalitarian and antidemocratic implications of his economic vision. One has to wonder if the audiences in the Richard Rodgers Theater would be as enthusiastic about a musical openly affirming such convictions. No founder of this country more clearly envisioned the greatness of a future empire enabled by drastic inequalities of wealth and power."

28 Nichols, "You Should Be Terrified That People Who Like 'Hamilton' Run Our Country."

29 Ibid.

30 Hartman and Wilderson, III, "The Position of the Unthought."

31 See: Erica Armstrong Dunbar, *Never Caught: The Washingtons' Relentless Pursuit of Their Runaway Slave, Ona Judge* (New York: Simon & Schuster, 2017); and Marcus Rediker, *The Fearless Benjamin Lay: The Quaker Dwarf Who Became the First Revolutionary Abolitionist* (Boston: Beacon Press, 2017).

32 Jodi Byrd and Justin Leroy, "Structures and Events: A Monumental Dialogue," *Bully Bloggers*, September 20, 2017, https://bullybloggers.wordpress.com/2017/09/20/structures-and-events-a-monumental-dialogue/ (accessed June 21 , 2018).

Chapter 7

1 Keeanga-Yamahtta Taylor (ed.), *How We Get Free: Black Feminism and the Combahee River Collective* (Chicago: Haymarket Books, 2017), 10–11.

2 Kirstine Taylor, "Untimely Subjects," 56.

3 Tom Shatel, "The Unknown Barry Switzer—Poverty, Tragedy Build Oklahoma Coach into a Winner," *Chicago Tribune*, December 14, 1986, http://articles.chicagotribune.com/1986-12-14/sports/8604030680_1_big-eight-coach-aren-t-many-coaches-oklahoma (accessed June 21, 2018). It should be noted that, according to Wikipedia, author Ralph Keyes does not attribute this quote to Switzer but "to an unknown author following an investigatigation in his book": https://en.wikiquote.org/wiki/Barry_Switzer (accessed October 5, 2018).

4 Daniel R. Smith, "The Meritocracy is a Smokescreen for Inherited Privilege," *The Conversation*, January 10, 2017, http://theconversation.com/the-meritocracy-is-a-smokescreen-for-inherited-privilege-70948 (accessed June 21, 2018).

5 See Cheryl I. Harris, "Whiteness as Property," *Harvard Law Review*, vol. 106, no. 8 (June 1993): 1707–1791.

6 For a comprehensive scholarly treatment of the United States' racial wealth gap, see Thomas M. Shapiro, *Toxic Inequality: How America's Wealth Gap Destroys Mobility, Deepens the Racial Divide, and Threatens Our Future* (New York: Basic Books, 2017).

7 "The Road to Zero Wealth," *Institute for Policy Studies*, September 11, 2017, http://www.ips-dc.org/wp-content/uploads/2017/09/The-Road-to-Zero-Wealth_FINAL.pdf (accessed June 21, 2018).

8 See Janelle Jones, John Schmitt, and Valerie Wilson, "50 years after the Kerner Commission," *Economic Policy Institute*, February 26, 2018, http://www.epi.org/publication/50-years-after-the-kerner-commission/ (accessed June 21, 2018); and Valerie Wilson and Janelle Jones, "Working Harder or Finding it Harder to Work," *Economic Policy Institute*, February 22, 2018, https://www.epi.org/publication/trends-in-work-hours-and-labor-market-disconnection/ (accessed June 21, 2018).

9 Ryan Cooper and Matt Bruenig, "Foreclosed: Destruction of Black Wealth During the Obama Presidency," *People's Policy Project*, December 2017, http://peoplespolicyproject.org/wp-content/uploads/2017/12/Foreclosed.pdf (accessed June 21, 2018); see: Michael Powell, "Bank Accused of Pushing Mortgage Deals on Blacks," *New York Times*, June 6, 2009, http://www.nytimes.com/2009/06/07/us/07baltimore.html (accessed June 21, 2018); Algernon Austin, "A good credit score did not protect Latino and black borrowers," *Economic Policy Institute*, January 2012, https://www.epi.org/publication/latino-black-borrowers-high-rate-subprime-mortgages/ (accessed June 21, 2018), cited in Cooper and Bruenig.

10 For a compelling history and analysis of the racial elements of welfare reform, see: Frances Fox Piven and Richard Cloward, *Regulating the Poor: The Functions of Public Welfare* (New York: Vintage, 1993); and Kenneth J. Neubeck and Noel A. Cazenave, *Welfare Racism: Playing the Race Card Against America's Poor* (New York: Routledge, 2001).

11 Antonio Moore, "The Racial Wealth Gap in 60 Seconds," *Inequality.org*, April 10, 2017, https://inequality.org/research/racial-wealth-gap-60-seconds/ (accessed June 21, 2018); see also Joshua Holland, "The Average Black Family Would Need 228 Years to Build the Wealth of a White Family Today," *The Nation*, August 8, 2016, https://www.thenation.com/article/the-average-black-family-would-need-228-years-to-build-the-wealth-of-a-white-family-today/ (accessed: June 21, 2018).

12 Ivana Kottasová, "The 1%Grabbed 82% of all Wealth Created in 2017," *CNN Money*, January 22, 2018, http://money.cnn.com/2018/01/21/news/economy/davos-oxfam-inequality-wealth/index.html (accessed June 21, 2018).

13 Heike Paul, *Myths that Made America* (Bielefeld, Germany: Transcript-Verlag, 2014), 369–370.

14 Cooper and Bruenig, "Foreclosed."

15 Lisa Guerrero, "One Nation under a Hoop: Race, Meritocracy, and Messiahs in the NBA," in *Commodified and Criminalized: New Racism and African Americans in Contemporary Sports*, eds. David J. Leonard and C. Richard King (Lanham, MD: Rowman & Littlefield Publishers, 2010), 141.

16 Kooijman, *Fabricating the Absolute Fake*, 48.

17 Yvette Carnell, "Even Black Celebs Are Broke," *Breaking Brown*, April 4, 2016, http://breakingbrown.com/2016/04/even-black-celebs-broke-martin-actress-tisha-campbell-martin-husband-200-cash/ (accessed June 21, 2018).

18 Matt Taibbi, "Hurricane Sandy and the Myth of the Big Government-vs.-Small-Government Debate," *Rolling Stone*, November 1, 2012, https://www.rollingstone.com/politics/news/hurricane-sandy-and-the-myth-of-the-big-government-vs-small-government-debate-20121101 (accessed June 21, 2018).

19 Ibid.

20 Christine E. Ahn, "Democratizing American Philanthropy," in *The Revolution Will Not Be Funded: Beyond the Non-Profit Industrial Complex*, ed. INCITE! (Durham: Duke University Press, 2017), 66.

21 Heike Paul, *Myths*, 378. See also: Bassichis, Lee, and Spade, "Building an Abolitionist Trans and Queer Movement with Everything We've Got," 27: "Oprah's well-publicized giveaways—as well as a range of television shows that feature 'big wins' such as makeovers, new houses, and new cars—have helped to create the image of social change in our society as individual acts of 'charity' rather than concerted efforts by mass groups of people to change relationships of power. These portrayals affirm the false idea that we live in a meritocracy in which any one individual's perseverance and hard work are the only keys needed to wealth and success. Such portrayals hide realities like the racial wealth divide and other conditions that produce and maintain inequality on a group level, ensuring that most people will not rise above or fall below their place in the economy, regardless of their individual actions. In reality, real social change that alters the relationships of power throughout history have actually come about when large groups of people have worked together toward a common goal."

22 For an excellent discussion of how marriage policies have served anti-black and anti-poor agendas, including how anti-illegitimacy laws have "prevented children born out of wedlock from accessing certain benefits and privileges have been used in the US to specifically target black people for exclusion," see Morgan Bassichis and Dean Spade, "Queer Politics and Anti-Blackness," in *Queer Necropolitics*, eds. Jin Haritaworn, Adi Kuntsman, and Silvia Posocco (New York: Routledge, 2014), 197–198.

23 Grimes, *Christ Divided*, 74.

24 Ira Katznelson, *When Affirmative Action Was White: An Untold History of Racial Inequality in Twentieth-Century* (New York: W. W. Norton & Company, 2006), 121.

25 "The King Philosophy," *The King Center*, http://www.thekingcenter.org/king-philosophy#sub4 (accessed: June 21, 2018).

26 Hartman and Wilderson, III, "The Position of the Unthought," 198.

27 Carole Boyce Davies, *Left of Karl Marx: The Political Life of Black Communist Claudia Jones* (Durham: Duke University Press, 2008), 217.

Chapter 8

1 Claudia Jones, "For the Unity of Women in the Cause of Peace!" *Political Affairs* 30, no. 2, (February 1951): 157.

2 See Tony Perucci, *Paul Robeson and the Cold War Performance Complex: Race, Madness, Activism* (Ann Arbor: University of Michigan Press, 2012), 162.

3 Tamara K. Nopper and Mariame Kaba, "Itemizing Atrocity," *Jacobin*, August 15, 2014, https://www.jacobinmag.com/2014/08/itemizing-atrocity/ (accessed June 22, 2018).

4 Oren Dorell, "U.S. $38B Military Aid Package to Israel Sends a Message," *USA* Today, September 14, 2016, https://www.usatoday.com/story/news/world/2016/09/14/united-states-military-aid-israel/90358564/ (accessed June 22, 2018).

5 "The Genocide of the Palestinian People: An International Law and Human Rights Perspective," *Center for Constitutional Rights*, August 25, 2016, https://ccrjustice.org/genocide-palestinian-people-international-law-and-human-rights-perspective (accessed June 22, 2018).

6 Kali Akuno, "Operation Ghetto Storm," November 2014, http://www.operationghettostorm.org/uploads/1/9/1/1/19110795/new_all_14_11_04.pdf (accessed June 22, 2018).

7 Adam Andrzejewski and Thomas W. Smith, "The Militarization of Local Police Departments," *Open the Books* Snapshot Report, May 2016, https://www.openthebooks.com/assets/1/7/OTB_SnapshotReport_MilitarizationPoliceDepts.pdf (June 22, 2018).

8 Alice Speri, "Israel Security Forces Are Training American Cops Despite History of Rights Abuses," *The Intercept*, September 15, 2017, https://theintercept.com/2017/09/15/police-israel-cops-training-adl-human-rights-abuses-dc-washington/ (accessed June 22, 2018).

9 "Invest-Divest," *The Movement for Black Lives*, https://policy.m4bl.org/invest-divest/ (accessed June 22, 2018).

10 "Black Lives Matter in Palestine to Protest US-Funded 'Genocide,'" *Telesur*, July 31, 2016, https://www.telesurtv.net/english/news/Black-Lives-Matter-in-Palestine-to-Protest-US-Funded-Genocide-20160731-0009.html (accessed June 22, 2018).

11 For a rich collection of essays on the subject, see Michael L. Butterworth (ed.), *Sport and Militarism: Contemporary Global Perspectives* (New York: Routledge, 2017). See also: Tricia Jenkins, "The Militarization of American Professional Sports: How the Sports–War Intertext Influences Athletic Ritual and Sports Media," *Journal of Sport and Social Issues* 37, no. 3 (2013): "In the case of the sports–war intertext, the military exploits sports to boost recruitment, to promote a sense of national unity, especially during times of conflict, to glorify its members through pageantry and athletic ritual, and to downplay the seriousness of combat by likening military service to sport. The military is not the only party involved in this type of exploitation of sports, however; fans, sports organizers, the media, and even athletes are complicit too," 258.

12 Emma Niles, "How the Pentagon Paid for NFL Displays of Patriotism," *Truthdig*, September 26, 2017, https://www.truthdig.com/articles/pentagon-paid-nfl-displays-patriotism/ (accessed June 22, 2018).

13 Sheryl Gay Stolberg, "Senate Passes $700 Billion Pentagon Bill, More Money Than Trump Sought," *New York Times*, September 18, 2017, https://www.nytimes.com/2017/09/18/us/politics/senate-pentagon-spending-bill.html (accessed: June 22, 2018).

14 Nick Turse, "Tomgram: Nick Turse, A Wider World of War," *TomDispatch*, December 14, 2017, http://www.tomdispatch.com/blog/176363/tomgram%3A_nick_turse%2C_a_wider_world_of_war (accessed June 22, 2018).

15 Les Neuhaus, "US Military Stretched Thin in 50 African Nations," *Observer*,

December 1, 2017, http://observer.com/2017/12/us-military-has-presence-in-50-of-54-african-countries/ (accessed June 22, 2018).

16 David Theo Goldberg, "Militarizing Race," *Social Text 129*, vol. 34, no. 4 (December 2016): 30.

17 As P. Khalil Saucier and Tryon P. Woods note: ". . . we follow black radical thought in viewing legal abstractions like 'democracy' in relation to material political practices . . . As such, democracy proves to be embedded within enslavement rooted in captivity, and a leitmotif for social parasitism. Democracy first emerges as a political value only among the Western European societies that were already deeply invested in the slave trade, and struggles internal to these societies for democratic inclusion were premised upon the concomitant expansion of slaveholding." "Introduction," in *Conceptual Aphasia in Black: Displacing Racial Formation*, ed. P. Khalil Saucier and Tryon P. Woods (Lanham, MD: Lexington Books, 2016), 14.

18 Michael Harriot, "Google Just Dropped $11,000,000 to Make Sure #BlackLivesMatter," *The Root*, February 24, 2017, https://www.theroot.com/google-just-dropped-11-000-000-million-to-make-sure-b-1792711820 (accessed June 22, 2018).

19 Christina Sharpe, "Blackness, Sexuality, and Entertainment," *American Literary History*, vol. 24, no. 4 (Winter 2012): 829.

20 See: Andrea J. Ritchie, *Invisible No More: Police Violence Against Black Women and Women of Color* (Boston: Beacon Press, 2017); Joe Macaré, Maya Schenwar, and Alana Yu-lan Price (eds.), *Who Do You Serve, Who Do You Protect? Police Violence and Resistance in the United States* (Chicago: Haymarket Books, 2016); and Kristian Williams, *Our Enemies in Blue Police and Power in America* (Oakland: AK Press, 2015).

21 Barbara Ransby, *Eslanda*, 278.

22 Carole Boyce Davies, *Left of Karl Marx*, 217. See also: Erik S. McDuffie, *Sojourning for Freedom: Black Women, American Communism, and the Making of Black Left Feminism* (Durham: Duke University Press, 2011); and Ashley D. Farmer, *Remaking Black Power* (Chapel Hill: University of North Carolina Press, 2017): "Increased contact with African, Asian, and Latin American liberation struggles and leaders, coupled with the intractable problem of black poverty at home, propelled activists toward political ideologies that could account for the interrelationship of racism, capitalism, and imperialism . . . As women in these organizations often noted, however, they rarely accounted for their

gender-specific experiences with imperialist politics and economic oppression." 184–185.

23 See Chapter 7 of this book.

24 Tony Perucci, "The Red Mask of Sanity: Paul Robeson, HUAC, and the Sound of Cold War Performance," *TDR/The Drama Review*, vol. 53, issue 4 (Winter 2009): 34. See also Penny M. Von Eschen, *Race Against Empire: Black Americans and Anticolonialism, 1937–1957* (Ithaca: Cornell University Press, 1997), 103, cited in Perucci, "Red Mask," 34.

25 For excellent resources on the importance of internationalist visions to Black radical thought, See Keisha N. Blain, *Set the World on Fire: Black Nationalist Women and the Global Struggle for Freedom* (Philadelphia: University of Pennsylvania Press, 2018); Robyn C. Spencer, *The Revolution Has Come: Black Power, Gender, and the Black Panther Party in Oakland* (Durham: Duke University Press, 2016); Ashley D. Farmer, *Remaking Black Power*; Brenda Gayle Plummer, *In Search of Power: African Americans in the Era of Decolonization, 1956–1974* (Cambridge: Cambridge University Press, 2012); Carol Anderson, *Eyes off the Prize: The United Nations and the African American Struggle for Human Rights* (Cambridge: Cambridge University Press, 2003); and Michael O. West, William G. Martin, Fanon Che Wilkins (eds.) *From Toussaint to Tupac; The Black International since the Age of Revolution* (Chapel Hill: University of North Carolina Press, 2009).

26 "Interview with Angela Davis," *Black Panther*, November 1, 1969, quoted in Robyn C. Spencer, "Merely One Link in the Worldwide Revolution: Internationalism, State Repression, and the Black Panther Party, 1966–1972," in Michael O. West, William G. Martin, and Fanon Che Wilkins (eds.), *From Toussaint to Tupac: The Black International since the Age of Revolution*, 220.

27 Barbara Ransby, *Eslanda*, 195.

28 See Sylvia Frey, "American Revolution," 47–71.

29 For an online archive of the *Third World Alliance* newsletter, *Triple Jeopardy*, see https://www.flickr.com/photos/27628370@N08/sets/72157605547626040/ (accessed June 22, 2018). Special thanks to Robyn Spencer for sharing this link.

30 Tony Perucci, *Paul Robeson*, 39.

31 Barbara Ransby, *Eslanda*, 186.

32 Lisa Lowe, *The Intimacies of Four Continents*, 170.

33 Billy Perigo, "How the U.S. Used Jazz as a Cold War Secret Weapon," *Time*,

December 22, 2017, http://time.com/5056351/cold-war-jazz-ambassadors/ (accessed June 22, 2018).

34 M. S. Handler, "Malcolm X Seeks U.N. Negro Debate," *New York Times*, August 13, 1964, https://www.nytimes.com/1964/08/13/malcolm-x-seeks-un-negro-debate.html (accessed June 22, 2018).

35 Joshua Bloom and Waldo E. Martin Jr., *Black against Empire: The History and Politics of the Black Panther Party* (Berkeley: University of California Press, 2016), 1.

36 Lisa Lowe, *The Intimacies of Four Continents*, 171. For an account of how impoverished Black women played a critical role in the intellectual formation of Black internationalist organizing, see Keisha N. Blain, *Set the World on Fire.*

37 Tom Miles, "U.S. Police Killings Reminiscent of Lynching, U.N. Group Says," *Reuters*, September 23, 2016, https://www.reuters.com/article/us-usa-police-un/u-s-police-killings-reminiscent-of-lynching-u-n-group-says-idUSKCN11T1OS (accessed June 22, 2018).

38 See: https://www.ecns.cn/2015/06–26/170804.shtml.

39 See homepage of "The Black Alliance for Peace," https://blackallianceforpeace.com/#overview (accessed June 22, 2018).

40 Von Eschen, *Race Against Empire*, 189.

Chapter 9

1 Joy James, *Seeking the Beloved Community*, 167.

2 Thora Siemsen, "On working with archives: An interview with writer Saidiya Hartman," *The Creative Independent*, April 18, 2018, https://thecreativeindependent.com/people/saidiya-hartman-on-working-with-archives/ (accessed June 22, 2018).

3 Audre Lorde, "A Litany for Survival," in Lorde, *The Black Unicorn*, (New York: W. W. Norton & Co., 1978), 31–32.

4 "World Press Freedom Index," *Reporters Without Borders*, https://rsf.org/en/ranking/2016 (accessed June 22, 2018).

5 Mathew Ingram, "Most Trump Supporters Don't Trust the Media Anymore," *Fortune*, Feburary 1, 2017, http://fortune.com/2017/02/01/trump-voters-media-trust/ (accessed June 22, 2018).

6 Dara Lind, "Unite the Right, the Violent White Supremacist Rally in Charlottesville, Explained," *Vox*, August 14, 2017, https://www.vox.com/2017/8/12/16138246/charlottesville-nazi-rally-right-uva (accessed June 22, 2018).

7 Dean Spade, *Normal Life*, 2.

8 Huey P. Newton, *War Against the Panthers: A Study of Repression in America* (New York: Harlem River Press, 1996), 4.

9 Ibid., 10.

10 Bruce Bartlett, *Wrong on Race: The Democratic Party's Buried Past* (New York: St. Martin's Griffin, 2008), 110.

11 Newton, *War*, 3.

12 Chandan Reddy, *Freedom With Violence* (Durham: Duke University Press, 2011), 2. For another example of how the U.S. state operates in such a way that the freedom of some depends on the state perpetrating violence against others, see Reddy's discussion of hate crimes legislation: "With the disproportionate arrests, convictions, and incarcerations of blacks and Latinos, it is fair to assume that these new penalties alongside the expansion of the federal government's policing power for the purposes of eradicating hate violence and enforcing civil rights laws will have a disproportionate impact on youth of color, or at least will deepen ideologies that advance the policing practices of the racialized liberal security state as an answer to the persistent contradictions, conflicts, and struggles of the radically uneven accumulation of wealth by race that characterizes US capitalism," 10.

13 Davies, *Left of Karl Marx*, 147–149.

14 Ibid., 185.

15 Cyril Briggs, testimony, in Hearings, 78. "Hearings before the Committee on Un-American Activities, House of Representatives, Eighty-fifth Congress, Second Session, Part 1," September 2 and 3, 1958 . Washington, D.C.: U.S. Government Printing Office, 1959. Quoted in Minkah Makalani, *In the Cause of Freedom: Radical Black Internationalism from Harlem to London, 1917–1939* (Chapel Hill: University of North Carolina Press, 2011), 225.

16 "COINTELPRO Revisited—Spying & Disruption," FBI Domestic Intelligence Activities, August 25, 1967, http://www.whatreallyhappened.com/RANCHO/POLITICS/COINTELPRO/COINTELPRO-FBI.docs.html (accessed June 22, 2018).

17 See Deborah Elizabeth Whaley, *Black Women in Sequence: Re-inking Comics, Graphic Novels, and Anime* (Seattle: University of Washington Press, 2016), 28–66.

18 See Barbara Ransby, *Ella Baker and the Black Freedom movement: A Radical Democratic Vision* (Chapel Hill: University of North Carolina Press, 2003), 129–130.

19 Andrew Lanham, "When W. E. B. Du Bois Was Un-American," *Boston Review*, January 13, 2017, http://bostonreview.net/race-politics/andrew-lanham-when-w-e-b-du-bois-was-un-american (accessed June 22, 2018).

20 "Complete Transcript of the Martin Luther King, Jr. Assassination Conspiracy Trial," http://www.thekingcenter.org/sites/default/files/KING%20FAMILY%20TRIAL%20TRANSCRIPT.pdf (accessed June 22, 2018).

21 Danny Haiphong, "Independent Journalist Corner: A Conversation with Daniel Patrick Welch," *Black Agenda Report*, March 7 2018, https://www.blackagendareport.com/independent-journalist-corner-conversation-daniel-patrick-welch (accessed June 22, 2018).

22 Saucier and Woods, "Introduction," in *Conceptual Aphasia in Black*, 6.

23 "Black Panther Greatest Threat to U.S. Security," *Desert Sun*, Number 296, July 16, 1969, https://cdnc.ucr.edu/cgi-bin/cdnc?a=d&d=DS19690716.2.89 (accessed June 22, 2018).

24 "Hoover Memo on Black Panthers' Breakfast for Children Program," *Federal Bureau of Investigation*, May 15, 1969, https://genius.com/Federal-bureau-of-investigation-hoover-memo-on-black-panthers-breakfast-for-children-program-annotated (accessed June 22, 2018).

25 See: Bloom and Martin, *Black Against Empire*; and Newton, *War Against the Panthers*.

26 Nikhil Pal Singh, "The Whiteness of Police," *American Quarterly*, vol. 66, no. 4 (December 2014): 1095.

27 For an excellent overview of state violence against women and gender-nonconforming people of color, especially the historical function of law enforcement officers in policing and punishing women's bodies, see Ritchie, *Invisible No More*.

28 Benjamin Franklin, "A Conversation Between an Englishmen, a Scotchman and an American on the subject of Slavery," *London Public Advertiser*, January 30, 1770. Quoted in Singh, "The Whiteness of Police," 1098.

29 Eric L. Muller, *American Inquisition: The Hunt for Japanese American Disloyalty in World War II* (Chapel Hill: University of North Carolina Press, 2007), 145.

30 Saucier and Woods, "Introduction," in *Conceptual Aphasia in* Black, 17.

31 Peter Maas, "Obama's Gift to Donald Trump: A Policy of Cracking Down on Journalists and Their Sources," *The Intercept*, April 6, 2016, https://theintercept.com/2016/04/06/obamas-gift-to-donald-trump-a-policy-of-cracking-down-on-journalists-and-their-sources/ (accessed June 22, 2018).

32 Leighton Akio Woodhouse, "Obama's Deportation Policy Was Even Worse Than We Thought," *The Intercept*, May 15, 2017, https://theintercept.com/2017/05/15/obamas-deportation-policy-was-even-worse-than-we-thought/ (accessed June 22, 2018).

33 Claudia Rankine, *Citizen: An American Lyric* (London: Penguin Books UK, 2015), 151.

34 See Simone Browne, *Dark Matters* (Durham: Duke University Press, 2015): "*Dark Matters* stems from a questioning of what would happen if some of the ideas occurring in the emerging field of surveillance studies were put into conversation with the enduring archive of transatlantic and its afterlife, in this way making visible the many ways that race continues to structure surveillance practices," 11.

35 Lisa Marie Cacho, *Social Death: Racialized Rightlessness and the Criminalization of the Unprotected* (New York: New York University Press, 2012), 6.

36 Ibid.

37 A. Naomi Paik, *Rightlessness: Testimony and Redress in U.S. Prison Camps since World War II* (Chapel Hill: University of North Carolina Press, 2016), 11.

38 For helpful resources that offer alternatives to policing, see INCITE! (ed.), *Color of Violence: The INCITE! Anthology* (Durham: Duke University Press, 2016); Andrea Smith, *Conquest*; Ching-In Chen, Jai Dulani, and Leah Lakshmi Piepzna-Samarasinha (eds.), *The Revolution Starts at Home: Confronting Intimate Violence Within Activist Communities* (Oakland: AK Press, 2016).

39 Kristian Williams, *Our Enemies in Blue*, 149. See also: Ritchie, *Invisible No* More; Jordan T. Camp and Christina Heatherton (eds.), *Policing the Planet: Why the Policing Crisis Led to Black Lives Matter* (Brooklyn: Verso, 2016).

40 See Alondra Nelson, *Body and Soul: The Black Panther Party and the Fight Against Medical Discrimination* (Minneapolis: University of Minnesota Press, 2011): "Following Fanon, the Panthers also recognized how medicine could serve as a vehicle of social control; indeed, it might be said that their mission to police the police was extended onto biopolitical terrain. The Panthers' characterization of the power exercised by the medical-industrial complex as neglect resulting in genocide signaled the group's sensitivity both to how the black body had been a site of domination historically—as expressed, for example, in its analogizing of the suffering of slavery with that of sickling—and to blacks' vulnerability to the constriction of health rights, to which the activists responded with clinics and initiatives," 187.

Chapter 10

1 Hartman and Wilderson III, "The Position of the Unthought," 193.

2 Christina Sharpe, "The Lie at the Center of Everything," *Black Studies Papers*, 1 (2014): 197.

3 See Travis J. Tritten, "Veterans Groups: NFL Players Who Kneel During National Anthem are 'Ungrateful,'" *Washington Examiner*, September 25, 2017, http://www.washingtonexaminer.com/veterans-groups-nfl-players-who-kneel-during-national-anthem-are-ungrateful/article/2635521 (accessed June 24, 2018) and Lee Moran, "Samantha Bee Skewers Fox News' Hypocrisy Over NFL Protests," *Huffington Post*, September 28, 2017, https://www.huffingtonpost.com/entry/samantha-bee-nfl-protests-fox-news_us_59cc9828e4b05063fe0f2276 (accessed June 24, 2018).

4 Moran, "Samantha Bee Skewers Fox News' Hypocrisy Over NFL Protests."

5 Brian R. Warnick, "Oppression, Freedom, and the Education of Frederick Douglass," *Philosophical Studies in Education*, vol. 39 (2008): 29.

6 Eugene D. Genovese, *Roll, Jordan, Roll: The World the Slaves Made* (New York: Vintage, 1976).

7 Josh Cole, "The Excuse of Paternalism in the Antebellum South: Ideology or Practice?," Paper written for Dr. Mark Voss-Hubbard HIS4940 "Early American History" class, Fall 2005, 31, http://www.eiu.edu/historia/Cole.pdf (accessed June 24, 2018).

8 Ibid., 38–39.

9 Hartman, "The Time of Slavery," 758.

10 Lisa Lowe, "History Hesitant," 86.

11 Shaun King, "When White Men Keep Lists of 'No-Good Niggers,'" *The Intercept*, September 26, 2017, https://theintercept.com/2017/09/26/nfl-national-anthem-pittsburgh-steelers-mike-tomlin-pennsylvania-fire-chief-donald-trump/ (accessed June 24, 2018).

12 Ibid.

13 Margaret Biser, "I Used to Lead Tours at a Plantation. You Won't Believe the Questions I Got About Slavery," *Vox*, August 28, 2017, https://www.vox.com/2015/6/29/8847385/what-i-learned-from-leading-tours-about-slavery-at-a-plantation (accessed June 24, 2018).

14 Ibid.

15 Thavolia Glymph, *Out of the House of Bondage: The Transformation of the Plantation Household* (Cambridge: Cambridge University Press, 2008).

16 Ibid., 163.

17 Joy James, *Seeking the Beloved* Community," 120–121. For similar narratives offered in the UK context, See Lisa Lowe, *The Intimacies of Four Continents*, 13: "liberal abolitionist arguments were less important to the passage of the Slave Trade Act and the Slavery Abolition Act than were the dramatic revolts and everyday practices of enslaved peoples themselves." See also Hartman, *Scenes of* Subjection; James C. Scott, *Weapons of the* Weak; and Dean Spade, *Normal Life.*

18 Calvin Warren, *Ontological Terror*, 92.

19 Connie Wun, "Racialized and Gendered Violence Permeates School Discipline," *Truthout*, November 2, 2015, http://www.truth-out.org/news/item/33481-racialized-and-gendered-violence-permeates-school-discipline (accessed June 24, 2018). See also Connie Wun, "Against Captivity: Black Girls and School Discipline Policies in the Afterlife of Slavery," *Educational Policy*, vol. 30, no. 1 (2016): 171–196.

20 Dave Zirin, "The NFL Chose to Tank Its Season Rather Than Sign Colin Kaepernick," *The Nation*, January 2, 2018, https://www.thenation.com/article/the-nfl-chose-to-tank-its-season-rather-than-sign-colin-kaepernick/ (accessed June 24, 2018).

Chapter 11

1 Neferti X. M. Tadiar, "Remaindered Life of Citizen-Man, Medium of Democracy," *Southeast Asian Studies*, vol. 49, no. 3 (December 2011), 468.

2 Gloria Wekker, *White Innocence: Paradoxes of Colonialism and Race* (Durham: Duke University Press, 2016), 17.

3 Scott A. Sandage, *Born Losers: A History of Failure in America* (Cambridge: Harvard University Press, 2006), 265.

4 Toby Miller, "US Imperialism, Sport, and 'the Most Famous Soldier in the War,'" in *A Companion to Sport*, ed. David L. Andrews and Ben Carrington (Hoboken, NJ: Blackwell Publishing, 2013), 229.

5 See: Katznelson, *When Affirmative Action Was White*; Douglas S. Massey and Nancy A. Denton, *American Apartheid: Segregation and the Making of the Underclass* (Cambridge: Harvard University Press, 1993); Richard Rothstein, *The Color of Law: A Forgotten History of How Our Government Segregated America* (New York: W. W. Norton & Company, 2017).

6 Howard Zinn, *A People's History of the United States* (New York: Harper Collins, 2015), 413.

7 Ibid.

8 Ibid., 417.

9 See, for example, Stephen Dillon's discussion of Assata Shakur and Angela Davis in "Possessed by Death," 114: "Although [Assata] Shakur's essay does not name neoliberalism explicitly, we can read it as a black feminist theorization of neoliberalism at the very moment of its emergence. Indeed, it is a narration of the drastic racialized and gendered restructurings of social and economic life in the 1970s United States from the perspective of someone detained for resisting those changes. Written by a captured member of the underground black liberation movement, the text names the discourses and (state) violence neoliberalism requires yet erases. Neoliberalism is most certainly an economic doctrine that prioritizes the mobility and expansion of capital at all costs, but its mechanisms exceed the liberation of the market from the repression of the state. By reading black feminist texts from the 1970s as implicit theories of neoliberalism, we can come to understand the formation and implementation of neoliberalism in a new light. Shakur not only connects an emergent neoliberalism to a rapidly expanding prison regime, she also links the contemporary prison to chattel slavery—an institutional, affective, and discursive connection apprehended by Angela Davis's phrase, 'From the prison of slavery to the slavery of prison.'"

10 Ibid., 117–118. See also Lisa Duggan, *The Twilight of Equality? Neoliberalism, Cultural Politics, and. the Attack on Democracy* (Boston: Beacon Press, 2003), 1–21, quoted in Dillon, 117.

11 See Social Security Administration, https://www.ssa.gov/cgi-bin/netcomp.cgi?year=2014 (accessed June 24, 2018).

12 Jill Cornfield, "Bankrate survey: Just 4 in 10 Americans have savings they'd rely on in an emergency," *Bankrate*, January 12, 2017, https://www.bankrate.com/finance/consumer-index/money-pulse-0117.aspx (accessed June 24, 2018).

13 Jay Shambaugh and Ryan Nunn, "Why Wages Aren't Growing in America," *Harvard Business Review*, October 24, 2017, https://hbr.org/2017/10/why-wages-arent-growing-in-america (accessed June 24, 2018).

14 Jenane Sahadi, "The richest 10% hold 76% of the wealth," *CNN Money*, August 18, 2016, http://money.cnn.com/2016/08/18/pf/wealth-inequality/index.html (accessed June 24, 2018).

15 "Statement on Visit to the USA, by Professor Philip Alston, United Nations Special Rapporteur on extreme poverty and human rights," *United Nations Human Rights Office of the High Commissioner*, December 15, 2017, http://www

.ohchr.org/EN/NewsEvents/Pages/DisplayNews.aspx?NewsID=22533 (accessed June 24, 2018).

16 Anupama Jacob, "The Supplemental Poverty Measure: A Better Measure for Poverty in America?" Policy Brief for *Center for Poverty Research*, University of California Davis, Volume 1, Number 6, https://poverty.ucdavis.edu/sites/main/files/file-attachments/jacob_poverty_measures_brief.pdf (June 24, 2018).

17 Alston, "Statement on Visit to the USA."

18 Jon Jeter, "It's Not the Dow, Stupid! Underpaid Workforce Imperils US and Global Economies," *MintpressNews*, February 2, 2018, https://www.mintpressnews.com/its-not-the-dow-stupid-underpaid-workforce-imperils-us-and-global-economies/237090/ (accessed June 24, 2018).

19 "A Pound of Flesh: The Criminalization of Private Debt," *American Civil Liberties Union*, February 2018, https://www.aclu.org/sites/default/files/field_document/022318-debtreport_0.pdf (accessed June 24, 2018).

20 Paula Chakravartty and Denise Ferreira da Silva, "Accumulation, Dispossession, and Debt: The Racial Logic of Global Capitalism—An Introduction," *American Quarterly*, vol. 64, no. 3 (September 2012): 362.

21 See Western Regional Advocacy Project, "Without Housing," 2006, https://wraphome.org//wp-content/uploads/2008/09/2010%20Update%20Without%20Housing.pdf (accessed June 24, 2018).

22 Craig Willse, "Neo-liberal Biopolitics and the Invention of Chronic Homelessness," *Economy and Society* vol. 39, no. 2 (May 2010): 173.

Chapter 12

1 Hartman, *Scenes of Subjection*, 4.

2 Shakur, "Women in Prison: How We Are," 60, quoted in Dillon, "Possessed by Death," 117.

3 *Malcolm X Speaks: Selected Speeches and Statements*, ed. George Breitman (New York: Grove Press, 1994), 8, quoted in Tryon P. Woods, "A Re-Appraisal of Black Radicalism and Human Rights Doctrine," in R. Khalil Saucier and Tryon P. Woods (eds.), *On Marronage* (Trenton, NJ: Africa World Press, 2015), 270.

4 For a representative sample of scholarly works analyzing the cultural politics of sports, see Janelle Joseph, *Sport in the Black Atlantic: Crossing and Making Boundaries* (London: Bloomsbury, 2015); Jessica Luther, *Unsportsmanlike Conduct: College Football and the Politics of Rape* (Brooklyn: Akashic Books, 2016); David J. Leonard, *Playing While White: Privilege and Power on and off*

the Field (Seattle: University of Washington Press, 2017); David L. Andrews and Michael L. Silk (eds.), *Sport and Neoliberalism Politics, Consumption, and Culture* (Philadelphia: Temple University Press, 2012); David J. Leonard, Kimberly B. George, and Wade Davis (eds.), *Football, Culture and Power* (New York: Routledge, 2016); Michael Silk, *The Cultural Politics of Post-9/11 American Sport: Power, Pedagogy and the Popular* (New York: Routledge, 2011); Stanley I. Thangaraj, Constancio Arnaldo, Christina B. Chin (eds.), *Asian American Sporting Cultures* (New York: New York University Press, 2016); Jorge Iber, Samuel Regalado, Jose Alamillo, and Arnoldo De Leon (eds.), *Latinos in U.S Sport A History of Isolation, Cultural Identity, and Acceptance* (Champaign, IL: Human Kinetics, 2011).

5 Glymph, *Out of the House of Bondage*, 6.

6 Ibid. Glymph continues: "The ideology of domesticity required enslaved women to work for the plantation household as if their own interests were involved. Their failure to do so made it hard for mistresses to meet the emerging standards of domesticity."

7 Ibid.

8 Dillon, "Possessed by Death," 121.

9 Ibid.,

10 See, for example, Robert Elias, *The Empire Strikes Out: How Baseball Sold U.S. Foreign Policy and Promoted the American Way Abroad* (New York: The New Press, 2010): "As a collaborator in U.S. expansionism, baseball had to be white as well. African Americans had been banned from MLB since the 1880's, and the last black played in the minor leagues in 1898—the inception date of America's rising new empire. At stake wasn't just who could *play* the game, but also who *owned* it . . . Baseball helped reinforce the white supremacy essential for rationalizing U.S. foreign policy. Combining gunboat and dollar diplomacy, the United States occupied one Latin American nation after another, usually to promote American financial interests in sugar, bananas, mining, and banking. Glorifying the benefits of the American way for local populations, U.S. companies routinely sponsored baseball as tangible proof of *gringo* superiority, hoping to Americanize their Latino workers along the way," 49. See also: James D. Cockcroft, *Latinos in Beisbol: The Hispanic Experience in the Americas* (Danbury, CT: Franklin Watts, 1996); Gerald R. Gems, "Sports, Colonialism, and United States Imperialism," *Journal of Sport History*, 33:1 (Spring 2006): 3–25; and Gerald R. Gems, "Sport, War and Ideological Imperialism," *Peace Review*, 11:4 (1999): 573–78.

11 Gilmore, *Golden* Gulag, 242.

12 Steven W. Thrasher, "Super Slaves," *Radical History Review*, vol. 2016, issue 125 (2016): 172; see William C. Rhoden, *$40 Million Slaves: The Rise, Fall, and Redemption of the Black Athlete* (New York: Broadway Books, 2007).

13 Matt Taibbi, "The NFL Draft, Decoded," *Men's Journal*, April 19, 2010, https://web.archive.org/web/20100421064046/http://www.mensjournal.com/the-nfl-draft-decoded.; quoted in Thrasher, 173; See also Daina Ramey Berry, *The Price For Their Pound of Flesh: The Value of the Enslaved from Womb to Grave, in the Building of a Nation* (Boston: Beacon Press, 2017).

14 Thomas Oates and Meenakshi Gigi Durham. "The Mismeasure of Masculinity: The Male Body, Race, and Power in the Enumerative Discourses of the NFL Draft," *Patterns of Prejudice*, Vol. 38, No. 3, 2004, 317.

15 Thrasher, "Super Slaves," 174.

16 Ibid., 175.

17 Ibid.

18 Ibid.

19 Ritchie, *Invisible No More*, 42.

20 Kelly Brown Douglas, *Stand Your Ground: Black Bodies and the Justice of God* (Maryknoll, NY: Orbis Books, 2015), 129.

21 Robin Bernstein, *Racial Innocence: Performing American Childhood from Slavery to Civil Rights* (New York: New York University Press, 2011), 94.

22 Ibid., 145.

23 Ibid., 243.

24 Donald McRae, "Jaylen Brown: 'Sport is a mechanism of control in America,'" *The Guardian*, January 9, 2018, https://www.theguardian.com/sport/2018/jan/09/jaylen-brown-boston-celtics-nba-interview (accessed June 25, 2018).

25 Shaun King, "The NCAA Says Student-Athletes Shouldn't Be Paid Because the 13th Amendment Allows Unpaid Prison Labor," *The Intercept*, February 22, 2018, https://theintercept.com/2018/02/22/ncaa-student-athletes-unpaid-prison/ (accessed June 25, 2018): "This is not just bad optics. It gets to the heart of what the multibillion-dollar enterprise that is the NCAA thinks not just of its athletes, but of its core business model. It is, in essence, admitting that student-athletes are working as slave laborers and, as such, do not deserve fair compensation."

26 Hartman, *Scenes of Subjection*, 24. See also Christina Sharpe, "Blackness, Sexuality, and Entertainment," where she comments on the work of Hartman,

Hortense Spillers, Frank Wilderson and Tavia Nyong'o who all examine "... a problematic of enjoyment in which pleasure is inseparable from subjection, will indistinguishable from submission, and bodily integrity bound to violence," 827–828.

27 See chapter 10.

28 Hartman, *Scenes of Subjection*, 7–8

29 Kimberly Juanita Brown, "Saving Mr. Jefferson: Slavery and Denial at Monticello," in *On Marronage*, ed. R. Khalil Saucier and Tryon P. Woods (Trenton, NJ: Africa World Press, 2015), 110.

30 Lisa Lowe,*The Intimacies of Four Continents*, 150.

31 Joy James, "Introduction," *The New Abolitionists*, xxiii. See also: Angela Davis, "From the Prison of Slavery to the Slavery of Prison: Frederick Douglass and the Convict Lease System," in *The Angela Y. Davis Reader*; David Oshinsky, *Worse Than Slavery*; Sarah Haley, *No Mercy Here*; Dylan Rodríguez, *Forced Passages: Imprisoned Radical Intellectuals and the U.S. Prison Regime* (Minneapolis: University of Minnesota Press, 2006); Dennis Childs, *Slaves of the State*; Alex Lichtenstein, *Twice the Work of Free Labor: The Political Economy of Convict Labor in the New South* (London: Verso, 1996); Ruth Wilson Gilmore, *Golden Gulags*; Loïc Wacquant, *Punishing the Poor: The Neoliberal Government of Social Insecurity* (Durham: Duke University Press, 2009).

32 Beth E. Richie, *Arrested Justice: Black Women, Violence, and America's Prison Nation* (New York: New York University Press, 2012), 103.

33 Maurice L. Johnson II, "A Historical Analysis: The Evolution of Commercial Rap Music," Master's Thesis (Florida State University), 2011, 5.

34 Connie Wun, "Anti-Blackness as Mundane: Black Girls and Punishment beyond School Discipline," in *Conceptual Aphasia in Black: Displacing Racial Formation*, ed. P. Khalil Saucier and Tryon P. Woods (Lanham, MD: Lexington Books, 2016), 81.

35 Ibid., 79.

36 Saidiya Hartman, *Scenes of Subjection*, 206.

37 Wun, "Anti-Blackness as Mundane," 80. See also Monique W. Morris, *Pushout: The Criminalization of Black Girls in Schools* (New York: New Press, 2017).

38 For a rich history of resistance and rebellions in Los Angeles prisons, See Kelly Lytle Hernández's discussion of the "rebel archive" in *City of Inmates*, 197: "Therefore, what the rebel archive guided me upriver to see was how currents of elimination flow through the nation's carceral core. The swells of imprisonment

and the attending realities of poverty, deportation, illness, and premature death, punctuated by all the police killings that surge through Native, black, and brown communities, are, in settler colonial terms, acts of elimination. From this perspective, disrupting the roots of mass incarceration in the United States will require addressing the structure of conquest, its eliminatory logic, and what it means for all of us, but especially for Native peoples and racialized communities targeted to 'progressively disappear n a variety of ways.'" See also Lorenzo Veracini, *Settler Colonialism A Theoretical Overview* (New York: Palgrave Macmillan, 2010), 16.

39 Stefano Harney and Fred Moten, *The Undercommons: Fugitive Planning and Black Study* (New York: Minor Compositions, 2013), 42.

40 Tryon P. Woods, "Something of the Fever and the Fret: Antiblackness in the Critical Prison Studies Fold," in P. Khalil Saucier and Tryon P. Woods (eds.), *Conceptual Aphasia in Black: Displacing Racial Formation* (Lanham, MD: Lexington Books, 2016), 149.

Chapter 13

1 Keeanga-Yamahtta Taylor, *From #BlackLivesMatter to Black Liberation* (Chicago: Haymarket Books, 2016), 29.

2 Michael Parenti, *The Face of Imperialism* (New York: Routledge, 2011), 4.

3 James Baldwin, "An Open Letter to My Sister, Angela Y. Davis."

4 Lisa Lowe, *The Intimacies of Four Continents*, 39.

5 See Neferti X. M. Tadiar, "Life-Times of Becoming Human," *Occasion: Interdisciplinary Studies in the Humanities*, vol. 3 (March 15, 2012): "It is in this context that I have described and continue to think about our political moment in terms of a complex, potentially antagonistic relation between a war to be human and becoming human in a time of war. The war to be human consists most spectacularly of the political-military project and the atrocities exemplified by the global war against terrorism, which continues to be waged by the United States and its subsidiary militaries throughout the world. The violence of this new imperial project to secure and further aggrandize the privileges and powers enjoyed as well as bequeathed by the already human within a capitalist order is amply documented and yet, woefully, so willfully ignored," 2.

6 See Neferti X. M. Tadiar, "Life-Times of Disposability within Global Neoliberalism," *Social Text* 115, vol. 31, no. 2 (Summer 2013): 19–47.

7 See Richard Peet, *Unholy Trinity: The IMF, World Bank and WTO* (London:

Zed Books, 2009); Michael Hudson, *Super Imperialism: The Origin and Fundamentals of U.S. World Dominance* (London: Pluton Press, 2003); Gloria Thomas Emeagwali (ed.), *Women Pay the Price* (Trenton, NJ: Africa World Press, 1995); Patrick Bond, *Against Global Apartheid – South Africa Meets the World Bank, IMF and International Finance* (Cape Town: University of Cape Town Press, 2004); Leo Zeilig (ed.), *Class Struggle and Resistance in Africa* (Chicago: Haymarket Books, 2009).

8 Asad Ismi, *Impoverishing a Continent: The World Bank and the IMF in Africa* (Halifax: Halifax Initiative, 2004), 11–13.

9 Kwame Nkrumah, *Neo-Colonialism: The Last Stage of Imperialism* (London: Thomas Nelson & Sons, 1965).

10 Karen McVeigh, "World is Plundering Africa's wealth of 'billions of dollars a year,'" *The Guardian*, May 24, 2017, https://www.theguardian.com/global-development/2017/may/24/world-is-plundering-africa-wealth-billions-of-dollars-a-year (accessed June 25, 2018).

11 "DR Congo: UN advises prudent use of abundant resources to spur development," *UN News*, October 10, 2011, https://news.un.org/en/story/2011/10/390912-dr-congo-un-advises-prudent-use-abundant-resources-spur-development (accessed June 25, 2018).

12 Mark Curtis, "Gated Development—is the Gates Foundation always a force for good?" *Global Justice Now*, June 2016, http://www.globaljustice.org.uk/sites/default/files/files/resources/gjn_gates_report_june_2016_web_final_version_2.pdf (accessed June 25, 2018).

13 Abram Lutes, "Empires of Aid and Compassion: Foundations as Architects of Neoliberalism," *Peripheral Thought*, February 5, 2018, https://peripheralthought.blog/2018/02/05/empires-of-aid-and-compassion-foundations-as-architects-of-neoliberalism/ (accessed June 25, 2018).

14 Colin Todhunter, "Gates Foundation is spearheading the neoliberal plunder of African agriculture," *Ecologist*, January 21, 2016, https://theecologist.org/2016/jan/21/gates-foundation-spearheading-neoliberal-plunder-african-agriculture (accessed June 25, 2018).

15 David Pilling, "Chinese investment in Africa: Beijing's testing ground," *Financial Times*, June 13, 2017, https://www.ft.com/content/0f534aa4-4549-11e7-8519-9f94ee97d996 (accessed June 25, 2018).

16 Maximilian Forte, *Slouching Towards Sirte: NATO's War on Libya and Africa* (Montreal: Baraka Books, 2012), 193.

17 See Dambisa Moyo, *Dead Aid: Why Aid Is Not Working and How There Is a Better Way for Africa* (New York: Farrar, Straus and Giroux, 2010).

18 Forte, *Slouching Towards Sirte*, 189.

19 Anthony Lake, Christine Todd Whitman, Princeton N. Lyman, and J. Stephen Morrison; "More Than Humanitarianism: A Strategic U.S. Approach Toward Africa," *Council on Foreign Relations* Task Force Report, January 2006, retrieved from: https://www.cfr.org/report/more-humanitarianism (accessed June 25, 2018), 8.

20 Forte, *Slouching Towards Sirte*, 198 and 21. See also: William T. Cavanaugh, "The Unfreedom of the Free Market," in David L. Schindler and Doug Bandow (eds.), *Wealth, Poverty, and Human Destiny* (Wilmington, DE: ISI Books, 2003).

21 For an excellent overview of AFRICOM, especially in its role with the U.S. invasion of Libya, see chapter 4 of Maximilian Forte, *Slouching Towards Sirte.*

22 Khaled Al-Kassimi, "The U.S informal empire: US African Command (AFRICOM) expanding the US economic-frontier by discursively securitizing Africa using exceptional speech acts," *African Journal of Political Science and International Relations*, vol.11, 11 (November 2017): 301–316.

23 Forte, *Slouching Towards Sirte*, 237, cited in Al-Kassimi, "The U.S informal empire," 309.

24 See AFRICOM's mission statement: http://www.africom.mil/ (accessed June 25, 2018).

25 See Forte, *Slouching Towards Sirte.*

26 Brad Hoff, "Hillary Emails Reveal True Motive for Libya Intervention," *Foreign Policy Journal*, January 6, 2016, https://www.foreignpolicyjournal.com/2016/01/06/new-hillary-emails-reveal-true-motive-for-libya-intervention/ (accessed June 25, 2018).

27 Forte, *Slouching Towards Sirte*, 258.

28 Thomas Mountain, "30,000 Bombs Over Libya," *Counterpunch*, September 2, 2011, https://www.counterpunch.org/2011/09/02/30000-bombs-over-libya/ (accessed June 25, 2018).

29 See Forte, *Slouching Towards Sirte*, where he exposes the double standard of the U.S. referring to Gaddafi's opponents as rebels: "In contrast, in Afghanistan, where NATO and the U.S. fund, train, and arm the Karzai regime in attacking 'his own people' (like they do in Pakistan), the armed opponents are consistently labelled 'terrorists' or 'insurgents,'" 260.

30 Ibid., 207.

31 Joeva Rock, "Militarized Humanitarianism in Africa," *Foreign Policy in Focus*, May 14, 2014, http://fpif.org/militarized-humanitarianism-africa/ (accessed June 25, 2018).

32 Scott Shane, "Western Companies See Prospects for Business in Libya," *New York Times*, October 28, 2011, http://www.nytimes.com/2011/10/29/world/africa/western-companies-see-libya-as-ripe-at-last-for-business.html (accessed June 25, 2018).

33 See Forte, *Slouching Towards Sirte*, 190.

34 Ibid., 196.

35 Ibid.

36 Ibid., 237.

37 Al-Kassimi, "The U.S Informal Empire," 306.

38 Whaley, *Black Women in Sequence*, 115.

Chapter 14

1 Joy James, *Seeking the Beloved Community*, 274.

2 Keeanga-Yamahtta Taylor, *From #BlackLivesMatter to Black Liberation*, 8.

3 Michael Parenti, "Foreword," in Gregory Elich, *Strange Liberators: Militarism, Mayhem, and the Pursuit of Profit* (Coral Springs, FL: Llumina Press, 2006), iii.

4 Dave Zirin and Jules Boycoff, "The US is not fit to host the Olympics," *Al Jazeera*, September 10, 2015, http://america.aljazeera.com/opinions/2015/9/the-us-is-not-fit-to-host-the-olympics.html (accessed June 25, 2018).

5 For a fascinating examination on how language of "consent" and "benevolent assimilation" is used to obscure U.S. imperial military violence in the Philippines, see Victor Román Mendoza, *Metroimperial Intimacies: Fantasy, Racial-Sexual Governance, and the Philippines in U.S. Imperialism, 1899–1913* (Durham: Duke University Press, 2015), 21 and 24: "The pervasive language around Philippine 'consent' to U.S. governance intimated a relationship of mutual hierarchical bonds. Such a trope, which no other colonial power at the time deployed, proves integral to U.S. exceptionalist discourse."

6 Joy James, *Seeking the Beloved Community*, 275.

7 Forte, *Slouching Towards Sirte*, 305.

8 Ibid.

9 For two notable critiques of human rights practice and discourse, see: Randall Williams, *The Divided World: Human Rights and Its Violence* (Minneapolis:

University of Minnesota Press, 2010); and Nicola Perugini and Neve Gordon, *The Human Right to Dominate* (Oxford: Oxford University Press, 2015).

10 Edward S. Herman and David Peterson, *The Politics of Genocide* (New York: Monthly Review Press, 2011), 22–23.

11 Forte, *Slouching Towards Sirte*, 297–298.

12 Herman and Peterson, *The Politics of Genocide*, 17–18.

13 Ibid., 18.

14 Daniel Kovalik, "Samantha Power, Henry Kissinger & Imperial Delusions," *Counterpunch*, June 16, 2016, https://www.counterpunch.org/2016/06/16/samantha-power-henry-kissinger-imperial-delusions/ (accessed June 25, 2018).

15 Herman and Peterson, *The Politics of Genocide*, 30–31.

16 Vanessa Beeley, "Examining the Truth about Syria and the White Helmets," *The Wall Will Fall*, January 30, 2018, https://thewallwillfall.org/2018/01/30/examining-the-truth-about-syria-and-the-white-helmets/ (accessed June 25, 2018).

17 Stephen Gowans, *Washington's Long War on Syria* (Montreal: Baraka Books, 2017).

18 Williams, *The Divided World*, xxxi.

19 Alana Abramson, "Here's How Many Nuclear Weapons the U.S. Has," *Time*, August 9, 2017, http://time.com/4893175/united-states-nuclear-weapons/ (accessed June 25, 2018).

20 Forte, *Slouching Towards Sirte*, 257.

21 For an important discussion of how the U.S. manipulates discourses of disability rights to further its imperial objectives, see Jasbir K. Puar, *The Right to Maim: Debility, Capacity, Disability* (Durham: Duke University Press, 2017), 71–72: ". . . [disability] exceptionalism renders the United States an advanced and progressive nation of disability awareness, accommodation, and incorporation while projecting backwardness and incapacity of modernity onto those Others elsewhere. Less examined, however, is how this transnational deployment of exceptionalism works not only as a process of Othering to retain copyright as the progenitor and arbiter of ableist modernity, but more trenchantly as camouflage of what I am calling the biopolitics of debilitation."

22 Michael Parenti, "The Logic of U.S. Intervention," in *Masters of War: Militarism and Blowback in the Era of American Empire*, ed. Carl Boggs (New York: Routledge, 2003), 24.

23 Forte, *Slouching Towards Sirte*, 291.

24 Glenn Greenwald, "Trump's Support and Praise of Despots Is Central to the

U.S. Tradition, Not a Deviation From It," *The Intercept*, May 2, 2017, https://theintercept.com/2017/05/02/trumps-support-and-praise-of-despots-is-central-to-the-u-s-tradition-not-a-deviation-from-it/ (accessed June 25, 2018).

25 Rich Whitney, "US Provides Military Assistance to 73 Percent of World's Dictatorships," *Truthout*, September 23, 2017, http://www.truth-out.org/news/item/42020-us-provides-military-assistance-to-73-percent-of-world-s-dictatorships (accessed June 25, 2018).

26 Forte, *Slouching Towards Sirte*, 304.

27 Perugini and Gordon, *The Human Right to Dominate*, 13.

28 See "The blockade remains in force and is tightening," *Granma*, October 25, 2017, http://en.granma.cu/cuba/2017-10-25/the-blockade-remains-in-force-and-is-tightening (accessed June 25, 2018).

29 See, for example, Maximilian Forte's introduction in Maximilian Forte (ed.), *Good Intentions: Norms and Practices of Imperial Humanitarianism* (Montreal: Alert Press, 2014), 28–29: "We should, if we are being honest with ourselves, also consider other norms and practices, such as Cuba's socialist internationalism. In the latter case, no permanent military bases resulted from Cuba coming to the aid of Angola; Cuban assistance was requested and mutually understood as an act of solidarity; there was no lucrative, extractive gain as a result of Cuba mobilizing to send troops and doctors to Angola; and, Angola's sovereignty was not undermined, rather it was defended by Cuba. Therefore, a consideration of the stakes, aims, methods, and the whole politics of intervention need to be clearly thought out and articulated. What there should not be is any more of the reflex 'cries': 'something must be done,' 'we cannot stand idly by,' and so forth—complex situations require maturity and political acumen, not trivial passion."

30 Forte, *Slouching Towards Sirte*, 279.

31 Ibid.

32 Ben Norton, "Close U.S. ally Saudi Arabia kicks off 2016 by beheading 47 people in one day, including prominent Shia cleric," *Salon*, January 2, 2016, https://www.salon.com/2016/01/02/close_u_s_ally_saudi_arabia_kicks_off_2016_by_beheading_47_people_in_one_day_including_prominent_shia_cleric/ (accessed June 25, 2018).

33 Bryan Schatz, "The Obama Years Have Been Very Good to America's Weapons Makers," *Salon*, March/April 2016, https://www.motherjones.com/politics/2016/05/obama-international-arms-weapons-deals/ (accessed June 25, 2018).

34 Adam Weinstein, "The Real Largest State Sponsor Of Terrorism," *Huffington Post,* March 16, 2017, https://www.huffingtonpost.com/entry/the-real-largest-state-sponsor-of-terrorism_us_58cafc26e4b00705db4da8aa (accessed June 25, 2018).

35 See Jakob Reimann, "One Last Chance for Peace in Yemen," *Foreign Policy in Focus,* May 4, 2016, http://fpif.org/one-last-chance-peace-yemen/ (accessed June 25, 2018).

36 Medea Benjamin, "U.S. Weapons Sales Are Drenched in Yemeni Blood," *Foreign Policy in Focus,* August 24, 2016, http://fpif.org/u-s-weapons-sales-drenched-yemeni-blood/ (accessed June 25, 2018).

37 Whitney Webb, "U.S.' Role In Saudi's War On Yemen May Include Torture," *Mint Press News,* June 24, 2017, https://www.mintpressnews.com/unitedstates-saudi-war-yemen-torture/229215/ (accessed June 25, 2018).

38 Keeanga-Yamahtta Taylor, *From #BlackLivesMatter to Black Liberation*, 29.

39 Forte, *Good Intentions*, 17.

40 For a helpful scholarly resource addressing the question of how to "live in and with empire," see Carole McGranahan and John F. Collins (eds.) *Ethnographies of U.S. Empire* (Durham: Duke University Press, 2018).

Chapter 15

1 "Don't Liberate Me," in *Color of Violence*, ed. INCITE!, 118.

2 Teju Cole, "The White-Savior Industrial Complex," *The Atlantic*, March 21, 2012, https://www.theatlantic.com/international/archive/2012/03/the-white-savior-industrial-complex/254843/ (accessed June 25, 2018).

3 Césaire, Aimé. *Discourse on Colonialism*, 39.

4 Richard Stupart, "7 Worst International Aid Ideas," *Matador Network*, February 20, 2012, https://matadornetwork.com/change/7-worst-international-aid-ideas/ (accessed June 25, 2018).

5 Ibid.

6 Inderpal Grewal, *Saving the Security State: Exceptional Citizens in Twenty-First-Century America* (Durham: Duke University Press, 2017), 60.

7 Ibid., 66.

8 Cole, "The White-Savior Industrial Complex."

9 Ibid.

10 "Malala Yousafzai Fast Facts," *CNN*, March 29, 2018, https://www.cnn

.com/2015/08/20/world/malala-yousafzai-fast-facts/index.html (accessed June 25, 2018).

11 Jeffrey St. Clair and Alexander Cockburn, "How Jimmy Carter and I Started the Mujahideen," *Counterpunch*, January 15, 1998, https://www.counterpunch.org/1998/01/15/how-jimmy-carter-and-i-started-the-mujahideen/ (accessed June 25, 2018).

12 Grewal, *Saving the Security State*, 77.

13 James Risen, "U.S. Identifies Vast Mineral Riches in Afghanistan," *New York Times*, June 13, 2010, http://www.nytimes.com/2010/06/14/world/asia/14minerals.html (accessed June 25, 2018).

14 Nerida Chazal and Adam Pocrnic, "Kony 2012: Intervention Narratives and the Saviour Subject," *International Journal for Crime, Justice and Social Democracy*, 5(1) (2016), 103.

15 Sverker Finnström, "*KONY 2012*, Military Humanitarianism, and the Magic of Occult Economies," *Africa Spectrum*, vol. 47, no. 2/3 (2012), 130–131.

16 "Uganda: US Help Against Rebels Overdue," *Al Jazeera*, October 15, 2011, https://www.aljazeera.com/news/africa/2011/10/2011101591032110944.html (accessed June 25, 2018).

17 Keir Forgie, "US Imperialism and Disaster Capitalism in Haiti," in *Good Intentions*, ed. Maximilian Forte, 58.

18 Ibid., 70.

19 "Haitian Workers Fight for Higher Minimum Wage Suppressed by Clinton's State Department," *Telesur*, May 22, 2017, https://www.telesurtv.net/english/news/Haitians-Workers-Fight-for-Higher-Minimum-Wage-Suppressed-by-Clintons-State-Department-20170522-0037.html (accessed June 25, 2018).

20 Afua Hirsch, "Oxfam Abuse Scandal is Built on the Aid Industry's White Saviour Mentality," *The Guardian*, February 20, 2018, https://www.theguardian.com/commentisfree/2018/feb/20/oxfam-abuse-scandal-haiti-colonialism (accessed June 25, 2018).

21 Virgil Hawkins, "The Price of Inaction: The Media and Humanitarian Intervention," *Journal of Humanitarian Assistance*, May 14, 2001, https://sites.tufts.edu/jha/archives/1504 (accessed June 25, 2018).

22 See Dylan Rodriguez, "The Meaning of 'Disaster' Under the Dominance of White Life," in *What Lies Beneath: Katrina, Race, and the State of the Nation*, ed. South End Press Collective (Boston: South End Press, 2007).

23 See Grewal, *Saving the Security State*, 33–48.

24 Ibid., 46.

25 See Jordan Flaherty, *Floodlines: Community and Resistance from Katrina to the Jena Six* (Chicago: Haymarket Books, 2010).

26 Paul Buchheit, "Morbid Inequality: Now Just SIX Men Have as Much Wealth as Half the World's Population," *Common Dreams*, February 20, 2017, https://www.commondreams.org/views/2017/02/20/morbid-inequality-now-just-six-men-have-much-wealth-half-worlds-population (accessed June 25, 2018).

27 Richard Stupart, "7 Worst International Aid Ideas."

28 Belén Fernández, "Celebrity 'Charity': A Gift For a Vicious System," *Al Jazeera*, December 3, 2017, https://www.aljazeera.com/indepth/opinion/celebrity-charity-gift-vicious-system-171203082049847.html (accessed June 25, 2018).

29 Ifi Amadiume, *Male Daughters, Female Husbands: Gender and Sex in an African Society* (London: Zed Books, 1987), 7; cited in Maximilian Forte, "Introduction," in *Good Intentions*, ed. Maximilian Forte, 26–27.

30 "Introduction," in *Good Intentions*, ed. Maximilian Forte, 26.

31 Ben Suriano and William T. Cavanaugh, "The Nation State Project, Schizophrenic Globalization, and the Eucharist: An Interview with William T. Cavanaugh," *The Other Journal*, December 11, 2007, https://theotherjournal.com/2007/12/11/the-nation-state-project-schizophrenic-globalization-and-the-eucharist-an-interview-with-william-t-cavanaugh/ (accessed June 25, 2018).

32 See INCITE! (ed.) *The Revolution Will Not Be Funded: Beyond the Non-Profit Industrial Complex* (Durham: Duke University Press, 2017).

33 See Julie Wark and Daniel Raventós, *Against Charity* (Oakland: AK Press, 2018).

Chapter 16

1 Holsti, "Exceptionalism in American Foreign Policy," 384.

2 Boyd Cothran, *Remembering the Modoc War: Redemptive Violence and the Making of American Innocence* (Chapel Hill, University of North Carolina Press, 2014), 197.

3 Dylan Rodriguez, *Forced Passages*, 47.

4 Aaron Mehta, "The Pentagon is planning for war with China and Russia—can it handle both?" *Defense News*, January 30, 2018, https://www.defensenews.com/pentagon/2018/01/30/the-pentagon-is-planning-for-war-with-china-and-russia-can-it-handle-both/ (accessed June 25, 2018).

5 For an excellent account of how refusing to vote in the general election can serve as an effective anti-imperial act of resistance, see Jason Goldfarb, "The

Case For Not Voting: In Defense of the Lazy, Ungrateful, and Uniformed," *Counterpunch*, June 17, 2016, https://www.counterpunch.org/2016/06/17/the-case-for-not-voting-in-defense-of-the-lazy-ungrateful-and-uniformed/ (accessed June 25, 2018). Particularly compelling is how Goldfarb dismantles myths such as: "it's your duty to vote," "if you don't vote you can't complain," "voting for the lesser of the two evils," "what if *everyone* chose not to vote?", "change can't come about if you don't participate in the process," etc.

6 Roger Harris, "The Real Problem With US Elections Isn't Russia," *Counterpunch*, January 5, 2018, https://www.counterpunch.org/2018/01/05/the-real-problem-with-us-elections-isnt-russia/ (accessed June 25, 2018).

7 Jon Schwarz, "Jimmy Carter: The U.S. Is an 'Oligarchy With Unlimited Political Bribery,'" *The Intercept*, July 30, 2015, https://theintercept.com/2015/07/30/jimmy-carter-u-s-oligarchy-unlimited-political-bribery/ (accessed June 25, 2018).

8 Michael Doran, "The Real Collusion Story," *National Review*, March 13, 2018, https://www.nationalreview.com/2018/03/russia-collusion-real-story-hillary-clinton-dnc-fbi-media/ (accessed June 25, 2018).

9 Adam Entous, Devlin Barrett, and Rosalind S. Helderman, "Clinton campaign, DNC paid for research that led to Russia dossier," *Washington Post*, October 24, 2017, https://www.washingtonpost.com/world/national-security/clinton-campaign-dnc-paid-for-research-that-led-to-russia-dossier/2017/10/24/226fabf0-b8e4-11e7-a908-a3470754bbb9_story.html?utm_term=.242846282a10 (accessed June 25, 2018).

10 Daniel Kovalik, *The Plot to Scapegoat Russia: How the CIA and the Deep State Have Conspired to Vilify Putin* (New York: Skyhorse Publishing, 2017), 165.

11 Aamer Madhani, Brad Heath, and John Kelly, "WikiLeaks: CIA hacking group 'UMBRAGE' stockpiled techniques from other hackers," *USA Today*, March 7, 2017, https://www.usatoday.com/story/news/2017/03/07/wikileaks-cia-hacking-group-umbrage-stockpiled-techniques-other-hackers/98867462/ (accessed June 25, 2018).

12 Eric Bradner, "John Brennan defends CIA after torture report in rare press conference," *CNN*, December 12, 2014, http://www.cnn.com/2014/12/11/politics/john-brennan-defends-cia-after-torture-report/index.html (accessed June 25, 2018).

13 Stephen Kinzer, "Trump Is Gutting the National Endowment for Democracy, and That's a Good Thing," *Common Dreams*, March 15, 2018, https://www

.commondreams.org/views/2018/03/15/trump-gutting-national-endowment-democracy-and-thats-good-thing (accessed June 25, 2018).

14 Ibid.

15 "Background to 'Assessing Russian Activities and Intentions in Recent US Elections: The Analytic Process and CyberIncident Attribution," *Office of the Director of National Intelligence*, January 6, 2017, https://www.dni.gov/files/documents/ICA_2017_01.pdf (accessed June 25, 2018).

16 Ibid.

17 Joseph Tanfani, "Russians targeted election systems in 21 states, but didn't change any results, officials say," *Los Angeles Times*, June 21, 2017, http://www.latimes.com/politics/washington/la-na-essential-washington-updates-russians-targeted-election-systems-in-1498059012-htmlstory.html (accessed June 25, 2018).

18 Aaron Maté, "MSNBC's Rachel Maddow Sees a 'Russia Connection' Lurking Around Every Corner," *The Intercept*, April 12, 2017, https://theintercept.com/2017/04/12/msnbcs-rachel-maddow-sees-a-russia-connection-lurking-around-every-corner/ (accessed June 25, 2018).

19 Matt Taibbi, "The New Blacklist," *Rolling Stone*, March 5, 2018, https://www.rollingstone.com/politics/taibbi-russiagate-trump-putin-mueller-and-targeting-dissent-w517486 (accessed June 25, 2018).

20 Kevin Johnson, "FBI probing release of CIA hacking tools," *USA Today*, March 8, 2017, https://www.rollingstone.com/politics/taibbi-russiagate-trump-putin-mueller-and-targeting-dissent-w517486 (accessed June 25, 2018).

21 Patrick Martin, "The CIA Democrats: Part one," *World Socialist Website*, March 7, 2018, https://www.wsws.org/en/articles/2018/03/07/dems-m07.html (accessed June 25, 2018).

22 Tony Perucci, *Paul Robeson and the Cold War Performance Complex*, 27.

23 Gerald Horne, *Paul Robeson: The Artist as Revolutionary* (London: Pluto Press, 2016), 112.

24 Ibid., 60.

25 See Ransby, *Eslanda*.

Chapter 17

1 Keeanga-Yamahtta Taylor (ed.), *How We Get Free*, 10.

2 Hoda Katebi, "On International Working Women's Day, Please Understand Complexity," *Joojoo Azad*, March 8, 2018, http://www.joojooazad.com/2018/03/on-international-working-womens-day.html (accessed June 25, 2018).

3 Liza Featherstone, "Hillary Clinton's Faux Feminism," *Truthout*, February 28, 2016, http://www.truth-out.org/opinion/item/35006-hillary-clinton-s-faux-feminism (accessed June 25, 2018).

4 Donald E. Pease, *The New American Exceptionalism* (Minneapolis: University of Minnesota Press, 2009), 210.

5 Ibid., 210.

6 Pierre Wilbert Orelus, *Race, Power, and the Obama Legacy* (New York: Routledge, 2016), 138–139.

7 Keeanga-Yamahtta Taylor, "Black Faces in High Places," *Jacobin*, May 4, 2015, https://www.jacobinmag.com/2015/05/baltimore-uprising-protests-freddie-gray-black-politicians (accessed June 25, 2018).

8 Featherstone, "Hillary Clinton's Faux Feminism."

9 See Richie, *Arrested Justice.*

10 Diana Johnstone, *Queen of Chaos: The Misadventures of Hillary Clinton* (Petrolia, CA: Counterpunch, 2015), 26.

11 Hillary Clinton, "Why America is Exceptional," *Time*, October 13, 2016, http://time.com/collection-post/4521509/2016-election-clinton-exceptionalism/ (accessed June 25, 2018).

12 Nicholas Kristof, "Trump's Threat to Democracy," *New York* Times, January 10, 2018, https://www.nytimes.com/2018/01/10/opinion/trumps-how-democracies-die.html (accessed June 25, 2018).

13 For further critiques of this liberal nostalgia for how things were before Donald Trump, see Jedediah Purdy, "Normcore," *Dissent*, Summer 2018, https://www.dissentmagazine.org/article/normcore-trump-resistance-books-crisis-of-democracy (accessed August 3, 2018): "What unifies the crisis-of-democracy genre is the failure to understand this, that the present moment is not an anomalous departure but rather a return to the baseline—to the historical norm, one might say."

14 Martin Gilens and Benjamin I. Page, "Testing Theories of American Politics: Elites, Interest Groups, and Average Citizens," *Perspectives on Politics*, vol.12, issue 3 (September 2014), 564–581.

Chapter 18

1 Dean Spade, *Normal Life*, 139.

2 Keeanga-Yamahtta Taylor (ed.), *How We Get Free*, 12.

3 See Lisa Lowe, *The Intimacies of Four Continents*, 6–7: "We see the longevity

of the colonial divisions of humanity in our contemporary moment, in which the human life of citizens protected by the state is bound to the denigration of populations cast in violation of human life, set outside of human society. Furthermore, while violence characterizes exclusion from the universality of the human, it also accompanies inclusion or assimilation into it. Such violence leaves a trace, which returns and unsettles the apparent closure of the liberal politics, society, and culture that establish the universal. *Race* as a mark of colonial difference is an enduring remainder of the processes through which the human is universalized and freed by liberal forms, while the peoples who created the conditions of possibility for that freedom are assimilated or forgotten. The genealogy of modern liberalism is thus also a genealogy of modern race; racial differences and distinctions designate the boundaries of the human and endure as remainders attesting to the violence of liberal universality."

4 Eli Massey and Yasmin Nair, "Inclusion in the Atrocious," *Current Affairs*, March 22, 2018, https://www.currentaffairs.org/2018/03/inclusion-in-the-atrocious (accessed June 25, 2018).

5 Gordon Lubold, "U.S. Spent $5.6 Trillion on Wars in Middle East and Asia: Study," *Wall Street Journal*, November 8, 2017, https://www.wsj.com/articles/study-estimates-war-costs-at-5-6-trillion-1510106400 (accessed June 25, 2018).

6 Dean Spade, "Under the Cover of Gay Rights," 37 *N.Y.U. Review of Law and Social Change 79*, (2013): 87.

7 Glenn Greenwald, "GCHQ's Rainbow Lights: Exploiting Social Issues for Militarism and Imperialism," *The Intercept*, May 18, 2015, https://theintercept.com/2015/05/18/exploitation-social-issues-generate-support-militarism-imperialism / (accessed June 25, 2018).

8 See "StandWithUs Booklets and Brochures," http://www.standwithus.com/booklets/ (accessed June 25, 2018).

9 Dean Spade, "The Right Wing Is Leveraging Trans Issues to Promote Militarism," *Truthout*, April 5, 2017, http://www.truth-out.org/opinion/item/40109-the-right-wing-is-leveraging-trans-issues-to-promote-militarism (accessed June 25, 2018).

10 See http://www.standwithus.com/booklets/lgbt/ (accessed June 25, 2018).

11 See, for example, the website, "If Americans Knew," http://ifamericaknew.org/ (accessed June 25, 2018).

12 Spade, "Under the Cover of Gay Rights," 92. See also Reddy, *Freedom With Violence*.

13 Spade, *Normal Life*, 149.

14 Dean Spade, "Their Laws Will Never Make Us Safer," in *Against Equality: Queer Revolution, Not Mere Inclusion*, ed. Ryan Conrad (Oakland: AK Press, 2014), 5.

Chapter 19

1 Hoda Katebi, "Please Keep Your American Flags off my Hijab," *JooJoo Azad*, January 23, 2017, http://www.joojooazad.com/2017/01/keep-your-american-flags-off-my-hijab.html (accessed June 25, 2018).

2 Taylor, *From #BlackLivesMatter to Black Liberation*, 29.

3 Carolyn Marvin and David W. Ingle, *Blood Sacrifice and the Nation: Totem Rituals and the American Flag* (Cambridge: Cambridge University Press, 1999), 85. See also William T. Cavanaugh, *The Myth of Religious Violence: Secular Ideology and the Roots of Modern Conflict* (Oxford: Oxford University Press, 2009).

4 William T. Cavanuagh, "The Root of Evil," *America Magazine*, July 29-August 5, 2013, https://www.americamagazine.org/issue/root-evil (accessed June 25, 2018).

5 Carolyn Marvin and David W. Ingle, "Blood Sacrifice and the Nation: Revisiting Civil Religion," *Journal of the American Academy of Religion*, vol. LXIV, issue 4 (October 1 1996): 770.

6 Goldberg, "Militarizing Race," 33.

7 Tom Secker and Matthew Alford, "EXCLUSIVE: Documents expose how Hollywood promotes war on behalf of the Pentagon, CIA and NSA," *Medium*, July 4, 2017, https://medium.com/insurge-intelligence/exclusive-documents-expose-direct-us-military-intelligence-influence-on-1-800-movies-and-tv-shows-36433107c307 (accessed June 25, 2018).

8 Allison, "How to Recognize a War Film," 256.

9 Ibid., 257.

10 Mia Fischer, "Commemorating 9/11 NFL-Style: Insights Into America's Culture of Militarism," *Journal of Sport & Social Issues*, 38(3), 2014, 214.

11 Michael L. Butterworth and Stormi D. Moskal, "American Football, Flags, and 'Fun': The Bell Helicopter Armed Forces Bowl and the Rhetorical Production of Militarism," *Communication, Culture & Critique* 2 (2009): 429.

12 See http://www.armedforcesbowl.com/ (accessed June 25, 2018).

13 Sarah Lazare, "The Untold Story of Memorial Day: Former Slaves Honoring and Mourning the Dead," *AlterNet*, May 30, 2016, https://www.alternet.org/

civil-liberties/untold-story-memorial-day-former-slaves-honoring-and-mourning-dead (accessed June 25, 2018).

14 Sylvester A. Johnson, "African Americans, the Racial State, and the Cultus of War: Sacrifice and Citizenship," *Social Text* 129, vol. 34, no. 4, (December 2016): 62.

15 Alasdair MacIntyre, "A Partial Response to My Critics," in *After MacIntyre: Critical Perspectives on the Work of Alasdair MacIntyre,* ed. John Horton and Susan Mendus (Notre Dame, IN: University of Notre Dame Press, 1994), 303, cited in William T. Cavanaugh, *Migrations of the Holy: God, State, and the Political Meaning of the Church* (Grand Rapids: Eerdmans, 2011), 36–37. See also Paul W. Kahn, *Political Theology: Four New Chapters on the Concept of Sovereignty* (New York: Columbia University Press, 2012), 23: "In a crisis, it remains true today that the secular state does not hesitate to speak of sacrifice, patriotism, nationalism and homeland in the language of the sacred," Kahn writes. "The state's territory becomes consecrated ground, its history a sacred duty to maintain, its flag something to die for."

16 James Carden, "New Study: The Communities Most Affected by War Turned to Trump in 2016," *The Nation,* July 13, 2017, https://www.thenation.com/article/new-study-communities-most-affected-by-war-turned-to-trump-in-2016/ (accessed June 25, 2018).

17 Frederick Douglass, "What to the Slave is the Fourth of July?" July 5, 1852, http://teachingamericanhistory.org/library/document/what-to-the-slave-is-the-fourth-of-july/ (accessed June 25, 2018).

18 Zareena Grewal, "Lights, Camera, Suspension: Freezing the Frame on the Mahmoud Abdul-Rauf-Anthem Controversy," *Souls: A Critical Journal of Black Politics, Culture, and Society,* 9:2 (2007): 109–122.

19 Hoda Katebi, "Please Keep Your American Flags off my Hijab."

20 Ibid.

Chapter 20

1 Toni Morrison, *Playing in the Dark* (New York: Vintage Books, 1992), 46.

2 Lisa Lowe, *Immigrant Acts: On Asian American Cultural Politics* (Durham, NC: Duke University Press, 1996), 2.

3 Tamara K. Nopper, "Strangers to the Economy: Black Work and the Wages of Non-Blackness," in *Conceptual Aphasia in Black: Displacing Racial* Formation, ed. P. Khalil Saucier and Tryon P. Woods (Lanham, MD: Lexington Books, 2016), 101.

4 See: Mariana Ortega and Linda Martín Alcoff, *Constructing the Nation: A Race and Nationalism Reader* (New York: State University of New York Press, 2009); and Mayanthi L. Fernando, "Exceptional Citizens: Secular Muslim Women and the Politics of Difference in France," *Social Anthropology*, vol. 17, issue 4 (2009): 379–392.

5 Martha d. Escobar, "No One is Criminal," in *Abolition Now! Ten Years of Strategy and Struggle Against the Prison Industrial Complex*, ed. Critical Resistance (Oakland: AK Press, 2008), 64. See also Martha D. Escobar, *Captivity Beyond Prisons: Criminalization Experiences of Latina (Im)migrants* (Austin: University of Texas Press, 2016), 63.

6 See, for example, Nopper, "Strangers to the Economy," 87–102; and Katie Grimes' chapter, "Nonwhiteness Will Not Save Us: The Persistence of Antiblackness in the 'Brown' Twenty-First Century," in Grimes, *Christ Divided*, 147–176.

7 Escobar, "No One is Criminal," 57.

8 Ibid., 63.

9 Lisa Lowe, "The Gender of Sovereignty," *S&F Online*, issue 6.3 (Summer 2008), http://sfonline.barnard.edu/immigration/print_lowe.htm (accessed June 25, 2018).

10 See Woodhouse, "Obama's Deportation Policy Was Even Worse Than We Thought."

11 Aviva Chomsky, "Clinton and Obama Laid the Groundwork for Donald Trump's War on Immigrants," *The Nation*, April 25, 2017, https://www.thenation.com/article/clinton-and-obama-laid-the-groundwork-for-donald-trumps-war-on-immigrants/ (accessed June 25, 2018).

12 Dara Lind, "Hillary Clinton wants child migrants sent back. Here's what that would look like," *Vox*, June 19, 2014, https://www.vox.com/2014/6/19/5819076/hillary-clinton-deport-send-back-message-asylum-unaccompanied-expedited-border (accessed June 25, 2018).

13 For excellent resources on the intersection of American identity and queer immigrant archives, see: Martin F. Manalansan IV, "The 'Stuff' of Archives: Mess, Migration, and Queer Lives," *Radical History Review*, issue 120 (Fall 2014): 94–107; and Nayan Shah, *Stranger Intimacy: Contesting Race, Sexuality, and the Law in the North American West* (Berkeley: University of California Press, 2011).

14 Lisa Lowe, *Immigrant Acts*, 22.

15 Kelly Lytle Hernández, "Amnesty or Abolition? Felons, illegals, and the case for a new abolition movement," *Boom: A Journal of California*, vol. 1, no. 4 (2011): 57.

16 Ibid., 56.

17 "America's mass deportation system is rooted in racism," *The Conversation*, February 26, 2017, https://theconversation.com/americas-mass-deportation-system-is-rooted-in-racism-73426 (accessed June 25, 2018).

18 For an excellent historical overview of the U.S. border patrol, see Kelly Lytle Hernández, *Migra! A History of the U.S. Border Patrol* (Berkeley: University of California Press, 2010).

19 See Tina Takemoto, "Looking for Jiro Onuma."

20 Joel Olson, *The Abolition of White Democracy* (Minneapolis: University of Minnesota Press, 2004), xxi.

21 For one of the most perceptive critiques of multiculturalism, see Vincent Lloyd's discussion of Sylvia Wynter in Vincent W. Lloyd, *Religion of the Field Negro: On Black Secularism and Black Theology* (New York: Fordham University Press, 2016), 93.

22 Raúl Al-qaraz Ochoa, "Legalization Kills Revolution: The Case Against Citizenship," *Un Pueblo Sin Fronteras*, December 27, 2010, https://antifronteras.wordpress.com/2010/12/27/legalization-kills-revolution-the-case-against-citizenship/ (accessed June 25, 2018).

23 For an insightful analysis of how the liberal, racial, and gendered politics of movement operate in the Palestinian context, see Hagar Kotef, *Movement and the Ordering of Freedom: On Liberal Governances of Mobility* (Durham: Duke University Press, 2015).

24 David Bacon, "When NAFTA was passed two decades ago, its boosters promised it would bring 'First World' status for the Mexican people. Instead, it prompted a great migration north," *Political Research Associates*, October 11, 2014, https://www.politicalresearch.org/2014/10/11/globalization-and-nafta-caused-migration-from-mexico/ (accessed June 25, 2018).

25 James North, "How the US's Foreign Policy Created an Immigrant Refugee Crisis on Its Own Southern Border," *The Nation*, July 9, 2014, https://www.thenation.com/article/how-uss-foreign-policy-created-immigrant-refugee-crisis-its-own-southern-border/ (accessed June 25, 2018).

26 Lisa Lowe, *The Intimacies of Four Continents*, 6.

27 Andrea Smith, "The Indigenous Dream, 11."

28 Paisley Currah, "The State," *Transgender Studies Quarterly*, 1 (1–2) (2014), 197.

29 Bianca C. Williams, *The Pursuit of Happiness: Black Women, Diasporic Dreams, and the Politics of Emotional Transformation* (Durham: Duke University Press, 2018), 7.

30 Ibid., 11.

31 For an excellent example of how Indigenous communities seek to decolonize and create steps to create full communal autonomy from the nation-state (in this case, from Mexico), see Mariana Mora, *Kuxlejal Politics: Indigenous Autonomy, Race, and Decolonizing Research in Zapatista Communities* (Austin: University of Texas Press, 2018).

32 Andrea Smith, "Foreword," in Harsha Walia, *Undoing Border Imperialism* (Oakland: AK Press, 2013), xiii.

Chapter 21

1 Christina Sharpe, *In the Wake: On Blackness and Being* (Durham: Duke University Press, 2016), 22.

2 Hartman, *Lose Your Mother*, 100.

3 "Introduction," in *Octavia's Brood: Science Fiction Stories from Social Justice Movements*, ed. Adrienne Maree Brown and Walidah Imarisha (Oakland: AK Press, 2015), 3.

4 Rory Fanning, "Why Do We Keep Thanking the Troops?" *TomDispatch.com*, October 26, 2014, http://www.tomdispatch.com/post/175912/tomgram%3A_rory_fanning,_why_do_we_keep_thanking_the_troops/ (accessed June 25, 2018).

5 "Actor Morgan Freeman says the US is 'at war' with Russia," BBC, September 21, 2017, http://www.bbc.com/news/av/world-europe-41345249/actor-morgan-freeman-says-the-us-is-at-war-with-russia (accessed June 25, 2018).

6 Trevor McCrisken, *American Exceptionalism and the Legacy of Vietnam: US Foreign Policy Since 1974* (New York: Palgrave, 2003), 190.

7 Maximilian Forte, "A Flickr of Militarization: Photographic Regulation, Symbolic Consecration, and the Strategic Communication of 'Good Intentions,'" in *Good Intentions*, 188.

8 Belén Fernández, "Iraq, 15 years on: A toxic US legacy," *Middle East Eye*, March 16, 2018, http://www.middleeasteye.net/columns/iraq-15-years-toxic-us-legacy-1536228276 (accessed June 25, 2018).

9 Department of Justice Report, March 23, 2015, https://www.justice.gov/opa/pr/department-justice-releases-report-philadelphia-police-departments-use-deadly-force (accessed June 25, 2018).

10 See Dylan Rodriguez, "'Mass Incarceration' Reform as Police Endorsement," *Black Agenda Report*, February 28, 2018, https://www.blackagendareport.com/

mass-incarceration-reform-police-endorsement (accessed June 25, 2018). See also Micol Seigel, *Violence Work: State Power and the Limits of Police* (Durham: Duke University Press, 2018).

11 Lisa Lowe, "Reckoning Nation and Empire: Asian American Critique," in *A Concise Companion to American Studies*, ed. John Carlos Rowe (West Sussex, U.K.; Malden, MA: Wiley-Blackwell, 2010), 231.

12 Ibid.

13 Saidiya Hartman, "Slavery, Human Rights, and Personhood," presented at "Human Rights and the Humanities," *National Humanities Center*, March 20, 2014.

14 "Will losing health insurance mean more US deaths? Experts say yes," *The Guardian*, June 24, 2017, https://www.theguardian.com/us-news/2017/jun/24/us-healthcare-republican-bill-no-coverage-death (accessed June 25, 2018).

15 "Study: US is an oligarchy, not a democracy," *BBC*, April 17, 2014, http://www.bbc.com/news/blogs-echochambers-27074746 (accessed June 25, 2018).

16 Alston, "Statement on Visit to the USA."

17 Greg Robb, "Why American capitalism doesn't work for all Americans, says Nobel winner Angus Deaton," *Marketwatch*, December 14, 2017, https://www.marketwatch.com/story/nobel-prize-winning-economist-angus-deaton-model-of-american-capitalism-that-lifted-working-class-seems-to-be-broken-2017-12-13 (accessed June 25, 2018).

18 Gregg Zoroya, "Pentagon report justifies deployment of military spy drones over the U.S.," *USA Today*, March 9, 2016, https://www.usatoday.com/story/news/nation/2016/03/09/pentagon-admits-has-deployed-military-spy-drones-over-us/81474702/ (accessed June 25, 2018).

19 Fanning, "Why Do We Keep Thanking the Troops?"

20 Vincent Emanuele, "Veterans Day in Trump's America," *Counterpunch*, November 11, 2016, https://www.counterpunch.org/2016/11/11/veterans-day-in-trumps-america/ (accessed June 25, 2018). For a detailed study of "Lockheed Martin's campaign to scare us into spending more on defense," see William D. Hartung, *Prophets of War: Lockheed Martin and the Making of the Military-Industrial Complex* (New York: Nation Books, 2012), 270.

21 Sarah Jaffe, "Trump's Austerity Budget Increases Military Recruiters' Power to Prey on Youth," (Interview with Rory Fanning), *Truthout*, March 24, 2017, http://www.truth-out.org/opinion/item/39978-trump-s-austerity-budget-increases-military-recruiters-power-to-prey-on-youth (accessed June 25, 2018).

22 Henry A. Giroux, "Disney, Militarization and the National Security State After 9/11," *Truthout*, August 23, 2011, http://www.truth-out.org/news/item/2879:disney-militarization-and-the-national-security-state-after-911 (accessed June 25, 2018).

23 See, for example, Keisha N. Blain, *Set the World on Fire*; Anne Garland Mahler, *From the Tricontinental to the Global South: Race, Radicalism, and Transnational Solidarity* (Durham: Duke University Press, 2018); Gerald Horne, *Facing the Rising Sun: African Americans, Japan, and the Rise of Afro-Asian Solidarity* (New York: NYU Press, 2018).

24 Simeon Man, "Aloha, Vietnam: Race and Empire in Hawai'i's Vietnam War," *American Quarterly*, vol. 67, no. 4 (December 2015): 1105; see Haunani-Kay Trask, "Birth of the Modern Hawaiian Movement," *Hawaiian Journal of History*, vol. 21 (1987): 127. See also Simeon Man, *Soldiering through Empire: Race and the Making of the Decolonizing Pacific* (Berkeley: University of California Press, 2018).

25 Daniel Moattar, "Prisons Are Using Military-Grade Tear Gas to Punish People," *The Nation*, April 28, 2016, https://www.thenation.com/article/prisons-are-using-military-grade-tear-gas-to-punish-inmates/ (accessed June 25, 2018).

26 Belén Fernández, "Iraq, 15 years on."

27 Sarah Jaffe, "Trump's Austerity Budget."

28 Connie Wun, "Against Captivity," 173.

29 Aziz Rana, "The Left's Missing Foreign Policy," *N+1*, March 28, 2018, https://nplusonemag.com/online-only/online-only/the-lefts-missing-foreign-policy/ (accessed June 25, 2018).

30 Sara Ahmed, *The Cultural Politics of Emotion* (New York: Routledge, 2004), 189.

31 See Warren, *Ontological Terror*, 172, and Ashon T. Crawley, *Blackpentecostal Breath: The Aesthetics of Possibility* (New York: Fordham University Press, 2016).

32 Manalansan IV, "The 'Stuff' of Archives," 106.

Index